Self-Directed Employment

Self-Directed Employment

A Handbook
for Transition Teachers
and Employment Specialists

by

James E. Martin, Ph.D.
University of Oklahoma, Norman

Dennis E. Mithaug, Ph.D.
Columbia University
New York City

James V. Husch, M.A.
Pikes Peak Board of
Cooperative Education Services
Fountain, Colorado

John H. Oliphint, M.Ed.
City of Colorado Springs
Colorado

Eva S. Frazier, M.A.
Academy School District
Colorado Springs

Baltimore • London • Sydney

Paul H. Brookes Publishing Co., Inc.
Post Office Box 10624
Baltimore, Maryland 21285-0624

www.brookespublishing.com

Typeset by Auburn Associates, Inc., Baltimore, Maryland.
Manufactured in the United States of America by
Corley Printing Co., St. Louis, Missouri.

All of the case studies in this book are based on the authors' actual experiences. In all instances, names have been changed; in some instances, identifying details have been altered to protect confidentiality.

Library of Congress Cataloging-in-Publication Data

Self-directed employment: a handbook for transition teachers and employment specialists /
by James E. Martin ... [et al.].
p. cm.
Includes bibliographical references and index.
ISBN 1-55766-580-X
1. People with disabilities—Vocational guidance. 2. People with disabilities—Employment.
I. Martin, James, 1951–

HV 1568.5 .S45 2002
362.4′0484—dc21 2002016405

British Library Cataloguing in Publication data are available from the British Library.

Contents

About the Authors

James E. Martin, Ph.D., University of Oklahoma, Carpenter Hall, Room 111, 840 Asp Avenue, Norman, OK 73019

Dr. Martin is the Zarrow Endowed Professor in Special Education and Director of the Zarrow Center for Learning Enrichment at the University of Oklahoma. He received a bachelor of science degree and a master's degree in education from Eastern Illinois University, and he received a doctorate in special education with an emphasis on secondary transition from the University of Illinois at Urbana-Champaign. Prior to his current position, Dr. Martin served as a professor of special education and as the first Director of the Center of Self-Determination at the University of Colorado at Colorado Springs. Through the years, he has specialized in the development and implementation of self-determination methodology in educational, transitional, and supported employment programs. Dr. Martin has written extensively on special education, self-determination, and transition. He has also co-authored several instructional packages, including the *Self-Directed IEP Kit* (Martin, Huber Marshall, Maxson, & Jerman, Sopris West, 1996), *ChoiceMaker Self-Determination Assessment* (Martin & Marshall, Sopris West, 1995), and *Take Action: Making Goals Happen* (Huber Marshall, Martin, Maxson, Hughes, Miller, McGill, & Jerman, Sopris West, 1998).

Dennis E. Mithaug, Ph.D., Teachers College, Columbia University, 525 West 120th Street, New York, NY 10027

Dr. Mithaug is Professor of Education in the Department of Health and Behavior Studies at Teachers College, Columbia University. He received a bachelor of arts degree from Dartmouth College and a master's degree in education and a doctorate from the University of Washington. Dr. Mithaug's research includes issues related to the job preferences of adults with severe disabilities, school-to-work transition, self-determination of students with disabilities, and supported employment. He has published numerous research articles and book chapters, and he has authored and co-authored many books, including *Self-Determined Kids: Raising Satisfied and Successful Children* (Lexington Books, 1991); *Self-Regulation Theory: How Optimal Adjustment Maximizes Gain* (Praeger, 1993); *Equal Opportunity Theory: Fairness in Liberty for All* (Sage Publications, 1996); *Learning to Theorize: A Four-Step Strategy* (Sage Publications, 2000); and *Self-Determined Learning Theory: Construction, Verification, and Evaluation* (edited with Mithaug, Agran, Martin, & Wehmeyer, Lawrence Erlbaum Associates, 2002).

John H. Oliphint, M.Ed., City of Colorado Springs, Post Office Box 1817, Colorado Springs, CO 80903

Mr. Oliphint currently serves as Para Transit Coordinator for the City of Colorado Springs, analyzing transportation issues and supervising the city's transit program for people with disabilities. Previously, he served as Director of Martin Luther Homes, a comprehensive residential and supported employment agency serving children and adults with mental retardation. Mr. Oliphint also directed statewide employment training efforts and served as an employment placement specialist for the Self-Directed Employment Program for the Center of Self-Determination at the University of Colorado. He earned a master's degree in education from Memphis State University and a master's degree in public administration from the University of Colorado Springs. Throughout his career, in a variety of capacities, he has worked to better the lives of individuals with developmental disabilities.

James V. Husch, M.A., Pikes Peak Board of Cooperative Education Services, 301 East Iowa Avenue, Fountain, CO 80817

Mr. Husch coordinates the School to Work Alliance Program, which assists youth at risk for school failure and youth with disabilities in determining career goals and attaining successful employment. He earned a master's degree in special education from the University of Colorado at Colorado Springs. Previously, he served as Director of the Self-Directed Employment Program for the Center of Self-Determination at the University of Colorado. In this capacity, he was responsible for training the program staff, implementing the program goals, and assisting in procuring placement sites for the center's clients. He also serves as a professional research associate for self-determination projects at the university. Through the years, he has co-authored several articles and chapters and has frequently presented on the issues of supported employment and self-determination.

Eva S. Frazier, M.A., 1783 Mineola Avenue, Colorado Springs, CO 80915

Ms. Frazier provides special education support services to students with disabilities. She received a master's degree in special education from the University of Colorado at Colorado Springs. Previously, she served as the intake and assessment coordinator for the Self-Directed Employment Program for the Center of Self-Determination at the University of Colorado. In that capacity, she participated in the development of the assessment procedures featured in this book. In particular, she created almost all of the illustrations used in the book, which are available to download at www.brookespublishing.com/picturebank. She has presented the results of her work at numerous conferences, and she has co-authored many publications.

Foreword

In *No Pity*, Joseph P. Shapiro's compelling book concerning the disability rights movement, the chapter describing the self-advocacy movement begins with a scene from a meeting at the inaugural People-First convention in 1990. T.J. Monroe, a national leader in the self-advocacy movement, was trying to rein in a roomful of boisterous delegates with cognitive disabilities from across the country. Hammering his gavel on the podium to get the attention of the meeting attendees, Monroe shouted to be heard above the din, proclaiming that "one thing we're going to vote on is a revolution!" (Shapiro, 1993, p. 184).

As Shapiro observed, T.J. Monroe actually intended to say *resolution*, not *revolution*. But as Shapiro noted and as anyone who has become acquainted with the self-advocacy movement can readily attest to, revolution is really a more appropriate description of the changes in the disability movement since the 1980s. My colleague Hank Bersani and I have described the history of the field of disability services and supports as defined by three waves. The first wave was dominated by professionals, during which physicians, psychologists, social workers, and other professionals were thought to hold all the keys to knowledge about disability. The bleak history of the treatment of people with disabilities during the first half of the 20th century illustrated the serious limitations of this "professional only" vision and led to the second wave, the parent movement. In the optimism and prosperity that washed across America in the aftermath of World War II and with advances in science and in the treatment of diseases such as polio, parents of children with disabilities began to challenge the standard expectations for the outcomes for their sons or daughters. The parent wave had tremendous impact on disability services, perhaps most notably evidenced by the passage in 1975 of the Education for All Handicapped Children Act (PL 94-142). But even as the parent movement was at its peak, the third wave began to emerge, the self-advocacy movement.

This book is a product of the sweeping changes in disability services brought about by the third wave of the disability movement. It describes a revolution in the way we conceptualize services, moving away from programs designed by professionals toward programs characterized by self-directed supports. These supports are designed on the basis of the interests, preferences, and abilities of the person receiving the support and in such a manner to ensure that the person remains in control of the process. This process builds on another revolution, the revolution of supported employment.

Although the authors rightly note that it is not possible to pinpoint the exact moment of the birth of supported employment, many of us who have been in the field at least since the 1980s can identify the moment we were first introduced to the revolutionary idea that people with severe disabilities could hold competitive jobs. I was a classroom teacher working with adolescents with severe disabilities at the time, and literally overnight, my vision of what was possible for my students changed from sorting widgets by size, shape, and color in the sheltered workshop to working competitively for pay with colleagues without disabilities.

My responsibility as a teacher also changed with my exposure to the supported employment concept. The old way of doing things was no longer acceptable. I had been exposed to a new way of thinking about people with disabilities that required that I change both my practices and my expectations. Not responding to that new vision was, in my perspective, never a viable option. Once I saw that people with severe disabilities could, in fact, contribute to society through competitive, paid work and could become a part of the rich fabric that is the social milieu of work environments, it became my *obligation* to discard my previous assumptions and expectations and move toward this new way of thinking and seeing.

The literature has debated whether supported employment is a process or a procedure, but this book captures perhaps the most important aspect of supported employment: having high expectations for people and supporting them to pursue rich, fulfilling lives. Supported employment is about the promise of a better life.

Why, at the start of the 21st century, do we find that supported employment is largely unrealized among people with severe disabilities? Perhaps it is because we, as a field, did not pay enough attention to the self-determination component of supported employment from the onset. We worried about the procedures and processes and forgot that it was really about empowerment, enablement, and high expectations. Martin, Mithaug, Oliphint, Husch, and Frazier suggest that the supported employment movement has, itself, moved through three phases. They title these the "Get a Job—Any Job—and Keep the Individual at the Job" phase, the "Get a Job That Is a Match For the Individual" phase, and the "Self-Directed Employment" phase. These are, in my mind, more than just three phases. They represent two dichotomous visions of disability and disability services. The first two phases put the professional in control of the process, even when integrating innovative strategies such as natural supports into the mix of supported employment services. The third phase is distinct from the first two. It is consumer-controlled and self-directed, and it places the person with disabilities at the controls, not professionals.

If you have not already been exposed to the vision of the self-determination movement, reading *Self-Directed Employment* places you at a decision point in your professional career. Much as obtaining knowledge about supported employment obligated those of us working with people with severe disabilities to change our visions for the future and to change our expectations of the people we support, so too does knowledge about self-directed services and self-determination obligate us to act and to create a new vision. It is a vision that must encompass the totality of our interactions with people with disabilities.

Almost everyone has seen the ubiquitous faces/vase stereogram developed by Gestalt psychologists to illustrate the figure–ground phenomenon in perception. This stereogram is the black and white object that, when you first look at it, appears to be the image of a white vase on a black background. When, however, you shift your focus slightly, you can see that the black background actually forms two faces looking at one another with the facial features (nose, brow, chin) on either side forming the contour of the vase. From the point in time one sees the faces, it becomes almost impossible to see only the vase in the image. Likewise, as you read this book and begin to see the faces of self-determination and the third wave of the disability movement outlining the vase of best practice in supported employment, it should change not only the way you provide supported employment services, but indeed the way you look at all supports for people with disabilities. Like the faces/vase stereogram, we should no longer be able to conceptualize disability supports without seeing the vision of self-determination.

Does this new vision mean that there is no longer a role for professionals? Hardly. The chapters that follow detail strategies and procedures for professionals. You must become the catalyst to enable and empower people with severe disabilities to "get a job" or more expansively, "get a life." There are detailed instructions for implementation, photocopiable forms to individualize instruction and assessment, and, perhaps most important, stories of the lives of real people, like Joe, Richard, Nina, Martha, and others who have succeeded with self-directed employment. This chapter is written out of the authors' decade-long experiences providing these supports. It helps that two of the text's authors, James Martin and Dennis Mithaug, are leaders in defining and promoting the self-determination of people with disabilities and can intertwine stories and procedures in a way that is both inspirational and instructive—a rare combination!

Are there any drawbacks to pursuing this course of action? Only one. That is, reading this book and implementing the practices and procedures outlined therein is not the end, but only the beginning. That is the rub with providing supports that promote self-determination. People's preferences change. They want new and better jobs. Access to employment leads to greater demands for supporting people to live in their communities, to become home owners and contributing members of that community, and so forth. Of course, it is not really our choice, is it? Not following this course of action is not really an option. Fortunately, this course is both the right and effective path. So, read on and then lead on!

Michael L. Wehmeyer, Ph.D.
Beach Center on Families and Disability
University of Kansas, Lawrence

REFERENCES

Education for All Handicapped Children Act of 1975, PL 94-142, 20 U.S.C. §§ 1400 *et seq.*

Shapiro, J.P. (1994). *No pity: People with disabilities forging a new civil rights movement.* New York: Times Books.

Preface

Self-Directed Employment: A Handbook for Transition Teachers and Employment Specialists provides step-by-step instructions on how to infuse self-directed employment strategies into your school transition or agency-supported employment program. First, you will read about the evolving nature of employment supports for individuals with disabilities and the important role that self-determination plays in this evolution. After the steps are stories and data demonstrating the effectiveness of the Self-Directed Employment (SDE) methodology.

We realize that many of you reading this book are veteran teachers or employment specialists who want to enhance your existing self-determination practices. Others of you believe that the strategies presented in this book require too much work, involve too much data collection, or decrease the professional input you and your colleagues now give to the employment process. We ask you to approach the ideas in this book with an open mind and consider the methods as tools to produce better outcomes. Then, after reading the book, think about how you can infuse a few strategies from this book into your own program.

Some of you reading this book will be new to the field or studying to enter your first teaching or employment specialist position. Welcome to a very exciting and important profession in which your efforts will improve the quality of life for many individuals with disabilities. As you read the chapters, reflect on your previous studies and notice how the procedures use the best of what the field currently knows about effective instruction. As you begin your first position, find the strength needed to implement these procedures and do not be overcome by the tendency to simply do what has been done in the past.

This book consists of five major parts: a general discussion about employment and self-determination, assessment methodology, placement and follow-along methodology, data analysis, and photocopiable forms. The first two chapters summarize community employment and self-determination research. Chapter 3–7 present the steps for conducting an SDE assessment. Chapters 8 and 9 present information on placement and on-the-job problem solving. Chapters 2, 10, and 11 include case studies and summative data for the SDE methodology. Finally, the appendix contains photocopiable forms that enable the user to copy and implement the SDE methodology in schools or supported employment programs. Readers can download pictures from www.brookespublishing.com/picturebank to individualize the forms.

CHAPTERS 1 AND 2

Chapter 1, entitled "Get a Job," discusses two major points. This chapter reviews the revolutionary concept of community employment and explains how supported employment consists of a set of methods, not just a type of employment outcome. The chapter also examines the evolution of employment practices from the "get them any job" initial phase to self-directed employment. Chapter 2 explains how and why self-determination powers the SDE methodology presented in this book. Self-determination concepts from a macro and micro viewpoint are examined, followed by a discussion of two different self-determination definitional strands. Next, a unifying understanding of self-determination is presented after examining several definitions.

CHAPTERS 3–7

Chapter 3, entitled "Getting Started: An Implementation Overview," presents the SDE curriculum and explains the choice management and self-management outcomes. The organizational schema explains how to use Chapters 4–9. Finally, an implementation reference guide lists the forms needed to implement each curriculum objective. Chapters 4–7 explain the steps for implementing the choice management assessment process. Each chapter details how to complete each curriculum objective and fill out each form and compute results and provides "What If?" questions and answers that offer solutions to the most common problems found in implementing each objective.

CHAPTERS 8–9

Chapter 8, entitled "Introduction to Section II. Goal E: Finding a Job Matching Skills and Preferences," explains placement and on-the-job problem solving. This chapter shows how to engage individuals with disabilities in the placement process. It emphasizes achieving a match between interests, skills, and job demands before and after the person accepts a new position. Chapter 9, entitled "Introduction to Section II. Goal F: Solving On-the-Job Problems," explains how to apply basic self-management skills to adjusting to the demands of the work place.

CHAPTERS 10–12

We established a SDE program at the University of Colorado at Colorado Springs to develop and demonstrate the procedures described in this book. During the program's 11 years, we provided employment services to 751 youth and adults with severe disabilities, including individuals with mental retardation, traumatic brain injury, and mental illness. Chapter 10, "Stories," presents case studies. These real-life examples—with the names, identifying information, and circumstances changed—show the SDE methods in action. A few case studies describe situations that were not successful because they illustrate other variables (beside the SDE methods) that can affect success. Chapter 11 presents summative results of the SDE program from different points in time. Comparison between the SDE program and national demonstration projects show that when individuals make their own choices and solve their own problems using the SDE procedures, their results at least equal the results of efforts made by professionals and often exceed professional accomplishments. Chapter 12 summarizes ideas behind the SDE program.

APPENDIX

The appendix presents photocopiable forms used in Chapters 4–9. Purchasers are granted permission to photocopy the individual forms in the appendix. Each site must purchase its own book; master forms cannot be shared among sites. Electronic reproduction of any form is prohibited, and none of the forms may be reproduced to generate revenue for any program or individual. Photocopies may only be made from an original book. *Unauthorized use beyond this privilege is prosecutable under federal law.* You will see the copyright protection at the bottom of each photocopiable page.

Most forms have two versions: a version that uses mostly words and a version that is illustrated. Use the text versions with individuals who can read, and the illustrated versions with individuals whose disabilities are more severe. Many of the forms can also be adapted using illustrations that you can download from the Brookes web site: www.brookespublishing.com/picturebank. This option can help you increase the individualized nature of the program.

NOTE TO THE READER

We worked together for many years creating and implementing the strategies in this book. We argued, laughed, and skied our way through the years. The time we spent together solving problems and creating an effective employment agency represent a dynamic, exciting, and vibrant part of our professional lives. We have all moved on to other professional positions, but each of us carries on with the work we established together.

Acknowledgments

So many people supported our efforts to develop the procedures described in this book and to all of you, we say thanks. We give a special acknowledgment of thanks to six people who supported our efforts to create the Self-Directed Employment Program. Professor Frank Rusch at the University of Illinois suggested that we create a supported employment program to develop our emerging self-determination ideas. Maxine Riley and Glenn Perry from the Colorado Springs office of the Colorado Division of Rehabilitation, Don St. Louis, Director of the Rocky Mountain Resource and Training Office, and Bill Bowman, Director of the Colorado Springs community board for individuals with disabilities, shared a vision for community employment and a process that empowered individuals to direct their own future. They also secured initial funding to begin what later became the Self-Directed Employment Program. Dr. Peg Bacon, who was the Dean of the School of Education at the University of Colorado, Colorado Springs when we began this project, encouraged and supported all of our efforts.

Numerous graduate assistants left their own mark on the finished procedures. We learned so much from you. You saw problems, created solutions, and implemented procedures that enabled many individuals to secure and maintain employment. Most of you today are implementing self-determination practices in your own educational programs. Together, we did accomplish a lot!

A special acknowledgment must go to the families of the individuals who became involved in the Self-Directed Employment Program. You supported your adult sons and daughters as they made the transition from sheltered employment or high school into community jobs. At times, individual preferences differed from what you believed was a good future, yet seldom did this difference of opinion deter individual success. The people who became involved in the Self-Directed Employment Program came looking for a better future. Your efforts enabled us to understand what you wanted.

To our families and to the many individuals who supported our efforts and taught us so much about self-determination and employment practice

To ski trips, where many of our best ideas became reality

To napkins, where many of the ideas first saw the light of day

Self-Directed Employment

Get a Job

The beauty of supported employment lies in the strength of a very simple concept: Individuals with disabilities will obtain and maintain employment in competitive employment positions with planned supports (Brooke, Wehman, Inge, & Parent, 1995). This simple yet profound concept emerged gradually from three historical events (Rusch & Hughes, 1989). First, research from the 1970s demonstrated that individuals with mental retardation could learn complex job skills (Bellamy, Horner, & Inman, 1979; Gold, 1972; Mithaug, 1979). Second, demonstration projects depicted individuals with mental retardation being successfully employed in competitive, community-based, nonsheltered workshop positions (Rusch, Connis, & Sowers, 1978; Rusch & Mithaug, 1980; Wehman, 1981, 2001; Wehman, Hill, & Koehler, 1979). Third, a philosophical shift began when Whitehead (1979) reported that the sheltered workshop system prepared people for nonexistent jobs and that few people in sheltered employment left for competitive employment in the community (Bellamy, Rhodes, Mank, & Albin, 1988; Rusch & Schutz, 1979). As the supported employment concept grew from these three historical events, questions regarding the ability of individuals with disabilities to do a community job, which previously barred them from community employment, began to fade (Rusch & Hughes, 1989).

Before supported employment, vocational rehabilitation and educational programs used a train-and-place model. Clients in sheltered workshops were trained to "get ready" for community employment, but few ever left the sheltered workshop for competitive employment. The first supported employment model questioned the train-and-place approach. The place-and-train model (Rusch & Mithaug, 1980) first placed individuals into community-based competitive employment settings, then trained them to complete the job tasks ("New Directions," 1992).

The place-and-train model (Rusch & Mithaug, 1980) and a set of basic procedures (Wehman, 1981) set the stage for the formal introduction of the term *supported employment* in the landmark Developmental Disabilities Act of 1984 (PL 98-527). This law, and the later Rehabilitation Act Amendments of 1992 (PL 102-569), defined *supported employment* as paid employment for people with disabilities who require ongoing support to work at a community job setting (Rusch & Hughes, 1990). Wehman and Revell added clarity when they said,

> [Supported employment] is not readiness training in classrooms or work centers intended to develop generalized skills for use in a job sometime in the future. Supported employment focuses on wages, working conditions, job security, and job mobility. It values full participation of persons with significant disabilities in the community and assumes that each individual has the capacity to work if appropriate and individualized ongoing supports are made available. It utilizes rehabilitation technology, the resources of the employer, family, and community networks as well as the experience of a job coach as some of the many ways to provide supports (Parent, Unger, Gibson, & Clements, 1994). Supported employment creates opportunities for social integration and redirects the image of an individual with a disability away from a focus on dependency. (1997, p. 68)

This revolutionary concept shifted focus from questions of competence to the procedures, types, and amount of supports that individuals need in order to attain community-based, competitive employment (Rusch, 1986). The President's Committee on Employment of People with Disabilities summarized this major shift:

> Supported employment facilitates competitive work in integrated work settings for individuals with the most severe disabilities (i.e., psychiatric, mental retardation, learning disabilities, traumatic brain injury) for whom competitive employment has not traditionally occurred and who, because of the nature and severity of their disability, need ongoing support services in order to perform their job. Supported employment provides assistance such as job coaches, transportation, assistive technology, specialized job training, and individually tailored supervision.
>
> Supported employment is a way to move people from dependence on a service delivery system to independence via competitive employment. Recent studies indicate that the provision of on-going support services for people with severe disabilities significantly increases their rates for employment retention. (1998, p. 1)

SUPPORTED EMPLOYMENT AS A SET OF METHODS

The supported employment concept is manifested in the methods that schools and adult agency programs use to facilitate community employment. Moon, Inge, Wehman, Brooke, and Barcus considered it "a specific job placement and training approach" (1990, p. 1). Rusch and Hughes defined *supported employment* as "an intervention package containing several components" (1989, p. 354). Horner (1990) perceived *supported employment* as a behavioral technology for assisting people to become employed. Beyer and Kilsby (1997) thought that training by a skilled job coach was essential to a successful placement. These practices involve activities and procedures that take place before the person becomes employed and those that take place once the person becomes employed (Martin, Mithaug, Agran, & Husch, 1990). The outcome of supported employment practices is a competitive community job (Wehman & Kregel, 1998).

What are these methods, and what roles do individuals with disabilities play? How have supported employment methods changed since their inception in the 1980s? Supported employment methodology evolved through three major phases, with each subsequent phase including many of the best practices of those preceding it. These phases are Phase One: get a job—any job—and keep the individual at the job; Phase Two: get a job that you think is a match for the individual, and then use staff or natural supports to keep the job; and Phase Three: self-directed employment.

Each phase represents best practice as reflected by the predominant values, attitudes, and available methodology during that time period. This chapter examines these three phases by reviewing their prominent features. Dates for these phases are approximate. Practice does not move in a linear fashion, and as one phase begins, the previous phase often continues. A few employment programs still only use Phase One techniques, while others are implementing Phase Two or Three methodologies. Pancsofar and Steere (1997) noted that some employment programs still focus on readiness and use numerous means to classify individuals with disabilities as being unable to work at community jobs. Others still deny individuals with disabilities supported employment opportunities. For example, one lobbyist for sheltered workshops advocated placing individuals with disabilities in sheltered workshops instead of in community employment. *Mouth Magazine* suggested that if this happens, people with disabilities will continue to be put into positions of servitude instead of getting an actual community job ("Caught in the Act," 2001). As with any system change, overlap of evolving procedures exists.

Since its introduction in the early 1980s, supported employment methodology evolved from simply getting a person a job, to the emerging self-determination–oriented employment practices of today (Browning, 1997; Gilmore, Schuster, Timmons, & Butterworth, 2000; Wehman & Kregel, 1989). This chapter reviews these three phases and discusses who answered the following questions.

- What are the worker's job, task, and characteristic preferences and interest?
- What are the worker's skills and limits?
- Do the available jobs match the worker's interests and preferences?
- Do the available jobs match the worker's skills and limits?
- What job accommodations are needed?
- Can the worker do the job tasks?
- How does the worker do the job tasks?
- What are the worker's problems and how are they solved?
- Who established the on-the-job support network?
- Who determines if the worker should leave the job?

Those who answered these questions varied by phase. Yet, regardless of who, the simplicity and the revolutionary nature of the idea—get a job in a community setting—comes through in every phase. Choice initiates the self-directed employment process, and these questions frame the self-directed employment orientation. But how does choice manifest itself in the self-directed employment process?

CHOICE MAKING

Unlike any previous era, people with disabilities now have greater opportunities to participate in making choices about their own daily lives (Harchik, Sherman, Sheldon, & Bannerman, 1993). Transition and supported employment programs provide an excellent opportunity for individuals to learn to make choices (Stalker & Harris, 1998; West & Parent, 1992). In 1984, Shevin and Klein issued a strong call to the field to create opportunities for exercising choice for individuals with severe disabilities but warned this process would be undertaken in "relatively uncharted territory, without the comforts of traditional behavioral definitions and research methodologies" (p. 161). Fortunately, since 1984, the field has learned a lot about vocational choice making.

Choice-Making Roadblocks

Individuals with severe disabilities often have fewer choice opportunities in the course of their daily lives than do peers without disabilities (Kishi, Teelucksing, Zollers, Park-Lee, & Meyer, 1988; Sands & Kozleski, 1994). Their teachers often pay scant attention to expressions of preference, especially in instructional situations (Houghton, Bronicki, & Guess, 1987). Parents often assert that they know what their child wants or that their child does not have preferences (O'Brien, O'Brien, & Mount, 1997; Parsons & Reid, 1990; Stalker & Harris, 1998). These roadblocks to personal expression of preferences result in far too many youths and adults with severe disabilities not having an opportunity to make choices (Dattilo & Rusch, 1985; Mithaug, 1991). It should be no surprise then that often "employment programs unknowingly suspend basic employment rights that nonhandicapped workers enjoy" (Martin & Mithaug, 1990, p. 87).

The Choice-Making Process

Individuals with severe disabilities, like those without, have personal preferences, likes, and dislikes (Shevin & Klein, 1984). If provided with the opportunity, they use their everyday life choices to define their identity (Guess, Benson, & Siegel-Causey, 1985; O'Brien, 1987) by expressing their preferences (Parsons & Reid, 1990). *Choice making* is "an individual's selection of a preferred alternative from among several familiar options" (Shevin & Klein, 1984, p. 160). It involves uncoerced selection. That is, no consequences exist for selecting one choice over another except that which come from the characteristics of the choices themselves (Brigham, 1979). The choice-making process relies on three essential elements: 1) having options, 2) understanding the options, and 3) possessing the power to take action on these options (Stalker & Harris, 1998). To make a choice, individuals with disabilities must communicate their preference to others and receive support from teachers, parents, or significant others to facilitate choice-making opportunities (Rawlings, Dowse, & Shaddock, 1995). In order for choice making to become a critical aspect of the decision-making process, preference-based choice-making skills must be taught (Shevin & Klein, 1984; West & Parent, 1992), and opportunities for choice making must be provided for both daily and lifestyle decision making (Hughes, Pitkin, & Lorden, 1998).

A review of the choice research literature found that once a choice-making response is taught, "most people with severe developmental disabilities can cope with choice situations and perform choice responses" (Lancioni, O'Reilly, & Emerson, 1996, p. 402). The literature has also shown that choice making is purposeful, can be done successfully within the context of a person's daily routine, and positively affects performance and behavior (e.g., Lancioni et al., 1996). The choice-making process must be structured, too, so that the individual with severe disabilities makes an informed choice. This structured process fits well into a vocational assessment process.

Informed Vocational Choice

The type and quality of choice that a person with a disability makes are determined in part by the amount of practice the person has had in making choices (Rawlings et al., 1995). To yield an informed vocational choice, the process must involve multiple, individualized choice opportunities across time that become validated through community on-the-job experience (Bambara & Koger, 1995). An informed vocational choice for a person with severe disabilities requires direct exposure to and interactions with the requirements, duties, and characteristics of a job (Schaller & Szymanski, 1992).

Preference Assessment Preference assessment yields an individual's unique interests and expectations (Lohrmann-O'Rourke & Browder, 1998). Repeatedly collecting data during work sampling facilitates direct preference assessment (Bambara, Koger, Katzer, & Davenport, 1995; Windsor, O'Reilly, & Moon, 1993). This process enables individuals with severe disabilities to realize what their preferences are and to tell others. Research demonstrates that a person's own choice produces better outcomes than choices made by a significant other. Lohrmann-O'Rourke and Browder (1998) suggested that a preference assessment should include:

- Repeated opportunities to make choices
- Direct assessment rather than third-party (e.g., teacher, parent) reporting of preferences
- Mass trial assessment with observation in the actual environment where the choice exists
- Repeated assessment across days
- Periodic assessment across time to assess any preference changes
- Presentation of assessment stimuli in a manner individuals can use (e.g., actual item, picture)
- Identification of selection and rejection responses to assessment stimuli (e.g., picking up the object)
- Presentation of assessment stimuli in a paired format with limited time available to make the selection and produce a list of preferred and nonpreferred items.

Until opportunity expands to making lifestyle decisions, the self-determination of people with severe disabilities will remain limited (Brown, Belz, Corsi, & Wenig, 1993). Hughes and colleagues (1998) asserted that preference assessment must be extended to affect the lifestyle decisions made by individuals with severe disabilities. Lohrmann-O'Rourke and Browder (1998) cautioned that identifying preferences for long-range choices or lifestyle decisions becomes problematic because of the level of abstraction needed to think about oneself in the future. Still, opportunities must be provided for individuals with severe disabilities to make meaningful lifestyle choices, such as choosing a job (Brown et al., 1993).

LIFESTYLE DECISION: MAKING EMPLOYMENT CHOICES

In order for people with disabilities to begin to prepare for working lives, they must first choose a career (Wilcox, McDonnell, Bellamy, & Rose, 1988). Individuals' "career goals should be a driving force in the development of employment opportunities within integrated community environments" (Powell et al., 1991, p. 27). Each person's own work preferences should determine job placements (Neumayer & Bleasdale, 1996). The individual with a disability must be the one to select a career path after experiencing a variety of vocational experiences and supports. School transition and adult supported employment programs must become consumer-driven so that each person with a severe disability can select a job and make proactive decisions to retain or leave it (Brooke et al., 1995).

Yet, typical vocational assessment procedures, such as standardized testing, interest inventories, simulated job task evaluation, or job developer analysis of job characteristics, do not provide adequate assessment information to facilitate vocational placements (Culver, Spencer, & Gliner, 1990; Targett, Ferguson, & McLoughlin, 1998). Often high school transition and postsecondary supported employment programs use aptitude measurement, work samples, interest inventories, and behavior checklists to assess individuals with severe disabilities (Agran & Morgan, 1991). These tools are inappropriate for individuals with severe needs (Menchetti & Flynn, 1990). A single point-in-time interest or skill assessment simply does not provide a valid profile (Gaylord-Ross, 1986). Results from an interest inventory, for example, completed on one day can change as the individual with a severe disability gains additional experience the next day (Buschner, Watts, Siders, & Leonard, 1989). Verbal preference statements may not match the results of career interest inventories (Elrod, Sorgenfrei, & Gibson, 1989). The results of a single-use, picture-based interest inventory often produce questionable results, too (Buschner et al., 1989).

Rather than using traditional vocational assessment tools, school-based transition teachers and supported employment specialists must learn how to implement a self-directed situational assessment and job matching process (Agran, Test, & Martin, 1994; Test & Wood, 1995). Individuals with severe disabilities must make decisions by considering their needs, interests, skills, and limits when given the tools to do so (Agran et al., 1994; Mithaug & Hanawalt, 1978; Mithaug & Mar, 1980). A preference-oriented assessment process enables the individual with a severe disability to experience choice and control (Wehmeyer, Kelchner, & Richards, 1995).

Simply stating a preference by itself, however, does not constitute informed choice. Although many individuals with severe disabilities can express a preference if requested to do so, their choices may not match what they later discover to be important (Moon et al., 1990). A person with a cognitive disability must experience several different job conditions and environments—otherwise, the expressed preferences will not reflect an informed decision. People with limited or no previous vocational experience—regardless of their communication skills—are not be able to make valid, meaningful, and informed choices, but people who have hands-on experience with different jobs understand what they like and want. Individuals with severe disabilities need the opportunity to compare initial preferences with knowledge gained from experience in order to determine if initial preferences match what they learned through on-the-job experience (O'Brien et al., 1997).

Workers with severe disabilities can make consistent choices (Mithaug & Hanawalt, 1978; Mithaug & Mar, 1980). Preference for working specific tasks is one of the work conditions that must be given consideration in making job-choice decisions (Moon et al., 1990). "Various studies concerned with the vocational adjustments of youth with handicaps point out that work interests and motivation are far more critical variables than specific job capacities and skills" (Berkell, 1987, p. 68). The process of comparing choices to actual environmental experiences enables the individual with a severe disability to discriminate among work conditions, duties, and variables (Martin & Mithaug, 1990). Making a match between expressed preferences and actual environmental traits leads one to make an informed choice (Schaller & Szmanski, 1992). Yet, roadblocks to providing choice opportunities exist.

Ecological Perspective

If a mismatch between the person and the job environment occurs, the placement usually fails (Mank, 2000; Thurman, 1977). The self-directed employment approach avoids this problem by emphasizing the interrelationships between individuals with disabilities and their environments. The process produces a job choice based on the match between individually stated preferences and specific environments (Schalock & Jensen, 1986). It depends on the comparison of choices with the reality of the workplace. The match between the individual with a disability and the job increases the likelihood that on-the-job behavior meets the job and environmental expectations (Chadsey-Rusch & Rusch, 1988). An ecobehavioral job match allows self-examination of behavior–environment relationships in the natural environment and provides opportunities for the person to make informed job choices (Rogers-Warren & Warren, 1977). In other words, a person's opinion of different job settings can be determined through self-evaluation of numerous job dimensions including characteristics, activities, and setting (Chadsey-Rusch & Rusch, 1988).

Too many individuals with severe cognitive disabilities lack the vocational experience to make informed choices. Typical interest inventories—especially those presented only in writing—are not appropriate for individuals with severe support needs. Some suggest that teachers and supported employment specialists observe people with severe disabilities doing different jobs (McLoughlin, Garner, & Callahan, 1987). But at best, this is a choice by proxy—teachers or employment specialists make the choice, not the person with the disability. In Phase Three practice, input by the individual with the disability is the beginning of the match process. The individual with the disability examines the job, observes other workers, tries the tasks, and compares the attributes of one job to another. To make a choice, the person needs directed hands-on experience with different job options. We believe that individuals with severe disabilities must have the opportunity to choose their own jobs. This begins by answering the question: What job do I like? Those who answer this question have changed as supported employment practices have evolved.

PHASE ONE: GET A JOB—ANY JOB—AND KEEP THE INDIVIDUAL AT THE JOB

This first supported employment phase, which started in the late 1970s, emphasized inclusion of people with severe disabilities in the community workforce instead of segregated sheltered workshops, work activity centers, and isolated school programs (Rusch & Hughes, 1989). The supported employment pioneers faced numerous problems and issues that had never before been addressed, including lack of readily available models and methodology on which to draw. So these pioneers created new models and infused existing methods into these new models.

Phase One Methodology

The first supported employment demonstration projects showed that individuals with mental retardation could become employed and remain employed if provided with long-term support (Rusch & Schutz, 1979; Wehman, 1981; Wehman et al., 1979). Using these initial findings, Rusch and Mithaug (1980) created the *survey, train, and place employment model.* This began with employment staff surveying employers to find job placement sites and concluded with procedures to "help the trainee maintain employment" (Rusch & Mithaug, 1980, p. 185). This model encouraged employment specialists to

1. Conduct a telephone or mail survey to identify potential job placement sites
2. Complete a job analysis at the locations that expressed interest in hiring a trainee
3. Analyze employer, supervisor, and co-worker expectations
4. Develop a work performance evaluation form that staff will use to get information from the worksite about the trainee's performance
5. Place the trainee in the job
6. Follow-up after placement to evaluate performance, identify problems, and provide on-the-job interventions

The employment staff assessed job requisites, assessed trainees' skills in those job requisites, specified instructional objectives, developed materials and procedures to obtain those objectives, secured a job, and taught the worker any needed job and social skills.

Vocational training for individuals with severe vocational disabilities prior to the 1980s primarily consisted of "vague instructions and occasional prompts to stay on task" (Gifford, Rusch, Martin, & White, 1984, p. 287). To achieve productive employment levels, the survey, train, and place model used applied behavior analysis techniques to teach trainees the required work and social skills (e.g., Bellamy et al., 1979; Rusch & Mithaug, 1980).

Job Match Factor Approach

Moon, Goodall, Barcus, and Brooke (1986) suggested that employment specialists use specific worker factors to develop successful job placements. They listed 27 factors to consider when making a job placement.

1. Availability to work (e.g., days, weekends)
2. Availability of transportation to and from the jobsite
3. Initiative and motivation
4. Strength for lifting and carrying objects
5. Endurance (hours of continuous work)
6. Independence in work areas of different sizes
7. Physical mobility
8. Independent work rate
9. Appearance
10. Communication abilities
11. Appropriate social interactions
12. Absence of unusual behaviors
13. Attention to task and perseverance
14. Independent sequencing of job duties
15. Adaptation skills
16. Reinforcement needs
17. Family support
18. Individual's financial situation
19. Discrimination skills
20. Time awareness
21. Functional reading skills
22. Functional math skills
23. Financial support benefits the individual with disabilities needs or presently has
24. Independent street crossing skills
25. Ability to handle criticism/stress
26. Limited amount of aggressive behavior or speech
27. Travel skills

Employment specialists use these factors to make job placements decisions. Notice that individual worker preferences do not enter into the placement process and that interests do not appear among the 27 factors. Involvement in the job placement decision-making process by individuals with disabilities is nonexistent. According to Moon and colleagues,

> [The] results of the job/worker compatibility analysis determine which consumers are appropriate to interview for the position. If two or three individuals appear equally suitable, there is almost always a factor that tips the decision toward the selection of one individual over another (e.g., one person's family is more enthusiastic about employment than others, or a person lives closer to the job site, or a person has more experience related to the job). In addition, do not overlook your intuition or "gut feeling" as to which individual you feel may be the best match for the job opening. It is often said that there is art, as well as science, in the process of job placement. Once the job trainer has chosen a client for the job, arrangements are made for the employer to interview your candidate. (1986, p. 59)

Clearly, in this early model, job trainers choose jobs. They based their decisions on the 27 factors without giving systematic consideration to individual preferences. Moon and colleagues acknowledged worker choice but in a limited manner.

> When an individual states that he or she does not want to perform a certain job duty, such as operating a dishwasher, respect this decision. Do not pressure anyone to take a job, hoping that he or she will grow to like it. There are many demands and stresses during the initial phase of job training and a positive attitude on the part of the worker can be a crucial factor for success. (1986, p. 55)

Who Answers the Self-Directed Employment Questions?

Table 1.1 depicts typical Phase One answers to questions regarding self-directed employment. To be considered a self-directed employment practice, the worker with a disability must directly answer at least eight of the ten questions. During Phase One, the employment specialist answered eight of the questions. No one answered the two interest questions. Clearly, worker preference simply did not enter into the job match decision. Employment staff determined the individual's skills and limits, made a placement that matched the person's skill level, and provided all the training and support needed at the jobsite. Jobsite personnel answered only three questions regarding basic employment decisions. The individual with a disability answered none of these questions. He or she was simply told what job to do and where to go.

Phase One methodology did not use self-directed employment practices. The procedures did, however, begin the exodus of people with disabilities from sheltered workshop settings into community jobs. As practices evolved, individual preferences became more important, as demonstrated in Phase Two.

PHASE TWO: GET A JOB THAT IS A MATCH FOR THE INDIVIDUAL

By the 1980s and early 1990s, workers with disabilities from across the United States benefited from supported employment programs (Ellis, Rusch, Tu, & McCaughrin, 1990; Hill & Wehman, 1983; Kregel, Wehman, Revell, & Hill, 1990; McDonnell, Nofs, Hardman, & Chambless, 1989). These programs began to flourish across the world, too. Australia (Anderson & Wisener, 1996), Britain (Beyer, Kilsby, & Willson, 1995), Jamaica (Bent, 1997), Germany (Barlsen & Bungart, 1997), Norway (Blystad & Spjelkavik, 1997), Finland (Harkapaa et al., 1997), and Spain (Verdugo, Borja, Urries, Bellver, & Martinez, 1998) all established effec-

Table 1.1. Who answers the self-directed employment questions with the Phase One stage of supported employment?

Self-determination methodology question	Individual with disabilities	Employment specialist	Jobsite co-worker or supervisor
What are the worker's job, task, and characteristic preferences and interests?	no	no	no
What are the worker's skills and limits?	no	yes	no
Does the available job match the worker's interest and preferences?	no	no	no
Does the available job match the worker's skills and limits?	no	yes	no
What job accommodations are needed?	no	yes	no
Can the worker do the job?	no	yes	yes
How does the worker do the job?	no	yes	yes
What are the worker's problems and how are they solved?	no	yes	no
Who establishes the on-the-job support network?	no	yes	no
Who determines if the worker should leave this job?	no	yes	yes

tive supported employment programs. Texts regarding Phase Two supported employment issues and methodology appeared with titles such as:

- *Competitive Employment: Issues and Strategies* (Rusch, 1986)
- *Getting Employed and Staying Employed* (McLoughlin et al., 1987)
- *Vocational Preparation and Employment of Students with Physical and Multiple Disabilities* (Sowers & Powers, 1991)
- *Helping Persons with Severe Mental Retardation Get and Keep Employment* (Moon et al., 1990)
- *Supported Employment: Models, Methods, and Issues* (Rusch, 1990)
- *Supported Employment for Persons with Disabilities: Focus on Excellence* (Wehman & Kregel, 1989)
- *A Working Relationship: The Job Development Specialist's Guide to Successful Partnerships with Business* (Fabian, Luecking, & Tilson, 1994)
- *Natural Supports in School, at Work, and in the Community for People with Disabilities* (Nisbet, 1992)

Supported employment programs expanded from only securing community employment for workers with mental retardation to also include those with mental illness (Anthony & Blanch, 1987), physical and multiple disabilities (Sowers & Powers, 1991), and traumatic brain injury (Wehman, Kreutzer, Stonnington, & Wood, 1988). During the Phase Two years, methodology also received increased attention.

Phase Two Methodology

The vocational preferences of individuals with disabilities must direct job placement (Martin et al., 1990; Reid, Parsons, & Green, 1998; West & Parent, 1992). Phase Two methodology acknowledged this mandate but, as documented in the following examples, employment specialists answer the two interest questions—self-directed employment practices have not yet emerged. Numerous Phase Two examples exist, but discussion is limited here to four.

Example 1 Beyer and Kilsby (1997) described a five-step supported employment model representative of Phase Two methodology.

Step 1. Staff create a vocational profile for the applicant, which includes a description of ideal job characteristics.
Step 2. Staff canvass employers until a job is found that the staff believe matches the worker's interests, abilities, and needs.
Step 3. Staff analyze job tasks and work culture, compare worker traits to the job, and if a match, secure placement.
Step 4. Staff provide training and support, then fade to the lowest level possible to maintain performance with the use of natural supports.
Step 5. Staff continue monitoring, problem solving, and working on career development issues.

Beyer and Kilsby's (1997) model added two evolutionary steps to the Phase One methods, while keeping most of the Phase One components. Staff created a vocational profile that reflected each person's interests and skills and obtained jobs that matched each person's profile. Beyer and Kilsby recognized that as a person worked in his or her job, the profile changed, and the job would need to be changed to match the changed career aspirations. They continued the use of applied behavioral training techniques on the job and infused natural supports as a means to fade support and maintain the worker's employment.

Example 2 McLoughlin et al. (1987) also used vocational profiles to assist with job placement. Their profile "is a composite picture of a potential employee's skills, experiences, available supports, *preferences,* needs, and living situation" (p. 112; italics added). Preference factors included

> a.) type of work that applicant wants to do, b.) type of work that the parent/guardian feels is appropriate, c.) what the applicant enjoys doing at home, d.) observations of the kinds of work that the applicant likes to do best, and e.) observations of social situations that the applicant likes best. (p. 114)

Preference, however, does not drive the job match process. It is only one of ten profile factors, and staff make the final decisions. These steps illustrate what employment specialists must do:

1. Develop a vocational profile of each person
2. Target several employers who somewhat match the profile.
3. Develop the job site; assess the requirements; negotiate accommodations; and complete the Quality Checklist.
4. If the site represents the type described in Step 2:
   a. Compare the conditions and requirements of the job site with the profiles to determine if there are large discrepancies.
   b. If the match appears close, contact the applicant and arrange with the employer to have the employee begin working.
   c. If discrepancies exist that might turn out to be problematic, consider negotiating with the employer, discussing options with the applicant (and parents/guardian), and determining what accommodations are available by the agency to delimit or in some way reduce the importance of the identified discrepancies.
   d. If it is not possible to reconcile the discrepancies, look for another job site.
5. If the job site represents the type noted in Step 4 d:
   a. Review the profiles of other applicants and select one or more who seem to be consistent with the conditions and requirements of the employer.
   b. Narrow the list to one applicant by using local criteria (McLoughlin et al., 1987, p. 116).

Individual preference becomes a proxied choice. Staff members make the actual job placement decisions. The individual's input is minimal, and often others in the person's network make the choices when using a person-centered planning type approach (Hagner, Helm, & Butterworth, 1996; O'Brien et al., 1997).

According to Phase Two methodology, do individuals with disabilities choose their own job? According to Steps 4 a and b, the employment specialist determines whether there is a good match between the person's profile information and the qualities of the job. Individuals with disabilities do not choose; the employment specialist makes the final job decision. The profile guides the match, but individuals often have little direct input into the profile. The person's only choice is a reactive one—workers may directly or indirectly decide that they do not want the job. They can refuse to go to the job or express their displeasure once there through poor production or other unwanted behavior. This is negative empowerment—through an on-the-job veto—not proactive choice.

Example 3 Powell and colleagues (1991) developed a four-stage model: career planning, job development, instruction, and ongoing support. The first career plan stage establishes the foundation for subsequent action. It begins with a personal profile of an individual's likes, preferences, dislikes, special interests or activities, and personal choices. A partial profile for a sample employee, Mike, is illustrated in Figure 1.1.

The planning team, which includes the individual with a disability, uses the profile to determine employment outcomes and to identify top priorities. The individual with a disability comments on the selection of outcomes, and team members reach a consensus through subsequent discussion. Next, a subgroup meets to conduct a compatibility analysis to determine matches between priority outcomes and jobs. Of note, the individual with a disability is not a part of this subgroup. The analysis includes 1) proactive planning, 2) identification of job retention factors, 3) observation of employment options regarding priority outcomes and retention factors, 4) assessment of individuals regarding priority outcomes and retention factors, 5) development of matches between individuals with disabilities and jobs, 6) initial screening to determine general compatibility, 7) single-factor analyses to gather additional information from participants or employers regarding undecided factors, and 8) decisions by committee members regarding the match.

There are no formal computer generated answers for determining the ultimate feasibility of obtaining the best matches between participants and community employment sites. At best, a consensus occurs among team members to pursue a match that makes the most sense with the amount of information that is available. Team members weigh the pros and cons of each potential match and decide where to proceed from there. It is advisable to isolate the employment/participant factors that should receive more weight as being extremely critical to the long-term success of each participant. Initial planning of acquisition and

Mike's Profile

Likes and Preferences	Skills, Abilities and Competencies	Dislikes
Cleaning and assembly activities	Wants to come to work	Changes in routine without preparation
Helping others	Persistent	Having to wait to speak or to receive recognition
Shopping	Works without assistance for short periods of time; can work longer with assistance	Being corrected or criticized
Calling parents at home	Positive attitude: ready to work	Excessive work demands (especially too fast a pace)
Being by himself at times	Friendly to most people	
Working inside (not outside!)		
Music		

Figure 1.1. Mike's profile. (From Powell, T.H., Pancsofar, E.L., Steere, D.E., Butterworth, J., Itzkowitz, J.S., & Rainforth, B. [1991]. *Supported employment: Providing integrated employment opportunities for persons with disabilities* [p. 33]. White Plains, NY: Longman; adapted with permission.)

ongoing supports can be predicted based on the number of excellent, good, and poor matches that exist. (Powell et al., 1991, p. 51–52)

The driving force of this program is sound. Participants' likes, dislikes, special interests, and personal choices contribute to job matches. Personal profiles guide team discussions about employment goals and outcomes. Nevertheless, a familiar pattern emerges once again, as service providers take over, conducting compatibility analyses and making final decisions about the appropriateness of different jobs.

The individuals with disabilities have input but not the final choice. Input occurs at the beginning of the match process, but then it ends. Individuals with disabilities do not examine potential jobsites. They do not observe what other workers do. They do not compare different job visits to determine which is best for them. They do not talk with employees or supervisors. They do not try out tasks to get a feel for the kind of work they might perform. There is no need for the person to think, analyze, and decide what is best because, ultimately, the team decides.

Who Answers the Self-Directed Employment Questions?

The profile in Table 1.2 differs in many ways from the results in Table 1.1. In Phase Two, the employment staff answers all of the questions, whereas in Phase One, they only answered 80% of the questions. Employment site personnel answered only 30% of the Phase One questions, but in Phase Two, they played a bigger role, answering 60% of the questions. Unlike practices in Phase One, the employment specialists in Phase Two determined the worker's job, tasks, and characteristic preferences and matched this profile to available jobs. The role of the jobsite personnel expanded from simply answering a couple of questions about the workers' employment, to becoming involved in on-the-job training and long-term support functions. The individual with a disability, however, still did not substantially answer any of the questions.

Table 1.2 suggests that the focus of Phase Two clearly shifts from getting the person any job, which characterizes Phase One. In Phase Two, employment staff consider what they think

Table 1.2. Who answers the self-directed employment questions with the Phase Two stage of supported employment?

Self-determination methodology question	Individual with disabilities	Employment specialist	Jobsite co-worker or supervisor
What are the worker's job, task, and characteristic preferences and interests?	no	yes	no
What are the worker's skills and limits?	no	yes	no
Does the available job match the worker's interest and preferences?	no	yes	no
Does the available job match the worker's skills and limits?	no	yes	yes
What job accommodations are needed?	no	yes	yes
Can the worker do the job?	no	yes	yes
How does the worker do the job?	no	yes	yes
What are the worker's problems and how are they solved?	no	yes	yes
Who establishes the on-the-job support network?	no	yes	no
Who determines if the worker should leave this job?	no	yes	yes

the interests and preferences of the individual are and how these match available jobs. To facilitate fading of the employment staff from the jobsite, Phase Two methods enlist co-workers and supervisors to provide additional training and support (Hagner & DiLeo, 1993; Mank, Cioffi, & Yovanoff, 1997; Murphy & Rogan, 1994; Nisbet, 1992). These results indicate that Phase Two programs do not operate in a self-directed manner. The individual with a disability still does not answer the questions—staff or employment site co-workers or supervisors do. As we now know, these subjective opinions of support personnel are often inaccurate (Everson & Reid, 1997).

PHASE THREE: SELF-DIRECTED EMPLOYMENT

International policy, federal mandates, and best practice all call for the infusion of self-directed employment practices into transition and supported employment programs. Article 23 of the United Nations Universal Declaration of Human Rights (1948) declared that everyone has the right to free choice of employment. The Rehabilitation Act Amendments of 1992 (PL 102-569) mandated that supported employment programs establish informed choice and teach self-determination to individuals with severe disabilities. The Individuals with Disabilities Education Act (IDEA) Amendments of 1997 (PL 105-17) acknowledged that students must learn self-determination and advocacy skills in order to maximize empowerment and inclusion in their communities. Policymakers in the United Kingdom also established choice making as a fundamental concept underlying all practices for people with severe disabilities (Stalker & Harris, 1998).

Best practice suggestions for Phase Three emerged, too, from the Council for Exceptional Children's Division of Career Development and Transition (DCDT) when it stated that it "strongly believes that self-determination instruction during the elementary, middle, and secondary transition years prepares all students for a more satisfying and fulfilling adult life" (Field, Martin, Miller, Ward, & Wehmeyer, 1998b, p. 118). The American Association on Mental

Retardation (AAMR) advocated supporting the expression of citizens with disabilities to speak for themselves in making life choices, including work choices (Wagner, 2000).

Phase Three methods became clear when the Association of Persons in Supported Employment's (APSE) *Quality Indicators* (2001) called for supported employment practices to become self-directed. APSE wanted all individuals involved in supported employment programs to have opportunities to learn self-determination skills and engage in decision-making activities. To do this, APSE encouraged individuals with disabilities to learn the skills needed to lead and become active participants in their individualized education programs (IEPs) or their individualized plans for employment (IPEs). ASPE also advocated for self-determination–oriented employment practices through its *Ethical Guidelines For Professionals In Supported Employment* (DiLeo, McDonald, & Killam, 1996). These guidelines tell supported employment professionals to

- Provide opportunities for each individual to pursue his or her unique career path
- Realize that individuals receiving supported employment have varying interests, preferences, and aptitudes
- Provide each individual with disabilities with sufficient options related to his or her interests and desires so that each person may exercise control and autonomy over his or her life's direction
- Provide opportunities so the choices made by an individual are the result of being fully informed through direct personal experience
- Believe that individuals with disabilities (or at their invitation, family, friends, or co-workers) are the best source to personally convey information of their personal interests, preferences, skills and aptitudes, and life goals
- Provide a job placement that matches the personal interests, preferences, and abilities of the person with disabilities

Others join APSE in calling for infusion of choice and self-determination practices into employment programs for youth and adults with severe disabilities (Bodgan, 1996; Everson, 1996; Everson & Reid, 1997; Pumpian, Fisher, Certo, & Smalley, 1997; Rusch & Hughes, 1989). Clearly, strong support exists for putting vocational choice-making decisions into the hands of individuals with disabilities. Phase Three procedures use vocational choice making as the foundation of a self-determination oriented employment practice. It enables the dreams and goals in peoples' hearts to become a crucial aspect of the planning and implementation of employment programs (Callahan & Garner, 1997).

Self-Directed Employment Model

Wehman stated that "if individuals are to experience personal satisfaction and quality of life regardless of whether or not they have a disability, it is critical for them to have the right to make choices, express preferences, and exercise control in their lives" (1997, p. 1). This requires a structure and the time for the individual with disabilities and his or her vocational specialists or teachers to meet to discover job preferences and establish an employment plan (Brooke et al., 1995). Any shortcuts taken during the preference discovery period will most likely result in additional training and support needs, job loss, and worker and employer disappointment (Parent, Unger, & Inge, 1997).

Self-Determination Self-determined individuals know what they want and how to get it. They advocate for their own interests. From an awareness of personal needs, self-determined individuals choose goals. They doggedly pursue their goals. This involves asserting their presence, making their needs known, evaluating progress toward meeting their goals, adjusting their performance as needed, and creating unique approaches to solve problems (Martin & Mithaug, 1990). A self-determined individual makes decisions and acts on those decisions (Martin, Mithaug, Husch, Frazier, & Huber Marshall, 2002).

Since the early 1990s, we have developed and implemented a *choose, manage, evaluate, and adjust model* to teach secondary students and adults with disabilities vocational choice making and other self-determination skills (see Figure 1.2). We developed and tested this model through the Self-Directed Supported Employment Program located at the University of Colorado in Colorado Springs and then repli-

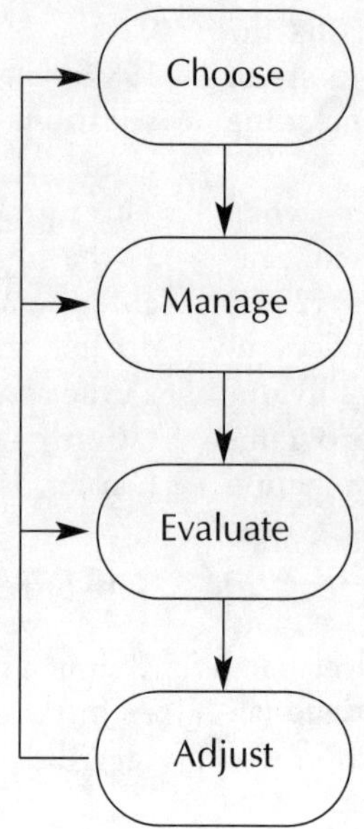

Figure 1.2. Choose, manage, evaluate, and adjust model.

cated the process across numerous sites both within Colorado and across the nation (Martin & Mithaug, 1990; Martin, Mithaug, Agran, & Husch, 1990; Martin, Oliphint, & Weisenstein, 1994). These procedures enable the individual to tell his or her team what he or she wants based on his or her own experiences (Cross, Cooke, Wood, & Test, 1999). This model uses a repeated-measures self-evaluation to produce a cumulative profile that depicts the individual's preferred choices (Gaylord-Ross, 1986).

The Self-Directed Supported Employment Program consists of three consecutive phases, with each having its own questions that the worker must answer (see Figure 1.3). The first is a structured community-based situational assessment, followed by a placement process, during which time the person learns situational specific problem-solving and self-management skills. Last, long-term follow-up and support facilitates job success or change management. Individuals systematically complete a structured curriculum as they progress from one phase to the next. The procedures help each person think about and then reliably answer critical vocational questions, phase-by-phase.

Methodology

Assessment The assessment process uses an ecological approach that provides the opportunity for individuals with disabilities to learn

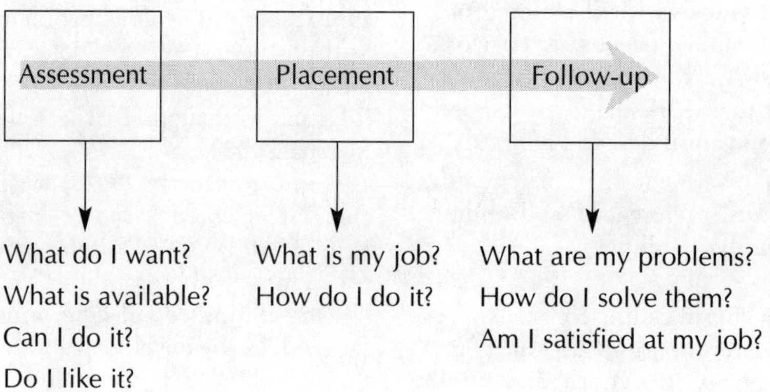

Figure 1.3. Self-Directed Employment questions.

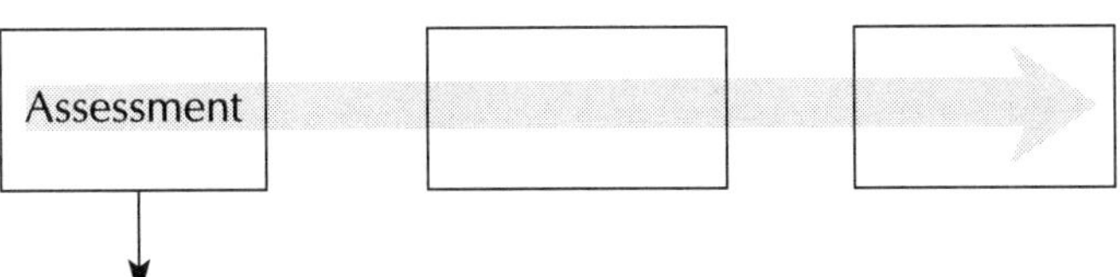

What do I want?

- Job choices method
- "Characteristics I like" method

What is available?

- "Job Characteristics I like versus those at the site" method
- Shadowing method

Can I do it?

- Work, social, personal, and task improvement method
- Job needs and accommodations method
- Self-determined improvement method

Do I like it?

- "Job Characteristics I like versus those at the site" method
- Task choice method

Figure 1.4. Assessment stage questions and methods.

what they like, can do, and how to match these characteristics to available community jobs. The individual with disabilities begins by making many choices. Through a series of structured community-based experiences, the individual then narrows his or her selections to two jobs that match stated preferences and market availability.

The Self-Directed Assessment process enables individuals with disabilities to answer four questions listed in Figure 1.4. Structured opportunities enable individuals with disabilities to determine 1) what do I want? 2) what's out there? 3) can I do it? and 4) do I like it? Upon entry into the program, individuals make initial job, task, and characteristic choices. Second, they explore these choices and choose again based on their recent experiences. Third, they complete a series of working on-the-job assessments to get a hands-on "feel and taste" of the job duties, characteristics, and demands. Then they choose again on the basis of what they learned. Individuals repeat this process many times across available entry-level jobs until a consistent profile emerges.

Placement Placement secures a job through a three-stage process. It starts at the end

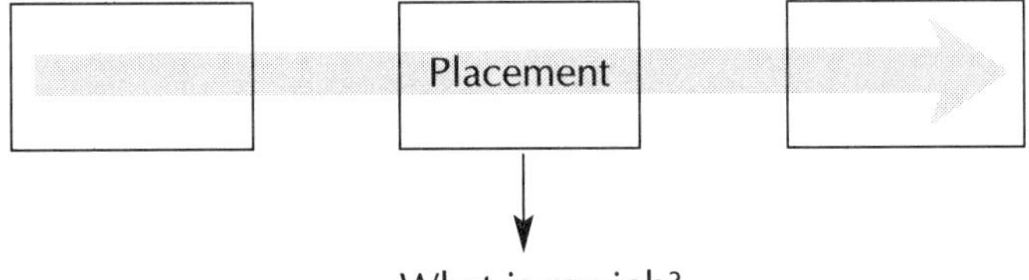

What is my job?

- "Can I do the job?" method
- "Job characteristics I like versus those at the site" method

How do I do it?

- Improvement contract method

Figure 1.5. Placement stage questions and methods.

of assessment and continues until the placement is considered successful. During placement, workers answer two basic questions: 1) What is my job? and 2) how do I do it? (see Figure 1.5).

Stage 1 This phase secures the person a preferred job. Employment specialists do not simply place the person in a job that matches the choices made during assessment. Because large environmental differences may often exist from site to site within the same job class, each person must answer specific questions about any potential jobsite. Using structured forms and systematic procedures, the person decides whether he or she can do the job and whether the characteristics at the site match his or her preferences.

Stage 2 During this phase, the worker learns how to do the job. The actual process is site dependent. Usually co-workers train the needed skills. In difficult training situations, employment specialists or peer job coaches enter to facilitate skill development. They help restructure the environment, teach the person self-management strategies (e.g., self-instructions), or provide trainer-directed instruction. Unlike the traditional job coaching model, the trainer teaches the individual to use self-management skills to cope with changing situations. Program staff do not do the work for the individual, as each person must assume responsibility for his or her assigned job duties.

Stage 3 This phase focuses on fluency, maintenance of learned skills, and adjustment to changing on-the-job demands. As the worker nears mastery of the required job duties, Phase 3 begins. Central to this phase is the "thinking process" depicted in Figure 1.6. Based on supervisor feedback from the previous day, the worker uses improvement contracts to establish a short-range plan to solve the problems, implements the plan, self-evaluates his or her performance, states any adjustments that are needed in either the plan or his or her actual performance and then repeats the cycle.

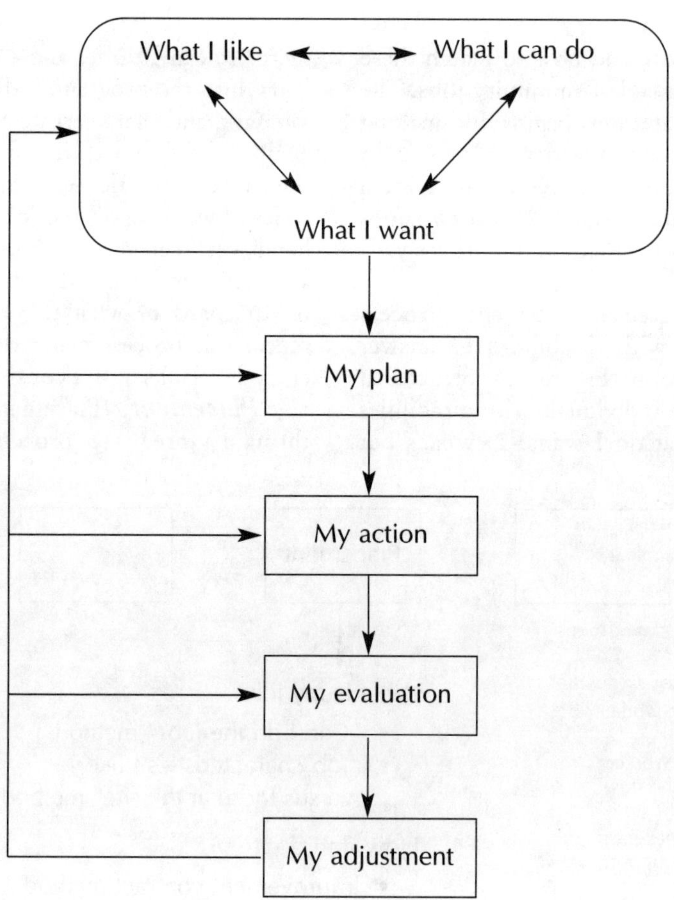

Figure 1.6. Self-Directed Employment process of thought.

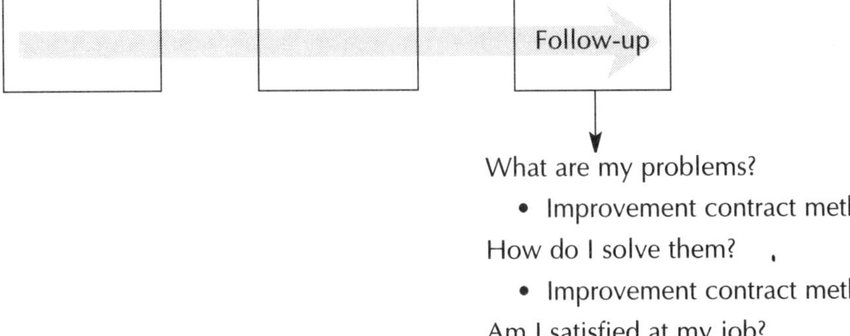

What are my problems?

- Improvement contract method

How do I solve them?

- Improvement contract method

Am I satisfied at my job?

- Change plan method

Figure 1.7. Follow-up stage questions and methods.

Follow-Up Individuals, as depicted in Figure 1.7, answer three questions during this phase: 1) What are my problems? 2) how do I solve the problems? and 3) am I satisfied at my job? During this phase, individuals continue to use their Improvement Contracts each week to identify and solve problems. In addition, the person completes a structured format to facilitate on-going career development. Through the use of a Change Plan, which is completed biannually, the individual compares what he or she wants with what is available at the job site. If discrepancies exist, the person implements a plan to remove the discrepancies. This may involve, for instance, getting another job, securing a promotion, or earning more pay.

Who Answers the Self-Directed Employment Questions?

The profile in Table 1.3 differs substantially from the results in Table 1.1 and Table 1.2. In Phase Three, the individual with disabilities answers all of the questions. Employment specialists and jobsite personnel do not answer any of the questions,

Table 1.3. Who answers the self-directed employment questions with the Phase Three stage of supported employment?

Self-determination methodology question	Individual with disabilities	Employment specialist	Jobsite co-worker or supervisor
What are the worker's job, task, and characteristic preferences and interests?	yes	no	no
What are the worker's skills and limits?	yes	assists	assists
Does the available job match the worker's interest and preferences?	yes	assists	assists
Does the available job match the worker's skills and limits?	yes	assists	assists
What job accommodations are needed?	yes	assists	assists
Can the worker do the job?	yes	assists	assists
How does the worker do the job?	yes	assists	assists
What are the worker's problems and how are they solved?	yes	assists	assists
Who establishes the on-the-job support network?	yes	assists	assists
Who determines if the worker should leave this job?	yes	assists	assists

but they do assist the individual with answering nine of the ten questions. The individual with disabilities substantially answers all of the questions. Table 1.3 shows how decision making shifts from the employment specialists–directed answers in Phase Two. In Phase Three, both the staff and job-site personnel facilitate answers. They set the occasion for the individual to determine what to do. These results indicate that Phase Three programs do operate in a self-directed manner. Why? The individual with disabilities answers the questions—not staff or co-workers. Rather than others making the decisions, the voice of the person with disabilities is heard and acted upon.

SUMMARY

Supported employment practices have evolved through three distinct phases. The methodology has gone from staff telling the person what job he or she will do to listening to what each individual wants to do. Although the methodology has changed, the purpose of supported employment remains the same. The heart of supported employment lies in the strength of a very simple concept: Individuals with disabilities can obtain and maintain employment in competitive positions with planned support.

2

Self-Determination

The Concept Powering Self-Directed Employment Practices

Self-determination is the most important skill that programs must teach (Ward, 1996). Secondary educational and supported employment programs, which typically have not taught self-determination skills (Phelps & Hanley-Maxwell, 1997), must now infuse self-determination methods into their daily operations so that people with disabilities can learn these crucial skills (Browning, 1997; Halloran, 1993; West, 1995). The self-directed employment questions posed in Chapter 1 represent operational self-determination concepts. The answers to these questions tracked two types of changes—the noticeable evolution in practice and the switch to self-determination oriented practices in Phase Three.

Phase One methodology got people community jobs, but individuals with disabilities made no decisions—they simply went where they were told. These practices did not teach or provide opportunities for individuals to develop their self-determination skills. Phase Two procedures, which initiated staff-directed job match procedures, produced better outcomes than Phase One methods (McDonnell et al., 1989), but the individuals still did not make the decisions. In Phase Three, practices evolved so that individuals with disabilities made their own employment decisions. Initial results indicate that this approach produces better results than Phase Two procedures (Martin et al., 2002). Programs that utilize Phase Three methods directly teach self-determination skills and provide opportunities for individuals to learn and practice these empowering behaviors.

Each self-directed employment question from Chapter 1 operationalized one or more self-determination concepts. Table 2.1 shows the self-determination concepts represented by each question. Two address self-awareness issues: choice and learning about one's strengths and weaknesses. The others focus on self-advocacy, decision making, self-evaluation, adjustment, and independent performance factors. Together, these self-determination concepts power Phase Three self-directed employment practices.

This chapter examines self-determination, reviews two self-determination strands, compares five self-determination instructional mod-

Table 2.1. Self-directed employment questions and corresponding self-determination concepts

Self-directed employment questions	Self-determination concept
What are the worker's job, task, and characteristic preferences and interests?	Self-awareness
What are the worker's skills and limits?	Self-awareness
Does the available job match the worker's preferences?	Decision making Self-evaluation
Does the available job match the worker's skills and limits?	Decision making Self-evaluation
What job accommodations are needed?	Decision making Self-evaluation
Can the worker do the job?	Decision making Self-evaluation
How does the worker do the job?	Decision making Independent performance (IP) Self-evaluation
What are the worker's problems and how are they solved?	Adjustment Decision making IP Self-evaluation
Who establishes the on-the-job support network?	Self-advocacy
Who determines if the worker should leave this job?	Adjustment Decision making Self-advocacy

els, shows that the self-determination components common to all the models are the same factors powering Phase Three self-directed employment practice, and provides examples of how self-determination concepts affect people with and without disabilities.

CONCEPT OF SELF-DETERMINATION

Discussions about self-determination date back several hundred years and lead to a macro- and micro-level understanding of this concept. The philosopher John Locke stated in 1715 that "the idea of men and self-determination appear to be connected" and that "men can determine themselves" (p. 293). Individual conceptualizations of self-determination grew into ideas of collective self-government. Since the days of the American Revolution, self-determination has served as a central concept in American ideology (Unterberger, 1996). The concept of self-determination has enabled high school students with disabilities to participate in decisions that affect their lives (Ward & Kohler, 1996) and adults with disabilities to assume financial control for the purchase of services from social service agencies (Pennell, 2001).

Individual Capacity for Self-Determination

Capacity for self-determined behavior derives from each person's social life, the sociopolitical process affecting each person's opportunity for self-direction, and three person-specific factors (Mithaug, 1996). First, "self-knowledge and self-awareness of personal needs, interests, and abilities" vary from person to person and affect each person's ability to seize opportunities to achieve goals that match his or her self-understanding. Second, the capacity for self-determination varies by the degree that an individual learns and manages his or her skills and motivation to get what he or she wants out of life. Third, the degree of access to personal, social, economic, and technical resources and supports either hinders or facilitates each person's capacity to achieve his or her self-selected goals. These three factors interact with each other, and each may be increased through specific instruction, opportunities, and supports. The larger society (macro-level) in which each person lives interacts with each individual's unique (micro-level) capacity to become and act self-determined.

Macro- and Micro-Levels of Self-Determination

Self-determination exists at macro- and micro-levels. *Macro-level self-determination* "refers to the right of a people to determine their own political destiny" (Unterberger, 1996, p. 926). Self-determination empowers societies and groups of people to take control of their own affairs and direct their own future. The American Revolution represents the first "assertion of the right of national and democratic self-determination in the history of the world" (Unterberger, 1996, p. 927). President Woodrow Wilson championed the right of self-determination to bring peace to Europe following the end of World War I (*Wilson's Address,* 1918). In contrast, societies that devalue groups of people and keep them in subservient roles produce individuals who lack the skills and attitudes for self-direction and goal-oriented behavior (Gilson & Tulser, 1997). Dictatorial governments that control all decision making, for example, never allow their citizens to learn and then use the self-determination skills needed for group goal-directed behavior and effective self-government. Many countries that attempt to become democratic struggle with self-government and occasionally lapse back into their previous, yet familiar dictatorial ways, in which the citizens are told what to do and how to do it. Indigenous Americans today still struggle with self-determination in educational systems (Snyder-Joy, 1992) and local, state, and federal government after not being allowed to make their own societal decisions for many generations (Smith, 1992).

Micro-level self-determination affects the individual. Self-determined individuals choose their own goals and attempt to attain their goals while using supports they have chosen (Field & Hoffman, 1994; Martin et al., 1994). Conversely, many people with disabilities—who may always have been told where to go, what to do, how they did, and what they have to do next—lack the level of self-determination needed to plan and achieve their desired dreams (Bodgan, 1996). These individuals need school transition and employment programs that embrace a self-determination philosophy and methods, so that they can learn and apply their self-determination skills (Mittler, 1995).

Increasing numbers of people with disabilities now realize that they need to advocate for themselves in order to achieve community and individual goals (Miller & Keys, 1996; Ward, 1996). Dudley noticed this change:

> Some labeled people are ready to break out of traditional consumer roles that characterize them as passive recipients of services. In place of these roles, they wish to take on new roles that involve more responsibility and risk-taking. These new roles can be "empowering" because they result in people assuming more control over their lives. (1997, p. 162)

These empowering behaviors enable individuals to organize into advocacy groups, which seek empathetic understanding and desired societal change (Rogovsky, 1997; Wilson, 1997).

An Applied Example In 1996, the Robert Wood Johnson Foundation funded pilot programs nationwide to change the delivery system for adults with developmental disabilities. These pilot sites collaboratively created a service support system that simultaneously facilitated political self-determination and supported individuals' self-directed lifestyle decision making on the basis of each person's self-knowledge of preferences (Pennell, 2001). The change in the social service system (on the macro level) enabled individuals (on the micro level) to shift decision-making power from the existing social service structure to the person. In these national pilot programs, individuals choose how they will live and the supports they will use to attain their goals. This macro-level system reform effort provides individuals with disabilities with the skills and information needed to make their own major life decisions. The pilot programs changed their expectations and, by so doing, provided the opportunity for individuals to increase their self-determination capacity. Pennell (2001) believed that the macro-level changes enabled self-determined actions so that individuals would be able to do the following:

- Freely choose family and friends, and plan a life with needed supports and control of their own service dollars (rather than purchase a preplanned program from the current system)
- Control their own service dollars to purchase the desired level of support
- Arrange their own supports

The Robert Wood Johnson Foundation projects had such an effect that many service providers, family members, and adults with disabilities now view self-determination as simply the means to control services. To these people, *self-determination* means that control over the services and supports that are offered to people with developmental disabilities should rest with the person receiving those services (Moseley, 1999). Clearly, controlling one's services represents a self-determined action or behavior, but self-determination manifests itself through more than just control of services.

SELF-DETERMINATION POLICY INITIATIVES AND MANDATES

A fundamental right of all people is the right to self-determination (United Nations, 1997). The National Agenda for Achieving Better Results for Children and Youth with Disabilities included this recognition in its call for a vision of education that "begins with images of children and youth with disabilities having access to supports and services that leads to self-actualization, self-determination, and independence" (as cited by Wolman, Campeau, DuBois, Mithaug, & Stolarski, 1994, p. 3). International and national leaders include self-determination concepts in policies and laws. The International Covenant on Civil and Political Rights, adopted by the General Assembly of the United Nations (UN), advocated that all people should have the right to self-determination and that all countries participating in the UN should promote and respect that right (United Nations, 1997).

United States and United Kingdom Government Policies

Government policies in the United States and the United Kingdom include self-determination outcomes and practices in disability legislation and regulations. The United States' Rehabilitation Act Amendments of 1992 (PL 102-569) "signaled a new era in disability service delivery and, indeed, in the way in which disability itself is viewed by society" (Wehmeyer & West, 1995, p. 277). The act indicates that people with disabilities should enjoy the rights to make choices and to enjoy self-determination. The goals of the United States, therefore, include providing individuals with the tools necessary to make informed choices and decisions and to become self-determined.

The 1991 and 1997 reauthorizations of the United States' IDEA (PL 102-119 and PL 105-17) require that school transition services be outcome-oriented; that is, current educational activities must focus on students' preferred post-school future. The law prescribed specific student-level self-determined activities, and its regulations mandated that if students' transition issues are going to be discussed, students must be invited to participate. More important, perhaps, is that decisions made about any student's transition activities must reflect that student's preferences and interests.

The United Kingdom's *Special Education Needs: Code of Practice* (1997) likewise mandated that self-determined student behaviors be present in the transition plan. The code required schools to answer these and other questions in their transition plans:

- "What information do young people need in order to make informed choices?"
- "How can young people be encouraged to contribute to their own transition plan and make positive decisions about their future?"
- "What are the young person's hopes and aspirations for the future, and how can these be met?" (Special Education Needs: Code of Practice, 1997, p. 118)

Special education laws in both the United States and the United Kingdom agree that students need to learn several self-determination behaviors prior to their transition plan meeting. Schools must teach students these behaviors. Student preferences and interests must guide the transition process. Mithaug, Wolman, and Campeau poignantly summarized these developments by saying "for the first time, the mandated condition is for student preferences to drive service delivery" (1992, p. 7).

To meet student involvement mandates in educational planning, students must learn self-determination skills (Wehmeyer, Agran, & Hughes, 1998). The intent of both the American and the British laws are that students become equal players in the educational planning and implementation process. To do this, students need to become self-determined (Wehmeyer et al., 1998).

The Division on Career Development and Transition Policy Statement

The Council for Exceptional Children's Division on Career Development and Transition (DCDT) published a self-determination transition policy statement. In this position statement, Field and colleagues wrote that self-determination is the transition foundation:

> We strongly believe that self-determination oriented instruction during the elementary and secondary transition years prepares all students for a more satisfying and fulfilling adult life. There is substantial evidence that encouraging self-determination for all youth could help them be more successful in their educational programs as well as helping them to develop lifelong success skills. (1998b, p. 118)

This policy reaffirms an earlier DCDT transition policy statement in which Halpern (1994) said that an emerging component of transition must be "a sense of student empowerment which eventually enhances student self-determination within the transition planning process. . ." (p. 118).

Association for Persons in Supported Employment Guidelines

The Association for Persons in Supported Employment (APSE) advocated for self-determination programs in its *Ethical Guidelines for Professionals in Supported Employment* (DiLeo et al., 1996). The ethical foundation of this organization demands that professionals

- Provide opportunities for each person to pursue his or her own career path
- Acknowledge each individual's unique set of interests, preferences, and aptitudes
- Provide options so that individuals may make informed choices
- Believe that individuals with disabilities are the best source of personal interests, preferences, skills, aptitudes, and life goals

Many have called for the infusion of self-determination practices in supported employment programs, but few self-determination supported employment practices exist (Bodgan, 1996; Everson, 1996; Everson & Reid, 1997; Pumpian et al., 1997; Rusch & Hughes, 1989).

SELF-DETERMINATION STRANDS

Discussions of self-determination and its importance to people with disabilities date back to the early 1970s. In this context, *self-determination* is not a trait or characteristic of individuals. It consists of a set of skills that are constantly being taught, learned, applied, and adapted within and across settings (Deci, Vallerand, Pelletier, & Ryan, 1991; Nowak, Laitinen, Stowitschek, & Affleck, 1995; Wehmeyer, 1999). Two major definitional strands emerge from these works: 1) the choice strand and 2) the goal setting and attainment strand.

Choice Strand

Nirje (1972) considered choice important from a disability rights perspective. Deci and Ryan (1985) discussed choice from a psychological motivational framework. Wehmeyer (1992) and Schloss, Alper, and Jayne (1994) stressed the human rights dynamic within a psychological construct perspective. Several others considered the intersection between self-determination and choice as well (see Table 2.2).

Vocational Choice Policies and legislation define vocational choice making by individuals with cognitive disabilities as a fundamental, international right. Article 23 of the United Nations' Universal Declaration of Human Rights (1948) declared that everyone has the right to employment choices. The United States' Rehabilitation Act Amendments of 1992 (PL 102-569) required that informed choice and self-

Table 2.2. Definitions of self-determination in the choice strand

Source	Definition
Nirje (1972)	Self-determination is a critical component of the normalization principle. Choices, wishes, and aspirations of people with disabilities must be taken into consideration in actions affecting them.
Deci and Ryan (1985)	Self-determination is the capacity of individuals to choose and then have these choices be the driving force behind their action. Choice initiates the self-determination process.
Williams (1990)	We already know what self-determination means—it is just a $10 word for choice.
Wehmeyer (1992, 1996)	Self-determination refers to the attitudes and abilities required to act as the primary causal agent in one's own life and to make choices regarding one's actions free from undue external influence.
Schloss et al. (1994)	Self-determination is a person's capacity to choose and to have those choices be the determinants of one's actions.

determination become central principles that U.S. employment programs follow. Policymakers in the United Kingdom established vocational choice making and self-advocacy as fundamental practices (Stalker & Harris, 1998; Wood & Trickey, 1996). The European Community wants the "widest possible choices of personally appropriate opportunities" to be provided as people with disabilities make the transition into the mainstream workforce (European Centre for the Development of Vocational Training, 1986).

Choice Making Denied These choice policy mandates stem from a history of abuse. Historically, people with cognitive disabilities have not been allowed to choose their own jobs because "employment programs unknowingly suspend basic employment rights that nonhandicapped workers enjoy" (Martin & Mithaug, 1990, p. 87). Just as experts once believed individuals with disabilities would not benefit from inclusive education or be able to work productively in competitive community-based employment, many failed to recognize the individual's right to control his or her own life through decision making, and self-advocacy (Inge & Tilson, 1997; Johnson, McGrew, Bloomberg, Bruininks, & Lin, 1997; Neumayer & Bleasdale, 1996).

Individuals with disabilities often had little to say about the jobs they found through school-based transition programs or adult agency–supported employment programs (Ficker-Terrill & Rowitz, 1991). The assessment process that schools and vocational programs used to match interests did not produce valid results (Agran & Morgan, 1991). The one-shot vocational interest and aptitude tests, checklists, and other forms that give cut-off scores for acceptable and unacceptable job placements do not work (Parker, Szymanski, & Hanley-Maxwell, 1989). The assessment process *was* systematic, objective, and replicable; however, it is invalid because the person actually is not making an informed choice (Beyer & Kilsby, 1997; Menchetti & Flynn, 1990; Parent, 1996). Even the person-centered planning process, which began as a means to listen to what people with developmental disabilities wanted, often does not facilitate real individual choice making because others typically make the decisions (O'Brien et al., 1997). Edgerton said,

> Individual choice among available options is essential if there is to be any meaningful improvement in peoples' lives, we must assure that it is persons with mental retardation who choose what they want, not we who choose for them. And if their choices do not invariably bring them a greater sense of well being, we should not then impose our choices on them. They, like the rest of us, should have the right to strive for satisfaction in life in their own way. And we must understand that some of them, like the rest of us, will be more successful than others. (1990, p. 158)

The procedures in Chapters 4–9 of this book provide teachers and employment staff the methods that empower individuals to make their own choices.

Goal Setting and Attainment Strand

The process of achieving goals that satisfy needs and match interests define this strand (Wehmeyer, Palmer, Agran, Mithaug, & Martin, 2000). This understanding emerged from several sources, including an analysis of the business and sport psychology "success" literature, developments within the independent living movement, an understanding of the instructional power of self-control and goal-setting strategies to assist in skill acquisition and generalization, and follow-up studies and interviews with individuals with disabilities (Mithaug, Martin, & Agran, 1987). These definitions in this strand are included in Table 2.3.

Toward a Unifying Understanding

Much of what we know about self-determination comes from the effort to teach these skills (Eisenman, 2001). Martin and Huber Marshall (1995) developed their self-determination curriculum on a framework provided by the earlier Adaptability Model (Mithaug et al., 1987). They added to this framework additional constructs discovered through an extensive literature search, interviews, and surveys of parents, professionals, and adults with disabilities. Together, they produced a comprehensive list of 37 self-determination concepts grouped into seven constructs: 1) self-awareness, 2) self-advocacy, 3) self-efficacy, 4) decision making, 5) independent performance, 6) self-evaluation, and 7) adjustment. From these, Martin and Huber Marshall (1995) created their self-determination curriculum.

Wehmeyer (1992); Field and Hoffman (1994); Serna and Lau-Smith (1995); and Mithaug, Wehmeyer, Agran, Martin, and Palmer (1998) followed similar procedures in creating their definitions by building their definitions from their identified constructs. For example, Wehmeyer, Kelchner, and Richards summarized their development efforts by saying

> In operational terms, self-determined actions reflect four essential characteristics: autonomy, self-regulation, psychological empowerment, and self-realization. These four essential characteristics emerge as individuals acquire component elements of self-determination, including choice and decision-making, problem-solving, goal setting, and attainment skills; internal locus of control orientations; positive self-efficacy and outcome expectancies; and self-knowledge and understanding. (1996, p. 632)

When laid side by side, the choice strand and the goal setting and attainment strand merge. Table 2.4 presents the constructs of five of the

Table 2.3. Definitions of self-determination in the goal and attainment strand

Source	Definition
Ward (1988)	Self-determination is the attitude and ability that lead individuals to define goals for themselves and to take the initiative in achieving those goals.
Martin, Huber Marshall, and Maxson (1993)	Self-determined individuals know what they want and how to get it. From an awareness of personal needs, self-determined individuals set goals, then they doggedly pursue *their* goals. This involves asserting *their* presence, making *their* needs known, evaluating progress toward meeting *their* goals, adjusting *their* performance as needed, and creating unique approaches to solve problems.
Wolman, Campeau, DuBois, Mithaug, and Stolarski (1994)	Self-determined people know and can express their own needs, interests, and abilities. They set appropriate goals, make choices, and plans in pursuit of their goals, and make adjustments as needed to achieve their goals.
Field and Hoffman (1994, 1995)	Self-determination is a person's ability to define and achieve goals from a base of knowing and valuing oneself.
Serna and Lau-Smith (1995)	Self-determination refers to a person's awareness of his or her strengths and weaknesses, his or her ability to set goals and make choices, to be assertive, and to interact with others in a socially competent manner. The outcome is a person who is able to obtain his or her own goals without infringing on the rights, responsibilities, and goals of others.
Mithaug, Wehmeyer, Agran, Martin, and Palmer (1998)	Self-determination is the repeated use of skills necessary to act on the environment in order to attain goals that satisfy self-defined needs and interests.
Wehmeyer et al. (2000)	People who are self-determined will regulate their own problem solving to attain their own goals.

Table 2.4. Self-determination concepts in the choice strand, keyed to Martin and Huber Marshall's conceptualization (1995)

Martin and Huber Marshall (1995)	Field and Hoffman (1994)	Wehmeyer, Agran, and Hughes (1998)	Serna and Lau-Smith (1995) (from their self-determination skills list)	Mithaug, Wehmeyer, Agran, Martin, and Palmer (1998)
Self-awareness Identify needs Identify interests Identify and understand strengths Identify and understand limitiations Identify own values	*Know yourself* Dream Know strengths, weaknesses, needs, and preferences Know options Decide what's important *Value yourself* Accept self Respect one's own rights and duties	*Choice making* Selecting between alternatives based on individual preferences *Self-awareness and self-knowledge*	not present in model	Identify interests and preferences
Self-advocacy Assertively state wants Assertively state needs Determine support needs Pursue needed support Obtain and evaluate needed support Conduct own affairs	not present in model	not present in model	not present in model	*Self-advocacy instruction*
Self-efficacy Expects to obtain goals	not present in model	*Positive attributions of efficacy and outcome expectancy*	not present in model	not present in model
Decision making Assess situational demands Set goals Set standards Identify information needed to make decisions Consider past solutions for new situations Generate new, creative solutions Consider options Choose best option Develop a plan	*Plan* Set goals Plan actions to meet those goals Anticipate results Be creative Visually rehearse	*Decision making* *Problem solving* *Goal setting and attainment*	*Self-direction skills* Action planning Goal setting Goal planning Self-management Evaluating outcomes	*Take action* Determine opportunities and barriers Set goals Determine a plan of action Identify instructional strategies Set goals Determine focus of action Prioritize learning needs

Independent performance Initiate tasks on time Complete tasks on time Use self-management strategies Perform tasks to standard Follow through on own plan	*Act* Take risks Communicate Access resources and support Negotiate Deal with conflicts and criticism Be persistent	*Independence, risk taking, and safety skills* *Self-instruction skills*	*Persistence and risk taking* Persistence through problem solving Risk taking through decision making	*Set schedule* *Self-directed learning*
Self-evaluation monitor task performance Compare performance to standard Evaluate effectiveness of self-management strategies Determine if plan is completed and goal met	*Experience outcomes and learn* Compare outcome to expected outcome Compare performance to expected performance	*Self-observation, self-evaluation, and self-reinforcement*	*Self-evaluation* Evaluating present skills Evaluating skills needed for future goals	*Self-regulation* Self-monitor Evaluate progress Compare progress Decide if goal is achieved
Adjustment Change goals Change standards Change plan Change strategies Change support Persistently adjust	*Experience outcomes and learn* Make adjustments	not present in model	not present in model	Revise goal if necessary Revise action if necessary Revise action plan if necessary
not present in model	*Value yourself* Accept and value yourself Admire strengths that come from uniqueness Recognize and respect rights and responsibilities Take care of yourself	*Internal locus of control*	*Social skills* Giving positive feedback Giving criticism Accepting criticism Resisting peer pressure Negotiation Following instruction Conversation Problem solving	not present in model

self-determination definitions aligned to the Martin and Huber Marshall (1995) conceptualization. Each of the definitional schemes included several of the constructs identified by Martin and Huber Marshall. All but one contains a construct that Martin and Huber Marshall did not identify. Comparisons of these constructs find that

- Four of the five models included self-awareness, with two including interests and limitations and two only focusing upon preferences.
- Out of the five models, Martin and Huber Marshall solely considered self-advocacy a self-determination construct. Later, Wehmeyer and colleagues extended this belief and concluded that individuals with disabilities "need to learn how to advocate for their own needs and interests by taking action to change circumstances that pose obstacles to their pursuits" (Wehmeyer et al., 2000, p. 441).
- Two of the five included self-efficacy.
- All five considered decision making a needed construct.
- All five included independent performance constructs, often emphasizing the use of self-management strategies.
- All five had self-evaluation as an essential self-determination concept.
- Three included adjustment components.

All four of the models included constructs that Martin and Huber Marshall did not. The analysis of these show

- Field and Hoffman and Wehmeyer et al. included one construct that Martin and Huber Marshall did not address. Field and Hoffman had "valuing yourself" as a major construct. Likewise, Wehmeyer et al. included a locus of control construct.
- Serna and Lau-Smith's model highlighted several constructs no other model included: prerequisite social skills, networking skills, and collaboration skills.

The Serna and Lau-Smith model matches the Martin and Huber Marshall model on three out of seven (43%) self-determination constructs. Both the Field and Hoffman and Wehmeyer et al. models match the Martin and Huber Marshall's conceptualization on five out of seven (71% agreement) concepts, and the Mithaug and colleagues (1998) Self-Determination Learning Model matches six out of seven (86%) concepts.

Using Martin and Huber Marshall's definitional framework, these models agreed at least once that self-determination consists of seven constructs. These are

- Self-advocacy
- Self-awareness
- Self-efficacy
- Decision making
- Independent performance
- Self-evaluation
- Adjustment

These self-determination concepts power the Self-Directed Employment procedures detailed in Chapters 4–9.

STUDIES ON SELF-DETERMINATION

Self-determination is the most important factor for a person with disabilities to achieve (Nirje, 1972). Self-determination is the ultimate goal of education (Halloran, 1993). Ward (1988) said that it is critical for individuals with disabilities to become self-determined. Why do these policy leaders demand in such strong language that self-determination is so important? Studies of individuals who were peak performers and studies of individuals with disabilities illustrate the importance of these concepts. As you read these summaries, note the match between the identified skills and seven self-determination constructs from the previous section.

Results from the Study of Peak Performers

Since the 1940s, considerable research on peak performers in the business and sport communities reached the same conclusion. Peak performers set goals, believe they can accomplish their goals, develop plans, initiate action on that plan, evaluate outcomes, make adjustments, and advocate for their own interests. Numerous sources result in these findings.

The Garfield Study Garfield (1986) identified the skills and strategies of more than 500 high achievers and compared them across business, science, sports, and the arts. Amongst other factors, he found

- Peak performers' decisions included 1) choosing a mission that leads to action; 2) envisioning and communicating a clear mission; and 3) following with an action plan of specific goals and benchmarks to evaluate the timing, quality, and quantity of the results. Peak performers follow with action plans that include goals, resource development, and timelines.
- Peak performers believed they could accomplish their goals. They had the ability to "see oneself as the originator of actions in one's life . . . [viewing] events in life as opportunities for taking action and [seeing] themselves as the agents who must precipitate action" (Garfield, 1986, p. 141).
- Peak performers self-evaluated; that is, they used their ability to seek out feedback and used the feedback positively to adjust subsequent performance.
- Peak performers used self-control strategies. For instance, they rehearsed by making mental images of the roles they would play in important events.
- Peak performers had the ability to adapt.

Garfield's characteristics also differentiated between adjustments that keep one on course and major changes that lead to new plans, goals, or even missions.

Garfield's peak performers distinguished themselves by

1. Defining and pursuing missions that motivate
2. Developing plans and engaging in purposeful activities directed toward achieving goals that contribute to the mission
3. Engaging in self-observation and effective thinking, which assures maximum performance
4. Correcting and adjusting activities to remain on the critical path to the goal
5. Anticipating and adapting to major change while maintaining momentum within an overall game plan

The Gallup Study Gallup and Gallup (1986) described the ability of top performers to overcome adverse conditions and to learn from mistakes. Successful people ". . . tend to be realistic about their talents and their abilities as well as about their weaknesses. So they are in a position to learn from their mistakes, even as they *expect* to reach their goals" (Gallup & Gallup, 1986, p. 81).

The Robbins Formula Anthony Robbins (1997) wrote that successful people follow a consistent path. The path begins by knowing what one wants.

> If you look at successful people, you'll find they followed these steps. They started with a target, because you can't hit one if you don't have one. They took action, because just knowing isn't enough. They have the ability to read others, to know what response they were getting. And they kept adapting, kept adjusting, kept changing their behavior until they found what worked. (Robbins, 1997, p. 12)

Results from Studies of People with Disabilities

Successful people set goals, develop plans, initiate action on that plan, evaluate outcomes, and make adjustments. But do individuals with disabilities have these skills? Gerber, Ginsberg, and Reiff (1992) interviewed a group of adults with learning disabilities. Much to their credit, Gerber and associates asked different questions than previous follow-up studies. They found out, among other things, that successful individuals with learning disabilities had

- A desire to succeed
- Well thought-out goals
- Persistence
- A social support network that facilitated their success

These researchers concluded that the successful individuals with disabilities wanted to succeed, set achievable goals, and confronted their learning disabilities. One participant in their survey said, "Successful people have a plan. You have to have a plan, goals, strategy, otherwise you are flying through the clouds and then you hit the mountain" (Gerber et al., 1992, p. 480).

Wehmeyer and Schwartz (1997) also conducted a follow-up study of former high-school youth with mental retardation or learning disabilities. They collected data regarding each person's level of self-determination before graduation and again one year after graduation. The people who were more self-determined as students had more positive adult outcomes, including being employed at a higher rate and earning more per hour than peers who were not as self-determined.

SUMMARY

Self-determination has become an educational, vocational, and major human rights issue. Individual self-determination competency is a function of the person's skill level and the opportunities that he or she has had in which to learn and practice those skills. The operationalized components of most contemporary self-determination models in the disability literature agree on seven major constructs: self-awareness, self-efficacy, decision making, self-advocacy, independent performance, self-evaluation, and adjustment.

The time has come to teach self-determination behaviors to individuals with disabilities and to provide opportunities to master self-determination skills. To do this, self-determination practices must be infused into educational transition practices and adult agency supported employment programs. The purpose of the next seven chapters is to describe the steps for infusing self-determination concepts into existing transition vocational and supported employment programs.

3

GETTING STARTED

An Implementation Overview

This chapter summarizes the self-directed employment (SDE) procedures, and it can be used as a reference tool for future use. First, it introduces the SDE curriculum, which depicts the 6 goals and 24 objectives divided into broad assessment and placement sections. Second, it answers assessment and placement questions (i.e., "Why we do it?" and "What is it?"). Third, it presents the Self-Directed Employment Staff Profile. This curriculum-referenced tool asks employment specialists and teachers to rate their responses to three questions for each objective of the SDE curriculum. The resulting profile indicates whether the teachers or employment specialists believe they know how to do the procedures, whether the procedures are currently implemented, and whether their school or employment programs value these concepts and actions. The data from this assessment provide useful information for staff development and program planning information. Fourth, the organizational schema and the notation used in Chapters 4 through 9 are presented. Fifth and finally, a detailed reference guide depicts the entire SDE process. Listed by each goal and objectives are corresponding forms by name and number, plus an estimated amount of time required to complete that objective.

A NOTE ABOUT TIME

Throughout Chapters 3 through 9, estimations of the amount of time needed to complete an objective are given. These estimates were determined from experience in developing and implementing these procedures in an agency-based supported employment program. Your actual time will vary on the basis of experience, adding to or taking away from the recommended procedures, and other factors. Please consider these numbers as only estimates. Your actual time will most likely differ at least slightly from these estimates.

SELF-DIRECTED EMPLOYMENT CURRICULUM

The SDE curriculum consists of two sections containing a total of 6 goals and 24 objectives. Section I addresses the *Assessment: Choice Management* goals and objectives. Section II addresses the *Placement and Follow Along: Self-Management* goals and objectives. Table 3.1 is a curriculum guide that summarizes the procedures in Chapters 4–9 and can enhance your understanding of the whole process. Refer to this curriculum guide often as you learn the SDE procedures.

Section I. Assessment: Choice Management

The assessment approach uses an ecobehavioral, repeated measure, structured situational assessment approach driven by each individual's choices. The starting point of assessment is the choices expressed by the person, and consequently, choice-making power resides with the individual.

Experiences gained through community job shadowing and internships provide opportunities for the individual to explore preferences in depth, to practice tasks, and to learn crucial decision-making skills. Repeated self-evaluation opportunities enable the individual to learn to match his or her behavior to jobsite requirements. Choice, decision making, and performance data are graphically presented to permit each individual and the support team to learn what the job seeker wants and can do. This teaching and assessment process sets up a foundation for individuals to advocate for their self-determined vocational preferences and choices or, in other words, to manage their own choices.

The *Assessment: Choice Management* process matches the individual's skills and preferences to jobs available in the local community. Figure 3.1 demonstrates this principle. The shaded triangular patch shared by all three circles represents the best vocational job match. The curriculum guide presents the 4 goals and 15 objectives of *Assessment: Choice Management.* Typically, 6–8 weeks and 40–45 staff hours are needed to complete the job match process. At the end, a completed Self-Determined Job Match Summary provides a graphic representation of the individual's choices, preferences, and skills.

Goal A: Making Choices The purpose of this goal is to generate a menu of initial interests and preferences to investigate later. The individual, the individual's family, the staff, and other helping professionals get to know each other. Initial organizational procedures such as consent and confidentiality forms are signed, and logistics are arranged. An orientation is provided to the individual and significant others. Past work history, education, and home details are gathered. Staff need to arrange three 1-hour meetings over a 2-week period. These meetings will be used to identify the individual's initial preferences for different jobs and characteristics. A summary of the individual's initial job and task choices is then made (see Figure 1.1).

Goal B: Exploring Choices The summary produced in Goal A is used to arrange preferred community job shadowing experiences. During shadowing, each individual observes workers doing jobs and tasks in community businesses. Once at the worksite, each person determines whether the skills required by the job match his or her skills. The individual once again decides if this is still a preferred job after seeing it, feeling it, smelling it, and hearing it. If a job is not easily observable, information may be gathered by interviewing a worker or supervisor from a preferred jobsite. Together, the individual and the staff develop a detailed shadowing summary of resulting job choices and preferences. This summary is used to determine internship sites that the individual will test in Goal C.

Goal C: Testing Choices For this goal, the individual completes at least a 3- to 4-hour working experience over 3 days in two or three pre-

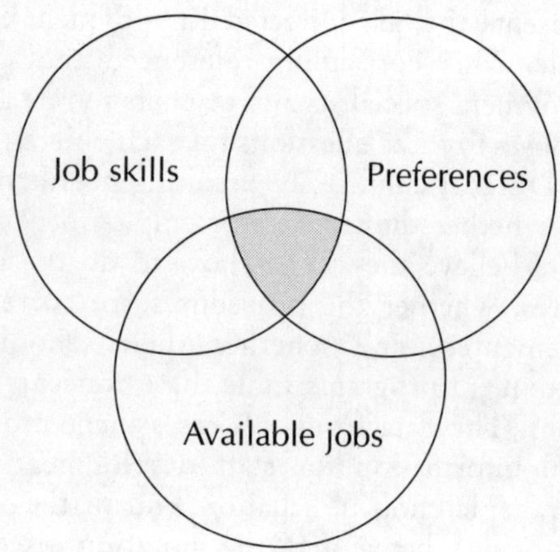

Figure 3.1. The requirements for a job match.

Table 3.1. Self-directed employment curriculum guide

Goals	Objectives				
Section I. Assessment: Choice Management					
A. Making Choices	1. Getting Started	2. Completing the Jobs I Want to Do: Form A or B	3. Completing the Characteristics I Like: Form A or B	4. Summarizing Making Choices	5. Constructing a Résumé
B. Exploring Choices	6. Completing Shadowing Skill and Preference Match	7. Completing the Characteristics I Like versus What Is Here: Form A or B	8. Doing the Situational Interview (optional)	9. Completing the Shadowing Summary	
C. Testing Choices	10. Facilitating Internships	11. Completing the Characteristics I Like versus What Is Here: Form A or B	12. Doing the Improvement Forms	13. Completing the Job Requirements and Accommodations: Form A or B	
D. Final Choices	14. Completing the Job Internship Summary Graphs	15. Facilitating Postassessment Staffing			
Section II. Placement and Follow-Along: Self-Management					
E. Finding a Job Matching Skills and Preferences	16. Individualizing Job Development	17. Collecting and Evaluating Supervisor Feedback	18. Completing the Do I Have the Job I Like? Forms	19. Completing the Can I Do This Job? Forms	20. Completing the My Employment Plan
F. Solving On-the-Job Problems	21. Checking Supervisor Match	22. Teaching a Problem-Solving System	23. Teaching Ongoing Adjustments	24. Monitoring Changes and Adjustments	

ferred jobs. At each site, the individual determines his or her work, social, personal, and task strengths and weakness. He or she also decides if this type of work matches his or her preferences. A graphic summary analysis of the individual's internship performance and choices is then produced.

Goal D: Final Choices Each individual helps produce the Self-Directed Job Match Summary. It contains graphs of the individual's preferences, work skills, social skills, personal skills, task skills, independent decision making, requirements and accommodations, and choices made throughout the assessment process. The individual's first and second ranked job choices, support recommendations, and suggestions are generated. Recommendations for facilitating postassessment staffing are provided. This summary of the assessment process is shared with the individual, the family, and supporting agencies.

Section II. Placement and Follow-Along: Self-Management

The purpose of this section is to teach the workers to self-manage their own jobs. It consists of a placement and follow-along process. *Placement* is a process of supporting people to secure employment in a job that matches their work skills and preferences. *Follow-along* is the process of maintaining a successful employment relationship and helping workers advance in their chosen career field.

Because large environmental differences exist from site to site within the same job class, each person must answer specific questions about any potential jobsite. Using a structured process and systematic procedures, the person decides if he or she can do the job and if the characteristics of the site match his or her preferences. Only after reaffirming the match does the person learn how to do the job and meet the employer's expectations.

At a growing number of businesses, coworkers provide training for the needed skills. In others, employment specialists enter the jobsite to facilitate skill development and build natural supports. They help restructure the environment, teach the person self-management strategies, build natural supports, or provide trainer-directed instruction. Unlike the traditional job coaching model, an employment specialist or a teacher using this approach teaches each worker to use self-generated self-management and problem-solving skills to cope with the changing work, social, and personal demands. Employment specialists using the approach do not do the work for the individual, as each person is responsible for assuming responsibility for the assigned job duties. A good job match ensures that this occurs.

Follow-along provides a structured format to facilitate career development. Through continued skill development, use of self-management, and a biannual preference check, the individual compares what he or she wants to do with what is available at his or her current jobsite. If discrepancies exist, the person implements a plan to remove the discrepancies. This may involve, for instance, getting another job, securing a promotion, getting additional education, or earning more pay.

Supported employment programs need to find jobs that match each individual's preferences and skills—not simply get jobs for the person. The approach offers the opportunity for individuals to develop career goals and secure a job that will be satisfying and rewarding. Section II of the curriculum contains the *Placement and Follow-Along: Self-Management* procedures. Goal E's objectives show how to find a job that matches skills and preferences. In most cases, a job match should be obtained within the first 3 months following the end of assessment. Timelines are not carved in stone; they depend on many variables, including the individual job choices, their availability, the demands of each job, and the needs of each individual. Goal F teaches individuals to solve on-the-job problems for immediate and continued success. Follow-along will likely continue for the vocational life of each individual, and its appearance will change with the needs and growth of each participant.

Goal E: Finding a Job Matching Skills and Preferences The purpose of this goal is to secure a job that matches the worker's skills and preferences. Once a job is found that matches the assessment profiles, the individual evaluates it to determine whether the skills and preferences of the job match present preferences. Also, a supervisor feedback process is introduced to the employer to determine if the worker is meeting the job requirements. The employment specialist works with the individual and coworkers to develop on-the-job supports.

Goal F: Solving On-the-Job Problems The objectives in Goal F teach each worker to use self-management skills to solve his or her own on-the-job problems. Several formats are provided to teach this process. The lessons teach a simple method:

1. Solicit supervisor feedback.
2. Identify problems.
3. Identify solutions.
4. Replace problems with solutions.
5. Follow through on adjustment.

As an individual becomes proficient in problem solving, an employment maintenance and career advancement strategy is introduced.

SELF-DIRECTED EMPLOYMENT STAFF PROFILE

The Self-Directed Employment Staff Profile contains 61 items and is divided into three sections (see pp. 281–284). A blank profile is available in Appendix A: Blank Forms. For each item, three questions are presented:

- Have I learned this?
- Do I do this?
- How important is this to my program?

Staff and administrators use a four-point response scale from 0 to 3 to rate themselves across each item and question. See Table 3.2 for information that may help in answering these questions. By totaling the number of points at the bottom of each section and then graphing the resulting raw scores on the profile, a picture of the responses for each section appears.

The Self-Directed Employment Staff Profile may be used in several ways. Ask supported employment staff, teachers, and their administrators to complete it to determine

- How much the philosophy is valued
- How much they know about the procedures
- How much they use the procedures

In our training of teachers and employment staff, we often used the profile as a pre/post measurement to determine values, knowledge, and practice information. One of the first things we do is request all involved staff and administrators to complete the profile. Six months to a year later, the staff completes the profile again. When compared with the first measure, this last measure shows how much gain occurred across the profile areas. The profile can also be used for each staff to establish yearly performance measures and for administrators to help monitor program quality and staff effectiveness.

ORGANIZATIONAL SCHEMA

Chapters 4 through 9 present the details of the SDE curriculum. This section explains how each of these chapters are organized. Each chapter follows the same format.

Reference Box

A reference box is located in the top left corner of each objective and on each form. Use the reference box to guide you through the curriculum (see Figure 3.2). You may wish to cross-reference each numbered box using the Implementation Reference Guide (Table 3.3).

Materials Needed List

As you read the first page of each objective, note the Materials Needed list. This list summarizes the forms you need to complete the objective.

Table 3.2. Questions and answers about the Self-Directed Employment Staff Profile

What does "Have I learned this?" mean?	Let's take item "I. Facilitate job choices" as an example. As a result of your previous training and experience, do you feel that you have learned how to facilitate someone in making job choices? Rank your response based on how well you have learned this. A rank of 0 means "Not very well." A rank of 3 means "Very well."
I work in an administrative position. How do I respond to "Do I do this?"	If the item is not relevant to your current job description or is not something that you do, circle 0. Make sure you have filled in your title at the top of the page.
What does "How important is this to my program?" mean?	In general, considering the cultural climate of your organization, how important do you think this item is to your program? Is this an item that your program really values?

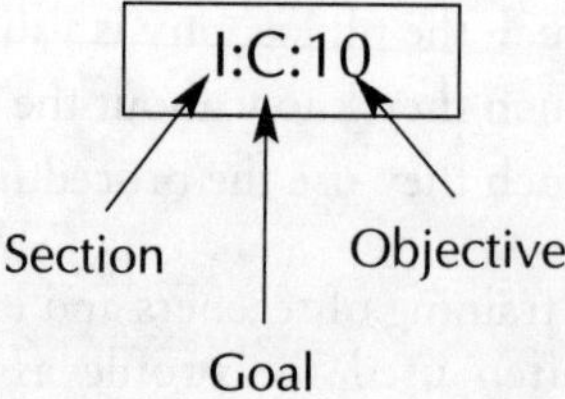

Reference boxes on forms have a fourth number. This number indicates the form number.

Figure 3.2. Key to the reference box.

Some of the forms listed for each objective are brand-new; others may have already been completed in previous objectives.

What If?

Following each objective, you will find a section labeled "What If?" We provide examples of the most common roadblocks that may occur. Although this is not a complete list of all of the possible situations, you may find that this section includes many answers to difficulties you may encounter. If your particular question is not included, those that are listed may still provide some insight regarding what to do.

IMPLEMENTATION STRATEGIES

The procedures and methodology are easily infused in existing transition and supported employment programs. The methodology enhances the structures and adds many new decision points. To ensure success, staff time and job descriptions may need to be modified. The Implementation Reference Guide addresses the goals, objectives, and the average amount of time that staff can expect to spend accomplishing each objective for one individual.

Each agency may have specific preferences for structuring the staffing patterns within their organization. It is generally efficient to have staff specialize by phase. Staff members who have an aptitude for detail and are very thorough may prefer the assessment process. Those staff who enjoy marketing and sales may do well with job development. Employees who implement the self-management and problem-solving procedures and who are invested in the long-term success of individuals are excellent job coaches. Many smaller organizations are limited to a few staff, however, and others choose a holistic approach in which each staff person does everything. Either organizational structure works just as well. Develop one that fits your organizational culture and needs.

Time Needed to Complete the Major Phases

The time estimates used in Chapters 4 through 9 assume an individually delivered supported employment program. School programs and other supported employment delivery options will most likely develop different time patterns. Typically, once staff become proficient with the procedures, you may expect an average of 40–45 direct and indirect staff hours to complete Section I with an individual. Likewise, approximately 45 hours may be needed to develop and build on-the-job supports. Of course, follow-along and career development are ongoing, and the time needed vary with the individual and jobsite.

As you read this book, you may notice a definite learning curve. Initially, you may be challenged by the objectives. Read through each of them more than once before attempting implementation. Make sure you feel comfortable with the instructions and the forms before you begin. You may wish to start with a small number of individuals (e.g., three or four). Schedule completion time over a 3-month period. Each quarter, you should think about adding three or four more individuals, with a goal of 12 for the year. By using this suggested timeline, you will have the first group finishing the first section as a new group begins. Keep the process going. As each group works through choices, staff will become more proficient with the procedures. The more you use the job match assessment procedures, the more efficient you will become. The same is true for Section II.

Implementation Reference Guide

Table 3.3 contains an Implementation Reference Guide, listing the goals, objectives and forms contained in this book. In addition, it provides the form numbers and the approximate time it will take to complete each objective. This reference guide is provided as a graphic organizer to aid in your understanding and successful implementation.

Table 3.3. Implementation Reference Guide

Goal	Objectives	Forms	Numbers	Time
Section I. Assessment: Choice Management				
A. Making Choices	All objectives	All forms		About 2 weeks
	1. Getting Started	Self-Directed Employment Orientation Matrix	I:A:1:1	1 to 2 hours
	2. Completing the Jobs I Want to Do: Form A or B	Jobs I Want to Do: Form A or Jobs I Have Done and Jobs I Want to Do: Form B	1:A:2:1 I:A:2:2 I:A:2:3	Three 1.5 hour sessions
	3. Completing the Characteristics I Like: Form A or B	Characteristics I Like: Form A or Characteristics I Like: Form B	I:A:3:1 I:A:3:2	Completed in Objective 2
	4. Summarizing Making Choices	Initial Job Preferences Graph Initial Task Preferences Graph Characteristics Summary Graph Four Most Important Characteristics Graph	I:A:4:1 I:A:4:2 I:A:4:3 I:A:4:4	1 hour
	5. Constructing a Résumé	Application for Employment Sample Résumé 1 Sample Résumé 2 Sample Résumé 3	I:A:5:1 I:A:5:2 I:A:5:3 I:A:5:4	2 hours
B. Exploring Choices	All objectives	All forms		About 1 month
	6. Completing Shadowing Skill and Preference Match	Assessment Event Organizer Questions for Shadowing Shadowing: Form A Shadowing: Form B	I:B:6:1 I:B:6:2 I:B:6:3 I:B:6:4	2.5 hours for each of the 3–4 jobsites shadowed plus jobsite development time
	7. Completing the Characteristics I Like versus What Is Here: Form A or B	Characteristics I Like versus What is Here: Form A or Characteristics I Like versus What is Here: Form B	I:B:7:1 I:B:7:2	Completed in Objective 6
	8. Doing the Situational Interview (optional)	Situational Interview Situational Interview Summary	I:B:8:1 I:B:8:2	2.5 hours
	9. Completing the Shadowing Summary	Shadowing Summary Graph Characteristics Summary Graph Four Most Important Characteristics Graph	I:B:9:1 I:A:4:3 I:A:4:4	2 hours

(continued)

Table 3.3. (*continued*)

Goal	Objectives	Forms	Numbers	Time
C. Testing Choices	All objectives	All forms		About 1 month
	10. Facilitating Internships	Assessment Event Organizer	I:B:6:1	Internship jobsite development time
	11. Completing the Characteristics I Like versus What Is Here: Form A or B	Characteristics I Like versus What is Here: Form A	I:B:7:1	Completed in Objective 12 (30 minutes)
		or		
		Characteristics I Like versus What is Here: Form B	I:B:7:2	
	12. Doing the Improvement Forms	Work Improvement: Form A	I:C:12:1	4–5 hours per internship site
		Social Improvement: Form A	I:C:12:2	
		Personal Improvement: Form A	I:C:12:3	
		Task Improvement: Form A	I:C:12:4	At least 2–3 sites should be developed
		or		
		Work Improvement: Form B	I:C:12:5	
		Social Improvement: Form B	I:C:12:6	
		Personal Improvement: Form B	I:C:12:7	
		Task Improvement: Form B	I:C:12:8	
		or		
		Self-Determined Improvement Form	I:C:12:9	
	13. Completing the Job Requirements and Accommodations: Form A or B	Job Requirements and Accommodations: Form A	I:C:13: 1	Completed the last day of each internship (30 minutes)
		or		
		Job Requirements and Accommodations: Form B	I:C:13:2	
D. Final Choices	All objectives	All forms		About 1 week
	14. Completing the Job Internship Summary Graphs	Work Strength Evaluation Graph	I:D:14:1	3–4 hours
		Social Strength Evaluation Graph	I:D:14:2	
		Personal Strength Evaluation Graph	I:D:14:3	
		Task Strength Evaluation Graph	I:D:14:4	
		Job Requirements and Accommodations Graph	I:D:14:5	
	15. Facilitating Postassessment Staffing	Evaluation Across Internships Graph	I:D:15:1	
		Adaptability Summary	I:D:15:2	
		Adaptability Graph	I:D:15:3	
		Internship Preference Graph	I:D:15:4	
		Initial Support Ratio Graph	I:D:15:5	
		Self-Determined Job Match Summary	I:D:15:6	

Section II. Placement and Follow-Along: Self-Management

E. Find a Job Matching Skills and Preferences	All objectives	All forms		About 1–2 months
	16. Individualizing Job Development	Preplacement Information Job Development Information Job Development Record	II:E:16:1 II:E:16:2 II:E:16:3	
	17. Collecting and Evaluating Supervisor Feedback	Supervisor Evaluation Cards: Form A or Supervisor Evaluation Cards: Form B Monitor Supervisor Feedback Graph	II:E:17:1 II:E:17:2 II:E:17:3	First day of the job and ongoing
	18. Completing the Do I Have the Job I Like? Forms	Characteristics I Like versus What is Here: Form A or Characteristics I Like versus What is Here: Form B Jobs and Tasks I Like: Form A or Jobs and Tasks I Like: Form B Do I Have the Job I Like? Summary	II:E:18:1 II:E:18:2 II:E:18:3 II:E:18:4 II:E:18:5	One week after job starts Collect for 5 or more days
	19. Completing the Can I Do This Job? Forms	Can I Do This Job? Form A or Can I Do This Job? Form B Can I Do This Job? Summary	II:E:19:1 II:E:19:2 II:E:19:3	Collect for 5 days or more
	20. Completing the My Employment Plan	My Employment Plan: Form A or My Employment Plan: Form B Job Termination Follow-Up Report	II:E:20:1 II:E:20:2 II:E:20:3	Optional: once a week or until consistent

(continued)

Table 3.3. *(continued)*

Goal	Objectives	Forms	Numbers	Time
F. Solve On-the-Job Problems	All objectives	All forms		Ongoing: on-the-job
	21. Checking Supervisor Match	Basic Match Contract	II:E:21:1	Optional: for as long as needed
		or		
		Match Contract: Alternate 1	II:E:21:2	
		or		
		Match Contract: Alternate 2	II:E:21:3	
		Match Data Summary	II:E:21:4	
	22. Teaching a Problem-Solving System	Problem and Solutions List	II:E:22:1	
		Basic Improvement Contract	II:E:22:2	Ongoing: on-the-job
		or		
		Improvement Contract: Alternate 1	II:E:22:3	
		or	II:E:22:4	
		Improvement Contract: Alternate 2	II:E:22:5	
		or		
		Improvement Contract: Alternate 3	II:E:22:6	
		or		
		Improvement Contract: Alternate 4	II:E:22:7	
	23. Teaching Ongoing Adjustments	Improvement Contract Data Summary	II:E:23:1	At least monthly
		Quarterly Placement Summary	II:E:23:2	
	24. Monitoring Changes and Adjustments	My Change Plan: Form A	II:E:24:1	Every 3–6 months or as needed
		or		
		My Change Plan: Form B	II:E:24:2	

4

INTRODUCTION TO SECTION I.

Goal A: Making Choices

To begin the SDE job match assessment, you should make sure that all of your organizational start-up procedures are processed appropriately. Chapter 3 outlines some of the necessary information needed to progress smoothly through the job match assessment process. When you meet with the individual with disabilities and concerned others, summarize what will be taking place. Make sure that support roles are well established and that the individual understands your role: You will be a guide, leading the way through a variety of experiences while the individual is making, exploring, and testing choices about jobs that exist in the local community.

Meet with the individual for three 1-hour sessions during a period of 2 weeks in order to identify initial job choices. Some individuals may need one or two more sessions to develop their initial choices. During these sessions, teach the person to identify preferred work characteristics—those distinguishing traits found at a job (e.g., does the person want a job where he or she works inside or outside? Does the person prefer to stand or sit?). During this process, ask the individual to describe past work experiences and to identify the preferred ones. It is important to identify a criterion with which to explore past work experiences. If the person has had paid job experiences, then make paid job experiences the criterion for gathering information. If you have read the files, talked with the individual's parents, and found out that the individual has not had paid job experiences, then identify the tasks the individual has done at home and in other settings. Your criterion can then be nonpaid work experiences. Be sure to consider volunteer experiences, too.

After determining past work experiences, find out what jobs the person would like to do. These choices can be previous jobs or new ones. What would the person like to do on each job? What do they imagine the job to be? Find out what is attractive about the choices. What specifically does the individual like about the job? Is there a friend or relative that currently has a similar job? Has he or she ever seen someone performing this job? After each session, encourage the individual to think about the choices just made. Explain that it is acceptable to make changes. Instruct the person to go home, talk to friends and relatives, walk through the community, and think about jobs.

This initial 2-week period is also a good time to schedule meetings in order to gather information that will be needed to complete future forms. This information should be compiled into a résumé that describes past experiences and interests. If a person has not had much paid experience, use volunteer work or work done around the house. At the end of the 2 weeks, create a summary of initial choices. Graphing the choices creates an initial picture of the individual's preferences. Share the summarized information with the individual, and determine with the individual that the information shown is representative of his or her choices. Finally, determine the jobs and tasks the individual would most like to shadow. (*Note:* Initial choices may not reflect the person's final choices. Do not lock the person into these choices. These choices can and often do change!) This graphic organizer will assist you through the process found in this chapter.

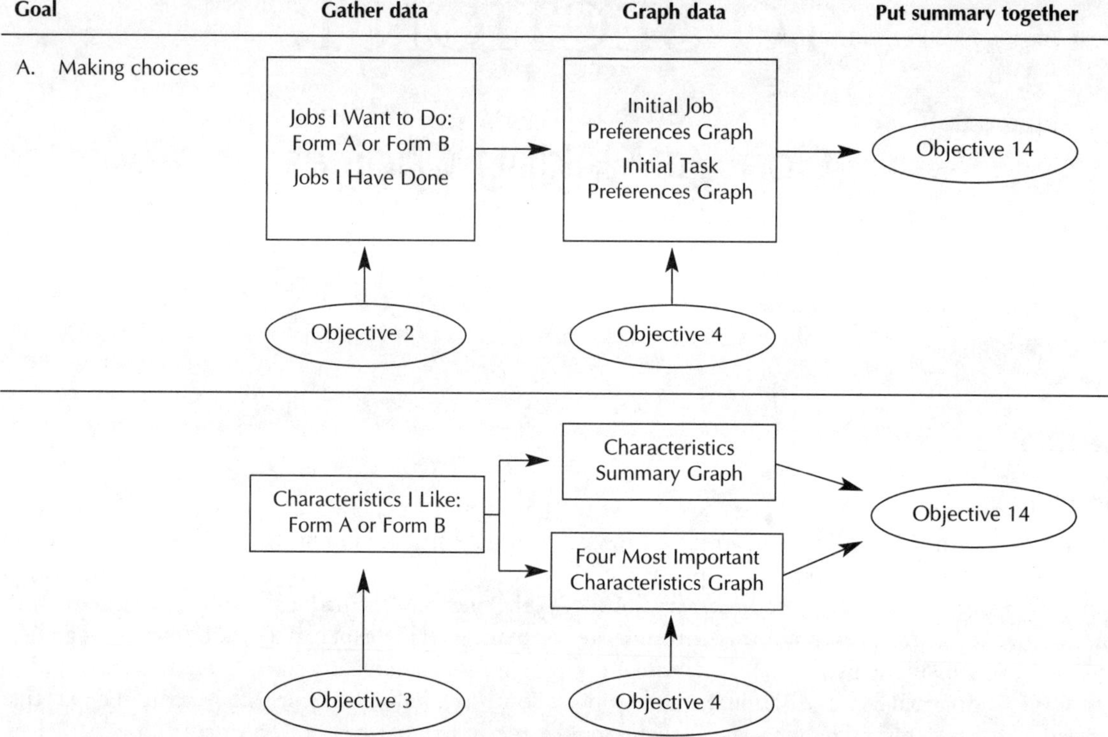

Section I. Assessment: Choice Management
Goal A: Making Choices

Objective 1: Getting Started

CONTENTS

Review files
First meeting: Intake
Second meeting: Orientation

MATERIALS NEEDED

Case history file
Your program's administrative forms
Self-Directed Employment Orientation Matrix (I:A:1:1)

PURPOSE

To understand background information and to introduce the individual and his or her significant others to the Self-Directed Employment Program

LOCATION

Office

Review files

Materials Needed
- Case history file
- Your program's administrative forms

A. Read the new individual's file. Answer as many of the following questions as possible:

1. Does this individual want to work?
2. What are this individual's job interests?
3. What is this individual's job history?
4. Does this individual have a history of bizarre, explosive, emotional, or otherwise inappropriate work behaviors, including criminal or job abandonment behaviors? If yes, what appears to prompt them? What works to control them?
5. Who will pay for services?
6. Does this individual have medical concerns or prescriptions that require special consideration?
7. Is this individual his or her own guardian? If not, who is?
8. What form of transportation does this individual use (e.g., bus, car, friend's car)?
9. What are this individual's work attendance patterns?
10. How will earnings affect benefits?

First meeting: Intake

A. Set an appointment to meet this individual. Make sure other service professionals, parents, guardians, or significant others are invited to the meeting.

1. Discuss the two purposes of this meeting: It provides an opportunity for the individual to find out about the Self-Directed Employment Program, and it provides an opportunity for the staff to get to know the individual.
2. Gather new information, and ask questions raised from an earlier review of the individual's file.
3. Explain that the individual will use a series of decision-making forms to help him or her choose the best job, learn the job, and do what is needed to keep his or her job.
4. Make an effort to establish rapport with the individual. If parents are present, answer questions they may have about the program. Enlist their support. Use them as a resource, but make sure that they understand that the input of the individual counts the most.
5. Decide the role of each person and agency.
6. Stress the importance of regular attendance at scheduled appointments.
7. Find out if this individual wants to be involved in the Self-Directed Employment Program.

B. Assist the individual or guardian in reading and signing program administrative forms that may include

1. A rights statement
2. A consent form to collect and enter data under conditions of confidentiality
3. Enrollment of the individual into the agency's liability insurance to allow coverage for community working assignments
4. A description of productive working internships and his or her pay

C. Schedule the Self-Directed Employment orientation meeting.

Second meeting: Orientation

Materials Needed
Self-Directed Employment Orientation Matrix

A. At the Self-Directed Employment orientation meeting, follow these steps:

1. Explain again the purpose of the Self-Directed Employment Program (see First meeting: Intake).
2. Give a copy of the Self-Directed Employment Orientation Matrix to the individual and his or her parents (and significant others) (see p. 285). Write the phases and other information shown in the matrix on a chalkboard. Dis-

cuss the information as you write. Relate the discussion to your knowledge of the person.

3. Describe the Choice Management Assessment as a job match process in which the individual chooses several jobs to explore, shadows the chosen jobs, and completes on-the-job internships. Appointments are set on the basis of the individual's needs and the employers' schedule.

4. Explain that the length of the assessment process depends on scheduling, past job experience, and the match between the individual and jobs he or she chooses. Most people complete the job match process in 1–3 months by attending the program one to four times per week.

5. Explain that during the placement phase the individual will learn decision-making and problem-solving skills needed to keep their job.

6. Discuss long-term follow-along details and what happens once the person learns how to do his or her job. This information will be unique to each supported employment program and to each individual.

Objective 1: What If?

What if individuals, parents, or significant others are afraid of losing Social Security benefits?

Provide an income analysis to the individual and family regarding benefits and payments. Contact your local Social Security Office to obtain a definitive consultation.

What if the individual refuses to give out personal or disability-related information?

Explain that if you know little about the individual's history, it is very hard to coordinate a good job match. With signed consent, contact active agencies, therapists, physicians, and other professionals to discuss your supported employment program and how it may affect the individual. Be sure to find out if the individual has a history of recent aggressive or criminal behavior so that you can make appropriate plans.

What if parents or significant others answer all questions during the initial meeting and do not provide the individual an opportunity to reply?

Gently but firmly explain that this program is for the individual, and it's the individual's opinion that counts. Address most of your remarks or questions to the individual.

Section I. Assessment: Choice Management
Goal A: Making Choices

Objective 2: Completing the Jobs I Want to Do: Form A or B

CONTENTS

Present forms
Complete Jobs I Want to Do: Form A
Complete Jobs I Want to Do: Form B and Jobs I Have Done
Schedule
Discuss choices

MATERIALS NEEDED

Jobs I Want to Do: Form A (I:A:2:1)
Jobs I Have Done (I:A:2:2)
Jobs I Want to Do: Form B (I:A:2:3)

PURPOSE

To make initial tentative community job choices

LOCATION

Office

Present forms

Materials Needed
Jobs I Want to Do: Forms A and B

A. The purpose of the Jobs I Want to Do form is to help individuals begin thinking about the community jobs they may like to do and to make initial, tentative job choices. The preferred jobs will be explored later to determine skill and preference matches.

B. Show the Jobs I Want to Do: Forms A and B to the individual (see pp. 286 and 288). Ask the individual to choose the form he or she likes best. Explain that Form A provides a greater degree of freedom to choose jobs, but choices will need to be generated directly by the individual since the form is open ended. A menu of sample jobs is given, but the individual is not limited to those. Form B is more structured and offers a set menu of illustrated jobs and tasks from which to choose. If needed, customize the form so the choice menu matches local employment conditions using pictures downloaded from www.brookespublishing.com/picturebank.

Note: Some individuals may benefit from using Form A and then Form B during different sessions. Form B may stimulate discussion of realistic job choices more than Form A. However, the open-ended nature of Form A may allow some individuals to better express their preferences for jobs not given in a menu format.

C. During this phase of the job match process, forms are not designed for the individual to complete independently. Staff should facilitate ongoing discussion. Make sure your comments do not influence the individual's choices.

Note: The Characteristics I Like form introduced in the next objective is completed simultaneously with the Jobs I Want to Do: Forms A and B introduced in this objective. The two objectives are described separately to aid your understanding.

Complete Jobs I Want to Do: Form A

Materials Needed
Jobs I Want to Do: Form A

A. Instruct the individual to choose four job types and write them in the second column (the first column remains blank until you work through the form). Example job types are provided at the bottom of the form. In general, a job type is a broad area of employment interest such as a store, factory, or child care. An example of Jobs I Want to Do: Form A is on page 49.

B. Ask the individual to choose a preferred job title matching the job type they chose. Example job titles include cashier, line worker, or child care aide. If the person does not know a specific job title, then leave the section blank.

C. Find out if the person did this job before, and ask the person to circle the appropriate answer in the "Have I done this job?" column.

D. If the person has done the chosen job before, ask him or her to circle "Yes" in the "Did I like this job?" column if he or she liked the job. Circle "No" if he or she did not.

E. Ask the individual to list four related job tasks for each job type. Example job tasks are listed at the bottom of the form. If the person can't list four tasks matching the job type, discuss the job with him or her to develop more tasks. If four tasks still cannot be elicited, accept what is given. If the person cannot name any job tasks, leave the section blank.

F. Instruct the individual to circle any tasks listed that were previously performed. If the task was previously performed, did the individual like doing this task? If so, check the circled task. If he or she did not like the task, do not check the circled task.

G. From all the job tasks listed across job types, ask the individual to rank in order of preference of 1 to 4 their four most preferred job tasks. A rank of 4 indicates the task that is best liked. A task rated 1 is liked more than those not ranked.

H. From all the job types listed, ask the individual to rank in order of preference his or her chosen job types from 1 to 4 in the far left column. A ranking of 4 indicates the type that is best liked.

1:A:2:1

Jobs I Want to Do: Form A

Making Choices

Name: Kelly Sample   Date: March 10, 2002

For the first and last columns, rank the jobs 1–4, with 4 indicating the job you like most.

Rank each job	Job type	Job title	Have I done this job?	Did I like this job?	Job tasks (list four)	Rank best tasks
2	Car wash	Car cleaner	Yes / No (circled)	Yes / No	Vacuum car Get trash out Dry cars ____	4 ____ 1 ____
4	Maid service	Room attendant	Yes / No (circled)	Yes / No	Clean restrooms Sweep Make beds Vacuum	3 2 ____ ____
1	Food service	Bus person	Yes / No (circled)	Yes / No	Wipe tables Wash dishes Tend salad bar Sweep and mop	____ ____ ____ ____
3	Janitorial work	Custodian	Yes (circled) / No	Yes (circled) / No	Clean restrooms Sweep and mop Dust Vacuum	____ ____ ____ ____

Can't think of choices? Here are some examples:

Some job types	Some job tasks		
Store work Laundry work Food service (restaurant) work Maid service work Janitorial work Factory work Office work Child care work Animal care work	Stocking and pricing items Bringing carts inside Running a cash register Folding laundry Pressing laundry Wiping tables Serving food Washing dishes Cleaning a kitchen	Working on an assembly line Bussing tables Cooking or baking Cleaning bathrooms Vacuuming Making beds Dusting Washing windows Mopping floors	Emptying trash Typing Mailing Filing Answering phones Playing with children Talking with children Disciplining children Watching children Cleaning animal cages

Complete Jobs I Want to Do: Form B and Jobs I Have Done

Materials Needed
- Jobs I Have Done
- Jobs I Want to Do: Form B

A. If the individual chooses Form B, complete both the Jobs I Want to Do: Form B and the Jobs I Have Done form. Make sure the illustrations represent entry-level jobs available in your community. You may need to customize the forms. An example of a filled-out Jobs I Want to Do: Form B is on page 51.

B. Complete Jobs I Have Done (see p. 287).

1. In the "Circle jobs you have done" section, explain row by row what job type each picture represents. After explaining each row, ask the individual to circle all jobs previously performed. Complete this process until all illustrations are explained. Ask the individual if he or she has worked at any job type not depicted. If the individual names a job type that is not depicted, add it to the open box and circle it.

2. In the "Circle tasks you have done" section, explain row by row which task each picture represents. After explaining each row, ask the individual to circle all previously performed tasks. Complete this process until all tasks are explained. Ask the individual if he or she performed any tasks not depicted. If he or she names any tasks that are not depicted, add the tasks to the open boxes and circle them.

C. Complete Jobs I Want to Do: Form B (see p. 288).

1. Explain, row by row, which job type each picture represents. After explaining each row, ask the individual to circle at least four preferred job types. Complete this process until all types in the first section are explained. Ask the individual if he or she prefers a job type not depicted. If the individual names a job type that is not depicted, add it to the open box and circle it.

2. Ask the individual to rank four jobs he or she would most prefer from 4 to 1. A ranking of 4 indicates the job that is best liked. Write the number beside each job circled.

3. In the second section, explain row by row which task each picture represents. After explaining each row, ask the individual to circle at least four preferred tasks. Complete this process until all tasks in the section are explained. Ask the individual if he or she prefers any tasks not depicted. If he or she names any tasks that are not depicted, add the tasks to the open boxes and circle them.

4. Ask the individual to rank the four tasks he or she would most like to do from 4 to 1. A ranking of 4 indicates the task that is best liked. Write the number beside each task circled.

I:A:2:3	**Jobs I Want to Do: Form B**	Making Choices

Name: Pat Sample Date: March 10, 2002

Circle at least four jobs you like. Rate them 1–4. A rank of 4 shows the job you like best.

Store work	Laundry	1 Food service	4 Maid service	Child care	3 Janitorial work
Animal care	2 Outdoor maintenance	Warehouse work	Office work	Factory work	Other

Circle tasks you like. Rate them 1–4. A rank of 4 shows the task you like best.

$ .39 Pricing	Folding	Ironing	Wiping tables	Serving food	4 Vacuuming
Cooking/baking	Washing dishes	Washing cars	2 Making beds	Dusting	Mowing lawns
Sanding	Taking out trash	Dusting videos	Carrying boxes	Weedeating	Gathering carts
Mailing	Working with machines	Washing windows	Watching children	Mopping/ sweeping 3	Cleaning bathrooms 1
Disciplining children	Bagging groceries	Filling condiments	Straightening books	Playing with children	Stocking
Other	Other	Other	Other	Other	Other

Schedule

A. Present the Jobs I Want to Do: Form A *or* the Jobs I Want to Do: Form B *and* Jobs I Have Done at least three times during a 2-week period. Plan on each of the three sessions taking 60–90 minutes. (See the Implementation Reference Guide for more details.) These forms should be presented simultaneously with the Characteristics I Like form explained in Objective 3. This repetition allows the individual to think about his or her choices and make changes at each meeting.

Discuss choices

A. Every time the individual completes Jobs I Want to Do: Form A or Form B, the staff should get as much information as possible. Explore the individual's understanding of each job and task choice. For example, if an individual is interested in working as a cashier, ask, "What do you think it would be like to work at K-Mart? At 7-Eleven? At Sears?" After each discussion, ask the individual if the choices remain attractive. Find out which is the most attractive and why. For each choice, provide examples of possible employment sites. Note any unique reactions and comments in the margins of the form.

Objective 2: What If?

What if the individual wants to choose fewer than four jobs?

Explain to the individual that two jobs will eventually be chosen. At this time, the more jobs chosen to explore, the better the chance there will be of finding an available job that matches his or her skills and preferences. If an individual continues to choose less than four jobs, accept his or her response. Often, the number of choices will increase with exposure to job options.

What if the individual chooses Form A but cannot read it?

Read the form to the person and help him or her fill it out.

What if the individual cannot use Form B?

Read the form. Point to the picture that best illustrates what you are saying. Prompt the individual to point to the picture that best represents his or her choice. If the person does not reliably point to the pictures in Form B, customize the form by using photographs of actual settings or use actual items from that setting. Also, try limiting the number of illustrations on a page. If this still doesn't work, begin picture discrimination instruction.

What if the individual wonders why choices need to be made more than once?

Explain to the individual that as he or she begins to think about the jobs, he or she may change his or her mind and refine his or her choices. This is okay and is encouraged so that many choices are explored.

What if the job that the individual wants is not on the picture Form B?

Customize the form by using the illustrations in the Picture Bank online at www.brookespublishing.com/picturebank, ask the individual to draw an illustration depicting a preferred job, or provide a custom-made drawing or photograph.

What if the individual cannot think of any job choices?

Explore past jobs or work experiences and ask what conditions and duties were preferred. Suggest jobs that fit these preferences. If an individual has no previous work history, explore some of the things he or she likes do. Perhaps you might begin choosing task preferences before naming jobs or complete Objective 3 first.

What if the individual only chooses jobs that match previous experience when using Form B?

Change the form presentation order, or accept what is chosen. The job internship experiences may confirm or disprove these first choices. You may sense that an individual is hesitant because he or she does not want to get stuck in an unfamiliar job he or she does not want. Reassure him or her that this is only a tentative initial choice.

Try to get the individual to think about jobs he or she likes but has not done before. Perhaps there is a job he or she would like to do that a friend has or a job has caught his or her eye that he or she would like to know more about.

What if the individual does not understand when you ask him or her to rank his or her preferences from 4 to 1?

Ask the individual to assign 4 points to the item liked the most, 3 points, 2 points, then 1 point. Or ask the person to point to the job or task he or she likes best.

What if the individual using Form A is unsure of his or her job preferences?

Talk informally about the information presented on Form A. Provide more individual job exploration experiences. Some effective resources might include newspaper classified ads, Internet job exploration, the annual update to the Dictionary of Occupational Titles handbook, manufacturer indices available at public libraries, standardized interest inventories, and assistance available at the local Job Service office.

What if the individual does not comprehend the meaning of the illustrations?

Substitute photographs or the person's own drawings for the illustrations. If this does not work, take the individual to an array of community jobsites and use photographs to implement basic picture discrimination instruction.

Section I. Assessment: Choice Management
Goal A: Making Choices

Objective 3. Completing the Characteristics I Like: Form A or B

CONTENTS

Complete Characteristics I Like: Form A or B
Schedule

MATERIALS NEEDED

Characteristics I Like: Form A (I:A:3:1) or Form B (I:A:3:2)

PURPOSE

To explore and tentatively choose characteristics that are important to the individual

LOCATION

Office

Complete Characteristics I Like: Form A or B

Materials Needed
Characteristics I Like: Form A and Form B

A. Explain that the purpose of the Characteristics I Like form is to explore and tentatively choose preferred job characteristics. Ask the individual to choose the format that will meet his or her needs. Form A requires reading (see p. 289). Form B requires picture discrimination skills (see p. 290). An example of a filled-out Characteristics I Like: Form A is on page 56.

B. The Characteristics I Like items are presented as contrasting pairs. Using the form that the individual has chosen, instruct him or her to circle the preferred item out of each pair.

1. Discuss each characteristic chosen by asking the meaning of each selected item. Circle the preferred item in each pair.
2. If an individual is undecided about the item to choose, ask him or her to choose neither or circle both. Do not suggest this ahead of time, as some individuals may use this as an alternative to making decisions.
3. Individuals may prefer characteristics that are not listed. Write these in the blank spaces labeled "Other."
4. From the circled characteristics, ask the individual to draw a star beside 10 of the most important characteristics in the column labeled "★."
5. From the column, ask the individual to check the four most preferred characteristics he or she would like in a job in the section labeled "Top four."
6. Once again, discuss the final four characteristics chosen by asking the individual the meaning of each selected item.

I:A:3:1

Characteristics I Like: Form A

Making Choices

Name: Kelly Sample Date: April 4, 2002

First, circle the preferred item in each pair. Second, draw a star in the ★ column for the 10 characteristics that are most important to you. Third, check your four most preferred characteristics in the "Top Four" column.

Characteristics		★	Top four
Work alone	Work with others	☆	✓
Work in a quiet workplace	Work in a noisy workplace		
Work part-time	Work full-time	☆	
Work weekdays only	Works weekends, too		
Work at a hard job	Work at an easy job		
Work inside	Work outside	☆	
Have few rules	Have well-defined rules	☆	✓
Work standing up	Work sitting down	☆	
Work mornings	Work evenings	☆	
Work in an attractive place	Looks of place do not matter		
Dress up for work	Do not dress up	☆	
Do physical work	Do thinking work	☆	✓
Detail is important	Detail is not important		
Do the same tasks every day	Do different tasks every day	☆	✓
Work with people	Work with things		
Working fast is important	Speed does not matter		
Work with little supervision	Work with a lot of supervision	☆	
Work in the daytime	Work at night		
Work in a small business	Work in a large business		
Other:			
Other:			
Other:			
Other:			

7. Assist the individual with any of these steps only when appropriate and necessary.

Schedule

A. Present the Characteristics I Like forms at least three times during a 2-week period. Complete the Characteristics I Like form immediately following each presentation of Jobs I Want To Do: Form A *or* Jobs I Want To Do: Form B *and* Jobs I Have Done (introduced in Objective 2).

B. Individuals' responses may not be consistent on the Characteristics I Like form. This is acceptable since their experience in a job environment may be limited. Their responses will become more consistent over time. The opportunity to choose characteristics will be repeated several more times through the Choice Management assessment process.

Objective 3: What If?

What if the individual chooses only characteristics that match jobs he or she has had in the past?	*Accept what is chosen. The job internship experiences may confirm or disprove these first choices.*
What if the individual says the characteristics of the job he or she wants do not matter to them?	*This will be addressed later during shadowing and the job internship experiences. Explain that if the individual wants a preferred job, it is important to tell what characteristics define a good job.*
What if the individual consistently states that he or she wants, for example, a store job, but the characteristics chosen by the individual do not match this job choice?	*This will be addressed during shadowing and the job internship experiences.*
What if the individual cannot narrow the characteristics he or she likes to four?	*Accept the top 10 characteristics chosen. Attempt to get the individual to prioritize them.*
What if the individual chooses only characteristics that match a job he or she has in mind?	*Explain that it is in his or her best interest to be honest about preferences. This will be further addressed during shadowing and job internship experiences.*
What if an individual cannot choose the 10 characteristics he or she likes most?	*Keep progressing through the objectives. After the shadowing and internship experiences, consistent characteristic choices usually occur.*
What if the individual consistently circles both characteristics?	*Explain that you are trying to discover the individual's preferences. It is important for the individual to begin to make choices by circling one item.*

Section I. Assessment: Choice Management
Goal A: Making Choices

Objective 4: Summarizing Making Choices

CONTENTS

Summarize initial job choices
Determine top-ranked job preferences
Summarize task choices
Determine top-ranked task preferences
Summarize characteristics most often chosen
Summarize four most important characteristics

MATERIALS NEEDED

Initial Job Preferences Graph (I:A:4:1)
Initial Task Preferences Graph (I:A:4:2)
Characteristics Summary Graph (I:A:4:3)
Four Most Important Characteristics Graph (I:A:4:4)
Completed:
Jobs I Want to Do: Form A (I:A:2:1)
Jobs I Have Done (I:A:2:2) and Jobs I Want to Do: Form B (I:A:2:3)
Characteristics I Like: Form A (I:A:3:1) or B (I:A:3:2)

PURPOSE

To summarize initial vocational preferences and to develop an action plan for exploring these preferences

LOCATION

Office

Summarize initial job choices

Materials Needed
Initial Job Preferences Graph
Initial Task Preferences Graph

Completed:
Jobs I Want to Do: Form A or B

A. Complete both the Initial Job Preferences Graph and the Initial Task Preferences Graph (see pp. 291–292). Assist the individual to complete the forms or complete them yourself, if appropriate. An example of a filled-out Initial Job Preferences Graph is on page 60.

1. Referring to the first day's completed Jobs I Want to Do: Form A or Form B, write each job type chosen in the column labeled "Job" in the Initial Job Preferences Graph. In the column labeled "Rank," enter the rank in the column labeled "Day 1."

2. For the second day's completed Jobs I Want to Do: Form A or B, enter in the column labeled "Job" any different job types not chosen on the first form. In the column labeled "Rank," enter the rank for all jobs the individual chose on the second day (4 indicates the job that is best liked).

3. Repeat this procedure for the column labeled "Day 3."

I:A:4:1

Initial Job Preferences Graph

Making Choices (circled)
Final Choices

Name: Pat Sample

Date: April 4, 2002

Job	Rank Day 1	Rank Day 2	Rank Day 3	Check if done	Job preference graph (shaded through)
Car wash	2				1 2 3 4 5 6 7 8 9 10 11 12 (shaded 1–2)
Maid service	4	4	2		1 2 3 4 5 6 7 8 9 10 11 12 (shaded 1–10)
Food service	1				1 2 3 4 5 6 7 8 9 10 11 12 (shaded 1)
Janitorial work	3	3	1	✓	1 2 3 4 5 6 7 8 9 10 11 12 (shaded 1–7)
Office work		1			1 2 3 4 5 6 7 8 9 10 11 12 (shaded 1)
Factory work		2	3		1 2 3 4 5 6 7 8 9 10 11 12 (shaded 1–5)
Work with plants			4		1 2 3 4 5 6 7 8 9 10 11 12 (shaded 1–4)
					1 2 3 4 5 6 7 8 9 10 11 12
					1 2 3 4 5 6 7 8 9 10 11 12
					1 2 3 4 5 6 7 8 9 10 11 12
					1 2 3 4 5 6 7 8 9 10 11 12
					1 2 3 4 5 6 7 8 9 10 11 12

Four top-ranked jobs	Have I done this job?	Do I need to shadow this job?
Maid service	Yes (No)	(Yes) No
Janitorial work	(Yes) No	Yes (No)
Factory work	Yes (No)	(Yes) No
Work with plants	Yes (No)	(Yes) No

4. If a listed job was not ranked on a given day, leave the "Rank" column empty.

5. Complete the "Check if done" column. If the individual completed Jobs I Want to Do: Form A, find the column labeled "Have I done this job?" For each job that the individual circled "Yes," check the corresponding job that was entered in the job column. If the individual completed Jobs I Want to Do: Form B, match the jobs ranked 4–1 to those jobs circled on the Jobs I Have Done form. For each job, the individual wants to do and has done, check the "Check if done" column.

Determine top-ranked job preferences

A. Complete the bar graphs.

1. Complete the bar graph for each job listed by adding the ranked scores of 1 to 4 for each day. Shade in the amount of squares that match the total. For example, if an individual ranked a job "1" for 3 days, shade in three squares beside that job type.

B. Determine jobs to shadow.

1. At the bottom of the page, locate the area labeled "Four top-ranked jobs." List the job with the highest score from the Initial Job Preference Graph in the first blank. An easy way to see this is to tell the individual to pick the job with the most shaded squares or the one with the longest line. Record the jobs with the second, third, and fourth highest scores as well.

2. For each top-ranked job listed, refer to the "Check if done" column, and circle the corresponding answer in the "Have I done this job?" column.

3. If the individual has done a top-ranked job before, then it is likely that he or she will not need to shadow this job. If the individual has not done this job before, he or she will need to shadow the job. Circle the answer in the "Do I need to shadow this job?" column accordingly. Individuals who have worked at a job that is one of their top preferences probably know more about that particular job than a 1-hour shadowing would reveal. Discuss the job with the individual to determine if shadowing is needed.

4. Discuss the summary findings with the individual. Remember that the final decision to shadow any particular jobsite should be the choice of the individual.

Summarize task choices

Materials Needed
Initial Task Preferences Graph

Completed:
Jobs I Want to Do: Form A or
Jobs I Want to Do Form: B
and Jobs I Have Done

A. Begin the Initial Task Preferences Graph.

1. Referring to the first day's completed Jobs I Want to Do: Form A or B, write each task type chosen in the column labeled "Task" in the Initial Task Preferences Graph. In the column labeled "Rank," enter the rank in the column labeled "Day 1."

2. For the second day's completed Jobs I Want to Do: Form A or B, enter in the column labeled "Task" any new and different task types not chosen on the first day. In the column labeled "Rank," enter the rank for all tasks the individual chose on the second day. A rank of 4 indicates the task that is best liked.

3. Repeat this procedure for the column labeled "Day 3."

4. If a listed task was not ranked on a given day, leave the ranking box empty.

B. Complete the "Check if done" column.

1. If the individual completed Jobs I Want to Do: Form A, find the column labeled "Tasks" on those forms. For each task the individual circled and ranked, check the "Check if done" column beside the corresponding task that was entered in the "Task" column."

2. If the individual completed the Jobs I Want to Do: Form B, match the tasks ranked 4–1 to those tasks circled on the Jobs I Have Done forms. For each task the individual wants to do and has done, check the "Check if done" column.

Determine top-ranked task preferences

A. Complete the bar graphs.

1. Complete the bar graph for each task listed by adding the scores of 1 to 4 for each day. Shade in the amount of squares that match the total. For example, if an individual ranked a task as "2" for 3 days, shade in six squares beside that task name.

B. Determine the tasks the person will shadow.

1. At the bottom of the page, locate the area labeled "Four top-ranked tasks." List the task with the highest score in the first blank. An easy way to show this is to tell the individual to pick the task with the most shaded squares or the longest line. Continue to record the tasks with the second, third, and fourth highest scores.

2. For each top-ranked task listed, refer to the "Check if done" column and circle the corresponding answer in the "Have I done this task?" column.

3. If the individual has done a top-ranked task before, then it is likely that he or she will not need to shadow this task. If the individual has not done this task before, he or she will need to shadow this top-ranked task. Circle the appropriate answer in the "Do I need to shadow this task?" column. Individuals who have worked at a task that is one of their top preferences probably know more about that particular task than a 1-hour shadowing would reveal. Discuss the task with the individual to determine if a shadowing is needed.

4. Summarize and discuss the results with the individual. Remember that the final decision to shadow any particular jobsite should not be the assessment staff person's choice. It is up to the individual to decide. As a person decides whether he or she wants to complete a shadowing experience, the objective data reported in the Initial Job and Task Preference Graphs should only serve as a guideline. For instance, a person who acquired a traumatic brain injury may decide to shadow a jobsite even if the graphs indicate that he or she liked a previous experience or if he or she suggests a new job or task choice the day the graphs were completed. The Making Choices process helps begin the assessment process. The data should not be used to make concrete job decisions. The guiding rule is to be flexible. Listen to what the individual tells you. Discuss preferred jobsites for shadowing, the jobsites that do not need to be shadowed, and reasons for each.

5. Have the individual choose at least three jobsites to shadow.

Summarize characteristics most often chosen

Materials Needed
Characteristics Summary Graph

Completed:
Characteristics I Like: Form A or Form B

A. To summarize the characteristics the individual chose most frequently, gather the Characteristics I Like forms that were completed during the three Making Choices sessions. Help the individual complete the Characteristics Summary Graph or complete the form yourself, if appropriate (see p. 293). An example of a filled-out Characteristics Summary Graph is on page 64.

1. In the upper right corner of the Characteristics Summary Graph, circle "Making Choices." This indicates that you have entered the data from the three Characteristics I Like: Forms A or B.

2. For each characteristic circled for the first day, shade in one box. Leave boxes blank for those characteristics that were not circled. Continue to record the individual's choices similarly for the second and third day.

3. Use this form as you progress through each goal of the Choice Management job match assessment process. When all goals have been completed, the Characteristics Summary Graph becomes a part of the individual's assessment summary.

1:A:4:3

Characteristics Summary Graph

Making Choices (circled)
Exploring Choices
Testing Choices
Final Choices

Name: Pat Sample

Date: April 29, 2002

Work alone	1	2	3	4	5	6	7	8	9	10	11	12	13	14	15	16	17	18
Work with others	1	2	3	4	5	6	7	8	9	10	11	12	13	14	15	16	17	18
Work in a quiet workplace	1	2	3	4	5	6	7	8	9	10	11	12	13	14	15	16	17	18
Work in a noisy workplace	1	2	3	4	5	6	7	8	9	10	11	12	13	14	15	16	17	18
Work part-time	1	2	3	4	5	6	7	8	9	10	11	12	13	14	15	16	17	18
Work full-time	1	2	3	4	5	6	7	8	9	10	11	12	13	14	15	16	17	18
Work weekdays only	1	2	3	4	5	6	7	8	9	10	11	12	13	14	15	16	17	18
Works weekends, too	1	2	3	4	5	6	7	8	9	10	11	12	13	14	15	16	17	18
Work at a hard job	1	2	3	4	5	6	7	8	9	10	11	12	13	14	15	16	17	18
Work at an easy job	1	2	3	4	5	6	7	8	9	10	11	12	13	14	15	16	17	18
Work inside	1	2	3	4	5	6	7	8	9	10	11	12	13	14	15	16	17	18
Work outside	1	2	3	4	5	6	7	8	9	10	11	12	13	14	15	16	17	18
Have few rules	1	2	3	4	5	6	7	8	9	10	11	12	13	14	15	16	17	18
Have well-defined rules	1	2	3	4	5	6	7	8	9	10	11	12	13	14	15	16	17	18
Work standing up	1	2	3	4	5	6	7	8	9	10	11	12	13	14	15	16	17	18
Work sitting down	1	2	3	4	5	6	7	8	9	10	11	12	13	14	15	16	17	18
Work mornings	1	2	3	4	5	6	7	8	9	10	11	12	13	14	15	16	17	18
Work evenings	1	2	3	4	5	6	7	8	9	10	11	12	13	14	15	16	17	18
Work in an attractive place	1	2	3	4	5	6	7	8	9	10	11	12	13	14	15	16	17	18
Looks of place do not matter	1	2	3	4	5	6	7	8	9	10	11	12	13	14	15	16	17	18
Dress up for work	1	2	3	4	5	6	7	8	9	10	11	12	13	14	15	16	17	18
Do not dress up	1	2	3	4	5	6	7	8	9	10	11	12	13	14	15	16	17	18
Do physical work	1	2	3	4	5	6	7	8	9	10	11	12	13	14	15	16	17	18
Do thinking work	1	2	3	4	5	6	7	8	9	10	11	12	13	14	15	16	17	18
Detail is important	1	2	3	4	5	6	7	8	9	10	11	12	13	14	15	16	17	18
Detail is not important	1	2	3	4	5	6	7	8	9	10	11	12	13	14	15	16	17	18
Do the same tasks every day	1	2	3	4	5	6	7	8	9	10	11	12	13	14	15	16	17	18
Do different tasks every day	1	2	3	4	5	6	7	8	9	10	11	12	13	14	15	16	17	18
Work with people	1	2	3	4	5	6	7	8	9	10	11	12	13	14	15	16	17	18
Work with things	1	2	3	4	5	6	7	8	9	10	11	12	13	14	15	16	17	18
Working fast is important	1	2	3	4	5	6	7	8	9	10	11	12	13	14	15	16	17	18
Speed does not matter	1	2	3	4	5	6	7	8	9	10	11	12	13	14	15	16	17	18
Work with little supervision	1	2	3	4	5	6	7	8	9	10	11	12	13	14	15	16	17	18
Work with a lot of supervision	1	2	3	4	5	6	7	8	9	10	11	12	13	14	15	16	17	18
Work in the daytime	1	2	3	4	5	6	7	8	9	10	11	12	13	14	15	16	17	18
Work at night	1	2	3	4	5	6	7	8	9	10	11	12	13	14	15	16	17	18
Work in a small business	1	2	3	4	5	6	7	8	9	10	11	12	13	14	15	16	17	18
Work in a large business	1	2	3	4	5	6	7	8	9	10	11	12	13	14	15	16	17	18
Other:	1	2	3	4	5	6	7	8	9	10	11	12	13	14	15	16	17	18
Other:	1	2	3	4	5	6	7	8	9	10	11	12	13	14	15	16	17	18
Other:	1	2	3	4	5	6	7	8	9	10	11	12	13	14	15	16	17	18
Other:	1	2	3	4	5	6	7	8	9	10	11	12	13	14	15	16	17	18

Summarize four most important characteristics

Materials Needed
Four Most Important Characteristics Graph

Completed:
Characteristics I Like: Form A or Form B

A. To summarize the four characteristics that the individual chose most frequently, gather the Characteristics I Like forms that were completed during the three Making Choices sessions. Help the individual to complete the Four Most Important Characteristics Graph or complete the form yourself, if appropriate (see p. 294).

1. In the upper right corner of the Four Most Important Characteristics Graph, circle "Making Choices." This indicates that you have entered the data from the three Characteristics I Like: Forms A or B.

2. Look at the first day's Characteristics I Like: Form A or B. For each characteristic the individual checked, indicating a top preference, shade in one box. Leave boxes blank for those characteristics that were not most preferred. Continue to record the individual's four most preferred characteristics similarly for the second and third day.

3. Use this form as you progress through each goal of the Choice Management assessment process. During Goal D, the four blanks labeled "Four most important characteristics" will be filled out. When all goals have been completed, the Four Most Important Characteristics Graph becomes a part of the individual's assessment summary.

Objective 4: What If?

What if the individual chooses jobs that he or she has performed in the past?	*If the individual has had and liked past job experiences, skip the shadowing process and go straight to the internship phase. Use Objective 6: Completing Shadowing Skill and Preference Match to determine the best internship location.*
What if, when trying to determine what to shadow, there is a tie between two or three job choices?	*Ask the individual what he or she likes best. Let the individual break the tie and determine what to shadow.*
What if the individual chooses completely different jobs each session?	*Try to find the commonalties that exist in the group of jobs. Discuss similar tasks that may be performed in each job choice. Choices from the Characteristics I Like forms can be very helpful here. An additional Original Choice session may be needed in order to clarify what jobs the individual is most interested in shadowing.*
What if the individual has an equal preference for more than four jobsites?	*Discuss the importance of each jobsite. Determine with the individual why each site is important. It may be to the individual's advantage to shadow all of these sites in order to get more information about the chosen jobs.*

Section I. Assessment: Choice Management
Goal A: Making Choices

Objective 5: Constructing a Résumé

CONTENTS

Gather information
Complete a job application
Construct a résumé

MATERIALS NEEDED

Written past job information
Application for Employment (I:A:5:1)
Sample Résumé 1 (I:A:5:2)
Sample Résumé 2 (I:A:5:3)
Sample Résumé 3 (I:A:5:4)

PURPOSE

To strengthen rapport, learn about the individual's history, and prepare an individualized résumé

LOCATION

Office

Gather information

A. Talk with the individual about his or her vocational and educational history as well as any hobbies. This discussion should cover

1. All previous education and training
2. Work-study experiences
3. Summer youth employment
4. Volunteer work
5. Types of work accomplished in sheltered workshops
6. Responsibilities around the house
7. Informal work experiences (e.g., mowing lawns, babysitting)
8. Previous jobs

Complete a job application

Material Needed
Application for Employment

A. The day before this session, ask the individual to bring in any résumés, written recommendations, task descriptions, and past job evaluations.

B. Assist the individual in completing a sample application (see pp. 295–296). Explain that this process will be used to collect needed information for the résumé and future applications.

The individual will need to bring in names, addresses, and telephone numbers of past employers. If available, include the name of the supervisor, work dates, and wages earned. Parents or other caregivers may be a great source of information about past job experiences—use them!

C. The finished application will be used to verify information gained during the initial job choices process and to assist with job development.

Construct a résumé

Materials Needed
Sample Résumés 1–3

A. Choose a résumé format (see pp. 297–299). Sample Résumé 1 combines education, work, and volunteer experiences. Sample Résumé 2 shows how education and work experience can be shown. Each begins with the person's career objective.

B. Consider a functional résumé for those individuals with large gaps in their employment history (see Sample Résumé 3). A functional résumé lists and describes work experience, but dates are not given.

1. Be sure to describe job duties in positive but honest terms. Inflated résumés are usually easily detected and may do the individual a disservice.

2. Put work experience first. Educational experience is usually not nearly as important if one is looking for entry-level employment.

C. Always print the résumé on a good grade of bonded paper.

D. The finished résumé will be used to assist with job development.

Objective 5: What If?

What if the individual has had no competitive job experiences?

Ask the individual or others close to him or her about what work he or she has performed in the workshop, at school, or in the home, including paid or unpaid experience. Also include any civic or volunteer experiences in the résumé. These might include the 4-H Club, Boy Scouts, and Candy Stripers. Hobbies and special interests can also be mentioned. Sometimes individuals begin to remember work experiences as they progress through shadowing and the internship phases. Revise the résumé to include this information.

What if the individual has been fired from every job he or she has attempted?

Focus on one or two of the most successful experiences. From the array of tasks completed at the terminated position, write a functional résumé with a focus on experience by job category rather than specific jobs held.

What if, after having some shadowing and internship experiences, the individual develops an interest in a specific job area?

Revise the résumé to reflect this interest.

Introduction to Section I.

Goal B: Exploring Choices

Goal A helped you to determine the individual's initial job and task preferences. In Goal B, you should further explore choices by setting up shadowing opportunities at jobsites matching the individual's choices. The purpose of exploring choices by shadowing is to facilitate informed choice making by providing first-hand experiences at preferred jobs. When setting up sites to shadow, let local businesses know what you are trying to accomplish. Tell them about the self-directed supported employment concepts and procedures. Most businesses are glad to participate in the shadowing process. They generally appreciate the opportunity to give something back to the community in a way that does not require a monetary donation. Once businesses understand that you only want to observe some of their employees work, you will find that most are happy to show you what they do. Business people love to talk about their successes. Capitalize on this pride.

Explain that the purpose of your visit is to explore what it would be like to have a job in a business similar to theirs. For example, you may say:

Hello! My name is ______________. I work for ______________. My organization serves people who need a little extra help with getting employed. My job is to help them figure out what job best matches what they like and can do. We have found that the best way to do this is to give people the opportunity to see what jobs look and feel like.

Explain the following points:

- You need 20 minutes or less to conduct a quick interview, and you will stay about 1 hour to watch an employee perform the required tasks.
- The person determines what characteristics he or she likes versus what is at this site.
- The person determines which skills are needed and matches his or her skills to those of the employee.
- The person determines if this job matches what he or she would like to do.
- You are not there to get a job for anyone at this time. You are there with the individual to shadow an employment site.

- It is important to you and your organization not to interfere with the daily operation of the business in any way.
- You and any individual you bring are insured by your program.

Once employers understand exactly what you are trying to accomplish, most will arrange a convenient shadowing time.

When you are done shadowing at the jobsite, leave a good impression. If a store site is set up and there is a good rapport between your agency and the store manager, it may become a site that you can return to. Observation of specific tasks can be negotiated with the manager to meet an individual's needs. For instance, a store may offer a wide variety of tasks, such as taking carts in, sacking, stocking, processing returns, pricing, working as a cashier, or providing customer service. Tailor the tasks that you need to observe to the individual's choices. Get to know each manager of each jobsite.

While shadowing, keep in mind that the purpose is to provide information about vocational interests to the individual. Be careful not to tell the individual that he or she cannot do a particular job. Let each person discover what he or she can or cannot do through the match process. If you do tell a person that he or she cannot do a particular job, chances are that person will not believe you. As you become more skilled at setting up sites for shadowing, you will be able to better match each individual's needs to the appropriate site and its environment.

After shadowing, summarize the individual's experiences on the Shadowing Summary Graph (see p. 310). Involve the individual as much as possible. Record and graph each shadowing site per the instructions. When analyzing the summary form, pay attention to both the individual's preferences and the skills the person believes he or she possesses. Keep in mind that some individuals may overestimate the skill match when there is a high preference for that job. Pay attention especially to the individual's preference match, particularly if the person chooses a job that is impossible to explore further or if the person does not have the skills to do the tasks.

Note: As you read through the procedures, you may notice that neither marketing plans nor job prospecting ideas are addressed. We believe that most organizations have already begun to network in their community. If not, there are many good books that explain how to do marketing.

As you read the procedures, note that each individual makes site choices at three points: before, during, and after each shadowing experience. Be sure to follow the directions given for each of these steps. You may notice that at one point in Objective 6, the instructions direct you to begin Objective 7. These objectives should be presented at roughly the same time because the information that each objective provides is necessary to the completion of the other. You may want to refer to the Implementation Reference Guide in order to keep organized (Table 3.3).

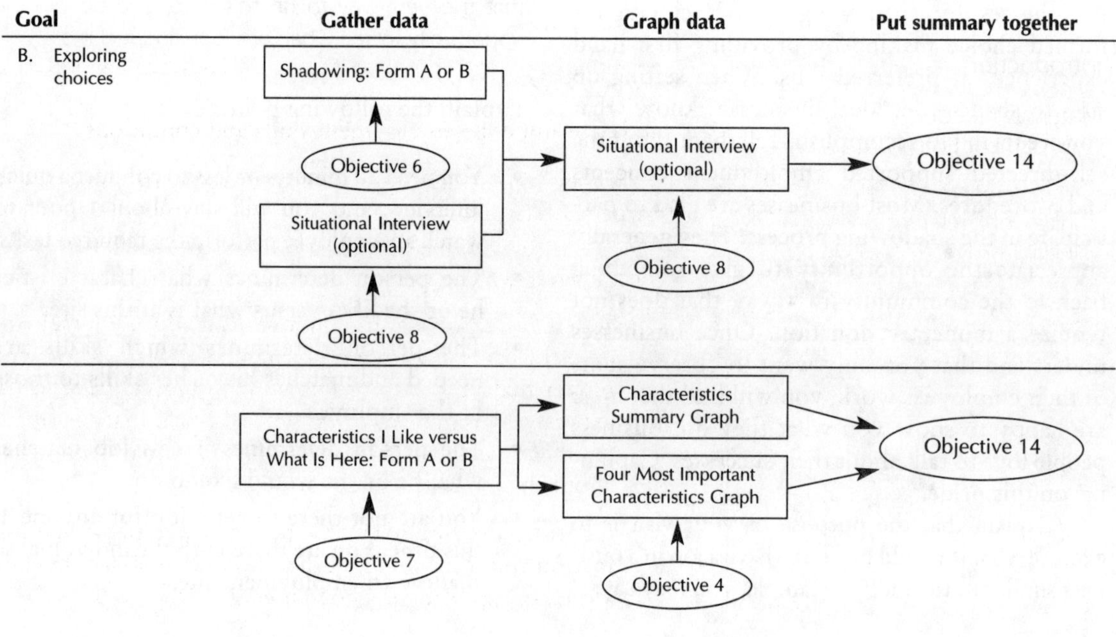

Section I. Assessment: Choice Management
Goal B: Exploring Choices

Objective 6: Completing Shadowing Skill and Preference Match

CONTENTS

MATERIALS NEEDED

Telephone book
Newspaper classified advertisements
Local Chamber of Commerce business directory
Assessment Event Organizer (I:B:6:1)
Questions for Shadowing (I:B:6:2)
Shadowing: Form A (I:B:6:3) or Form B (I:B:6:4)
Characteristics I Like versus What Is Here: Form A (I:B:7:1) or Form B (I:B:7:2)
Completed:
Initial Job Preferences Graph (I:A:4:1)
Initial Task Preferences Graph (I:A:4:2)

PURPOSE

To provide opportunities for the individual to match his or her skills and work condition preferences with a job of his or her choice

LOCATION

Office
Shadowing site

Introduction

Materials Needed
Assessment Event Organizer

Completed:
Initial Job Preferences Graph
Initial Task Preferences Graph

A. Set up shadowing appointments at the individual's preferred jobsites. Once at the site, the individual will observe workers and determine the employment skills and conditions.

B. To set up shadowing appointments, talk with managers or owners of community businesses that match the jobs and tasks identified in the Initial Job Preferences Graph and Initial Task Preferences Graph.

1. When you talk with the employer, introduce yourself and describe your employment program. Explain to the employer that you are working with an individual who has expressed an interest in the type of work that his or her company performs. However, the individual is uncertain about the job duties and work conditions.

2. Consider the employer an expert who can provide information about the job. Ask the employer to assist the individual in exploring this job choice.

3. Explain that the purpose of shadowing an employee is to provide the individual with an opportunity to observe the skills and conditions that exist on the job and to determine the match between the actual job and his or her work preferences.

4. Schedule a time when the employee who is to be shadowed is working on tasks that exemplify the job.

5. Make sure that the time is convenient for the employer and the individual with whom you are working.

C. To schedule the shadowing appointments, you may wish to use the Assessment Event Organizer to facilitate the job match process (see p. 300). This form is a time and event organizer designed to manage the shadowing experiences of numerous people.

Preparing for Shadowing

Materials Needed
- Questions for Shadowing
- Shadowing: Form A and Form B
- Characteristics I Like versus What Is Here: Form A and Form B

Completed:
Initial Job Preferences Graph

A. Once a shadowing site is developed, you should locate the Characteristics I Like versus What Is Here: Forms A and B, Shadowing: Forms A and B, and the Questions for Shadowing form. These three forms should be used at each shadowing site (see pp. 301–303). Step 4 directs you to begin Objective 7.

1. Complete the "What I like" section in Part 2 of the Shadowing: Form A or item 1 on Form B. Ask the individual to state the two jobs he or she likes the most. You may need to prompt the individual by using the Initial Job Preferences Graph (see Objective 4). If the individual chooses jobs he or she has not chosen before, that is okay. If necessary, help the individual fill in the box labeled "Two jobs I like most" with his or her preferences.

2. Similarly ask the individual to state the two tasks he or she likes most in the "What I like" section in Part 2 of Shadowing: Form A or item 2 on Form B. You may need to prompt the individual by using the Initial Task Preferences Graph (see Objective 4) to show what tasks he or she chose before. If the individual chooses tasks not chosen before, assist the individual to fill in the box labeled "Two tasks I like most" with their preferences. If appropriate, help write in the information.

3. Review with the individual the questions that will be asked at the shadowing site. These questions are found on the Questions for Shadowing form. If necessary, change the questions to fit the needs of the individual and the site. For instance, a person with a chronic mental illness may want to ask about job sharing or permitted time away.

4. Complete the "What I like (Before)" section of the Characteristics I Like versus What Is Here: Form A or B, found in Objective 7.

Interview and Observe

Materials Needed
Questions for Shadowing

A. As you enter the site to begin the shadowing experience, introduce yourself and the individual to the manager. Ask which employees should be observed to see a full range of entry-level work.

B. Go where directed and introduce yourself and the individual to the employees on the job. Explain to them why you are there. Establish rapport. Small talk works well. Make sure to address the employees with respect.

C. Encourage the individual to ask the manager and employees for information that describes the job and addresses the questions found in the Questions for Shadowing form. Use this form to help prompt questions.

D. The individual should observe the employees working at a variety of tasks for at least 45 minutes to 1 hour. Take detailed notes regarding answers given to the questions. Use this information to assist the individual in completing the Questions for Shadowing form immediately after the individual stops observing the employee.

E. While observing the work being performed, point out the following skills to the individual if he or she does not appear to notice them:

1. Main factors describing this job
2. Characteristics of a person who is good at this job
3. Duties of this job
4. Daily routines

F. After interviewing and observing the employees, help the individual to complete the Questions for Shadowing form. Find a quiet place to sit down at the jobsite to discuss what you and the individual have just shadowed. Completing the forms at the site is preferred—use a break room or other out-of-the way location. If necessary, prompt the individual with the information from your notes. If you assist by writing the answers to the questions, write the information in the person's own words. An example of a filled-out Questions for Shadowing form is on page 76.

Using Shadowing: Form A

A. Immediately after completing the Questions for Shadowing form, complete either Shadowing: Form A or B (see pp. 302–303). If the person can read, write, and understand abstract concepts such as the work skills, use Form A; otherwise, use Form B. A completed example of Form A is in page 78.

I:B:6:2

Questions for Shadowing

Exploring Choices

Name: Kelly Sample

Date: May 9, 2002

Jobsite: Do Drop Inn

Interviewee: John Patel

Main factors describing this job (Required work skills)

Clean bathrooms
Change bed linens
Put out fresh towels and hand soap
Vacuum rooms
Dust and empty trash
Take soiled linen to the laundry room

Characteristics of a person who is good at this job (Required social and personal skills)

Honest (must turn in items left in rooms)
Dependable and timely
Able to keep up a fast pace
Able to follow a supervisor's directions
Friendly and courteous to customers even when they aren't

Duties of this job (Required task skills)

Complete one room in 30 minutes
Complete eight rooms per shift
Deep cleaning is done during the winter.

Daily routines

Arrive no later than 9:00 a.m.
Check in at the office and get a room schedule
Get the cart and needed cleaning supplies
Report damages when cleaning the rooms

Experience, licenses, and education required for this job

None, but must have good references

How often do you hire for this position? Other positions?

Once a month during the summer; every three months during the winter

How much does a person doing this job get paid?

$5.25 per hour

Shadowing: Form A: Part 1. What I Can Do

Materials Needed
Shadowing: Form A

Completed:
Questions for Shadowing

A. Use the Questions for Shadowing to acquire information for the column called "Skills I need for this job" in Part 1 of Shadowing: Form A. List the most crucial work-related (quality and quantity), social (interpersonal interaction), personal (self-care), and task-related (equipment use and step completion) skills. A number of skills may fit more than one category. For example, in child care, talking to children is a work-related social skill. Put the skill in the category that balances examples across the crucial skill areas needed to do the job. Observe the worker completing several representative job tasks for at least 1 hour.

1. Use directed questioning to assist the individual in listing observed skills. The content of the questions should give clues to the answer. Questions might include "What do you have to be able to do to work at this job? What things do you have to be able to do to get along with people at this job?"
2. List required items in the section labeled "Job experiences, licenses, and education" at the bottom of the "Skills I need for this job" section. These could include special licenses, transportation, skill in operating special machines, special hours, and so forth.
3. Within each category skill box, number each listed skill. For each skill box, begin numbering with 1.

B. For each numbered skill identified in the "Skills I need for this job" section, ask the individual whether he or she possesses this skill. If the individual says he or she has the skill, write the number corresponding to this skill in the "Skills I have" column. Repeat this procedure for each skills category.

Shadowing: Form A: Part 1. What I Can Do: Calculations

A. Count the numbers listed in each category in the "Skills I have" column. Put the count to the left of the slash (as the numerator) in the "Matches" column. Count the number of skills listed in each category in the "Skills I need for this job" section. Write each total to the right of the slash (as the denominator) in the "Matches" column.

B. Add all the numbers that are to the left of the slash and write this total in the blank labeled "Skills I have" in the "Average skill match" box. Add all the numbers that are to the right of the slash and write this total in the blank labeled "Skills I need" in the "Average skill match" box. Divide the number to the left of the slash by the number to the right of the slash. Write the resulting decimal number to the right of the equal sign. The result should be equal to one or less.

C. Multiply the answer by 100 to calculate the percentage of skill match, and write the percentage in the "Percentage of average skill match" shaded box.

I:B:6:3	**Shadowing: Form A**	Exploring Choices

Name: Kelly Sample Jobsite: Do Drop Inn Date: May 3, 2002

Part 1: What I can do

Skills I need for this job (Get the answers from the Questions for Shadowing Form)	Skills I have (write the number of each)	Matches
Work skills 1. Work at a fast pace 2. Be timely 3. Deep clean	2	1/1
Social skills 1. Be friendly to customers when they aren't friendly		0/1
Personal skills 1. Be honest (turn stuff in) 2. Be dependable 3. Wear a clean uniform	1, 2, 3	3/3
Task skills 1. Clean restrooms 2. Change bed linens 3. Vacuum 4. Put out fresh linens and soap 5. Get cart and cleaning equipment 6. Dust and empty trash	1, 3, 4, 5, 6	5/5
Job experience, licenses, and education 1. Good references	1	1/1

Skills I have: 10 / Skills I need: 14 = .71 x 100 = 71 % Percentage of average skill match

Part 2: What I like

Two jobs I like most	Is this job one of my top choices?	Matches
1. Maid service 2. Janitorial	(Yes) No	1/1 = 1 Site match

Two tasks I like most	Is this task performed here?	Matches
1. Vacuum 2. Sweep and mop	(Yes) No (Yes) No	2/2 = 1 Task match

Site match + Task match + Characteristics match*: 2.71 / 3 = .90 x 100 = 90 % Percentage of average preference match

**From the Characteristics I Like versus What Is Here Form*

Shadowing: Form A: Part 2. What I Like

A. Complete the "Part 2: What I Like" section.

1. Direct the individual to refer to the box labeled "Two jobs I like most." Ask if the job that he or she just shadowed is one of the top two choices written in the box. If appropriate, help the individual choose the appropriate answer in the box labeled "Is this job one of my top choices?"
2. Direct the individual to refer to the box labeled "Two tasks I like most." Ask if the tasks performed at this site match the two tasks written in the box. If appropriate, assist the individual to circle the appropriate answer in the box for each task labeled "Is this task performed here?"

Shadowing: Form A: Part 2. What I Like: Calculations

A. Perform the following calculations.

1. If this job is one of the individual's two top-ranked choices, then put a 1 to the left of the slash in the first row of the column labeled "Matches." Perform the division to get the "Site match." The answer will be 1 or 0.
2. If both of the tasks are performed at this site, put a 2 to the left of the slash in the column labeled "Matches." If one of the tasks is performed at this site, write a 1 in this space. If none of the top-ranked two tasks are performed here, write a 0 in this space. Perform the division to get the "Task match." The answer will be 1, .5, or 0.
3. From the calculation field of the Characteristics I Like versus What Is Here: Form A or B (see Objective 7), transfer the decimal number from the blank labeled "Characteristics match" to the "Characteristics match" blank.
4. Add the "Site match," "Task match," and "Characteristics match" numbers. Divide the total by 3 to get the average preference match for this site. Write the answer in the blank at the bottom of the page.
5. Multiply the average preference match by 100 to get the percentage for the average preference match for this site. Write the answer in the shaded box labeled "Percentage of average preference match."

Using Shadowing: Form B

Materials Needed
Shadowing: Form B
Characteristics I Like versus What Is Here: Form A or Form B

Completed:
Questions for Shadowing
Initial Job Preferences Graph
Initial Task Preferences Graph

A. Always try to complete Form A with individuals first. Form B is designed for individuals who cannot complete Form A. Once a shadowing site is developed, you should locate the Questions for Shadowing form, Shadowing: Form B, and the Characteristics I Like versus What Is Here: Form A or B. These three forms will be used at each shadowing site. Typically, individuals who use Form B cannot independently identify work skills and tasks at a shadowing site. They need concrete examples to make decisions. The illustrations provided in Form B aid understanding. An example of a filled-out Shadowing: Form B is on page 81.

B. Before going to the shadowing site with the individual, prepare the illustrated Shadowing: Form B:

1. Review the Initial Job Preferences Graph from Objective 4. Using the "Four top-ranked jobs" section, select the four jobs most frequently chosen by the individual. Place illustrations of the preferred choices on line 1, line 3, and line 8 of Shadowing: Form B. (You can download pictures from www.brookespublishing.com/picturebank for use with this form.)

2. Using the Initial Task Preferences Graph, select the tasks most frequently chosen by the individual in Objective 4. Place pictures of the preferred tasks on line 2.

3. When setting up the shadowing site, be sure to arrange which tasks will be observed with the manager. Place selected pictures of the major tasks on lines 4, 5, 6, and 7 of Shadowing: Form B in order to individualize the form. Place one picture per box. You may leave some boxes empty.

C. Before going the shadowing site, ask the individual to select his or her most preferred jobs and tasks.

1. Circle the two jobs he or she likes the most on line 1, "Jobs I like (Before) and the two tasks he or she likes the most on line 2, "Tasks I like (Before)."

2. In Objective 7, locate Characteristics I Like versus What Is Here: Form B and then complete the "What I like" section.

3. Review the questions found on the Questions for Shadowing. The individual will need to become familiar with these questions in order to interview the manager at the jobsite being shadowed. If appropriate, change the questions to fit the needs of the individual or the site. For instance, a person with a physical limitation may want to ask about job sharing or task exchanges with co-workers.

D. After arriving at the shadowing site:

1. Ask the individual to confirm the site that is being shadowed by circling the appropriate box on line 3, "This job here."

2. Meet the manager, and have the individual ask the questions listed on the Questions for Shadowing. You may need to prompt or assist the individual with the questions. Write the responses under each respective question.

3. While observing an employee at the jobsite, assist the individual to list the tasks that the employee is doing. Prompt the individual to generate as many tasks as possi-

I:B:6:4

Shadowing: Form B

Exploring Choices

Name: Pat Sample Jobsite: UltraPlastics Date: May 9, 2002

Row	
	Jobs I like (Before): Circle two.
1	
	Tasks I like (Before): Circle two.
2	
	The job here: Circle one.
3	
	Tasks here: Circle all the tasks that are here.
4	
	Tasks here I can do: Circle all the tasks you can do.
5	
	Tasks here I have done: Circle all the tasks you have done.
6	
	Tasks here I like: Circle all the tasks you like.
7	
	Jobs I like (After): Circle two.
8	

1. Matches for Rows 1 and 3 = 1
2. Matches for Rows 1 and 8 = 0
3. Items circled in Row 2 divided by total of Row 7= .29
4. Characteristics match (from I.B.7.2) = .58

Sum of 1–4: / 4 = .47 x 100 = 47% Percentage of preference match

5. Items circled in Row 5 divided by total of Row 4 = .86
6. Items circled in Row 6 divided by total of Row 4 = .29

Sum of 5 and 6: / 2 = .58 x 100 = 58% Percentage of skill match

ble. Direct the individual to circle the major tasks illustrated on line 4, "Tasks here." Continue to shadow the worker until either the worker has run out of tasks to do, or the 1-hour observation is complete.

E. Immediately after shadowing, find a quiet place at the jobsite, if possible. You may need to assist the individual by going through each task one-by-one on each line. Help the individual complete the following steps:

1. Confirm the tasks he or she saw performed and circled on line 4, "Tasks here." If there are blank boxes and the person wants to add a new task that was not illustrated, ask the individual to draw a picture of the new task in the blank box.
2. Circle tasks he or she can do on line 5, "Tasks here I can do."
3. Circle the tasks he or she has done on line 6, "Tasks here I have done."
4. Circle the tasks he or she likes on line 7, "Tasks here I like."
5. Circle two jobs he or she likes on line 8, "Jobs I like (After)."

F. Complete the Characteristics I Like versus What Is Here: Form B found in Objective 7.

Shadowing: Form B: Calculations

A. Assist the individual to perform the calculations at the bottom left side of the page in the box.

1. On item 1, assist the individual to match the items circled on line 1, "Jobs I like (Before)" and line 3, "The job here." If one of the two jobs circled in line 1 matches one of the two jobs circled in line 3, write a 1 in the blank provided. Otherwise, write a 0.
2. On item 2, assist the individual to match the items circled in line 1, "Jobs I like (Before)" and line 8, "Jobs I like (After)." If one of the two jobs circled in line 1 matches one of the two jobs circled in line 8, write a 1 in the blank provided. Otherwise, write a 0.
3. On item 3, assist the individual to count the number of circled tasks on line 2, then count the total number of pictured tasks in the boxes on line 7, "Tasks here I like." Divide the numbers, and place the decimal number after the equal sign.
4. From the Characteristics I Like versus What Is Here: Form B, transfer the decimal number in the blank labeled "Characteristics match" to line 4 of the Shadowing: Form B.
5. Finally, add all four numbers together and divide by 4. Your answer will be a decimal number. Multiply this number by 100 to find the "Percentage of preference match."

B. Assist the individual to perform the calculations at the bottom right side of the page.

1. For item 5, assist the individual to count the number of items circled in line 5, "Tasks here I can do." Assist the individual to count the number of items circled in line 4, "Tasks here." Divide line 5 by line 4, and write the decimal number after the equal sign.

2. For item 6 of the box, assist the individual to count the number of items circled in line 6, "Tasks here I have done." Assist the individual to count the number of items circled in line 4, "Tasks here." Divide line 6 by line 4, and write the decimal number after the equal sign.

3. Finally, add the two numbers together and divide by 2. Your answer should be a decimal number. Multiply this number by 100, and fill in the blank labeled "Percentage of skill match."

C. Discuss the preference match and the skills match with the individual.

1. As a general guide, you use a criterion of 75%–80% to determine a strong preference and skills match.

2. How strong is the individual's preference for doing this type of job? What characteristics exist that make the job attractive?

3. What skills does the individual feel he or she has to do the job? What skills will be needed?

4. Review the responses from the Questions for Shadowing to determine an overall subjective match.

Objective 6: What If?

What if the individual is interested in work that is not easily observable? For example, the individual wants to be an airline pilot?

Set up a situational interview (see Objective 8). Do not use the process described in Objectives 6 and 7.

What if you cannot find an employer willing to let you shadow the job the individual is interested in?

Shadow all other choices first. The individual may find that he or she likes a different job. Attempt to find a similar jobsite to shadow. If this is not possible, see the response to the first question.

What if the individual indicates he or she has the skill to do the tasks at the shadowing site, but you don't agree?

Accept the individual's response. Ask the individual to explain why he or she can do the skill. If this becomes a preferred site, the individual will have an opportunity to demonstrate this skill when an internship is arranged.

What if, when using Form B, the individual is not able to verbalize the tasks he or she sees at the site?

You can verbalize the task list or have the individual point to preselected pictures of the tasks.

What if, while using Form B, you run out of room to list tasks?

Try to group tasks together. List the tasks that are done most often.

What if there is a high skills match but a low preference match?

Let the preference match guide your efforts toward the individual's job choice.

What if the individual expresses frustration after finding that the jobs shadowed pay only entry-level wages?

Explain to the individual that these jobs may serve as stepping stones to higher paying jobs.

What if the individual lists a work skill as a social skill?

List the skill in the category that the individual chose.

Section I. Assessment: Choice Management
Goal B: Exploring Choices

Objective 7: Completing the Characteristics I Like versus What Is Here: Form A or B

CONTENTS

Choose characteristics
Determine match
Characteristics I Like versus What Is Here:
Form A: Calculations

MATERIALS NEEDED

Characteristics I Like versus What Is Here:
Form A (I:B:7:1) and Form B (I:B:7:2)

PURPOSE

To determine the match between the characteristics that individuals like and the characteristics that are available at different shadowing sites

LOCATION

Office
Shadowing site

Choose characteristics

Materials Needed
Characteristics I Like versus What Is Here: Form A and Form B

Note: Introduce Objective 7: Completing the Characteristics I Like versus What Is Here Forms and the Shadowing Forms from Objective 6 at the same time.

A. Explain to the individual that the purpose of the Characteristics I Like versus What Is Here forms is to
   1. Explore characteristics central to a preferred job
   2. Identify characteristics that exist at the jobsite
   3. Compare the characteristics that are important to the individual with the characteristics that exist on a jobsite

B. Choose the appropriate format to meet the needs of the individual.
   1. Form A requires the ability to read.
   2. Form B requires picture discrimination skills. It is designed for individuals whose reading skills are limited or nonexistent.

C. The items in the Characteristics I Like versus What Is Here Form are presented as contrasting pairs (see pp. 304–306). Instruct the individual to choose the preferred item out of each pair.
   1. Teach this form by first reading the contrasting pairs, explaining the terms, and then asking the person to choose one. Repeat this for the first two or three pairs.

2. The individual may be able to complete this form independently. Give him or her the opportunity to do so. If help is needed, read and briefly explain each item.

3. If the individual is undecided about which item to choose, ask him or her to circle neither or both.

D. Before going to the jobsite, follow these steps.

1. Ask the individual to complete the column labeled "What I Like (Before)" in Characteristics I Like versus What Is Here: Form A or B by circling the item that he or she prefers in each pair.

2. Add any additional preferred characteristics in the blank boxes noted during Objective 3: Teaching Characteristics I Like at the bottom of the form next to "Other."

3. Using the circled characteristics, assist the individual, if necessary, to draw a star next to the 10 most important characteristics in the column labeled "★."

4. Next, assist the individual to check the four most important characteristics in the column labeled "✓".

5. Once again, discuss the final four characteristics chosen by asking the individual to describe the important features of each selected characteristic. If the individual wants to change the top-ranked characteristics, the final choice must be his or hers. *Do not* try to influence the decision.

E. Complete the shadowing session in Objective 6. Then, ask the individual to complete the "What is here (After)" section of the Characteristics I Like versus What Is Here Form. The individual should circle the characteristic that best describe the jobsite from each of the contrasting pairs.

Determine match

A. Next, the individual completes the "Matches" column. Assist the person to determine the match between "What I like" and "What is here" for each characteristic. For each row, have the individual indicate a match by circling "Yes" in the "Matches" column. If the circled characteristics do not match, have the individual circle "No," indicating no match.

Characteristics I Like versus What Is Here: Form A: Calculations

A. Help the individual to complete the calculations as directed. An example of a completed Characteristics I Like versus What Is Here: Form A is on page 87.

1. Divide the total number of "Yes"s by the total number of matches available. The total will be a decimal number. (This is also the number that should be transferred to the appropriate blank on the Shadowing Form in Objec-

I:B:7:1

Characteristics I Like versus What Is Here: Form A

Exploring Choices
Testing Choices

Name: Kelly Sample Jobsite: Do Drop Inn Date: May 20, 2002

What I like (Before)		★	✓	What is here (After)		Matches	
Work alone okay	Work with others	☆	✓	Work alone	Work with others	Yes	No
Quiet workplace	Noisy workplace			Quiet workplace	Noisy workplace	Yes	No
Part-time	Full-time	☆		Part-time	Full-time	Yes	No
Weekdays only	Weekends, too			Weekdays only	Weekends, too	Yes	No
Hard job	Easy job			Hard job	Easy job	Yes	No
Work inside	Work outside	☆		Work inside	Work outside	Yes	No
Few rules	Defined rules	☆	✓	Few rules	Defined rules	Yes	No
Work standing up	Work sitting down	☆		Work standing up	Work sitting down	Yes	No
Mornings	Evenings			Mornings	Evenings	Yes	No
Attractive place	Looks of place do not matter			Attractive place	Looks of place do not matter	Yes	No
Detail is important	Detail is not important			Detail is important	Detail is not important	Yes	No
Dress up for work	Do not dress up	☆		Dress up for work	Do not dress up	Yes	No
Physical work okay	Thinking work	☆	✓	Physical work	Thinking work	Yes	No
Important to work fast	Speed is unimportant			Important to work fast	Speed is unimportant	Yes	No
Same tasks every day okay	Different tasks every day	☆	✓	Same tasks every day	Different tasks every day	Yes	No
Work with people	Work with things			Work with people	Work with things	Yes	No
Little supervision	A lot of supervision	☆		Little supervision	A lot of supervision	Yes	No
Daytime work	Nighttime work			Daytime work	Nighttime work	Yes	No
Small business	Large business	☆		Small business	Large business	Yes	No
Other:	Other:			Other:	Other:	Yes	No
Other:	Other:			Other:	Other:	Yes	No

Number of characteristics matches: 17

Number of matches available: 19

= .89

Characteristics match

x 100

= 89%

Percentage of characteristics match

100%	
Good match	89%
75%	75%
Okay match	
50%	
Poor match	
25%	
Not a match	
0%	

After determining the four top-ranked characteristics and checking them, write "okay" beside each checked item that matches the characteristic circled in the "What is here" column.

Number of okays: 3

4

x 100 = 75%

Percentage of most important characteristics match

tive 6.) Multiply this number by 100. Write the percentage in the blank provided. Use this percentage to mark the scale.

2. For each of the four characteristics checked in the "✓" column that matches the site in the "What is here" column, write "Okay" beside the item. Divide the total number of "Okays" by four. The total will be a decimal. Write this number on the appropriate line, and multiply by 100. The number you get will give the percentage for the "Percentage of most important characteristics match." Write this number in the labeled blank, and use it to mark the scale.

3. Discuss the scores with the individual. Review the "Characteristics match" score with the individual. Using the graph, determine if the match is a strong score. Review the characteristics that the individual likes and the characteristics that the individual said was there. What items made this jobsite attractive to the individual? What items made this jobsite unattractive to the individual? What were the individual's most important characteristics? What was the final score? Ask the individual why the chosen items are most important to have at a job.

Objective 7: What If?

What if the individual chooses "Weekends, too" and the job is on weekdays only?	*These choices should be considered a match.*
What if the individual chooses "Looks of place do not matter," but the jobsite is characterized as an "Attractive place"?	*These choices should be considered a match.*
What if the individual chooses both characteristics by circling both of the contrasting items in a section? For example, the individual chooses "Working with things" and "Working with people." Employees at the jobsite that was shadowed work with things.	*This would be considered a match. The opposite is also a match.*
What if the individual does not indicate a preference?	*The section would not be counted as an available match. This section would be excluded in the match calculation.*
What if the individual's characterization of the jobsite is different from yours? For example, you perceive the site as being relatively loud, and the individual perceives it as being quiet.	*Ask the individual to explain why he or she chose to describe the jobsite as quiet. Do not try to persuade, and make sure your questions are neutral. After the individual explains why he or she chose that characteristic, accept his or her characterization.*
What if the jobsite can be described by both contrasting pairs? For example, the job requires working in the morning and the afternoon.	*Circle both items. This is always a match.*
What if the individual has a strong preference for a jobsite and forces a match between "What I like (Before)" and "What is here (After)?"	*When the individual completes the "What is here (After)" section, cover the "What I like (Before)" section with a piece of paper.*
What if, when completing the "What is here (After)" section, the individual does not know when the job is performed?	*Instruct the individual get the needed information from a co-worker or the manager.*
What if the paired comparison characteristic does not apply to this job?	*Leave blank or scratch through the comparison. The match would not be available for calculation.*

Section I. Assessment: Choice Management
Goal B: Exploring Choices

Objective 8: Doing the Situational Interview (Optional)

CONTENT

Prepare
Introduce the Situational Interview
Interview
Determine matches and calculate
Use the Situational Interview Summary
Situational Interview Summary: Part 2. What I Like: Calculations
Situational Interview Summary: Part 1. What I Can Do
Situational Interview Summary: Part 1. What I Can Do: Calculations

MATERIALS NEEDED

Situational Interview (I:B:8:1)
Situational Interview Summary (I:B:8:2)

PURPOSE

To enable individuals who are interested in jobs that are either impossible or inconvenient to shadow to gain information about that job

LOCATION

Office
Interview site

Prepare

A. For an individual who is interested in a job that cannot be shadowed, the situational interview may be more appropriate. The process described in this objective replaces that described in Objectives 6 and 7. We found that this process works well for people who had previous professional careers and acquired their disabilities in adulthood.

B. Make an appointment to interview the manager or personnel director at a preferred jobsite.

   1. Explain that the individual has expressed an interest in the kind of work performed at the business.

   2. Explain that the individual needs to gain information about the job to determine if his or her skills match those required by the job.

Introduce the Situational Interview

Materials Needed
- Situational Interview
- Situational Interview Summary

A. Before going to the interview site, follow these steps:

1. Take time to review the two-page Situational Interview form and the Situational Interview Summary (see pp. 307–309). The individual must be familiar with these forms in order to understand the interview process and the information he or she will be expected to gather. If the individual cannot read the questions, then you should read them out loud.
2. Ask the individual to circle his or her preferred characteristics in the "What I like" side of the "Work characteristics questions" section on the first page.
3. Fill out the "Part 2: What I like" section of the Situational Interview Summary. Ask the individual to fill out the box labeled "Two jobs I like most." You may need to prompt the individual by using the Initial Job Preferences Graph (see Objective 4). If the individual chooses jobs he or she has not chosen before, that is okay. Assist the individual to fill in the section, if appropriate.

Interview

A. Be sure to bring two copies of the Situational Interview form with you to the interview so that both you and the individual can make notes.

B. When meeting with the manager, use the Situational Interview form to ask questions about the skills and job conditions. Specifically ask the company culture questions on the first page and the skills-oriented questions on the second page.

C. Both you and individual should take notes by filling in the blank next to each question during the interview.

D. Cordially ask for a tour to get additional information about work conditions.

Determine matches and calculate

A. After the interview and tour, find a quiet place or return to the office. Ask the individual to complete the "What is here" side of the "Work characteristics questions" section on the first page of the Situational Interview form.

1. Instruct the individual to determine the match between "What I like" and "What is here" for each characteristic.
2. The individual should circle "Yes" in the "Matches" column whenever "What I like" and "What is here" match. Circle "No" if they do not match.

B. Assist the individual to complete the calculations at the bottom of the section.

1. Write the total number of "Yes"s in the space labeled "Number of characteristics match."

2. Write the number of characteristics available in the space labeled "Number of available matches."
3. Perform the division, and write the decimal number in the blank.
4. Multiply this number by 100. Write the answer in the shaded box labeled "Percentage of characteristics match."

C. Discuss the characteristics matches with the individual.

D. Look at the company culture answers from the Situational Interview. If the individual likes the answer, write "Okay" in the labeled column. If not, write "Not okay."

1. Assist the individual to count up the number of "Okay"s. Write this number in the blank labeled "Number of culture items okay."
2. Assist the individual to count up the number of culture questions that were answered and write this number in the space labeled "Number of available answers."
3. Perform the division and write this decimal number in the blank. Multiply by 100, and write this number in the shaded box labeled "Percentage of culture match."

Use the Situational Interview Summary: Part 2. What I like: Calculations

A. Complete the calculations to determine the preference match.

1. If one of the preferred jobs is the job here, then write a 1 to the left of the slash in the first row of the column labeled "Matches." If not, write a 0. Perform the division to get the number for the "Site match."
2. Assist the individual to transfer the "Culture match" number from the first page of the Situational Interview to the second row of the "Matches" column labeled "Culture match."
3. From the "Work characteristics questions" section on the first page of the Situational Interview, transfer the decimal number from the "Characteristics match" section to the "Characteristics match" box on this form.
4. Add the site, culture, and characteristics match numbers. Divide the total by 3. Write this number on the blank line.
5. Multiply the answer by 100, and write this percentage into the blank next to "Percentage of average preference match."

B. Discuss the results of the situational interview with the individual. Find out what things about the culture of the organization were appealing. Did the characteristics exist at this job that the individual needs? What was the "Percentage of average preference match" score? Does this person have a strong preference for this type of job? Find out why.

Use the Situational Interview Summary: Part 1. What I Can Do

Materials Needed
- Situational Interview
- Situational Interview Summary

A. Using the notes taken on the second page of the Situational Interview, complete the Situational Interview Summary. An example of a completed Situational Interview Summary is on page 95.

1. Review and compare notes written on the second page of the Situational Interview.
2. Using the skills-oriented answers on the second page of the Situational Interview, list all of the required skills in the "Skills I need for this job" column on the Situational Interview Summary. Let the individual recall the skills, and prompt the individual to list the skills in the appropriate work, social, personal, or task boxes.
3. List the most crucial job requirements in the box labeled "Job needs, requirements, and conditions." These could include special licenses, transportation, skill in operating special machines, and so forth.
4. Use directed questioning to help the individual list skills that have not been addressed. Questions might include "What do you have to be able to do to work at this job? What things do you have to be able to do to get along with people at this job?" Add the answers to the directed questions to the appropriate box.
5. Within each box, number each skill. Begin numbering with 1. (Numbers do not have to correspond with numbers on the Situational Interview.)
6. For each skill identified in the "Skills I need for this job" column, ask the individual whether he or she possesses this skill. If the individual feels he or she does, write the number corresponding to this skill in the same category in the "Skills I have" column. Repeat this procedure for each category presented on the form.

Use the Situational Interview Summary: Part 1. What I Can Do: Calculations

A. Perform the calculations.

1. Count the numbers listed in each category in the "Skills I have" column. Write the total to the left of the slash (as the numerator) in the "Matches" column.
2. Count the number of skills listed in each category in the "Skills I need for this job" column. Write each total to the right of the slash (as the denominator) in the "Matches" column.
3. Add all the numbers that are to the left of the slash and write this total on the line labeled "Skills I have." Add all the numbers that are to the right of the slash and write this total next to "Skills I need." Compute the fraction, and write the resulting decimal number in the blank provided.
4. Multiply this number by 100, and write the percentage in the screened box labeled "Percentage of average skill match."

I:B:8:2

Situational Interview Summary

Exploring Choices

Name: Kelly Sample   Jobsite: Fancy Nursery   Date: May 31, 2001

Part 1: What I can do

Skills I need for this job (Get the answers from the Situational Interview Form)	Skills I have (write the number of each)	Matches
Work skills 1. Be on time 2. Work fast 3. Follow directions 4. Use feedback to do a better job	1, 2, 3	3 / 4
Social skills 1. Get along with others 2. Help others out 3. Have a positive attitude	3	1 / 3
Personal skills 1. Dress is casual 2. Aprons and boots are provided	1, 2	2 / 2
Task skills 1. Fill flats and pots with soil 2. Trasplant plants 3. Water 4. Clean work area 5. Clean bathrooms and break area	1, 2, 3, 4, 5	5 / 5
Job needs, requirements, and conditions 1. A lot of standing 2. A lot of walking 3. A lot of bending and reaching 5. The job is part time afternoons at $4.35 per hour	1, 2, 3, 4, 5	5 / 5

Skills I have: 16 / Skills I need: 19 = .84 x 100 = 84% Percentage of average skill match

Part 2: What I like

Two jobs I like most	Is this job one of my top choices?	Site match
Maid service Working with plants	(Yes) No	1 / 1 = 1

Site match + Culture match[a] + Characteristics match[b]: / 3 = .89 x 100 = 89% Percentage of average preference match

[a] *From the Situational Interview (page 1)*
[b] *From the Characteristics I Like versus What Is Here Form*

Objective 8: What If?

What if the individual has identified the job of his or her dreams but learns that employment opportunities are rare or nonexistent in your community?

Assessment staff should find out what parts of the job are appealing. Explore other jobs that possess similar characteristics.

What if the individual identified the job of his or her dreams, but certifications are required that the person does not have?

Explore possibilities for jobs in the same area that do not require certification, or look into educational programs in which the person could earn the needed certificate.

What if, after arriving at the prearranged interview site, the employer tells you that the meeting has to be cut short, and you are not able to ask the full set of questions?

The assessment staff should ask the questions and write the answers as quickly as possible. Choose specific questions that you know will be most important for the individual to hear the answers to. Ask the individual if there are any further questions that he or she would like to ask the employer.

What if, during the interview, you discover that the employer is not giving information that is critical to the job and will have a direct effect on the individual. For example, you are interviewing the owner of a cabinet shop, and the owner does not emphasize the fact that precise measurement is critical. You know that measuring skills are not a strength of the individual you are working with.

Specifically ask the employer to elaborate on the required measuring skills. Ask questions about the required skill, such as "What are the specific tools used to attain accurate measurement?" If possible, ask the employer to give examples or show you both some completed work.

What if the employer says that there is a checklist that the individual can use to compare his or her skills to those that are needed at the jobsite?

Complete the checklist with the individual, but also set up an interview at that site if possible. If this is not possible, attempt to arrange an interview at a similar jobsite.

Section I. Assessment: Choice Management
Goal B: Exploring Choices

Objective 9: Completing the Shadowing Summary

CONTENTS

Summarize the Shadowing Forms (corresponds with Objectives 6 and 7)
OR
Summarize the Situational Interview Summary Forms (corresponds with Objective 8)
Determine the results of shadowing sites
Determine top-ranked characteristics

MATERIALS NEEDED

Shadowing Summary Graph (I:B:9:1)
Completed:
- Characteristics Summary Graph (I:A:4:3)
- Four Most Important Characteristics Graph (I:A:4:4)
- Shadowing: Form A (I:B:6:3) or Form B (I:B:6:4)
- Characteristics I Like versus What Is Here: Form A (I:B:7:1) or Form B (I:B:7:2)
- Situational Interview (I:B:8:1)
- Situational Interview Summary (I:B:8:2)

PURPOSE

To provide a process for individuals to find out the shadowing sites or interview sites that best matched their skills and preferences

LOCATION

Office

Summarize the Shadowing Forms

Materials Needed
Shadowing Summary Graph

Completed:
Shadowing: Form A or Form B

A. Collect all the completed Shadowing Forms that the individual used to shadow his or her preferred jobsites.

B. Along the top row of the Shadowing Summary Graph (see p. 310), fill in the names of each shadowed jobsite in the boxes labeled "Shadowed site 1" through "Shadowed site 6." (An individual may shadow up to six jobsites, but it is unlikely that he or she would need to shadow more than six.)

C. For each completed Shadowing Form, follow these steps.

1. Locate the section called "Part 1: What I can do." Find the box labeled "Percentage of average skill match." Transfer the decimal number to the box labeled "Skill match" on the Shadowing Summary Graph.

2. Locate the section called "Part 2: What I like," and find the box labeled "Percentage of average preference match." Transfer the decimal number to the box labeled "Preference match" on the Shadowing Summary Graph.

3. Repeat this procedure for each site where the Shadowing Form was used. The box labeled "Culture match" remains blank.

Summarize the Situational Interview Summary

Materials Needed
- Shadowing Summary Graph
- Completed:
  - Situational Interview
  - Situational Interview Summary

A. Collect all of the Situational Interviews and Situational Interview Summaries that the individual used.

B. For each Situational Interview Summary, complete these steps.

1. Locate the section called "Part 1: What I can do," and find the box labeled "Average of total skill match." Transfer the decimal number to the box labeled "Skill match" on the Shadowing Summary Graph.

2. Locate the section called "Part 2: What I like," and find the box labeled "Percentage of average preference match." Transfer the decimal number to the box labeled "Preference match" on the Shadowing Summary Graph.

C. For each Situational Interview, find the box labeled "Percentage of culture match." Transfer the decimal number to the "Culture match" box on the Shadowing Summary Graph.

Determine the results of shadowing sites

Materials Needed
- Shadowing Summary Graph

A. After entering the skill, preference, and culture match scores for each site, shade in the graph in order to represent each score. The scale is located on the left side of the Shadowing Summary Graph. For each shadowed site, draw a column matching the score for each skill, preference, and culture match. Shade in each column up to the appropriate point.

B. At the bottom of the page is a section labeled "Three internship sites." After reviewing the scores by looking at the graph for each shadowed jobsite and discussing the results, determine the three top-ranked jobsites, and fill in the three blanks from the highest to lowest score. These will be internship jobsites in the next objective.

Determine top-ranked characteristics

Materials Needed
- Completed:
  - Characteristics Summary Graph
  - Four Most Important Characteristics Graph
  - Characteristics I Like versus What Is Here: Forms A or Forms B
  - Situational Interview

A. Collect all of the completed Characteristics I Like versus What Is Here forms and the completed Situational Interview.

B. To summarize the characteristics the individual chose most frequently, continue to add the individual's choices to the Characteristics Summary Graph. Circle "Exploring Choices" in the upper right corner of the form.

1. As before in Goal A, for each characteristic chosen for the first shadowed jobsite, shade in a blank box for the corresponding characteristic. Leave any characteristics not chosen blank.

2. Continue to record the individual's choices for each shadowed site. Help the individual to complete the form or complete it yourself, if necessary.

C. To summarize the four most important characteristics the individual chose most frequently, continue to add the individual's choices to the Four Most Important Characteristics Graph. For each characteristic form completed at the shadowed jobsite, shade in one box for each of the four checked items. Leave boxes blank for those characteristics that were not a top-ranked preference. Continue to record the individual's four top-ranked preferred characteristics for the second and third days. Help the individual to complete the form or complete it yourself, if appropriate.

D. Review the summarized characteristic information with the individual to determine the individual's top-ranked characteristic choices and the individual's four most important characteristics that must exist at a job.

Objective 9: What If?

What if an individual uses a combination of Form A for the Initial Job Preferences Graph and the Initial Task Preferences Graph and a combination of Shadowing: Form A and the Situational Interview form for shadowing?

Enter all per directions. To compare them, look for the averages. This is not unusual for an individual who acquired disabilities during adulthood.

What if there is a tie between two, three, or four shadowed jobsite scores on the Shadowing Summary Graph?

Ask the individual to make a choice. Where does he or she most want to intern? Have the individual choose his or her most preferred two or three sites.

What if, throughout the shadowing process, the individual has been insistent that he or she must have a job now?

Consult the individual's vocational rehabilitation counselor. Determine the true financial need. After reviewing the Shadowing Summary Graph, determine whether preferred internship sites have immediate job openings that are appropriate.

What if the individual has shadowed a job and has a high skill match but a low preference for the job?

Discuss the shadowed jobsite. Discuss skills and preference scores. Let the individual choose whether he or she wants to intern this job.

What if the individual has shadowed a job and has a low skill match but a high preference match?

Discuss the shadowed jobsite. Discuss skills and preference scores. Let the individual choose whether he or she wants to intern this job. When setting up the internship, try to arrange tasks that you feel the individual might perform well. Do not ignore the individual's preference. You do not want someone to believe that you never gave him or her a chance!

INTRODUCTION TO SECTION I.

Goal C: Testing Choices

Goal C continues the process covered in the previous chapters. From the Shadowing Summary Graph, identify several jobs for the individual to test during an internship. Then, arrange internships for each top-ranked job preference. The procedures outlined in Goal C provide the individual with an opportunity to spend 3–4 hours per day to test preferences and skills for a 3-day period. Internships are typically fully supervised by the assessment staff and insured by the local vocational rehabilitation agency. Interns are paid at least minimum wage for the work performed at each internship site. In some cases, we have found internships to be a good marketing tool for placement, if used wisely.

For each internship site, the individual determines his or her work, social, personal, and task strengths and weaknesses. Goals and plans are set for those items that the individual would like to improve. The intern performs the assigned tasks and then evaluates his or her own performance. For each work, social, personal, or task item, the intern determines if his or her evaluation matches the assessment staff's evaluation. After determining a match, the intern decides what adjustment is needed the next time the job is performed and whether the characteristics at the internship site match his or her preferences. On the last day of each internship, the intern identifies the major job requirements, whether he or she can meet those requirements, and what, if any, accommodations need to be made in order to have a job similar to the internship.

Assessment personnel support, supervise, and evaluate the individual. All interns should receive the same training normally given to new first-day employees. If necessary, provide individualized assistance. If assistance beyond the normal training is given, evaluate the individual accordingly: Did you model the task? Did you give verbal prompts? Did you need to physically prompt the intern? Did you correct some of the work performed?

Internships afford opportunities to sample many different job environments. Individuals need enough internships to develop their choice-making skills and to determine their first and second job choices. At the end of this phase, prepare a summary analysis of preferences and choices for each internship site. You may want to refer to the Implementation Reference Guide (Table 3.3).

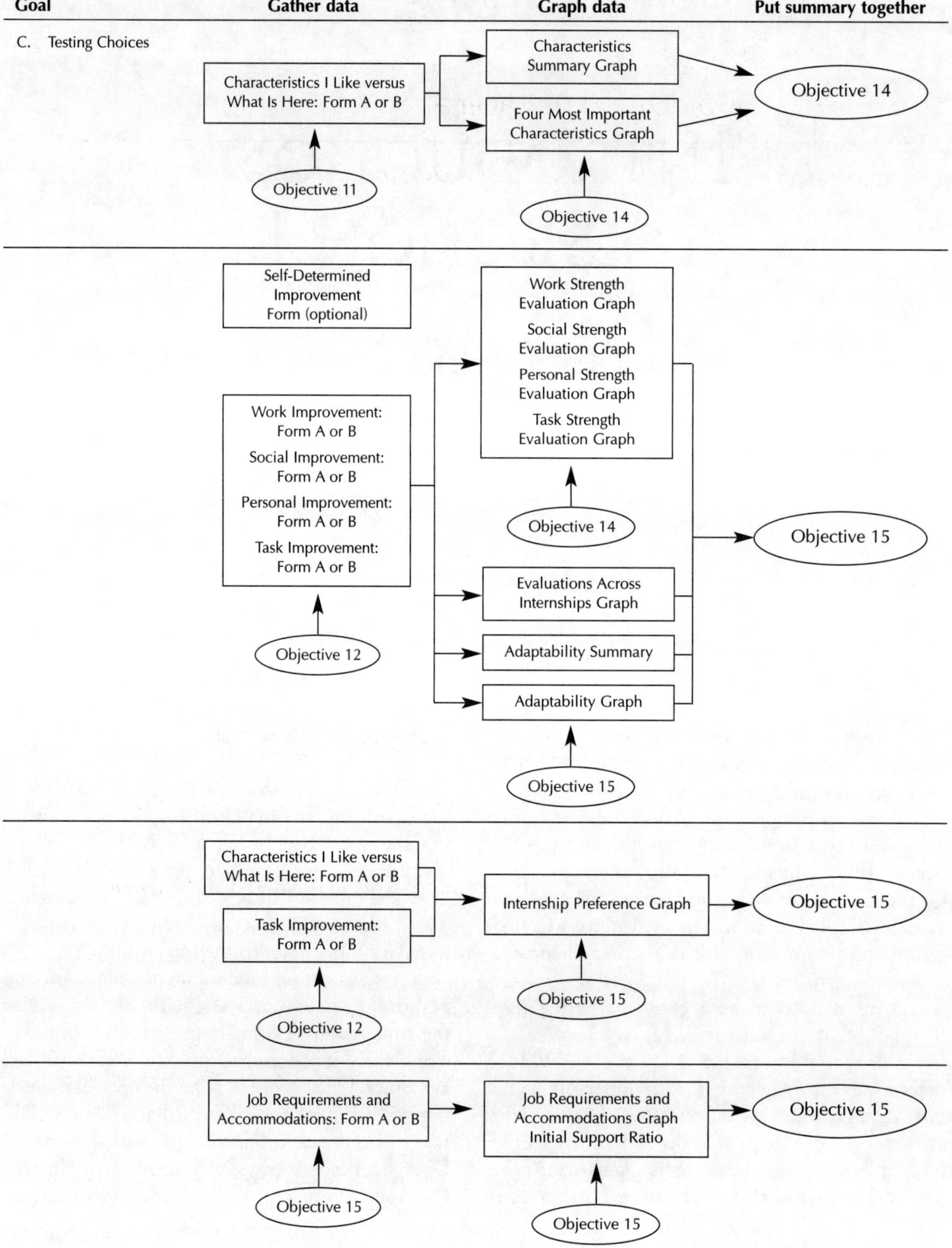

Section I. Assessment: Choice Management
Goal C: Testing Choices

Objective 10: Facilitating Internships

CONTENTS

Review information
Prospect sites

MATERIALS NEEDED

Completed:
Job reference sources
Assessment Event Organizer (I:B:6:1)
Shadowing Summary Graph (I:B:9:1)

PURPOSE

To obtain an opportunity for the individual to try out a job and determine the match between his or her preferred job, skills, and work conditions

LOCATION

Office
Internship site

Review information

Materials Needed

Completed:
Job reference sources
Assessment Event Organizer
Shadowing Summary Graph

A. Review the completed Shadowing Summary Graph with the individual to determine preferred internship sites.

B. Determine what type of internship is needed.

1. If the individual has no work experience in a field that matches his or her preferences and self-assessed skills or has had unsuccessful work experiences, then set up two or three internships matching the top-ranked choices—some people may need four or more internships to acquire sufficient information in order to make decisions.
2. If the individual possesses some experience in an employment area that matches his or her choices and is very sure about this job choice, then seek internships that provide the possibility of employment.
3. If the individual has substantial work experience, then he or she should explore his or her choices further or go to an immediate job opening matching past work experiences.
4. Arrange an internship at a business with a job opening if the individual has a firm understanding of his or her preferences and skills, worked in the job before, and wants to go to work quickly.

C. Find potential internship sites.

1. Gather job reference sources from newspaper classified ads, phone books, Chamber of Commerce publications, and so forth. Do not forget friends, family, and past employers.

2. List internship sites that match an individual's preferences and skills.

3. Involve the individual in this process. Ask him or her to look at the newspaper with you and to talk to his or her friends about job openings.

D. Use the Assessment Event Organizer to organize each individual's internship events (see p. 300). Schedule each internship for at least 3 hours per day during 3 consecutive days. Schedule the work experience during hours that are best for the employer. Usually, this will be a time when there may be work to do but the employer is not overwhelmed by a busy period.

Prospect sites

A. Contact prospects by phone or in person. Introduce your organization to the employer.

1. Tell the employer that the individual you are working with is interested in determining whether his or her skills match a job at the employer's site.

2. Indicate to the employer that an internship allows the individual to determine whether his or her skills match the job. The internship also provides an opportunity for the employer to prescreen a potential employee. However, make sure the employer realizes that, at this point, the individual is not asking for a job.

3. Explain that the intern will receive wages from your program for each hour he or she works at the site. We recommend that you pay the minimum wage or more for each hour the individual works—this will ensure compliance with all labor laws. See Simon and Halloran (1994) and Martin and Husch (1987) for discussions of labor laws and employment experiences.

4. Be prepared to answer questions from the employer about liability and workman's compensation insurance. If your program is paying the internship wages, assure the employer that your insurance will cover these items. Explain your agency's insurance coverage. The employer may require proof of insurance. Also check with your local or state vocational rehabilitation agency. Many provide on-the-jobsite insurance coverage for clients.

B. Set an appointment for the employer to meet the intern.

1. The employer may want to interview the individual before scheduling internship dates. Expect the dates and times to match the employer's schedule—not yours.
2. If the individual is inexperienced at work or there are doubts about the individual's productivity, make sure the employer understands that the intern is an extra worker rather than an integral part of the business for that day. Keep productivity expectations to a minimum.
3. Schedule one internship at a time. If the individual does well during the first internship, it may turn into a job.

Objective 10: What If?

What if the individual demands an immediate job because of dire financial conditions, even though previous experiences do not match present choices?

Contact your local rehabilitation counselor to assist in acquiring short-term financial aid. Proceed with the internship experiences. If the individual is sure about what he or she wants to do and you think it is a good match, arrange an internship that could turn into a job.

What if an employer wants to know who will supervise the intern?

This should be discussed with the employer. In some cases, they may want this responsibility. In most cases, your program will assume full supervisory responsibilities. You will need to be there to assist the individual to complete the internship learning process.

What if the individual and his or her parents expect an internship to be an actual long-term paid job?

Clarify with the individual and parents that internships are established for assessment purposes. The individual will be paid by the agency for the productive time spent doing tasks during the internship. The employer does not pay the individual for his or her work time, nor is the intern an employee of the business.

Section I. Assessment: Choice Management
Goal C: Testing Choices

Objective 11: Completing the Characteristics I Like versus What Is Here: Form A or B

CONTENTS

Choose characteristics
Determine match
Characteristics I Like versus What Is Here Form: Calculations
Summarize characteristics most often chosen
Summarize the four most important characteristics

MATERIALS NEEDED

Characteristics I Like versus What Is Here: Form A (I:B:7:1) or Form B (I:B:7:2)
Completed:
Characteristics Summary Graph (I:A:4:3)
Four Most Important Characteristics Graph (I:A:4:4)

PURPOSE

To determine the match between the characteristics that the individual likes and the characteristics that are available at different internship sites

LOCATION

Office
Internship site

Choose characteristics

Materials Needed
Characteristics I Like versus What Is Here: Form A or Form B

A. The Characteristics I Like versus What Is Here form was also used in Objectives 6 and 7. Use blank forms for this objective (see pp. 304–306). Review with the individual the purpose of the Characteristics I Like versus What Is Here form:

1. To further explore characteristic preferences
2. To identify characteristics that exist at the internship site
3. To compare the chosen characteristics with those that exist at the internship site

B. Choose the form format that will meet the needs of the individual. The individual is likely to use the format he or she used in Objectives 6 and 7.

1. Form A requires reading skills.
2. Form B requires picture discrimination skills. It is designed for individuals whose reading skills are limited or nonexistent.

C. Circle "Testing Choices" on the form (in the upper right-hand corner) to indicate that it corresponds with Objective 11. The items on this form are presented as contrasting pairs. Instruct the individual to circle the preferred item out of each pair.

1. Teach this form by reading the choices and then asking the person to choose one. Repeat this for the first two or three pairs.

2. Some individuals may be able to complete this form independently. Give them the opportunity to do so. If help is needed, read and briefly explain each item.

3. If the individual cannot decide which item to choose, ask him or her to circle both or none at all.

D. Before going to the internship site, complete these steps.

1. Ask the individual to circle the preferred items from the "What I like (Before)" section. This is the left column in both forms.

2. Instruct the individual to check the four most important circled characteristics in the column labeled "✓".

3. If an individual cannot immediately identify his or her four top-ranked characteristics, ask him or her to draw a star beside 10 of the most important characteristics in the column labeled with the "★". Then, ask the person to identify his or her four top-ranked characteristics by placing a checkmark in the "✓" column.

4. Once again, discuss the final four characteristics chosen by asking the individual to describe the important features of each selected characteristic. Note the answers on the form or in your notes.

5. If the characteristics checked do not match those previously chosen, discuss this with the individual. If the individual wants to change his or her top-ranked characteristics, the final choice must be the individual's. Do not try to influence this decision.

E. Parallel the introduction of the "What I like" section of the Characteristics I Like versus What Is Here form with the introduction of the internship forms in Objective 12. Go to Objective 12 now.

F. After completing Objective 12, ask the individual to complete the "What is here" section of the Characteristics I Like versus What Is Here form. Instruct the individual to consider the contrasting pairs and circle the characteristics that best describe the internship job.

Determine match

A. Have the individual complete the "Matches" section. Assist the person to determine the match between "What I like (Before)" and "What is here (After)" for each characteristic. For each row, the individual should indicate a match by circling "Yes" in the "Matches" column. If the circled characteristics do not match, circle the "No" to indicate no match.

Characteristics I Like versus What Is Here Form: Calculations

A. Assist the individual to complete the calculations as directed.

1. Divide the number of "Yes"s by the number of matches available. The total will be a decimal. Write this number in the blank labeled "Characteristics match." Multiply this number by 100. The answer you get will give you the "Percentage of characteristics match." Draw a line on the scale to match.
2. For each most preferred characteristic ranked in the "✓" column that matches the "What is here" column, write "okay" beside the "✓". Divide the total number of "okay"s by four. The total will be a decimal. Multiply this number by 100. The answer you get will give the "Percentage of most important characteristics match." Write this number in the space provided.
3. Discuss the matches with the individual.

Summarize characteristics most often chosen

Materials Needed

Completed:
Characteristics I Like versus What Is Here: Form A or Form B
Characteristics Summary Graph

A. To summarize the characteristics the individual chose most frequently, continue to add the individual's choices to the Characteristics Summary Graph (see p. 293).

1. In the upper right corner of the Characteristics Summary Graph, circle "Testing Choices" in order to indicate that you have entered the data from the three Characteristics I Like versus What Is Here forms completed in Objective 11.
2. For each characteristic circled for the first day, shade in one box. Leave boxes blank for those characteristics that were not circled. Continue to record the individual's choices the same way for the second and third day.
3. Use this form as you progress through each goal of the job match assessment process. When all goals have been completed, the Characteristics Summary Graph becomes a part of the individual's assessment summary.

Summarize the four most important characteristics

Materials Needed

Completed:
Characteristics I Like versus What Is Here: Form A or Form B
Four Most Important Characteristics Graph

A. To summarize the four most important characteristics the individual chose most frequently, gather the Characteristics I Like versus What Is Here forms that were completed during the three internships.

1. In the upper right corner of the Four Most Important Characteristics Graph, circle "Testing Choices" to indicate that you have entered the data from the three Characteristics I Like versus What Is Here forms completed in Objective 11.
2. Continue to add the individual's choices to the Four Most Important Characteristics Graph. For each characteristic form completed at the internship, shade in one box for

each of the four checked items. Leave boxes blank for those characteristics that were not a top-ranked preference. Continue to record the individual's four top-ranked preferred characteristics for the second and third internships. Help the individual to complete the form or complete it yourself, if appropriate.

3. Use this form as you progress through each goal of the job assessment process. When all goals have been completed, the Four Most Important Characteristics Graph becomes a part of the individual's assessment summary.

Objective 11: What If?

What if the individual says he or she likes to work outside but only in nice weather?

Instruct the individual to take into account the weather when it is cold and wet. While thinking about the weather conditions over all the seasons, the individual should reconsider whether he or she prefers to work inside or outside.

What if the individual states that he or she prefers a job where it is required to dress up but thus far the individual has worn jeans and t-shirts?

Find out how the individual defines "dress up for work." Clarify definitions. Cite examples of dressing up and environments where dressing up can be found.

What if the individual becomes agitated over needing to do this form again after seeing it in the shadowing process?

In order to determine what characteristics of a job the individual really likes, it is necessary to ask the individual many times what his or her choices are. Asking many times allows the individual to change his or her mind as many times as he or she would like. If the person is still agitated after you have tried to explain, a break may be in order. Stop and try again later. Make sure the individual knows that this is an opportunity to tell you exactly what he or she wants in a job.

SECTION I. ASSESSMENT: CHOICE MANAGEMENT
GOAL C: TESTING CHOICES

Objective 12: Doing the Improvement Forms

CONTENTS

Introduction to the Improvement Forms
Completing the Work, Social, Personal, and Task Improvement: Forms A: Before the Job
Completing the Work, Social, Personal, and Task Improvement: Forms A: During the Job
Completing the Work, Social, Personal, and Task Improvement: Forms A: After the Job
Completing the Work, Social, Personal, and Task Improvement: Forms A: Calculations
Completing the Work, Social, Personal, and Task Improvement: Forms B
Completing the Work, Social, Personal, and Task Improvement: Forms B: Before the Job
Completing the Work, Social, Personal, and Task Improvement: Forms B: During the Job
Completing the Work, Social, Personal, and Task Improvement: Forms B: After the Job
Completing the Work, Social, Personal, and Task Improvement: Forms B: Calculations
Completing the Self-Determined Improvement Form: Before the Job
Completing the Self-Determined Improvement Form: During the Job
Completing the Self-Determined Improvement Form: After the Job
Completing Self-Determined Improvement Form: Calculations

MATERIALS NEEDED

Work Improvement: Form A (I:C:12:1) and Form B (I:C:12:5)
Social Improvement: Form A (I:C:12:2) and Form B (I:C:12:6)
Personal Improvement: Form A (I:C:12:3) and Form B (I:C:12:7)
Task Improvement: Form A (I:C:12:4) and Form B (I:C:12:8)
Self-Determined Improvement Form (I:C:12:9)

PURPOSE

To evaluate self-directed goal setting, planning, evaluating, and adjusting at the internship site

LOCATION

Internship sites

Introduction to the Improvement Forms

A. The individual will begin to learn on-the-job decision-making skills. To do this, he or she will evaluate his or her job skills and match them to jobsite demands. You and the individual should review, discuss, and then choose the most appropriate internship forms (see pp. 311–318). Consider the following when deciding which forms to use:

1. Form A is for people with reading and writing skills; it allows for evaluation on a scaled gradient.

2. Form B provides illustrations for those people with limited or no reading and writing skills. Evaluation is concrete—it is done with a positive or negative response chosen from a menu.

3. The Self-Determined Improvement Form is designed for people who can successfully use an open-ended format.

4. Across all formats, the individual will set goals, make plans to meet these goals, evaluate daily performance, match his or her evaluations to yours, and make adjustments to the next day's goals.

5. With the individual's input, pick a format to begin the process. Remember, if this first format does not work, change to another.

6. To complete the improvement forms, the individual needs to arrive at the internship site 20–30 minutes before starting work.

Note: The Characteristics I Like versus What Is Here form introduced in Objective 11 is completed simultaneously with the forms introduced in this objective. The two objectives are described separately to aid your understanding.

Completing the Work, Social, Personal, and Task Improvement: Forms A: Before the Job

A. The individual will complete the Work, Social, Personal, and Task Improvement Forms for 3 days. Three consecutive sessions are preferred to allow familiarity with the internship tasks. An example of a completed Work Improvement: Form A is on page 115.

B. For each Work, Social, or Personal Improvement form, follow these steps:

1. Read together the goals listed on the left side of the page. Briefly explain the behaviors associated with each goal.

2. Ask the individual to circle the goal statements he or she wants to pursue for that day. The person may choose as many or as few goals as he or she wants. Make it clear to the individual that the number of goals chosen is his or her decision, not yours. *Explain that at the end of the work session, evaluations will be completed on all the goal statements.*

3. For each goal statement circled, ask the individual how he or she might achieve that goal. For example, if the individual chooses the "Follow company rules" goal, write the plan for doing this in the column labeled "Plan." One

I:C:12:1

Work Improvement: Form A

Testing Choices

Name: Pat Sample Jobsite: Fancy Nursery Date: May 1, 2002 Session: 1

Key: Score a "1" for "great!" ".67" for "okay," ".33" for "needs improvement," and "0" for "poor." I and .67 are positive scores; .33 and 0 are negative.

Goal	Plan (How will I do this?)	My evaluation	Job coach evaluation	Comments	Match	Improve next
Follow company rules		1 **.67** .33 0	1 **.67** .33 0		**Yes** No	Follow company rules
Come to work		**1** .67 .33 0	**1** .67 .33 0	Job coach picked me up and drove	**Yes** No	Come to work
Come to work on time		**1** .67 .33 0	**1** .67 .33 0	Job coach picked me up and drove	**Yes** No	Come to work on time
Call if you miss work		**1** .67 .33 0	**1** .67 .33 0		**Yes** No	Call if you miss work
Work accurately		1 **.67** .33 0	1 .67 **.33** 0		Yes **No**	**Work accurately**
Pay attention to work	I will watch what I'm doing and check my own work	1 **.67** .33 0	1 .67 **.33** 0		Yes **No**	**Pay attention to work**
Work at the right pace		1 .67 **.33** 0	1 .67 **.33** 0		**Yes** No	**Work at the right pace**
Work safely		**1** .67 .33 0	**1** .67 .33 0	Great job cleaning up!	**Yes** No	Work safely
Take specified breaks		1 **.67** .33 0	1 **.67** .33 0		**Yes** No	Take specified breaks
Listen and use feedback	Ask questions and listen to what the supervisor says	1 **.67** .33 0	1 **.67** .33 0		**Yes** No	Listen and use feedback

Number of matches with job coach: 8 / Available matches: 10 x 100 =

80 % Percentage of work matches

Note: Positive scores match as do negative scores.

Number of positive job coach answers: 7 / Available answers: 10 x 100 =

70 % Percentage of positive job coach work answers

Note: Score any evaluation of 1 or .67 as positive.

way to prompt the individual to make a goal is using the word "by" (e.g., "Today I will follow company rules by . . .").

4. If the individual is not able to think of a plan for each goal, that's okay! This assessment process evaluates whether the individual can set plans to meet his or her goals.

5. Repeat this process for each of the Work, Social, and Personal Improvement: Forms A.

Note: Do not modify an individual's plan, even if the plan does not seem to be a reasonable way to achieve the goal! What may not seem to be a good plan to you may be a good plan for the individual, or at least a necessary step in his or her reasoning process.

C. Present the Task Improvement: Form A. An example of a completed Task Improvement: Form A is on page 117.

1. Ask the individual to list the job tasks previously arranged with the employer—assist if it is appropriate. If more than four tasks are listed, write them on a second page.

2. Ask the individual to set goals for each task listed by circling "Independence," "Speed," or "Quality." The individual may choose more than one. Explain that at the end of the 3- to 4-hour work period, evaluations will be completed on all measures.

3. For each goal circled, ask the individual how he or she might achieve that goal. For example, if the individual chooses to increase his or her speed, write the plan to do this in the column labeled "Plan."

Note: If the tasks are not determined by the beginning of the first day, list them as they occur. Depending on the internship site, some tasks may change from day to day. Each day, try to find out what tasks will change before starting the job. Arrange to learn the tasks well enough yourself so that you will not need training from the employer. Maximizing benefits to the employer will increase your chance of maintaining this site as an ongoing internship site for the future.

Completing the Work, Social, Personal, and Task Improvement: Forms A: During the Job

A. After deciding the job goals and plans, the individual starts performing the internship tasks.

1. Instruct the intern using the company's standard procedures when possible. Make an effort to allow the intern to be independent. Modify employer training procedures only if the individual is not learning how to do the tasks.

I:C:12:4

Task Improvement: Form A

Testing Choices

Name: Kelly Sample   Jobsite: Fancy Nursery   Date: June 1, 2002   Session: 1

Goal	Concern	Plan	Criteria	My evaluation	Job coach evaluation	My performance was	Matches	Improve next	Like this task?
Task 1 Fill flats with soil	Independence	by: Keeping up with others	Independence	Yes **No**	Yes **No**	Great	**Yes** No	Independence	**Yes**
	Speed		Speed	**Yes** No	Yes **No**	**Okay**	Yes **No**	**Speed**	No
	Quality		Quality	**Yes** No	**Yes** No	Not good	**Yes** No	Quality	
Task 2 Fill pots with soil	Independence	by: Keeping up with others	Independence	Yes **No**	Yes **No**	Great	**Yes** No	Independence	**Yes**
	Speed		Speed	**Yes** No	Yes **No**	**Okay**	Yes **No**	**Speed**	No
	Quality		Quality	**Yes** No	**Yes** No	Not good	**Yes** No	Quality	
Task 3 Water plants	Independence	by: Following directions	Independence	Yes **No**	Yes **No**	Great	**Yes** No	Independence	**Yes**
	Speed		Speed	Yes **No**	Yes **No**	**Okay**	**Yes** No	Speed	No
	Quality		Quality	Yes **No**	Yes **No**	Not good	**Yes** No	**Quality**	
Task 4 Clean up area	Independence	by: Doing a good sweeping job	Independence	**Yes** No	Yes **No**	**Great**	Yes **No**	Independence	**Yes**
	Speed		Speed	**Yes** No	**Yes** No	Okay	**Yes** No	Speed	No
	Quality		Quality	**Yes** No	**Yes** No	Not good	**Yes** No	Quality	

Tasks I like: 4 / Tasks I did: 4 = 1 x 100 = 100% Percentage of task preference matches (TP)

Matches made: 9 / Available matches: 12 = .75 x 100 = 75% Percentage of task matches (TM)

Positive job coach 4 / Tasks I did: 12 = .33 x 100 = 33% Percentage of positive job coach task answers (PA)

100%
Good match
75%
Okay match
50%
Poor match
25%
Not a match
0%

TP
TM
PA

2. If appropriate, first model the task to be performed. Second, ask the intern to perform it independently. Third, provide additional instruction as needed.

3. You should *not* do the job for the intern. Working beside the intern is acceptable and can be an effective way to teach required skills.

4. When coaching, imagine yourself in the role of the manager. How would you want the work to be done?

Completing the Work, Social, Personal, and Task Improvement: Forms A: After the Job

A. Find a quiet place to sit down and complete the remaining sections of the Work, Social, and Personal Improvement Forms.

1. In the column labeled "My evaluation," ask the intern to circle the option that best evaluates his or her performance for each corresponding item in the "Goal" column. Instruct him or her to circle a 1 if his or her performance was great, .67 if it was okay, .33 if he or she needs improvement, and 0 if his or her performance was poor. Ensure that all the goals are evaluated, even if they were not circled for improvement. The intern should evaluate him- or herself on each item listed, not just the items he or she chose as goals. Find out the intern's reasons for his or her evaluations.

2. Allow the individual to evaluate him- or herself without interference. For example, if an individual circled a 1 for "Use good grooming skills" on a Personal Improvement Form, but you disagree, allow the individual to circle his or her choice.

3. Next, complete the "Job coach evaluation" column for all of the forms. Do this for all goal items, not just those the individual circled. As you complete the evaluation, provide specific examples when giving both positive (1 or .67) and negative (.33 or 0) scores on Form A. Indicate your reasons briefly in the "Comments" column.

4. After your evaluation is finished, ask the individual to determine the match between his or her evaluation and yours. In the "Matches" column, the individual should circle "Yes" if there is a match and "No" if there is not a match. Two positive evaluations match, as do two negatives. For example, evaluations rated 1 and .67 are considered to match. Evaluations of .67 and .33 do not match.

5. Ask the intern to circle the goals he or she prefers to work on the next time in the column labeled "Improve next." Again, make sure the individual makes these choices, not you.

B. Now, complete the remaining sections of the Task Improvement Form.

1. In the column labeled "My evaluation," ask the individual to circle "Yes" or "No" for "Independence," "Speed," and "Quality." Repeat this process for each task. To evaluate his or her performance, the individual should answer the question, "Did I meet the minimum requirements of an entry-level employee for independence? Speed? Quality?"
2. Next, ask the individual to complete the "My performance was" column by deciding how well he or she performed the task. The individual should circle "Not good," "Okay," or "Great." Repeat this process for each task.
3. Next, evaluate how well the individual performed each task in the "Job coach evaluation" column. Evaluate his or her performance as compared with a typical worker beginning that job. Remember that all employees' work, speed, and quality vary, but also keep in mind that management maintains a starting standard.
4. After your evaluation, have the individual determine whether his or her evaluation matches yours. In the "Matches" column, the individual should circle the appropriate answer. Once again, two positive evaluations match, as do two negatives.
5. Instruct the individual to indicate the goals he or she prefers to work on next time by circling the corresponding goals in the column labeled "Improve next." Again, ask the individual to make these choices—not you.
6. In the column labeled "Like this task?" instruct the individual to circle the appropriate answer.

Completing the Work, Social, Personal, and Task Improvement: Forms A: Calculations

A. For each Work, Social, Personal, and Task Improvement: Form A, assist the individual to calculate each of the following steps.

1. Calculate the percentage of matches between your responses and the individual's. Add the total number of matches in the column labeled "Matches." Write this number in the blank labeled "Number of matches with job coach." Using the "Matches" column again, count the total matches available and write this number in the blank labeled "Available matches." Divide the "Available matches" number into the "Number of matches with job coach." Multiply your answer by 100, and write it in the shaded box labeled "Percentage of work matches."

2. Calculate the percentage of positive job coach evaluations. Add the total number of positive "Job coach evaluation" answers (i.e., scores of .67 or 1) in the column labeled "Job coach evaluation." Write this number in the blank labeled "Number of positive job coach answers." Using the "Job coach evaluation" column again, count the total positive answers available, and write this number in the blank labeled "Available answers." Divide the "Available answers" number into the "Number of positive job coach answers." Multiply your answer by 100, and write it in the shaded box labeled "Percentage of positive job coach work answers."

3. Calculate the "Task preference matches" on the Task Improvement Form by counting the number of "Yes"s in the column labeled "Like this task?" Write this number in the blank labeled "Tasks I like." In the blank labeled "Tasks I did," write the total number of tasks performed. Divide the "Tasks I did" into the "Tasks I like." Your answer will be a decimal number. Write the answer in the blank. Multiply your answer by 100, and write it in the shaded box labeled "Percentage of task preference matches (TP)."

4. On the graph at the bottom right corner of the Task Inprovement form, draw a triangle for the "Percentage of task preference matches (TP)." Calculate the "Percentage of task matches (TM)" and the "Percentage of positive job coach task answers (PA)" as on previous improvement forms. Write "TM" for the "Percentage of task matches (TM)" and "PA" for the "Percentage of positive job coach task answers (PA)." Show the individual the results on the scale. Discuss positive and negative performance issues. In general, scores above 75% are considered a good match.

Completing the Work, Social, Personal, and Task Improvement: Forms B

A. If Form B was used in "Making Choices" or if the individual chooses an illustrated form, then introduce Form B. Form B is an illustrated format and should be used with individuals who demonstrate limited or no reading and writing skills. Form B evaluations are simpler. The individual chooses "Yes" or "No." An example of a completed Work Improvement: Form B is on page 121.

Completing the Work, Social, Personal and Task Improvement: Forms B: Before the Job

A. Have the individual complete Work, Social, and Personal Improvement: Forms B for the 3-day internship experience. Use the following directions to complete each form.

1. Describe the illustrations in the "Goal" column, located on the left side of the page. Point to each illustration, and provide sample behaviors associated with each goal.

2. Ask the individual to circle the illustrated goal statements he or she wants to improve. The person may choose as

I:C:12:5

Work Improvement: Form B

Testing Choices

Name: Pat Sample　　Jobsite: Motel 7　　Date: May 2, 2002　　Session: 1

Goal	Plan	Evaluation			Great	Match	Next
Follow company rules		I think / Job coach thinks	☑ Follow company rules ☑	☐ Break company rules ☐	✓	(Yes) No	
Come to work (M Tu W Th F ✓ ✓ ✓ ✓ ✓)		I think / Job coach thinks	☑ M Tu W Th F ✓ ✓ ✓ ✓ ✓ Come to work ☑	☐ M Tu W Th F ✓ X ✓ X X Miss work ☐		(Yes) No	
Come to work on time		I think / Job coach thinks	☑ Come to work on time ☑	☐ Come to work late ☐		(Yes) No	
Call if you miss work		I think / Job coach thinks	☑ Call if you miss work ☑	☐ Miss work without calling ☐		(Yes) No	
Work accurately		I think / Job coach thinks	☑ Work accurately ☐	☐ Make mistakes ☑		Yes (No)	✓
(Pay attention to work)	Do task I am told to do	I think / Job coach thinks	☑ Pay attention to work ☑	☐ Pay little attention ☐		(Yes) No	
(Work at the right pace)	Keep up with coworkers	I think / Job coach thinks	☑ Work at the right pace ☑	☐ Work too fast or too slow ☐		(Yes) No	
Work safely		I think / Job coach thinks	☑ Work safely ☑	☐ Work unsafely ☐	✓	(Yes) No	
Take specified breaks		I think / Job coach thinks	☑ Take specified breaks ☑	☐ Take too many breaks ☐		(Yes) No	
Listen and use feedback		I think / Job coach thinks	☑ Listen and use feedback ☑	☐ Reject feedback ☐		(Yes) No	

Number of matches: 9 / Available matches: 10 = .90 x 100 = 90% Percentage of work matches

Number of positive job coach answers: 9 / Available answers: 10 = .90 x 100 = 90% Percentage of positive job coach work answers

many goals as he or she likes, but at least one needs to be chosen. Explain to the individual that at the end of the work period, evaluations will be completed for all goal areas.

3. For each goal circled, ask how he or she might achieve that goal. For example, if he or she chooses to follow company rules, write the plan to do this in the column labeled "Plan."

4. If the individual is not able to think of a plan for each goal, that is okay! One of the skills that the assessment process evaluates is whether the individual can set plans to meet his or her goals.

5. Repeat this process for each of the Work, Social, and Personal Improvement Forms.

B. Present the Task Improvement: Form B. At the beginning of the internship, consult with the employer to determine the tasks that the individual will do.

1. Before the internship begins, place pictures of the predetermined tasks in the column labeled "Task." If more than two tasks are performed, use an additional page. Illustrations can be found on the Paul H. Brookes Publishing Company web site at www.brookespublishing.com/picturebank.

2. Before starting work, ask the individual to circle the tasks he or she wants to improve. Next, ask him or her to set goals by circling the pictures for "Independence," "Speed," or "Quality." The intern may choose more than one.

3. For each goal circled, ask the individual how he or she might achieve that goal. For example, if the individual chooses to increase his or her speed, write the person's plan, not your suggestion, in the column labeled "Plan." If he or she does not have a plan, leave the plan blank. Do not try to influence the individual.

4. Review with the intern the task he or she chose to improve; whether he or she is going to improve independence, quality, or speed; and his or her plan for improving the task.

Completing the Work, Social, Personal, and Task Improvement: Forms B: During the Job

A. After deciding the job goals and plans, the individual will start performing the internship tasks.

1. Train the intern to perform the tasks by using the company's standard procedures when possible. Allow the intern to be as independent as possible. Modify employer training procedures only if the individual is not learning how to do the tasks.

2. If appropriate, first model the task to be performed. Second, ask the intern to perform it independently. Third, provide additional instruction as needed.

3. You should not do the job for the intern. However, working beside the intern is acceptable and can be an effective way to teach required skills.

Completing the Work, Social, Personal, and Task Improvement: Forms B: After the Job

A. Find a quiet place to sit down and complete the remaining sections of the Work, Social, and Personal Improvement: Forms B.

1. In the column labeled "Evaluation," ask the intern to choose the pictures that best describe his or her behavior for that day. For example, on Personal Improvement: Form B, if an individual believes he or she has good grooming, he or she should mark the "I think" box next to the picture of the person looking in the mirror. Individuals should evaluate themselves on each item listed, *not* just the items they circled as goals to improve.

2. Allow the individual to evaluate him- or herself without interference. Even if, for example, an individual marked the box for good grooming and you disagree, allow the individual to mark his or her choice. Your evaluation will come later.

3. Next, mark the boxes next to the picture in the boxes labeled "Job coach thinks." Talk about specific examples to illustrate your positive and negative evaluations.

4. If the intern performed particularly well, check the "Great" column for that item. Tell the individual why he or she did so well.

5. Next, ask the intern to determine the match between his or her evaluation and yours. In the "Matches" column, tell the intern to circle the appropriate answer. Two positive evaluations match, as well as two negatives. You may need to prompt the intern by pointing to the marked boxes.

6. Last, the intern should indicate the goals he or she prefers to work on next time by circling the corresponding goals in the column labeled "Next." Make sure the individual makes these choices.

B. Now, complete the remaining sections of the Task Improvement: Form B.

1. In the column labeled "My evaluation," ask the intern to evaluate his or her performance for each task by circling a "Yes" or a "No" for "Independence," "Speed," and "Quality." Provide a brief explanation of each term. The individual should determine the right answer by asking

him- or herself, "Did I meet the entry-level requirements for doing this task today?"

2. Next, evaluate how well the intern performed each task in the "Job coach evaluation" column. Evaluate the intern's performance based on the performance of an average beginning worker. Remember that all employees' work, speed, and quality vary, but also keep in mind that businesses maintain a general performance standard. Did the individual meet or exceed that standard?

3. Ask the intern to determine whether his or her evaluation matches yours. In the "Matches" column, the individual should circle the appropriate answer. Two positive evaluations match, as do two negatives.

4. Ask the intern to indicate his or her next day's goals by circling the illustrations in the "Improve next" column. Again, make sure the individual makes these choices, not you.

5. Finally, in the column labeled "Like this task?" ask the intern to circle the appropriate answer.

Completing the Work, Social, Personal, and Task Improvement: Forms B: Calculations

A. For each Work, Social, Personal, and Task Improvement: Form B, assist the individual to calculate the results using the following steps.

1. Calculate the percentage of matches between your answers and the individual's. Add the total number of matches in the column labeled "Matches." Write this number in the blank labeled "Number of matches." Using the "Matches" column again, count the total matches available and write this number in the blank labeled "Available matches." Divide the "Available matches" into the "Number of matches." Write this decimal number in the blank. Multiply your answer by 100, and write it in the shaded box labeled "Percentage of work matches."

2. Calculate the percentage of positive job coach evaluations. Add the total number of positive "Job coach evaluation" answers. Write this number in the blank labeled "Number of positive job coach answers." Using the "Job coach evaluation" column again, count the total number of positive job coach answers available, and write this number in the blank labeled "Available answers." Divide the "Available answers" number into the "Number of positive job coach answers." Write this decimal number in the blank. Multiply your answer by 100 and write it in the shaded box labeled "Percentage of positive job coach work answers."

C. In addition, on the Task Improvement Form, complete the Preference Summary calculation.

1. In the column labeled "Like this task?" count the number of circled "Yes"s. Write this number in the blank labeled "Tasks I like." In the blank labeled "Tasks I did," write the total number of tasks performed.

2. Divide the "Tasks I did" into the "Tasks I like." Your answer will be a decimal number. Write the answer in the blank provided. Multiply your answer by 100, and write it in the shaded box labeled "Percentage of task preference match."

3. On the graph, write "TP" to represent the percentage of task preference matches. Show the individual his or her results on the scale. Discuss the individual's overall preference rating.

Note: Go back and complete Objective 11 if you have not done so already.

Completing the Self-Determined Improvement: Form: Before the Job

A. The Self-Determined Improvement Form is designed for individuals who have had successful work experiences (see p. 319). This form provides open-ended goal choices rather than a fixed menu. From our experience, some interns find the Improvement: Forms A too simple. The open-ended format of the Self-Determined Improvement Form provides these individuals with a more challenging format. An example of a completed Self-Determined Improvement Form is on page 126.

B. The first column is labeled "Goals." It is divided into categories of work, social, personal, and task-related behaviors.

1. On the first day of the internship, ask the intern to identify and list the most important work-related, social, personal, and task-related behaviors to improve. If more space is needed, use an additional form. Some individuals may do this independently, and others may need some prompting.

2. Have the individual select his or her goals by circling the behavior he or she chooses to improve that day.

3. Ask the intern to write how he or she plans to accomplish each behavior in the column labeled "Plan."

4. The Task Improvement Form can be used with the Self-Determined Improvement Form. If some tasks at the internship site do not lend themselves to the Task Improvement Form, build the appropriate set of forms based on the individuality of the jobsite and the intern.

I:C:12:9

Self-Determined Improvement Form

Testing Choices

Name: Kelly Sample   Jobsite: Bud's Jewelry   Date: June 7, 2002   Session: 2

Goal: List the behaviors you want to improve	Plan	My evaluation	Job coach evaluation	Matches	Improve next
Work behavior Setting a work schedule	Get into a routine.	Great 1 Okay .50 (circled) Not at all 0	Great 1 Okay .50 (circled) Not at all 0	Yes (circled) No	
Work behavior Avoiding mistakes	Don't rush to get the job done.	Great 1 Okay .50 Not at all 0 (circled)	Great 1 Okay .50 Not at all 0 (circled)	Yes (circled) No	✓
Social behavior		Great 1 Okay .50 Not at all 0	Great 1 Okay .50 Not at all 0	Yes No	
Social behavior		Great 1 Okay .50 Not at all 0	Great 1 Okay .50 Not at all 0	Yes No	
Personal behavior Motivating myself to get things done on time	The job coach will call with a reminder.	Great 1 Okay .50 (circled) Not at all 0	Great 1 Okay .50 (circled) Not at all 0	Yes (circled) No	
Personal behavior Making sure I have things for work	Use self-reminders.	Great 1 Okay .50 (circled) Not at all 0	Great 1 Okay .50 (circled) Not at all 0	Yes (circled) No	
Task-related behavior		Great 1 Okay .50 Not at all 0	Great 1 Okay .50 Not at all 0	Yes No	
Task-related behavior		Great 1 Okay .50 Not at all 0	Great 1 Okay .50 Not at all 0	Yes No	

Matches made: 4 / Available matches: 4 = 1 x 100 = 100% Percentage of task matches (TM)

Positive job coach answers: 3 / Available answers: 4 = .75 x 100 = 75 % Percentage of positive job coach task answers (PA)

100%	Good match	75%	Okay match	50%	Poor match	25%	Not a match	0%

TM   PA

Completing the Self-Determined Improvement Form: During the Job

A. Remind the intern to think about his or her goals and plans.

B. The intern who uses the Self-Determined Improvement Form may sometimes not need job coaching that is as intensive as others may need, and some may find it demeaning to have you looking over their shoulders. If the intern does not need intensive job coaching and a supervisor on the job is willing to give honest performance feedback, let the intern work with the supervisor.

C. Review the goals and plans with the supervisor if you have arranged with the employer to leave the site.

Completing the Self-Determined Improvement Form: After the Job

A. After the work is done, ask the intern to evaluate his or her performance. In the column labeled "My evaluation," request the intern to evaluate *all* behaviors listed in the "Goals" column regardless of whether he or she chose the behavior for a goal. Ask the intern to circle "Great," "Okay," or "Not at all" for each behavior.

B. Complete the "Job coach evaluation" section. If you left the site, base the evaluation on the supervisor's feedback.

C. In the column labeled "Matches," ask the intern to write in the appropriate answer: "Yes" if the two evaluation answers match, "No" if they do not. Two positive evaluations match, as do two negatives. For items that do not match, discuss discrepancies with the intern. Come to an agreement about what an appropriate evaluation would include.

D. In the "Improve next" column, instruct the intern to check the boxes corresponding to the behaviors he or she will work on the next day.

Completing the Self-Determined Improvement Form: Calculations

A. Count the number of "Yes"s in the "Matches" column. Write this number in the blank labeled "Matches made." Add the total matches available from the "Matches" column, and write this number in the blank labeled "Available matches." Divide the "Available matches" into "Matches made." Write the decimal number in the space provided. Multiply your answer by 100, and write the percentage in the shaded box labeled "Percentage of task matches (TM)."

B. Count the number of items marked "Great" or "Okay" in the "Job coach evaluation" column. Write this number in the blank labeled "Positive job coach answers." Determine the positive answers available by counting the number of behaviors evaluated. Write this number in the blank labeled "Available answers." Divide the "Available answers" into "Positive job coach answers." Write the decimal number in the blank. Multiply it by 100, and put the percentage in the shaded box labeled "Percentage of positive job coach task answers (PA)."

C. At the bottom right of the page, find the graph and write "TM" to represent the "Percentage of task matches." Write "PA" on the graph to correspond with the "Percentage of positive job coach task answers." Discuss the evaluation ratings with the intern.

Objective 12: What if?

What if the internship includes working on an assembly line, and the job coach models the task and gives instruction, but the individual is not able to do the task to company standards?

The intern must not hinder other workers. Provide whatever assistance is needed to reach correct production levels. Circle "No" when evaluating independence and speed on the Task Improvement Form. If your combined efforts are not enough to get the job done, terminate the internship quickly.

What if a work, social, or personal item does not apply to the internship site?

When calculating the percentage of matches or positive answers, subtract these items from the total matches possible.

What if you discover behaviors that are important to the success of the internship, but these are not listed in the goal section of the Improvement Form?

Add the item to the goal list.

What if the individual does not choose a daily goal or a goal for next time?

Prompt one time. If a goal is still not chosen, accept his or her decision.

What if you are at the internship site the first day and the employer offers a job to the individual?

Discuss the positive and negative attributes of the job with the individual. Ask the employer if 2 more days of the internship could be finished before a decision is made. If the individual really likes the job and it is a good match, the individual should take the job. Be sure to finish the next 2 days of internship while the individual is working for the employer.

What if the individual works at the internship site for 30 minutes and then quits? Or if he or she becomes agitated and will not complete any more tasks?

Try to find out what the problems is. Tasks may need to be modified or different tasks arranged. If the situation escalates, leave the internship site immediately.

What if the individual has high expectations and feels the tasks that have been arranged are beneath him or her?

Explain that these tasks are part of an internship, and they may differ from those found at other jobsites. Remind the individual that one purpose of internship is to observe someone's work habits and that no matter what job title he or she ends up with, most entry-level employees will be required to do at least some entry-level tasks.

What if the employer is not able to tell you what tasks the intern will do until after the internship starts?

List the tasks at the end of the day on the improvement form. The intern will not be able to set goals or plans on the improvement form. Make sure the intern completes the rest of the improvement form for each task experience. Arrange with the employer to repeat the same tasks on the second and third day of the internship, if possible.

What if the tasks change from one day to the next at the internship site?

Try to arrange to repeat as many tasks as possible. You want the intern to gain experience with trying to improve his or performance from one day to the next by repeating tasks. If some tasks change, list the new tasks, and follow the directions for the Task Improvement Form. Some businesses may require frequent task changes from day to day.

What if the individual becomes irate as a result of negative job coach evaluations?

Stop the evaluation. Remember that nothing productive is gained in an argument. If things start to get out of control, leave the site. You may need to enter your evaluations without the individual present. Schedule a convenient time to review the internship results with the individual.

What if the individual sets a goal and then writes an illogical plan?

Accept the plan. Evaluate the individual on his or her performance of the task. After the evaluation, ask the individual if the plan worked. When recording the data, give the individual credit for the plan written.

What if the individual is having a really hard time with the tasks?

Remember that the assessment person is there to evaluate the individual's performance. Try to keep from assuming a job coaching or trainer role. If cues are given, make sure you keep track of them. Keep extensive notes or contact logs that will help you when writing the assessment summary.

What if you are confused about whether to circle "Great" or "Okay" when giving the intern a positive evaluation?

Circle "Great" unless you see that something is wrong but not significant enough for a negative evaluation. For example, if the individual is on time, then the evaluation should be "Great." The evaluation should be "Okay" for occasions when the individual's performance is not quite what it should be but you do not want to give a negative evaluation. For example, an individual might finish 40 buckles per hour at a helmet factory. This is good for a second day, but regular employees are expected to finish 70 per hour after 14 days of employment. The job coach's evaluation would be "Okay."

Section I. Assessment: Choice Management
Goal C: Testing Choices

Objective 13: Completing the Job Requirements and Accommodations: Form A or B

CONTENTS

MATERIALS NEEDED

Job Requirements and Accommodations: Form A (I:C:13:1) and Form B (I:C:13:2)

PURPOSE

To identify job requirements and accommodations needed to overcome limitations through the use of natural supports

LOCATIONS

Office
Internship site

Job Requirements and Accommodations: Form A

Materials Needed
Job Requirements and Accommodations: Form A

A. Individuals who used Improvement: Forms A or the Self-Determined Improvement Form should complete the Job Requirements and Accommodations: Form A (see p. 320). Schedule this form to be completed on the last day of each internship. An example of a completed Job Requirements and Accommodations: Form A is on page 132.

B. Help the intern to list the requirements of this job in the column labeled "Tasks required at this job."

C. After each requirement is listed, ask the individual to circle the appropriate answer in the "Can I do this now?" column.

D. Next, evaluate the intern's skills and resources by circling "Yes" or "No" in the column labeled "Job coach evaluation."

E. The intern determines the match between his or her evaluation and yours in the column labeled "Matches." Circle the appropriate answer in the "Matches" column. Discuss any conflicting responses, and attempt to reach an agreement. Both you and the individual are free to change responses. If no agreement can be reached, ask the jobsite manager to resolve the issue.

I:C:13:1

Job Requirements and Accommodations: Form A

Testing Choices

Name: Pat Sample Jobsite: Fancy Nursery Date: June 7, 2002 Session: 2

Tasks required at this job	Can I do this now?	Job coach evaluation	Matches	I can change	Plan	Who can help?	Can I do this with changes?
Transportation Can take last city bus	Yes No (circled)	Yes No (circled)	Yes (circled) No	The task My skills (circled) The tools I use	Learn how to take the bus independently	Job coach	Yes (circled) No
Hours 1:00 to 5:00	Yes (circled) No	Yes (circled) No	Yes (circled) No	The task My skills The tools I use			Yes No
Walking or climbing? Walking	Yes (circled) No	Yes (circled) No	Yes (circled) No	The task My skills The tools I use			Yes No
Lifting, pushing, or pulling? All	Yes (circled) No	Yes (circled) No	Yes (circled) No	The task My skills The tools I use			Yes No
Bending or reaching? All	Yes (circled) No	Yes (circled) No	Yes (circled) No	The task My skills The tools I use			Yes No
Standing or sitting? Standing all shift	Yes (circled) No	Yes (circled) No	Yes (circled) No	The task My skills The tools I use			Yes No
Find motor skills? Required for planting cuttings	Yes (circled) No	Yes (circled) No	Yes (circled) No	The task My skills The tools I use			Yes No
Other?	Yes No	Yes No	Yes No	The task My skills The tools I use			Yes No

6 (Tasks I can do now) + 1 (Tasks I can do with changes) = 7 (Tasks I can do)

Tasks I can do: 7 / Tasks required at this job: 7 = 1 x 100 = 100% Percentage of job requirements and accommmodations match

F. If there is a negative match, ask the intern to choose a response in the "I can change" column. If there is something else that could be changed, write this in the column labeled "Plan."

G. Accommodations are adaptations or adjustments that enable the individual to perform required tasks. For any item circled in the "I can change" column, brainstorm possible plans with the individual. Then, ask the individual to identify accommodations or other changes in the column labeled "Plan."

H. For any plan written in the "Plan" column, identify who can help meet this requirement in the "Who can help?" column. Emphasize the importance of using supports to meet job requirements.

I. Finally, in the "Can I do this with changes?" column, ask the individual to reevaluate the requirements assuming that changes can be made. For example, the individual just finished an internship at a store stocking shelves. This type of work is often performed very early in the morning or late at night. The bus that the individual rides to work is not available during these hours. The individual and job coach decide that the intern should change "Tools I use," and they plan for the individual to carpool with a co-worker. The name of the co-worker should be listed in the "Who can help?" column. If the strategy works, the transportation requirement can be met.

Job Requirements and Accommodations: Form A: Calculations

A. Perform the calculations.

1. Count the number of "Yes"s in the column labeled "Can I do this now?"
2. Write that number in the blank at the bottom left-hand side of the page labeled "Tasks I can do now."
3. Count up the number of "Yes"s in the column labeled "Can I do this with changes?" Put the total number of "Yes"s in the blank labeled "Tasks I can do with accommodations."
4. Add the two sums together and put the answer in the blank labeled "Tasks I can do."
5. Copy the "Tasks I can do" number into the next calculation field. Divide the "Tasks I can do" by the number of "Tasks required at this job." Write the answer in the blank provided.
6. Multiply your answer by 100, and write this answer in the shaded box labeled "Percentage of job requirements and accommodations match."

Requirements and Accommodations: Form B

Materials Needed
Job Requirements and Accommodations: Form B

A. Individuals who used Improvement: Forms B should complete the Job Requirements and Accommodations: Form B (see pp. 321–322). Schedule the individual to complete the form on the last day of the internship.

B. The purpose of Job Requirements and Accommodations: Form B is to enable individuals who cannot read or write to evaluate their skills compared with on-the-job requirements.

C. In the left column labeled "Required tasks," circle the pictured job requirements. For example, if the job requires a lot of bending and reaching, circle the corresponding picture.

D. For the column labeled "Can I do this now?" help the individual to circle the appropriate answer.

E. Next, evaluate the individual by circling "Yes" or "No" for the circled items you think the individual can or cannot do in the column labeled "Job coach evaluation."

F. Assist the individual to circle yes or no in the column labeled "Matches" when there is a match between your evaluation and the individual's evaluations.

Job Requirements and Accommodations: Form B (Page 1): Calculations

A. In the column labeled "Can I do this now?" count the circled "Yes"s. Write this number in the blank labeled "Tasks I can do now." In the column labeled "Required tasks," add the number of items circled, and write this number in the blank. Divide the number of "Tasks I can do now" by the number of "Tasks required at this job," and write this number in the blank provided. Multiply the result by 100, and write the answer in the shaded box labeled "Percentage of tasks I can do now." Draw a star beside the corresponding percentage on the graph below. Discuss the results with the intern.

Job Requirements and Accommodations: Form B (Page 2)

A. In the column labeled "Tasks I can't do now," you or the individual should circle all pictures evaluated with a "No" from the "Job coach evaluation" column on the first page.

B. Accommodations are adaptations or adjustments that enable the individual to perform required tasks. Discuss with the individual the accommodations needed to meet the job requirements. For instance, to overcome a lifting limitation, the individual may trade tasks with a co-worker or use an adaptive lifting device (e.g., a hand truck). If the individual thinks he or she can meet a requirement with some changes, help him or her to circle "Yes" in the column labeled "Can I do this with changes?" If not, help the individual to circle "No."

C. In the column labeled "Who can help?" help the individual to generate the name of someone who has the authority to modify each requirement or the resources to help overcome the limitation.

Job Requirements and Accommodations: Form B (Page 2): Calculations

A. Complete the calculations.

1. Add the number of "Yes"s circled in the "Can I do this with changes?" column. Write the total in the space labeled "Tasks I can do with accommodations."
2. From the first page, copy the number in the blank labeled "Tasks I can do now," and write that number in the blank with the same label on the second page.
3. Add the "Tasks I can do with accommodations" and "Tasks I can do now." Write the "Total number of tasks I can do now and with accommodations" in the blank. Divide this number by the number of "Tasks required at this job."
4. Multiply your answer by 100 to get the percentage of tasks the individual can do.

B. Draw a star beside the corresponding percentage on the graph below. Discuss the results with the intern.

I:C:13

Objective 13: What If?

What if the internship starts at 10:00 A.M. to do stocking tasks, but if this person would get a stocking job, most would start at 4:00 A.M.?

This internship was arranged at the convenience of the employer. Working at 4:00 A.M. would probably look a little different and would definitely cause a transportation problem. Indicate this scenario on the Job Requirements and Accommodations: Form A or Form B as a transportation barrier.

INTRODUCTION TO SECTION I.

Goal D: Final Choices

After all the internships are completed, complete the Self-Determined Job Match Summary. Procedures outlined in Objectives 14 and 15 will enable you to summarize the entire job match assessment process and make graphs that easily illustrate the individual's preferences, choices, strengths, weaknesses, and accommodations.

Arrange a time for a postassessment staffing. The job seeker, parents, significant others, the rehabilitation counselor, the assessment staff person, the case manager, the job developer, and other relevant agency staff should be invited. The individual and the assessment person should prepare for the postassessment staffing by discussing the results of the summary graphs and planning which points should be emphasized during the meeting.

The job seeker should direct the staffing by presenting as much information as possible. The assessment person should fill in by reviewing other relevant findings and coach the individual's performance. During this staffing, assessment personnel and the individual should present the results of the internship experiences. Ask the individual what he or she experienced during the assessment process. The job seeker should then present his or her preferences for tasks and specific job strengths, and explain how his or her limits will not prevent him or her from performing his or her job of choice. Discuss any needed accommodations, too. Agreement should be reached on the type and frequency of support required for the individual's job success. Coordinate the role of the employment specialist, residential staff, parents, and other individuals.

Discuss the local job market and how it may affect the individual's short- and long-term job choices. For example, an individual may have chosen a job for which he or she does not presently have the necessary experience. The individual may first want a job that requires fewer skills in order to secure a dream job later. Make sure you explain that the choices the individual currently makes are not expected to last forever. As the individual grows vocationally, new choices and preferences present themselves. New opportunities become available. Prepare a detailed benefit analysis before the meeting and review the possible effect the income will have on the benefits. Establish a tentative plan for transportation arrangements.

The employment specialist should review all information, attend the postassessment staffing, gather any new or needed information, and arrange a meeting to get to know the individual and his or her preferences. Job developers use the Self-Determined Job Match Summary to match individuals with their specific job choices. From the assessment information, employment specialists learn the strengths and weakness that affect job success. (See p. 102 for the graphic organizer for this chapter.)

Section I. Assessment: Choice Management
Goal D: Final Choices

Objective 14: Completing the Job Internship Summary Graphs

CONTENTS

Gather information
Determine top characteristics
Complete the Work, Social, and Personal Strength Evaluation Graphs
Complete the Task Strength Evaluation Graph
Complete the Job Requirements and Accommodations Graph

MATERIALS NEEDED

Work Strength Evaluation Graph (I:D:14:1)
Social Strength Evaluation Graph (I:D:14:2)
Personal Strength Evaluation Graph (I:D:14:3)
Task Strength Evaluation Graph (I:D:14:4)
Job Requirements and Accommodations Graph (I:D:14:5)
Completed:
Work Improvement: Form A (I:C:12:1)
Social Improvement: Form A (I:C:12:2)
Personal Improvement: Form A (I:C:12:3)
Task Improvement: Form A (I:C:12:4)
OR
Work Improvement: Form B (I:C:12:5)
Social Improvement: Form B (I:C:12:6)
Personal Improvement: Form B (I:C:12:7)
Task Improvement: Form B (I:C:12:8)
Self-Determined Improvement Form (I:C:12:9)
Characteristics I Like versus What Is Here: Form A (I:B:7:1) or Form B (I:B:7:2)
Job Requirements and Accommodations: Form A (I:C:13:1) or Form B (I:C:13:2)
Characteristics Summary Graph (I:A:4:3)
Four Most Important Characteristics Graph (I:A:4:4)

PURPOSE

To provide the individual with an opportunity to summarize all internship experiences and to determine the job that best matches his or her skills, preferences, and the local job conditions

LOCATION

Office

Gather information

A. You will need to block out 3–4 hours of your time to complete this objective. Gather all of the completed forms listed in the Materials Needed section. In some cases, the individual may have completed the Self-Determined Improvement Form in place of the Work, Social, Personal, and Task Improvement: Forms A.

B. For each site, identify and compile the completed set of internship forms. For example, one individual completed internships at the car wash and a grocery store. At each jobsite, he completed three work sessions. Sort the forms completed at each jobsite into two stacks.

Determine top characteristics

Materials Needed

Completed:
Characteristics Summary Graph
Four Most Important Characteristics Graph
Characteristics I Like versus What Is Here Forms

A. Collect all the completed Characteristics I Like versus What Is Here Forms.

B. To summarize the characteristics the individual chose most frequently, continue to add choices to the Characteristics Summary Graph that was used in Objective 4 and Objective 9. Assist the individual to complete the form or complete the form yourself, if appropriate.

1. Circle "Final Choices" in the top right corner to indicate that the information from the internships has been recorded.
2. For each session at the first internship site, find the characteristic circled on the Characteristics I Like versus What Is Here Form. Shade in a blank box for the corresponding characteristic. Leave any characteristics not chosen blank.
3. Continue to record the individual's choices similarly for each internship site and each session. Assist the individual in completing the form or complete the form yourself if appropriate.

C. To summarize the four most important characteristics the individual chose most frequently, continue to transfer the individual's choices to the Four Most Important Characteristics Graph used in Objective 4 and Objective 9. Circle "Final Choices" in the upper right corner to indicate that the information from the internships has been recorded. Help the individual to complete the form or complete the form yourself, if appropriate. For each Characteristics I Like versus What Is Here Form completed at an internship site, shade in one box for each of the four checked items.

D. Review the summarized characteristic information with the individual.

Complete the Work, Social, and Personal Strength Evaluation Graphs

Materials Needed
Work Strength Evaluation Graph

Completed:
Work, Social, and Personal Improvement: Forms A or B
Self-Determined Improvement Form

A. Gather the Work Improvement: Forms A or B or the Self-Determined Forms that were completed during the internship process. Arrange the forms in chronological order. On the evaluation graph, write the first day's information on the first row for the first internship. Repeat for each subsequent session. Continue this process for the second and third internship, if applicable. An example of a completed Work Strength Evaluation Graph is on page 141.

I:D:14:1

Final Choices

Work Strength Evaluation Graph

Name: Pat Sample Date: June 22, 2002

Graph (0%–100%)	Follow company rules	Come to work	Work safely	Listen and use feedback	Use the right pace for the job	Take specified breaks	Work accurately	Come to work on time	Pay attention to work	If I miss work, call
	89%	100%	100%	72%	78%	95%	45%	100%	78%	100%
Internship 1	Day 1 .67	Day 1 1	Day 1 1	Day 1 .67	Day 1 .33	Day 1 .67	Day 1 .33	Day 1 1	Day 1 .33	Day 1 1
	Day 2 .67	Day 2 1	Day 2 1	Day 2 .67	Day 2 .67	Day 2 1	Day 2 .67	Day 2 1	Day 2 .67	Day 2 1
	Day 3 1	Day 3 1	Day 3 1	Day 3 1	Day 3 .67	Day 3 1	Day 3 .67	Day 3 1	Day 3 .67	Day 3 1
Internship 2	Day 1 1	Day 1 1	Day 1 1	Day 1 1	Day 1 1	Day 1 1	Day 1 0	Day 1 1	Day 1 1	Day 1 1
	Day 2 1	Day 2 1	Day 2 1	Day 2 0	Day 2 1	Day 2 1	Day 2 1	Day 2 1	Day 2 1	Day 2 1
	Day 3 1	Day 3 1	Day 3 1	Day 3 1	Day 3 1	Day 3 1	Day 3 0	Day 3 1	Day 3 1	Day 3 1
Internship 3	Day 1	Day 1	Day 1	Day 1	Day 1	Day 1	Day 1	Day 1	Day 1	Day 1
	Day 2	Day 2	Day 2	Day 2	Day 2	Day 2	Day 2	Day 2	Day 2	Day 2
	Day 3	Day 3	Day 3	Day 3	Day 3	Day 3	Day 3	Day 3	Day 3	Day 3
	My score 5.34	My score 6	My score 6	My score 4.34	My score 4.67	My score 5.67	My score 2.67	My score 6	My score 4.67	My score 6
	Number of scores 6	Number of scores 6	Number of scores 6	Number of scores 6	Number of scores 6	Number of scores 6	Number of scores 6	Number of scores 6	Number of scores 6	Number of scores 6
	My average score 89%	My average score 100%	My average score 100%	My average score 72%	My average score 78%	My average score 95%	My average score 45%	My average score 100%	My average score 78%	My average score 100%

1. If you are using Form A, convert the raw data from the "Job coach evaluation" column. If 1 is circled, enter a 1 on the corresponding blank of the Work Strength Evaluation Graph and so on.
2. If you are using Form B, record the rating in the "Job coach evaluation" column for each item listed by entering a 1 for a positive evaluation or a 0 for a negative evaluation.
3. If you are using the Self-Determined Improvement Form, write under each work skill the behavior from the Self-Determined Improvement Form. Using the information in the "Job coach evaluation" column, record a 1 for "Great," a .50 for "Okay," and a 0 for "Needs improvement."
4. Find the column labeled "My score." Add the scores in this column, and divide them by the total number of scores. This will give you the average score for each behavior.
5. The last row is the "My average score" row. Place the average score for each behavior in the box.
6. For each average score, draw a line on the graph that best represents this score for each behavior. Write the number above the line. Shade in the column to the line. Repeat this procedure for each behavior.

B. For each internship session, gather the Social and Personal Improvement: Forms A or B or the Self-Determined Improvement Form. Repeat Steps A, B, and C to complete the Social Strength Evaluation Graph and the Personal Evaluation Graph (see pp. 324–325).

Complete the Task Strength Evaluation Graph

A. Refer to each completed Task Improvement: Form A or Form B to fill out the Task Strength Evaluation Graph (see p. 326). An example of a completed Task Strength Evaluation Graph is on page 143.

1. Using each completed Task Improvement: Form A or Form B, transfer the name of each task completed at all three intern sites to the row labeled "Task."
2. From the "Job coach evaluation" column of the Task Improvement: Forms A or Forms B, record the responses in the Task Strength Evaluation Graph by placing a 1 or 0 respectively for "Independence," "Quality," and "Speed" for each task performed at each session. If a task was not performed during a session, leave the space blank. More than one Task Strength Evaluation Graph page may be used.
3. To find the individual's average, add all the ones and zeros for each column to find the total, then multiply the number of days worked by 3, and divide this product into the total. Write this number in the "My average score" box at the bottom of each task column.

I:D:14:4

Final Choices

Task Strength Evaluation Graph

Name: Kelly Sample

Date: June 24, 2002

For each task, multiply the average score (listed in the last box of each column) by 100 and mark it on this graph.

100% / 75% / 50% / 25% / 0%

Graph		78%	78%	56%	78%	78%	67%				
Task		Fill flats with soil	Fill pots with soil	Water plants	Clean up area	Vacuum room	Dump trash				
Day 1	Independence	0	0	0	0	1	0				
	Speed	0	0	0	1	0	1				
	Quality	1	1	1	1	1	1				
Day 2	Independence	1	1	0	0	1	1				
	Speed	1	1	1	1	1	1				
	Quality	1	1	1	1	0	0				
Day 3	Independence	1	1	0	1	1	1				
	Speed	1	1	1	1	1	1				
	Quality	1	1	1	1	1	0				
Total: / Days worked x 3:		7/9	7/9	5/9	7/9	7/9	6/9				
Average score		78%	78%	56%	78%	78%	67%				

4. Draw a line on the graph that best represents the average score above the task name. Write the number above the line, and shade in the column to the line. Repeat this procedure for each task.

Complete the Job Requirements and Accommodations Graph

Materials Needed

Job Requirements and Accommodations Graph

Completed:
Job Requirements and Accommodations: Forms A or Forms B

A. Gather all the completed Job Requirements and Accommodations: Forms A or Forms B. On the Job Requirements and Accommodations Graph (see page 327), write in the name of each internship below the graph in the boxes entitled "Internship 1," "Internship 2," and "Internship 3." Below each internship label on the graph, transfer the information found in the summary section of each completed Job Requirements and Accommodations: Form A or Form B. Perform the following calculations in the corresponding graph calculation boxes. An example of a completed Job Requirements and Accommodations Graph is on page 145.

1. Divide the "Tasks required that I can do" by "Number of required tasks." Write the answer in the box labeled "Percentage of tasks I can do now."

2. Add the "Number of tasks I can do" and the "Number of tasks I can do with accommodations," and divide by the "Number of required tasks." Write the answer in the box labeled "Percentage of tasks I can do with accommodations."

3. Find the "Number of matches" and divide by the "Number of required tasks." Write the answer in the box labeled "Percentage of task matches."

B. Complete the graph section at the bottom of the page.

1. In the first column of "Internship 1," draw a line on the graph that corresponds with the "Percentage of tasks I can do now." Write the percentage above the drawn line, and shade the column up to the line.

2. In the second column of "Internship 1," draw a line on the graph that corresponds with the "Percentage of tasks I can do with accommodations." Write the percentage above the drawn line, and shade in the column to the drawn line.

3. In the third column of "Internship 1," draw a line on the graph that corresponds with the "Percentage of task matches." Write the percentage above the drawn line, and shade in the column to the drawn line.

C. Repeat steps A and B for Internships 2 and 3. If the individual participated in more than three internships, use an additional page.

I:D:14:5

Job Requirements and Accommodations Graph

Final Choices

Name: Pat Sample

Date: June 26, 2002

Internship 1: Fancy Nursery	Internship 2: Motel 7	Internship 3:
Tasks required that I can do: 6 / Number of required tasks: 7	Tasks required that I can do: 9 / Number of required tasks: 10	Tasks required that I can do: / Number of required tasks:
= .86 x 100 = 86% Percentage of tasks I can do now	= .90 x 100 = 90% Percentage of tasks I can do now	= . x 100 = % Percentage of tasks I can do now
Number of tasks I can do now: 6 + Number of tasks I can do with accommodations: 1 / Number of required tasks: 7	Number of tasks I can do now: 9 + Number of tasks I can do with accommodations: 1 / Number of required tasks: 10	Number of tasks I can do now: + Number of tasks I can do with accommodations: / Number of required tasks:
= 1 x 100 = 100% Percentage of tasks I can do with accommodations	= 1 x 100 = 100% Percentage of tasks I can do with accommodations	= . x 100 = % Percentage of tasks I can do with accommodations
Number of matches: 7 / Number of required tasks: 7	Number of matches: 10 / Number of required tasks: 10	Number of matches: / Number of required tasks:
= 1 x 100 = 100% Percentage of task matches	= 1 x 100 = 100% Percentage of task matches	= . x 100 = % Percentage of task matches

Percentage I can do now	Percentage I can do with accommodations	Percentage of matches	Percentage I can do now	Percentage I can do with accommodations	Percentage of matches	Percentage I can do now	Percentage I can do with accommodations	Percentage of matches
86%	100%	100%	90%	100%	100%			

Graph scale: 100%, 75%, 50%, 25%

Objective 14: What if?

What if the characteristics and task matches are low, but the preference for the job is high?

Additional sessions of the internship may be in order. Find out what the individual likes about this job. Take a close look at the tasks the individual performed. Are there steps in the task that the individual can do well? Perhaps other tasks should be considered. Review and discuss the individual's preference for each characteristic circled.

SECTION I. ASSESSMENT: CHOICE MANAGEMENT
GOAL D: FINAL CHOICES

Objective 15: Facilitating Postassessment Staffing

CONTENTS

Introduction
Complete the Evaluation Across Internships Graph
Complete the Adaptability Summary
Complete the Adaptability Graph
Complete the Internship Preference Graph
Complete the Initial Support Ratio Graph
Postassessment meeting

MATERIALS NEEDED

Evaluation Across Internships Graph (I:D:15:1)
Adaptability Summary (I:D:15:2)
Adaptability Graph (I:D:15:3)
Internship Preference Graph (I:D:15:4)
Initial Support Ratio Graph (I:D:15:5)
Self-Determined Job Match Summary (I:D:15:6)

Completed:
Initial Job Preferences Graph (I:A:4:1)
Initial Task Preferences Graphs (I:A:4:2)
Characteristics Summary Graph (I:A:4:3)
Four Most Important Characteristics Graph (I:A:4:4)
Shadowing Summary Graph (I:B:9:1)
Work Strength Evaluation Graphs (I:D:14:1)
Social Strength Evaluation Graphs (I:D:14:2)
Personal Strength Evaluation Graphs (I:D:14:3)
Task Strength Evaluation Graphs (I:D:14:4)
Job Requirements and Accommodations Graph (I:D:14:5)

PURPOSE

To summarize the progress and outcomes of the job match process for the individual, human services professionals, parents, and significant others

LOCATION

Office

Introduction

A. The information gained from the job match experiences will be used to produce a summative graphic document. Block out 3–4 hours to complete this objective. Gather and set aside all summary graph forms the individual has completed, including

1. Initial Job and Task Preferences Graphs
2. Shadowing Summary Graph
3. Characteristics Summary Graph
4. Four Most Important Characteristics Graph

5. Work, Social, Personal, and Task Strength Evaluation Graphs

6. Job Requirements and Accommodations Graph

Complete the Evaluation Across Internships Graph

Materials Needed

Evaluation Across Internships Graph

Completed:

- Work Improvement: Forms A or Forms B
- Social Improvement: Forms A or Forms B
- Personal Improvement: Forms A or Forms B
- Task Improvement: Forms A or Forms B
- Self-Determined Improvement Form

A. Once again, locate all the completed Work, Social, Personal and Task Improvement: Forms A or Forms B or the optional Self-Determined Improvement Form for each session of each internship. At the bottom of each of these forms, you will find the summary section. Look for the shaded boxes, and find the percentages.

B. Using page 1 of the Evaluation Across Internships Graph, write the name of each internship in the corresponding blanks labeled "Internship 1," "Internship 2," and "Internship 3" (see pp. 328–329).

C. Transfer the calculations from each Work, Social, Personal, and Task Improvement: Forms A or Forms B or the Self-Determined Improvement Form that correspond to the session number and internship site to the columns labeled "Work issues," "Social issues," "Personal issues," and "Task issues." Calculate the average number of positive answers for each column by adding and then dividing by the number of sessions. Write the numbers in the boxes.

D. At the bottom of the first page of the form, complete the calculations to find the "Overall average percentage of positive answers." Add all of the percentages from each session of each internship. This is the "Sum of all percentages of positive answers." Divide this total by the "Number of percentages of positive answers" to get the "Overall average percentage of positive answers." Write this number in the appropriate shaded box.

E. Next, find the "Overall average percentage of matches." Add all of the percentages from each session of each internship. This is the "Sum of all percentages of matches." Divide this total by the "Number of percentages of matches" to get the "Overall average percentage of matches." Write this number in the appropriate shaded box.

F. Graph each internship site's average percentage of positive answers for each work, social, personal, and task area on page 2 of the Evaluation Across Internships Graph. An example of a completed Evaluation Across Internships Graph is on pages 149–150.

1. Find the percentages of positive answers on all of the work improvement forms for Internship 1, add them together, and divide by 3. Repeat this process for the social, personal, and task improvement forms for Internship 1.

I:D:15:1

Evaluation Across Internships Graph (page 1)

Final Choices

Name: Kelly Sample

Date: June 30, 2002

To complete page 1, find the percentages of matches and positive answers for each session, find the percentages for each group of improvement forms, add them, and divide by the number of sessions. Record the percentages in the following tables. To find the average percentage of positive answers, add the percentages from the three sessions, and divide by the number of sessions.

Internship 1: Fancy Nursery — Job type interned: Gardening

	Work issues		Social issues		Personal issues		Task issues	
	Matches	Positive answers	Matches	Positive answers	Matches	Positive answers	Matches	Positive answers
Session 1	80 %	70 %	75 %	63 %	84 %	84 %	81 %	44 %
Session 2	80 %	100 %	75 %	100 %	84 %	84 %	81 %	81 %
Session 3	80 %	100 %	100 %	100 %	100 %	100 %	88 %	88 %
Average percentage of positive answers		90 %		88 %		89 %		71 %

Internship 2: Maid service — Job type interned: Janitorial

	Work issues		Social issues		Personal issues		Task issues	
	Matches	Positive answers	Matches	Positive answers	Matches	Positive answers	Matches	Positive answers
Session 1	90 %	90 %	88 %	75 %	50 %	50 %	67 %	67 %
Session 2	90 %	90 %	100 %	87 %	50 %	67 %	67 %	67 %
Session 3	90 %	90 %	88 %	63 %	100 %	100 %	84 %	84 %
Average percentage of positive answers		90 %		75 %		72 %		73 %

Internship 3: — Job type interned:

	Work issues		Social issues		Personal issues		Task issues	
	Matches	Positive answers	Matches	Positive answers	Matches	Positive answers	Matches	Positive answers
Session 1	%	%	%	%	%	%	%	%
Session 2	%	%	%	%	%	%	%	%
Session 3	%	%	%	%	%	%	%	%
Average percentage of positive answers		%		%		%		%

Sum of all percentages of positive answers: 567 / Number of percentages of positive answers: 8 = 71 % — Replace: Overall average percentage of positive answers

Sum of all percentages of matches: 1972 / Number of percentages of matches: 24 = 82 % — Match: Overall average percentage of matches

I:D:15:1

Evaluation Across Internships Graph (page 2)

Final Choices

To complete page 2, graph the "Average percentage of positive answers" for each issue across internships.

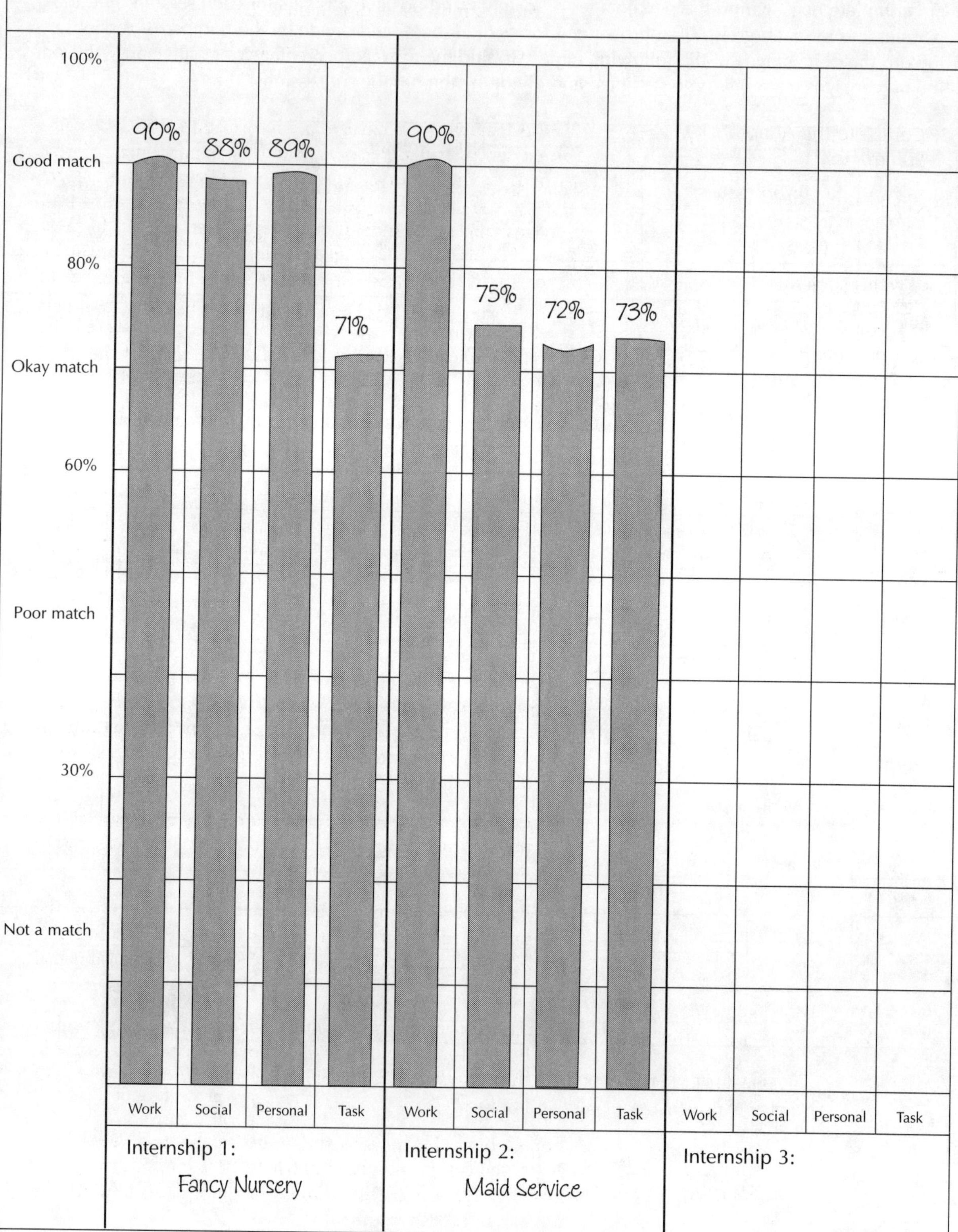

2. In the columns for "Internship 1," draw lines on the graphs that correspond with the percentages of positive evaluations for work, social, personal, and task issues. Write the percentages above the drawn lines, and shade in the columns to the drawn lines.

3. Repeat this process for "Internship 2" and "Internship 3."

Complete the Adaptability Summary

Materials Needed

Adaptability Summary

Completed:
- Work Improvement: Forms A or Forms B
- Social Improvement: Forms A or Forms B
- Personal Improvement: Forms A or Forms B
- Task Improvement: Forms A or Forms B
- Self-Determined Improvement Forms

A. The Adaptability Summary uses information from the completed Work, Social, Personal, and Task Improvement: Forms A or B or the optional Self-Determined Improvement Form (see pp. 330–331). The Adaptability Summary is divided into sections labeled "Session 1.3" through "Session 3.3." In most cases, "Session 1.1" through "Session 1.3" provide adequate space to include the 3 days of information gathered from Internship 1. Therefore, it is possible to get information about three internships on the form. If information was gathered differently, make adjustments. More than one copy of the form may be used.

B. Use the completed Work, Social, Personal, and Task Improvement: Forms A or B or the optional Self-Determined Improvement Form to complete the subsections. Complete Column A: "Negative answers last time" and Column B: "Goals set for negative answers."

1. For Sessions 1.1, 2.1, and 3.1, no previous evaluations would exist. That is why Columns A, B, and C are unavailable for those rows.

2. For all other sessions, look in the "Job coach evaluation" column of the improvement forms, and count the number of negative evaluations the individual received on each form. Write the total number of negative evaluations in the corresponding work, social, personal, and task rows of Column A.

3. For Column B, add the total number of goals circled for the negative evaluations received on the previous day. Do this for each Improvement Form.

4. For each row, divide the number in Column B by the number in Column A, and write the answer in Column C: "B divided by A." Your answer will be 1 or a decimal number.

5. Add the numbers in Column C, and divide this number by the total number of filled boxes. Write the average in the box labeled "Choose" at the end of the second page of the form.

C. For Column D, look in the "Goal" column of each Task Improvement Form (or optional Self-Determined Improvement Form). Count the number of goals circled. Write the number in each corresponding row.

D. To find the values for Column E, count the number of plans that were made in the "Plan" column of the Improvement Forms.

1. For each row, divide the number in Column E by the number in Column D, and write the answer in Column F. Your answer will be 1 or a decimal.

2. Add the numbers in Column E, and divide the answer by the total number of spaces that have numbers in them. (*Note:* If goals were not set for the Improvement Form during the first session, your divisor will be 11. If all the spaces were used, then your divisor will be 12.) Write the average in the box at the bottom of the second page of the form labeled "Manage."

E. Now, complete Columns G and H.

1. For Sessions 1, 2, and 3, look in the "Job coach evaluation" column of the Improvement Forms, and count the number of negative answers circled or checked. For each session, write the number of negative evaluations in Column G: "Negative answers today."

2. To find the values for Column H, count the number of items that were circled in the "Improve next" column of the Improvement Forms and place this number in the corresponding rows.

3. For each row, divide the number in Column H by the number in Column G, and write the answer in Column I. Your answer will be 1 or a decimal number.

4. Add the numbers in Column I, and divide the answer by the total number of spaces that have numbers in them. (*Note:* If goals were not set for the Improvement Form during the first session, your divisor will be 11. If all the spaces were used, then your divisor will be 12.) Write the average in the box at the bottom of the second page of the form in Column I labeled "Adjust."

Complete the Adaptability Graph

Materials Needed
- Adaptability Graph

Completed:
- Evaluations Across Internship Graph
- Adaptability Summary

A. Complete the Adaptability Graph (see p. 332). A completed sample is on page 153. Refer to the bottom of the Evaluation Across Internship Graph (page 1). Locate the two shaded boxes labeled "Replace: Overall average percentage of positive answers" and "Match: Overall average percentage of matches."

1. Find the corresponding columns labeled "Replace" and "Match" on the Adaptability Graph (columns three and five).

2. Draw a line across each labeled column to represent each score. Write the percentage above the drawn line, and shade in the column to the line.

I:D:15:3

Adaptability Graph

Final Choices

Name: Pat Sample

Date: June 7, 2002

To complete this graph, refer to the bottom of the first page of the Evaluation Across Internship Graph (I:D:15:1). Locate the two shaded boxes labeled "Replace: Overall average percentage of positive answers" and "Match: Overall average percentage of matches." Graph those percentage for Replace and Match in the appropriate columns. Then, find page 2 of the Adaptability Summary (I:D:15:2). Graph the percentages for Choose, Manage, and Adjust in the appropriate columns.

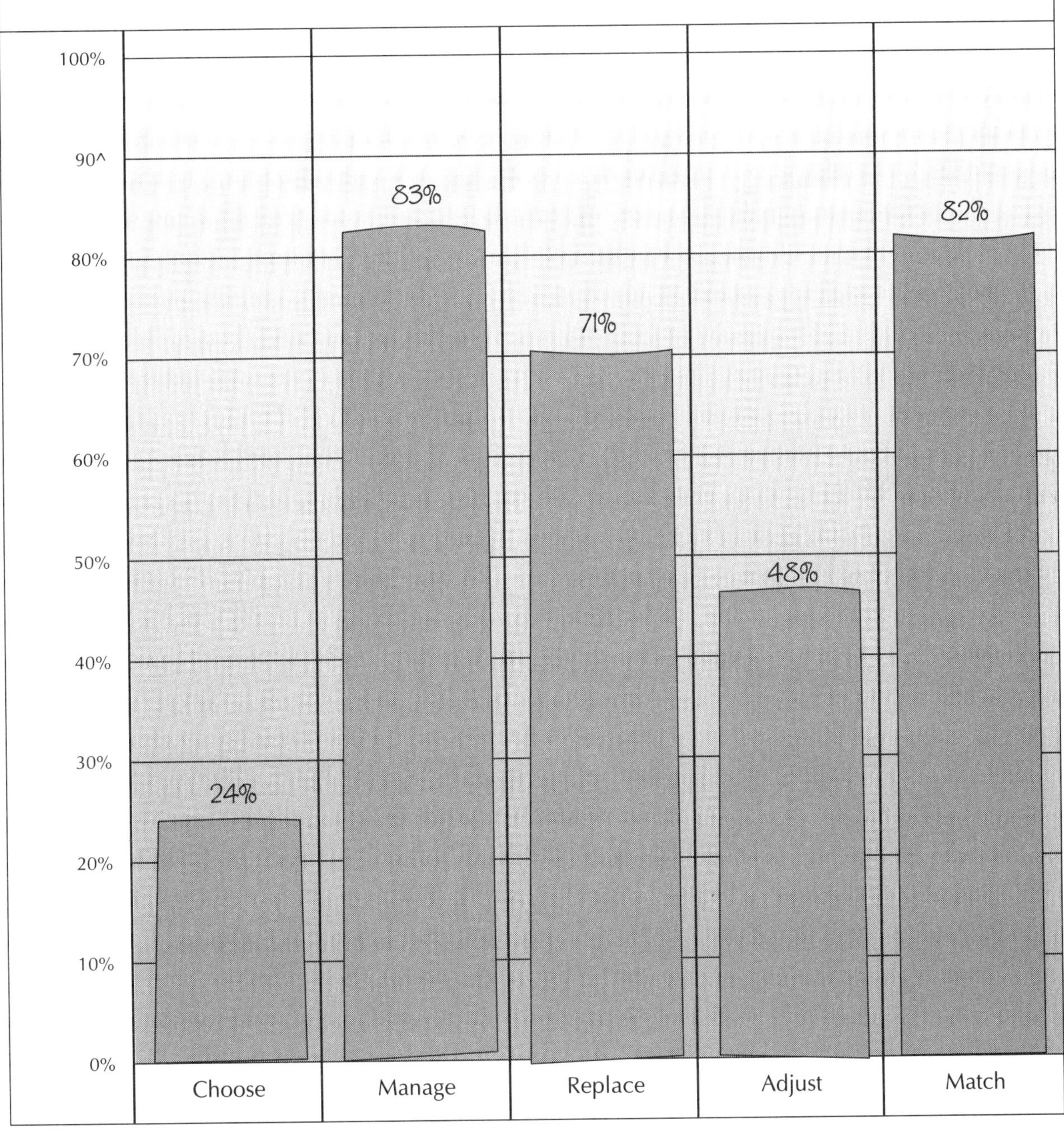

B. Refer to the bottom of the Adaptability Summary. Locate the three boxes labeled "Choose," "Manage," and "Adjust."

1. Find the corresponding columns labeled "Choose," "Manage," and "Adjust" on the Adaptability Graph (columns one, two, and four).

2. Draw a line across each labeled column to represent each score. Write the percentage above the drawn line, and shade in the column to the drawn line.

Complete the Internship Preference Graph

Materials Needed

Internship Preference Graph

Completed:
Characteristics I Like versus What Is Here: Form A or Form B
Task Improvement: Form A or Form B

A. You will need to gather all the completed Characteristics I Like versus What Is Here: Forms A or Forms B and the Task Improvement: Forms A or Forms B used by the intern for all sessions and internship sites. Fill in the names of the internship jobsites in the boxes above the graph.

1. In each Characteristics I Like versus What Is Here: Form A or Form B, locate the "Percentage of characteristics match." Write this percentage in the corresponding box under the graph for each session.

2. Add the percentages for all of the session for each internship and divide by the number of sessions to find the average. Write this number in the boxes at the bottom of the "Percentage of characteristics match" and the "Percentage of four most important characteristics match" columns for each internship.

B. From each completed Task Improvement Form, list the tasks from each internship in the corresponding blank on the bottom half of the Internship Preference Graph (see p. 333).

1. For each session the task was done, enter a 1 if the individual did the task and liked it or a 0 if the individual did the task and did not like it. This information may be found in the "Liked this task" column of the Task Improvement: Form A or Form B.

2. Divide the total of preference entries by the number of times the tasks were performed. Multiply by 100, and write your answer in the box at the bottom of the column in the shaded box labeled "Percentage of tasks match." Repeat this procedure for each internship.

C. To graph the preferences during each internship, locate the boxes for "Characteristics match," "Four most important characteristics match," and "Task match." In the graph section at the top of the page, draw a line to represent these percentages in the corresponding columns. Write the score above the lines, and shade in the columns to the drawn line. An example of a completed Internship Preference Graph is on page 155.

I:D:15:4

Internship Preference Graph

Final Choices

Name: Pat Sample   Date: July 2, 2002

	Internship 1: Fancy Nursery			Internship 2: Motel 7			Internship 3:		
	Characteristics match	Four most important characteristics match	Task match	Characteristics match	Four most important characteristics match	Task match	Characteristics match	Four most important characteristics match	Task match
Graph value	63%	50%	100%	84%	75%	100%			

Graph scale: 100%, 90%, 80%, 70%, 60%, 50%, 40%, 30%, 20%, 10%, 0%

	Percentage of characteristics match (Internship 1)	Percentage of four most important characteristics match (Internship 1)	Percentage of characteristics match (Internship 2)	Percentage of four most important characteristics match (Internship 2)	Percentage of characteristics match (Internship 3)	Percentage of four most important characteristics match (Internship 3)
Session 1	58%	50%	79%	75%		
Session 2	63%	50%	79%	75%		
Session 3	68%	50%	95%	75%		
Average	63%	50%	84%	75%		

Tasks at Internship 1	1	2	3	Tasks at Internship 2	1	2	3	Tasks at Internship 3	1	2	3
Fill flats with soil	1	1	1	Vacuum rooms	1	1	1				
Fill pots with soil	1	1	1	Dump trash	1	1	1				
Water plants	1	1	1								
Clean up area	1	1	1								

Internship 1	Internship 2	Internship 3
Total: 12 / Number of entries: 12 = 1 x 100 = 100% Percentage of tasks match	Total: 6 / Number of entries: 6 = 1 x 100 = 100% Percentage of tasks match	Total: ___ / Number of entries: ___ = ___ x 100 = ___% Percentage of tasks match

Complete the Initial Support Ratio Graph

Materials Needed

Initial Support Ratio Graph

Completed:

Job Requirements and Accommodations Graph

Evaluation Across Internships Graph

Adaptability Graph

Internship Preference Graph

A. By summarizing previous scores, this form provides an estimate of the percentage of time that the person may need for on-the-job support after starting a preferred job (see p. 334). An example of a completed Initial Support Ratio Graph is on page 157.

B. Complete Step 1 to find the "Average percentage of positive skill answers."

1. Using information in the Job Requirements and Accommodations Graph, add the "Sum of the percentages of tasks I can do with accommodations," and divide by the number of internships. This yields the "Average percentage of tasks I can do."
2. Add this percentage to the "Overall average percentage of positive answers" found at the bottom of the Evaluation Across Internships Graph, and divide by two. This yields the "Average percentage of positive skill answers."
3. Find the column for the "Average percentage of positive skill answers" (column 1) and graph this percentage. Draw a line that represents the average percentage. Shade in the column to the drawn line, and write the percentage above the line.

C. Complete Step 2 to find the "Average percentage of independent decision making."

1. Using the information in the Adaptability Graph, add the percentages in all five categories ("Choose, Manage, Replace, Adjust, Match"), and divide by 5.
2. Find the column for the "Average percentage of independent decision making" (column 2), and graph this percentage. Draw a line that represents the average percentage. Shade in the column to the drawn line, and write the percentage above the line.

D. Complete Step 3 to calculate the "Average percentage of task performance."

1. Using the information in the Internship Preference Graph, add the "Sum of the percentages of tasks match" for all the internships, and divide by the number of internships completed. This yields the "Average percentage of task performance."
2. Find the column for the "Average percentage of task performance" (column 3), and graph this percentage. Draw a line that represents the average percentage. Shade in the column to the drawn line, and write the percentage above the line.

I:D:15:5	**Initial Support Ratio Graph**	Final Choices

Initial Support Ratio Calculations Field

1	Use information in the Job Requirements and Accommodations Graph (I:D:14:5). Sum of the percentages of tasks I can do with accommodations: 200 / Number of internships: 2 = 100% Average percentage of tasks I can do Now, use information in the Evaluations Across Internships Graph (I:D:15:1) (Overall average percentage of positive answers + Average percentage of tasks I can do 171) / 2 = 86 % Average percentage of positive skill answers
2	Use information in the Adaptability Graph (I:D:15:3). Choose + Manage + Replace + Adjust + Match: 308 / 5 = 62 % Average percentage of independent decision making
3	Use information in the Internship Preference Graph (I:D:15:4). Sum of the percentages of task matchs: 200 / Number of internships: 2 = 100% Average percentage of task performance
4	Use information from the above numbers to find the Initial Support Ratio Sum of three averages on this page: 248 / 3 = Result: 83 % 100% – Result = 17 % Initial support ratio

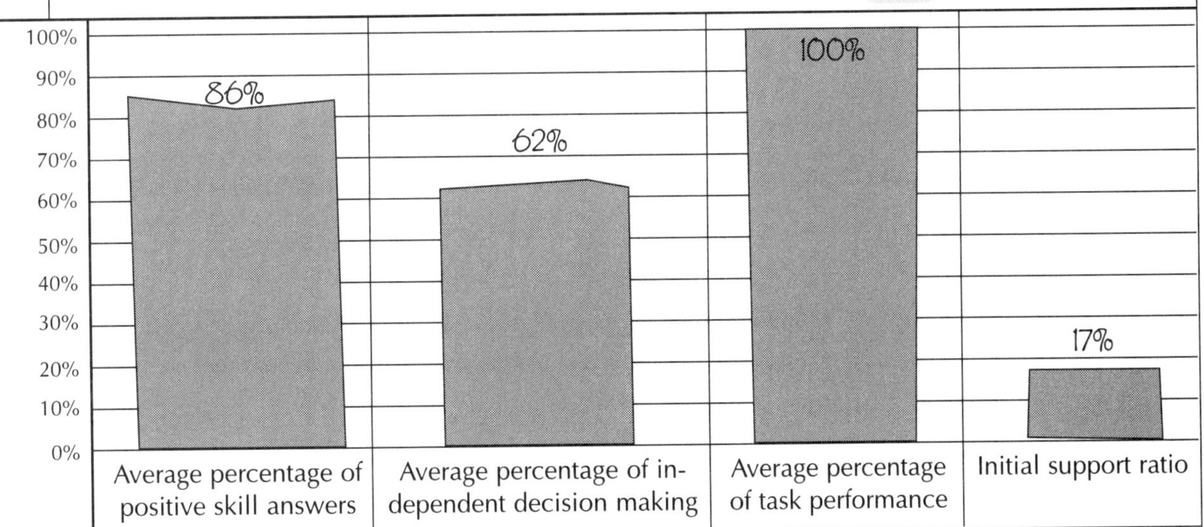

E. Calculate the "Initial support ratio."

1. Add the "Average percentage of positive skill answers," the "Average percentage of independent decision making," and the "Average percentage of task performance." Divide this number by 3, and multiply the answer by 100. Then, subtract this percentage from 100%. This yields the percentage of the "Initial support ratio."

2. Find the column for the "Initial support ratio" (column 4), and graph this percentage. Draw a line that represents the average percentage. Shade in the column to the drawn line, and write the percentage above the line.

Postassessment meeting

Materials Needed

Self-Determined Job Match Summary

Completed:

All summary and graph forms from Objectives 14 and 15

A. Set an appointment to meet with the rehabilitation counselor, the individual, and his or her significant others.

B. Complete the first page of the Self-Determined Job Match Summary (see pp. 335–336).

1. Gather all completed graph forms listed in the Materials Needed section from the first page of this objective.

2. Fill out the first sections of page 1, and summarize the major results by referring to the completed graphs. When completing the "Independent decision making skills" section on the bottom right side of page 1, the criterion for circling "Yes" is a score of 80% or better. Record the actual percentages. To answer the "Able to use forms" item, consider how much assistance the individual needed to complete the various forms. In the "Type of form recommended" section at the bottom of the page, circle the format the individual completed most independently.

C. Complete the second page of the Self-Determined Job Match Summary.

1. In the "Support recommendations and personal notes" section on page 2, estimate the initial placement support requirement. Base this estimate on the individual's support needs during the job match process. Present an estimated ratio of support to hours worked during the first, second, and third weeks of placement. For example, José Rueben may require 60% support the first week, 45% the second week, and 30% the third week. Once the person is actually on the job, a more precise ratio can be determined.

2. Include the salient points brought up by the summaries. Examples include particular preferences that are not negotiable for the individual or particular strengths he or she showed on the jobsite.

3. Mention other job-relevant behaviors or factors that came up during the job match process. For example, if the individual disappeared for long periods of time and was difficult to find, here is a good place to note this. Include positive outcomes or behaviors about the individual.
4. Complete the "What next?" section. Using your insight and experiences from the job match process, provide recommendations.
5. Attach copies of all summary and graph forms from Objectives 14 and 15 to the summary sheets.
6. Make enough copies so that everyone at the staff meeting has one.

C. At the postassessment staff meeting, assist the individual with presenting the Self-Determined Job Match Summary information as a starting point.

1. The job match information should be discussed in terms of vocational plans and realities. For example, if an individual says that he or she wants to work only in the daytime, only in a store, and only during the week, talk about the incompatibility of the preferences and how this may delay the individual's placement.
2. If an individual has had a difficult time making plans to fit his or her goals, discuss how his or her significant others might be able to help him or her with this in the future by discussing problems and some potential solutions.
3. Make sure the individual has a chance to comment on each piece of information as it is presented. It is likely that the individual may have some ideas or solutions that you have not considered. Keep in mind that this is the individual's meeting.

D. End the meeting by talking about what happens next. If the individual already has a job, discuss the long-term employment outlooks, including job coaching needs. If he or she does not, discuss your current level of job development activities.

E. Make sure that all of the necessary signature and date fields are filled out in the "FOR OFFICE USE ONLY" section. The recordkeeping that you do now in this simple step can potentially solve a lot of issues that can sometimes come up at the end of the process.

Objective 15: What If?

What if, when making up the final assessment summary and during the postassessment staffing, you find it hard to make positive statements about the individual's experiences during the assessment process?

Get on the individual's side. Although there may be negative outcomes to report, try to present these in a supportive manner. Establish that productive outcomes can be accomplished as a result of working on identified weakness. Do not let the negatives keep you from seeing the good worker that the individual could be.

What if the individual has Tourette syndrome and is a nonstop talker as a result of this disability?

Address the inappropriateness of nonstop talking in the work place. Remember that your evaluation should be based on what is expected of a typical entry-level worker.

What if the individual has overpowering bad breath but would need major dental work to correct it?

Address the inappropriateness of bad breath in the work place. Remember that your evaluation should be based on what is expected of a typical entry-level worker. Your outcomes may encourage the individual to get needed dental attention.

INTRODUCTION TO SECTION II.

Goal E: Finding a Job Matching Skills and Preferences

Contrary to what you may think about placement and job development, the activities for this goal do not begin when assessment ends—they begin while the person is completing the "Testing Choices" internships. Relationship building and learning about the worker's performance and preference characteristics must occur before job development begins.

Prior to the beginning of the individual's job, several steps must be accomplished. First, placement and assessment staff must meet to discuss the individual and transfer records. Second, the assigned employment specialist reviews all written material available, including personal files, assessment logs, and assessment reports. Third, the employment specialist reviews the Job Match Assessment Summary and attends the postassessment staffing. Fourth, within a week of the postassessment staffing, the employment specialist meets with the job seeker to gather information that will assist in writing a Job Development Plan. During this meeting, the employment specialist and the individual determines the steps each will take to enhance the chances for a successful placement.

Once a job match occurs and employment start-up procedures are accomplished, on-the-job supports steps need to be initiated. First, the supervisor feedback process is introduced. Second, the employment specialist facilitates on-the-job supports and on-site job orientation. Third, the employment specialist and the worker charts supervisor feedback to evaluate progress and to determine if there is a need for a structured problem-solving system. Fourth, the individual determines how well the job requirements match his preferences and skills. After the individual is on the job long enough to know its characteristics and requirements, he or she begins a 2–4 week process comparing job, task, and characteristic preferences with the employment site. Also the individual determines if he or she is meeting the essential job requirements. This information is summarized in an Employment Plan to determine if this particular jobsite is a match. If this site is not a match, then a Job

Termination Follow-Up Report is completed. Within this report, goals, plans, and strategies are developed for the next job. If the job site is a match, then proceed to the next chapter. You may want to refer to the "Implementation Reference Guide."

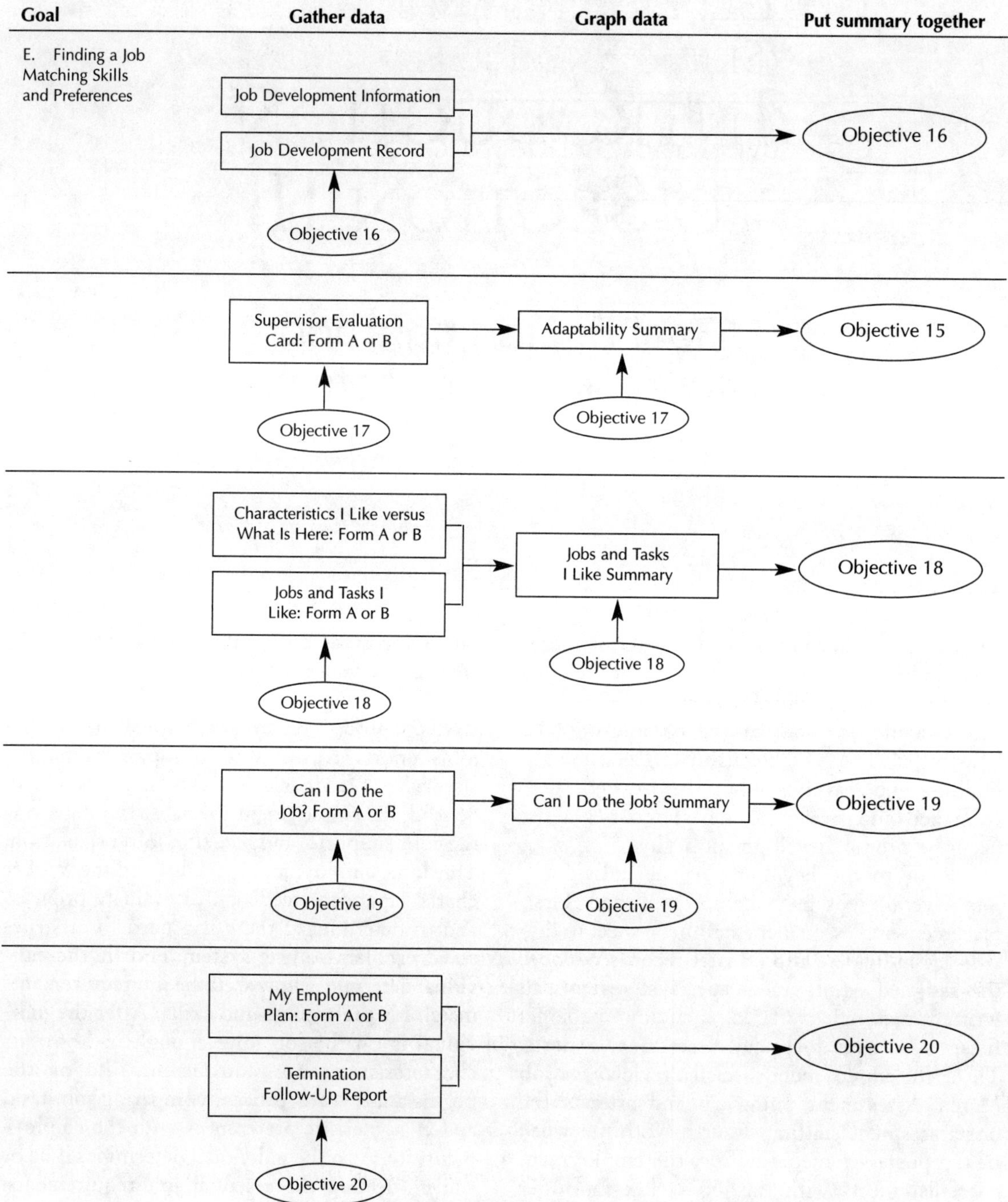

Section II. Placement and Follow-Along: Self-Management

Goal E: Finding a Job Matching Skills and Preferences

Objective 16: Individualizing Job Development

CONTENTS

Match an employment specialist
Review files
Attend postassessment staffing
Review files, including assessment summary
Review Job Match Assessment Summary
Meet with the job seeker
Follow through on the job development plan
Complete employment start-up procedures
Consider internships

MATERIALS NEEDED

Job seeker's file
Employment applications
Tax credit information
Employment benefit forms
Rehabilitation voucher
Preplacement Information (II:E:16:1)
Job Development Information (II:E:16:2)
Job Development Record (II:E:16:3)
Completed:
 Résumé
 Self-Directed Employment Orientation Matrix (I:A:1:1)
 Self-Determined Job Match Summary (I:D:15:6)

PURPOSE

To review assessment information, develop a plan for placement, follow through and assist with employer start-up requirements

LOCATION

Office
Employment site
Internship site

Match an employment specialist

A. As the individual nears completion of the internship assessment phase (Goal C: Testing Choices), the placement coordinator should meet with the assessment coordinator to review the individual's progress. Usually, this will be 2–3 weeks before the postassessment staffing. Based on the information gathered, assign an employment specialist to lead the placement process.

1. Match the personal style of the employment specialist to the individual.

2. Match the employment specialist's past work experiences and skills to the individual's job preferences.

3. If needed and appropriate, assign the employment specialist on the basis of the job seeker's stated or implied gender preference. For instance, the assessment staff may have determined that the presence of a male role model enhances this person's behavior.

Review files

Materials Needed
Preplacement Information
Job Development Information

A. The employment specialist should review the individual's files to answer the following questions:

1. What are the individual's top three job choices?
2. What are the individuals top two job characteristic preferences?
3. Where does the individual live?
4. What means of transportation will be used?
5. What educational and training experience has the individual had?
6. What limitations or restrictions might affect the job development process? What physical limitations exist? How does the individual adapt to physical demands?
7. How much are parents or significant others involved?
8. How much job coach support is needed or desired?

B. While reviewing the files, specific information should be gathered to complete the Preplacement Information and Job Development Information forms. Be sure to find out:

1. What events or circumstances produce success or failure?
2. Is the individual taking medications? If so, how might these medications affect specific vocational performance and behavior? When are medications scheduled?
3. Are there any medical concerns? How might these concerns affect specific vocational performance and behavior?
4. What interventions or accommodations have worked in the past?
5. What information does the vocational history offer?
6. Has the individual worked before? If so, what type of work was performed and for how long?
7. What success and problems did the individual have during assessment and on past jobs?

C. Confer with the individual's rehabilitation counselor to determine Social Security, employer tax credit, and employment training benefit status, if any.

Attend postassessment staffing

A. Attend the postassessment staffing to provide a smooth transition from assessment to the placement phase.

1. Participate in the postassessment staffing with the individual and the other team members present.
2. Clarify questions and verify the results from the assessment findings that may affect placement of the individual in a community job. Take notes.
3. Be sure to schedule a meeting with the individual and significant others to review the placement program and procedures, and to schedule future contacts.

Review files, including assessment summary

Materials Needed

Completed:
Assessment Summary

A. Review the assessment summary profiles completed during the "Final Choices" phase (see Chapter 7) and any notes taken during the postassessment staffing. You need the individual's Preplacement Information and a Job Development Information form to record the required information. If you have any questions or need clarification, consult the assessment staff. Collect sufficient information to identify job possibilities. Discussions should include these considerations:

1. The individual's preferences, their importance, and any discrepancies you might see
2. The preferred job and any job accommodations applicable
3. Current events affecting the individual's life such as medication changes, family, or residential dynamics
4. The individual's vocational history and reinforcers

Meet with the job seeker

Materials Needed
Preplacement Information
Job Development Information

Completed:
Self-Directed Employment Orientation Matrix
Résumé

A. Meet and begin the job development process with the individual and his or her significant others. You should use the Preplacement Information and Job Development Information forms to guide your efforts (see pp. 337–340).

B. Let the individual and his or her family know what to expect in the placement phase. Reintroduce the Self-Directed Employment Orientation Matrix (see p. 285). Give an overview of the placement procedures and time lines.

1. Establish rapport and common ground. Share events of *your* vocational life.
2. Review your agency's supported employment program's placement success data. Include an account of the number of placements, long-term successful placements, career advancement placements, and barriers to success.
3. Ask the individual about preferences for specific job settings.

4. Review the individual's résumé and letters of recommendation. Update the résumé, if necessary.

5. Discuss the availability of jobs in your community and how job availability may affect specific placement requests. If certain desired job choices will more than likely take longer to get, make sure the individual, parents, and significant others understand your local economy and job market. If the individual wants to pursue a job that is typically hard to find, ask how long he or she is willing to wait. Determine second and third job choices, if necessary.

C. Discuss subjective factors observed by personnel in assessment, including

1. Motivation
2. Work persistence
3. Attendance and punctuality
4. Willingness to work at jobs that match preferences
5. Learning time, independence, and speed

D. Discuss how the individual will get to work (e.g., car, bus, friend, agency-provided transportation).

E. Ask if the job seeker has a picture identification and Social Security card. If not, facilitate getting them. These items are required in order to obtain a job.

F. Check whether you have all the information needed for the completion of the Job Development Information and the Preplacement Information forms. If there is incomplete information, now is the time to discuss discrepancies and collect the needed information.

1. Verify preferred hours and work days.
2. Verify transportation needs and skills.
3. Verify needed accommodations.

G. Summarize your meeting. Ask the individual if there are any more questions you could answer.

Follow through on the job development plan

Materials Needed
Job Development Record

A. Begin prospecting by phone, networking, cold calls, newspaper leads, Job Service bulletins, and so forth to develop a job leads list. Individualize your efforts by using the Job Development Record (see pp. 341–342). The record can also document the time and strategies you used to secure the placement.

B. Identify potential employers and locations that match individual skills, preferences, and requests for specified work. Emphasize valued job settings.

C. Set appointments with employers to find out the employment needs of their businesses.

D. Sell your unique employment program and the job seeker's skills. Demonstrate how your job seeker can meet the needs of this business.

   1. Target shared or similar positions that exist within the work place. Incorporate overlapping or intersecting tasks with other co-workers as much as possible.

   2. Allow for flexibility of job duties with other co-workers to facilitate communication.

E. Assist the job seeker to fill out applications and meet résumé requirements.

F. Set a date for an interview.

G. Negotiate working internships or the start date of the job with employers. Emphasize the abilities of your job seeker, not his or her disability. If possible, attempt to fill a position without offering benefit packages (e.g., the vocational rehabilitation office paying for half of the individual's wage for the first 4 weeks) or monetary perks (e.g., a tax credit) to the employer as incentives to get the job.

Complete employment start-up procedures

Materials Needed
Preplacement Information
Job Development Information

A. Establish placement parameters with the business. Be sure to include the job seeker in this process. Review the Preplacement Information and Job Development Information forms to assist with upcoming decisions regarding the individual's placement. Answers to the following questions will help with this process.

   1. Who will provide the training: the business, the job coach, or a combination of both?

   2. What is the role of the job coach? How will the business train the job coach?

   3. What type and how much initial and long-term support will be needed?

   4. What is the frequency of supervisor feedback that will be needed by the job seeker? How often will the supervisor be able to provide feedback?

   5. What problem-solving procedures need to be followed by the employer and the job seeker?

   6. Who will conduct any needed task or job analyses?

B. Determine the specific pre-employment requirements. These might include:

   1. Drug screening test or other testing

2. Employment training and benefits (e.g., tax credit, job salary support, special accommodations)
3. Special license or certification
4. Employee back-ground check
5. Others as requested

C. If appropriate, help the individual with the initial employment procedures, including:

1. Filling out a W-4 and I-9
2. Reading the employer handbook
3. Fitting or picking up a uniform
4. Procuring special equipment

D. Facilitate transportation arrangements, including bus training, if necessary.

E. Contact the job seeker's rehabilitation counselor and significant others to inform them of the following information:

1. Jobsite and location
2. Job titles and duties
3. Job start date
4. Scheduled weekly work hours, pay and benefits, and on-the-job support arrangements
5. Employment training benefit arrangements to employer, if any

Consider internships

A. Some individuals can enhance their opportunities for employment by participating in an internship process. Consider an internship for individuals who

1. Have little or no work or community experience and need more experiences before placement is possible
2. Have not been successful in previous employment experiences
3. Have a history of poor attendance
4. Have questionable work tolerance or endurance
5. Have a history of severe behavior problems
6. Have a history of very poor socialization skills
7. Could use an internship to try out needed accommodations or adaptations
8. Need internships to reconfirm their job choice

B. When considering internships, follow these steps:

1. Determine the type and how much support will be provided.
2. Determine who will pay for the individual's wages and cover liability.
3. Determine who will provide the training: the business, the job coach, or a combination of both.
4. Determine whether a short-term or long-term internship is appropriate.
5. Initiate the self-determination procedures described in objectives found later in the next objective.

C. A *short-term internship* can last from 1 day to 2 weeks.

1. When prospecting, try for immediate employment. If the business is hesitant or leaning towards not hiring, offer a short 1- or 2-day internship. Internships are great marketing tools. They provide the employer and the individual with an opportunity to mutually preview possible long-term employment commitments.
2. After the agreed internship period, meet to decide whether the employer is ready to hire or additional internship time is needed. If additional time is needed or requested, offer another day or two. If the individual can benefit from an extended period of internship, arrange more time, up to 2 weeks.
3. During the internship period, determine if this site is working out. If the anticipated outcome is placement, discuss employment with the manager. Find out specifics, and address them. Confirm that the job matches the individual's job choice. Get the individual employed, or move on to another site.

D. A *long-term internship* can last from several weeks to several months.

1. Specifically prospect businesses who will facilitate a long-term internship. Inform them that your program will pay the individual's wages and cover liability.
2. Determine who will provide the training: the business, the job coach, or a combination of both.
3. Review the information found in the Preplacement Information and the Job Development Information forms. Offer suggestions to the business that will support the individual during the internship. Get the business involved. At least initially, the job coach will more than likely take the role of the supervisor to facilitate problem solving. However, try to get co-workers involved. You will want your efforts to fade at some point during the internship and natural supports to occur.

4. Complete the same procedures, contracts, and forms when doing internships as you would if the individual was employed in a job.

Objective 16: What If?

What if, after job developing, you discover that the top-ranked job choice is not readily available in your community?

Discuss the facts found as a result of your job development and let the individual know that finding the top-ranked job choice may take longer than anticipated, or it is not possible to find this job. Ask the individual to look at other choices. Let the individual know that you will still monitor the availability of his or her top-ranked choice.

What if, after developing a preferred job, you discover that there is strong competition from more experienced and more qualified individuals?

Discuss the facts found as a result of your job development and let the individual know that finding the top-ranked job choice may take longer than anticipated, and the individual may not be qualified for this position.

- *Offer agency job coaching and support, internships, and an employment benefits package (e.g., tax credits) to the employer.*
- *Try to carve out some tasks that will be cost effective to the employer.*
- *Suggest to the individual that this particular job area should be viewed as a career choice instead of an immediate job choice. If the individual agrees, begin working with him or her toward meeting needed qualifications. This could involve more work experience, training, and education. Look at the individual's second and third choices.*

What if you find the job of choice for the individual, but there is a transportation barrier?

Check the following possibilities:

- *What is the schedules of your local public transportation? Be sure to include city bus, independent vans or buses, or ride finders.*
- *Is co-worker carpooling available?*
- *Is the job close enough to ride a bike or walk?*
- *How about rides from family or friends?*
- *Can the individual take a taxi cab?*
- *If social security eligible, a Plan for Achieving Self-Support (PASS) or Impairment Related Work Expense (IRWE) will help subsidize the cost for transportation.*

What if you find that the individual does not seem interested in any of the jobs you find in his or her choice areas, or the individual performs poorly during interviews?

The individual may be anxious about work in general and may need some internship experience to overcome this fear.

What if the individual has a poor work record and history of employment?

If the employer is unsure about the individual's performance, perhaps an internship will offer an opportunity to alleviate any concerns.

What if you review the assessment summary with the assessment staff and discover that the individual wants a job in an area that is highly competitive and the individual does not have the needed qualifications?

Suggest that additional assessment time will be needed to discover the individual's other preferences and skills. Or refer the individual back to the rehabilitation counselor to arrange additional education.

What if the individual and the parents are unrealistic about the initial job placement? For example, the individual has worked in produce during high school and demands a similar job placement with full-time hours and benefits. Local grocery stores require new employees to start as part-time courtesy clerks and provide no benefits.

Discuss the reality of job market and the requirements to get a job in a grocery store. Work toward achieving the long-term goal, but realize that entry-level requirements exist. Work to discover the individual's major requirements. Is it the specific job, the hours worked, or the benefits that are most important? Perhaps all would be available in another type of store.

Section II. Placement and Follow-Along: Self-Management

Goal E: Finding a Job Matching Skills and Preferences

Objective 17: Collecting and Evaluating Supervisor Feedback

CONTENTS

Introduce
Develop supports
Develop baseline

MATERIALS NEEDED

Supervisor Evaluation Cards: Form A (II:E:17:1) and B (II:E:17:2)
Monitor Supervisor Feedback Graph (II:E:17:3)

PURPOSE

To provide a process for honest written feedback from the supervisor and to develop supports for the new employee

LOCATION

Employment site
Office

Introduce

Materials Needed
Supervisor Evaluation Card: Forms A and B

A. Introduce the Supervisor Evaluation Cards, and begin to establish support parameters the first day the individual starts the job. Two formats are available (see pp. 343–344). Present both to the individual, and have him or her choose which format to use. An example of a completed Supervisor Evaluation Cards: Form A is available on page 174.

1. Find a way to make the evaluation convenient and useful to the employer and the individual. Determine who will evaluate the individual. This can be the supervisor, a co-worker, or the job coach. Determine the best time for the evaluation to take place.

2. Discuss each section of the evaluation in detail. Make sure the evaluator is clear on its use. The evaluator should use the card to evaluate if the individual's daily performance met the minimum requirements of the job. Ask the evaluator to circle the appropriate answers in the work, social and personal categories of the "Requirements" section. *Note:* Emphasize the need to evaluate on the same criteria used to evaluate other employees.

Supervisor Evaluation Cards: Form A

Supervisor's Evaluation

Name: Pat Sample Date: June 7, 2002

Category	Requirements	Concern
Work	(Yes) No	Very good dry mopping today
Social	Yes (No)	Did not empty trash when told to do so. Needs to work on not being so stubborn and follow directions.
Personal	(Yes) No	

Supervisor's Evaluation

Name: ______ Date: ______

Category	Requirements	Concern
Work	Yes No	
Social	Yes No	
Personal	Yes No	

Supervisor's Evaluation

Name: ______ Date: ______

Category	Requirements	Concern
Work	Yes No	
Social	Yes No	
Personal	Yes No	

Supervisor's Evaluation

Name: ______ Date: ______

Category	Requirements	Concern
Work	Yes No	
Social	Yes No	
Personal	Yes No	

3. The evaluator should note positive and negative comments in the corresponding "Comment" (Form B) or "Concern" (Form A) space. Encourage the evaluator to note concerns that may not be a problem now but may cause a problem in the future. Positive comments are encouraged, too.

B. Instruct the individual to ask for the Supervisor Feedback Card on a daily basis. Instruct the evaluator to complete and give the card to the individual at the end of the work shift. Also, daily verbal feedback from the supervisor and the employment specialist is encouraged. If there is no one at the business available to complete the feedback card daily, then the job coach should evaluate the individual based on verbal feedback from the supervisor or co-workers. If a phone call to the supervisor works best, then fill out the evaluation card yourself. In some instances, the individual may be able to self-evaluate accurately and complete the card him- or herself.

C. Encourage the individual to ask the immediate supervisor for daily verbal feedback regarding job performance (e.g., "How did I do today? Is there something I need to do better?").

D. Some individuals may require feedback more often than once a day. In this case, devise a feedback schedule that is synchronized with the natural rhythms of the workplace.

Develop supports

A. The employment specialist should adopt a consulting role. Assist the individual to establish lines of support. The use of the daily feedback cards are a good tool to help facilitate employee and employer interactions in a structured and accommodating manner. We found that use of the daily Supervisor Evaluation Cards is an excellent tool to help establish natural on-the-job supports and effective communication. The following points will help you establish a consulting relationship.

   1. Find out who the key individuals are and who has been there the longest that know the informal but crucial rules. Use these people to determine the formal and informal norms and how do they operate in this work culture.

   2. Use the existing social networks within the organization. Enlist the help of co-workers for orientation and training. Establish lines of supervision to report problems or ask for help.

   3. Observe conversations. Find out the subjects of typical conversations that take place in gathering places.

   4. Encourage the individual to get information from co-workers. The individual should ask co-workers for information or suggestions that will help them do the job easier, better, or faster. Encourage individuals to use their break time to get to know who they are working with and

something about each co-worker. Make a friend for yourself and facilitate the same for the new employee.

Develop baseline

Materials Needed
Monitor Supervisor Feedback Graph

A. Develop the Monitor Supervisor Feedback Graph to chart the Supervisor Feedback Cards over time. Sit down with the individual and plot supervisor feedback received daily.

1. If the individual receives three consistent "No"s in the "Requirements" section or a combination of "No"s and "Yes"s with negative concerns in the "Comments" section over three days in the work, social, or personal categories, an intervention is needed.

2. If the negative evaluations are received because the individual is inconsistent in performance or behavior, start the individual on an appropriate problem-solving contract as discussed in Goal F: Objectives 21 and 22.

Note: A "Yes" in the "Requirements" section should be considered a negative answer if the evaluator wrote a negative concern in the "Comments" section.

Objective 17: What If?

What if the individual has been doing well but receives a negative evaluation with an immediate, job-threatening concern?

Do not wait for three negatives. Immediately introduce an appropriate problem-solving contract with the individual and develop intervention strategies that address the problem.

What if the business does not understand the importance of the self-determination process that the individual is trying to learn?

Explain that providing the new employee with timely and honest feedback will enhance that person's immediate and long-term success. When supervisor feedback is given promptly and there is a problem on the job, you will be able to provide immediate problem-solving systems and strategies for continued success.

What if the supervisor is not being honest in the feedback because he or she does not want to hurt the new employee's feelings?

Explain to the supervisor that not being honest is unfair and actually harms the employee. Without honest and timely feedback, the individual does not know what improvements to make or how to make the improvement, nor can he or she make the adjustments to his or her work performance that are needed to stay employed.

Section II. Placement and Follow-Along: Self-Management

Goal E: Finding a Job Matching Skills and Preferences

Objective 18: Completing the Do I Have the Job I Like? Forms

CONTENTS

MATERIALS NEEDED

Characteristics I Like versus What Is Here: Form A (II:E:18:1) and Form B (II:E:18:1)
Jobs and Tasks I Like: Form A (II:E:18:3) and Form B (II:E:18:4)
Do I Have the Job I Like? Summary (II:E:18:5)

PURPOSE

To provide an opportunity for the employee to determine whether this is a job that matches his or her preferred job, site characteristics, and tasks

LOCATION

Office
Employment site
Community setting

Characteristics I Like versus What Is Here: Form A or B: Schedule

Materials Needed
Characteristics I Like versus What Is Here: Forms A and B

A. Initiate the Characteristics I Like versus What Is Here form after 1 week of employment or when the individual is familiar enough with the job and its surroundings.

Note: Alternate the introduction of Objective 18: Completing the Do I Have the Job I Like? Forms with the introduction of Objective 19: Completing the Can I Do This Job? Forms.

B. Explain that the purpose of the Characteristics I Like versus What Is Here Form is to provide an opportunity to determine actual jobsite characteristics and match them to the employee's stated preferences.

C. Present the Characteristics I Like versus What Is Here: Form A or B (see pp. 346–348).

   1. Ask the employee who has prior community job experience to complete the form twice a week for a 2–3 week period. Collect at least 3–5 days of data or continue until the preference scores become consistent.

2. Ask the employee who has no or limited community job experience to complete the form every other day. Collect at least 5 days of data or continue until the preference scores become consistent.

Characteristics I Like versus What Is Here: Form A or B: Match

A. Complete the "What I like (Before)" section with the individual.

1. The items are presented as contrasting pairs. Instruct the individual to choose a preferred item out of each pair.

2. Individuals may or may not be able to complete this form independently. If appropriate, read and briefly explain each item of the "What I like" section.

3. Teach this form by verbally instructing the choice for the first few pairs.

4. If the individual is undecided about the item to choose, ask him or her to circle the item liked the most. If both are still chosen, then instruct him or her to circle both.

5. If the individual doesn't choose or says, "It doesn't matter," explain that a good job match depends on his or her ability to make a choice.

B. If needed, assist the individual to draw a star beside 10 of the most important characteristics from the circled characteristics in the "★" column. Some individuals may want to skip this step and check the top-ranked four characteristics immediately. That is great! Instruct the individual to check the four most preferred characteristics they would like to have in a job in the section labeled "✓".

C. Once again, discuss the final four characteristics chosen by asking the individual the meaning of each selected item.

D. Instruct the individual to complete the "What is here (After)" section. Instruct the individual to circle the characteristics that actually exist on the job. If necessary, instruct the individual to ask the supervisor to help identify characteristics that exist on the job.

E. Instruct the individual to complete the match by comparing preferred jobsite characteristics to actual jobsite characteristics. Circle "Yes" in the column labeled "Matches" beside each matching pair.

F. Discuss the differences between previously stated preferences and actual job characteristics.

G. If necessary, help the individual to identify the matches and to calculate the percentage of matches. Point out the number of matches for the individual. Encourage the individual to point out the matches when responding to question regarding the jobsite.

1. Divide the number of matches by the available matches, and multiply this answer by 100. This yields the "Percentage of characteristics match."
2. Graph this percentage.

H. For characteristics that are checked, determine how many exist at this job by looking at the "Matches" column. Calculate the percentage.

1. Count the number of okays, and divide by four. Multiply the answer by 100. This yields the "Percentage of most important characteristics match."
2. Graph this percentage.

Jobs and Tasks I Like: Form A or B: Schedule

Materials Needed

Jobs and Tasks I Like: Form A or B

Completed:
Job Match Assessment Summary

A. Initiate the Jobs and Tasks I Like: Form A or B after 1 week of employment or when the individual is familiar enough with the job and its surroundings (see pp. 349–350).

B. Form A requires reading. Form B requires picture discrimination skills. Form B is designed for individuals whose reading skills are limited or nonexistent. An example of a completed Jobs and Tasks I Like: Form B is shown on page 182.

C. Using the individual's top-ranked job and task preferences from the Job Match Assessment Summary, the employment specialist should write the preferences (Form A) or add illustrations (Form B) that depict the individual's preferences in the "Two top-ranked jobs from assessment" and the "Four top-ranked tasks from assessment" sections. Construct Form B by copying and pasting the illustrations that best match the person's preferences.

D. When filling out the form with the individual, first point out the "Two top-ranked jobs from assessment" to the individual. These choices should be considered when completing the "Four jobs I like" section.

E. If using Form A, the individual can write his or her four top-ranked job choices. If using Form B, ask the individual what four jobs he or she likes most and then choose pictures that represent these choices. Instruct the individual to place these pictures in the blank boxes provided. In the "This job" space, the employment specialist should identify the employee's present jobsite (Form A) or place an illustration (Form B) depicting the jobsite.

F. Ask individuals to compare the jobs in "Four jobs I like" section to the job listed in the "This job" section. If "This job" matches one of the preferences, instruct the employee to circle "Yes" in the "Match" section. If it does not, circle "No."

II:E:18:4

Finding a Job

Jobs and Tasks I Like: Form B

Name: Kelly Sample

Jobsite: Shady Grove Hotel

Date: June 24, 2002

Jobs

Two top-ranked jobs from assessment:

Four jobs I like

This job

Match

Yes No

Do I have a job I like?

Yes No

Do I have a job I said I wanted in assessment?

Yes No

Tasks

Four top-ranked tasks from assessment:

Tasks that are here (circle the ones you like):

$$\frac{\text{Tasks I like: } 6}{\text{Tasks at this job: } 7} = .86 \times 100 = 86\%$$

Percentage of tasks I like

0% Not a match 25% Poor match 50% Okay match 75% Good match 100%

86%

Do I like most of the tasks here?

Yes No

1. Verify the job preference by instructing the employee to ask him- or herself, "Do I have a job I like?" Ask the individual to circle the corresponding answer.
2. Referring to the "Two top-ranked jobs from assessment" section, verify the employee's job preference from assessment by instructing the employee to ask him- or herself, "Do I have the job I said I wanted in assessment?" Circle the corresponding answer.

G. Ask the employee to identify at least four important tasks that are performed on a typical work day in the "Tasks at this job" section. Encourage the individual to talk to the supervisor if he or she cannot identify four tasks. Involve the individual in the preparation process. Get him or her to write down the tasks or place the illustrations depicting the tasks.

H. For each task listed, ask the employee to circle "Yes" or "No" in the "Do I like this task?" column (Form A) or circle the picture of the tasks he or she likes (Form B). If necessary, assist the individual with this process. Discuss the results of the preferences.

I. Calculate the "Percentage of tasks I like" by adding the yeses (Form A) or the number of circles (Form B) and dividing the total by the number of tasks identified in the "Tasks at this job" section. Multiply the answer by 100. Write this percentage in the space provided.

J. Help the individual to mark the graph at the bottom of the page. If the score falls within the 50% to 100% range (i.e., okay or good match), ask the employee to circle "Yes" in the statement "Do I like most of the tasks here?" If the score is less than 50%, the individual should circle "No."

Summarize the data

Materials Needed
- Do I Have the Job I Like? Summary

Completed:
- Characteristics I Like versus What Is Here: Forms A or B
- Jobs and Tasks I Like: Forms A or B

A. After 3–5 days of data have been collected, gather all Characteristics I Like versus What Is Here forms and the Jobs and Tasks I Like forms. Group the forms by title to evaluate.

B. Arrange a meeting with each individual before or after work. Assist the individual to record the dates and match scores for each item as indicated on the Do I Have the Job I Like? Summary (see p. 351). Calculate the average match score across the Characteristics I Like versus What Is Here forms and the Jobs and Tasks I Like forms and place them in the spaces provided. An example of a completed Do I Have the Job I Like? Summary is shown on page 184.

1. Use the average scores from the boxes to calculate the individual's "Average percentage of preference for this job," located in the second section of this form.
2. Assist the individual to mark the preference percentage for this job on the scale.

II:E:18:5

Do I Have the Job I Like? Summary

Finding a Job

Name: Kelly Sample Jobsite: Motel 7 Date: April 25, 2002

Characteristics I like versus what is here		Job I like		Tasks I like	
Percentage of characteristics match	Date of match	Percentage of jobs I like (100 or 0)	Date of score	Percentage of tasks I like	Date of match
75%	4/6/02	100%	4/6/02	75%	4/6/02
79	4/8/02	100	4/8/02	75	4/8/02
75	4/10/02	0	4/10/02	63	4/10/02
84	4/13/02	100	4/13/02	75	4/13/02
75	4/14/02	100	4/14/02	75	4/14/02
Total score / Number of days = 78 % Average percentage of characteristics match		Total score / Number of days = 80% Average percentage of jobs I like		Total score / Number of days: = 73 % Average percentage of tasks I like	

Preference for this job

78 Average percentage of characteristics match + 80 Average percentage of jobs I like + 73 Average percentage of tasks I like = 231 Total average percentage

Total average percentage: / 3 = 77 % Average percentage of preference for this job

0% | Not a match | 25% | Poor match | 50% | Okay match | 75% | Good match | 100%

Do I have the job I like? Yes (circled) No

(Circle "Yes" for a score of 50% or higher.)

C. Discuss the findings and encourage feedback.

1. Discuss outcomes of the choices made by the individual.

2. Ask the individual to circle "Yes" or "No" to answer the question, "Do I have the job I like?"

Objective 18: What If?

What if the individual is trying to get a "good" score rather than being honest with him- or herself when completing the Characteristics I Like versus What Is Here form?

Explain that you are not concerned with high scores. Emphasize the importance of honest responses. They will provide needed information to determine if the current job matches work preferences. Your responsibility is to assist the individual to find a job that matches his or her preferences.

What if, after completing 5 days of the preference forms, the individual's preference scores are low?

Monitor the scores over the 5-day period. You may want to extend the number of days. Talk with the individual about his or her job, and review the characteristics that the individual does not prefer. Find out if he or she likes the overall job. If the individual likes the job, ask if he or she can tolerate specific characteristics in order to keep the job. There are realistic trade-offs that should be considered. For example, if the individual does not like to work weekends, but working in a store requires this, the person may need to choose a different job choice or tolerate working weekends.

What if, after completing 5 days of preference forms, the individual's scores are inconsistent?

Monitor the scores over the 5-day period, and consider collecting more data. Most likely the individual needs more time to determine his or her preferences. Talk with the individual about the job, and review the characteristics that the individual does not prefer. Try to find out if the individual understands how to complete the form and whether the format is appropriate.

Section II. Placement and Follow-Along: Self-Management

Goal E: Finding a Job Matching Skills and Preferences

Objective 19: Completing the Can I Do This Job? Forms

CONTENTS

Preparation
Action
Monitor and assist

MATERIALS NEEDED

Can I Do This Job? Form A (II:E:19:1) and Form B (II:E:19:2)
Can I Do This Job? Summary (II:E:19:3)

PURPOSE

To provide an opportunity for individuals to determine their skill strengths and weaknesses on-the-job and whether the requirements of the job can be met

LOCATION

Office
Employment site

Preparation

Materials Needed
Can I Do This Job? Forms A and B

A. Initiate the Can I Do This Job? Form A or B after 1 week of employment or when the individual is familiar enough with the job and job surroundings (see pp. 352–353).

Note: Alternate the introduction of Objective 18 with the introduction of Objective 19.

1. Ask the employee who has prior community job experience to complete the form once or twice per week over a 2–3 week period. At least 5 days of data need to be collected. The individual needs to score 80% or higher on 4 out of 5 days.

2. Ask the employee who has no or limited community job experience to complete the form every other day. Five days of data need to be collected. The individual needs to score 80% or higher on 4 out of 5 days.

B. Can I Do This Job? Forms A and B provide individuals with the opportunity to determine whether the job requirements can be met and whether any weaknesses in job performance need improvement.

C. Cooperatively, the job coach, the individual, and the supervisor (when available) select a sample of key job requirements that are needed to maintain the job. These should be items essential to successful long-term employment. Determine the requirements that are *most* important for the individual to evaluate.

D. Present the individual with Can I Do This Job? Forms A and B. Form A requires reading. Form B requires picture discrimination skills. It is designed for individuals whose reading skills are limited or nonexistent.

E. Prepare the appropriate form, and present it to the individual prior to his or her shift. Explain to the individual that he or she will need to evaluate him- or herself in the "My evaluation" section and then have the supervisor or job coach evaluate him or her on each requirement in the "Supervisor's evaluation" section.

Action

A. Instruct the individual to evaluate each requirement honestly. The supervisor or job coach also needs to evaluate how the individual is doing on each requirement. Assist with this process, if appropriate.

B. After all responses are circled, it is best to talk through and review each requirement and response with the individual. An explanation should be given of each requirement and reasons discussed for the evaluation given. Encourage discussion.

C. Review the completed Can I Do This Job? Form with the individual. Discuss strengths and areas that may need improvement. Engage the individual in his or her evaluation of strengths and needs. Often individuals may evaluate themselves with a "No" and find that the supervisor will give them a "Yes." Praise the individual on the requirements that received a "Yes" from the supervisor.

D. Discuss with the individual what actions can be taken to meet the requirements of the job.

Monitor and assist

Materials Needed
Can I Do This Job? Summary

A. Add the number of "Yes"s the individual gave him- or herself. Write this number in the second column.

B. If necessary, help the individual to determine the number of supervisor "Yes"s. Write number in the third column.

C. If necessary, help the individual to determine the number of matches between his or her evaluation and the supervisor's evaluation. Write this number in the last column.

D. The individual will need to get at least seven matches in order to give him- or herself a "Yes" on the final evaluation "Can I do this job?"

E. Record each day's performance results on the Can I Do This Job? Summary to evaluate the 5 days of work.

   1. Follow the directions for the calculation fields at the bottom of the page.

   2. Assist the individual to mark the graph according to the scores obtained. Place an "M" on the graph the represent the percentage of matches and a "P" on the graph to represent the percentage of positive answers.

F. If the individual scores less than 75% on 4 out of the 5 days recorded, the process should be extended for another 5 days. If the individual is still not meeting criterion, the employment specialist should consider carving the job in order to appropriately match required tasks with the individual's skill, or use procedures suggested in Objective 20.

Objective 19: What If?

What if, after 5 days, the individual is not able to meet the requirements of the job?

Check Supervisor Feedback Cards to look into how immediate or serious concerns are. If concerns are not immediate or serious, the individual might just need more time to learn or refine the skills required for the job. Assist the individual to improve skills in the needed area. You may also want to talk to the supervisor about accommodations or adaptations, changes in the job description, or carve the job into skills the individual can learn quickly. Finally, there is a possibility that this job may not match the individual's skills, and another placement may be most appropriate.

What if the individual is not matching the supervisor's evaluations on the Can I Do This Job? form?

It is important that the individual is able to recognize his or her skills and to match them realistically with the supervisor's evaluation. Perhaps the evaluator needs to be more specific in his or her explanation of negative evaluations. Provide specific examples for improvement. Explain to the individual that it is important to recognize and not ignore supervisor feedback and expectations.

What if the individual completing Form B does not understand the meaning of the picture?

Physically demonstrate each requirement that is pictured. Ask the individual to evaluate him- or herself for each task demonstrated, model completing the form, then coach form completion.

Section II. Placement and Follow-Along: Self-Management

Goal E: Finding a Job Matching Skills and Preferences

Objective 20: Completing the My Employment Plan

CONTENTS

Introduction
Use the plan
Monitor and assist with new plan
Determine the next step if the job ends

MATERIALS NEEDED

My Employment Plan: Form A (II:E:20:1) and Form B (II:E:20:2)
Job Termination Follow-Up Report (II:E:20:3)
Completed:
Do I Have the Job I Like? Summary (II:E:18:5)
Can I Do This Job? Summary (II:E:19:3)

PURPOSE

To provide an opportunity to review individual preferences and skills, to identify problem areas on the job, and to make job choice changes or to reaffirm the match at the current job

LOCATION

Office
Community jobsite

Introduce

Materials Needed
My Employment Plan: Forms A and B

A. My Employment Plan: Forms A and B offer the individual a format to review preferences and skills, to identify problem areas on a job, to make job choice changes, or to reaffirm the match of a current job (see pp. 355–357). My Employment Plan is found to be most effective when:

1. The individual is experiencing problems on the job that may be preference- or skill-related.
2. Inconsistent or subtle changes on the preference forms in Objective 18 or low scores on the skill forms in Objective 19 signaled the employment specialist that the individual may have a questionable job match.
3. The individual has lost his or her first job, and the employment specialist wants to investigate individual preferences further.

Use the plan

Materials Needed
My Employment Plan: Form A or B

Completed:
Characteristics I Like versus What Is Here: Forms A or B
Do I Have the Job I Like? Summary
Jobs and Tasks I Like: Forms A or B
Can I Do This Job? Forms A or B
Supervisor Feedback Card: Forms A or B
Monitor Supervisor Feedback Graph

A. You will need the preference and skill information obtained in Objectives 18 and 19. My Employment Plan should be used concurrently with the Job Termination Follow-Up Report. An example of a completed My Employment Plan: Form B is on pages 193–194.

B. Review the information from the completed Characteristics I Like versus What Is Here forms and the Do I Have the Job I Like? Summary from Objective 18. Ask individuals to choose his or her 10 most preferred characteristics and write them in the "Characteristics I like" section of My Employment Plan: Form A. For My Employment Plan: Form B, use illustrations. Discuss each choice and assist the individual, if necessary, to circle his or her four most important characteristics.

1. If the individual is employed, ask him or her to check the box next to each characteristic that exists on the job.

2. If the individual is not employed, ask him or her to check the box next to each characteristic that he or she would want on a job.

3. Count the number of matches (the number of check-marks), and divide by the number of characteristics listed. Multiply the answer by 100. This yields the "Percentage of characteristics matches."

C. Ask the individual to choose his or her preferred tasks, and write them in the "Tasks I like" section of My Employment Plan: Form A. For My Employment Plan: Form B, use pictures. Discuss each choice. Some individuals may need to review the Jobs and Tasks I Like forms and the Do I Have the Job I Like? Summary completed in Objective 18.

1. If the individual is employed, ask him or her to check the box next to each characteristic that exists on the job.

2. If the individual is not employed, ask him or her to check the box next to each characteristic that he or she would want on a job.

3. Count the number of matches (the number of check-marks), and divide by the number of characteristics listed. Multiply the answer by 100. This yields the "Percentage of tasks matches."

D. Ask the individual to choose his or her preferred job or jobs and write them in the "Jobs I like" section of My Employment Plan: Form A. For My Employment Plan: Form B, use pictures. Discuss each choice. Some individuals may need to review the Jobs and Tasks I Like: Forms A or B and the Do I Have the Job I Like? Summary completed in Objective 18.

1. If the individual is employed, ask him or her to check the box next to each characteristic that exists on the job.

II:E:20:2

My Employment Plan: Form B (page 1)

Finding a Job

Name: Pat Sample Jobsite: Carla's Date: June 25, 2002

If employed, check what's here and determine the match. If unemployed, check the boxes for the items that you want in your next job.

Characteristics I like

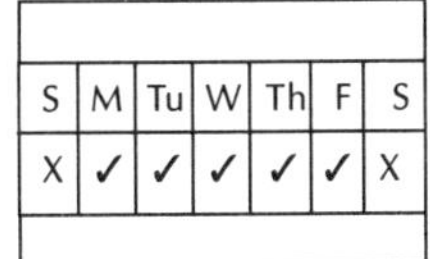

[Y] 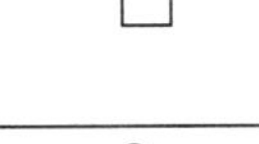    [Y]

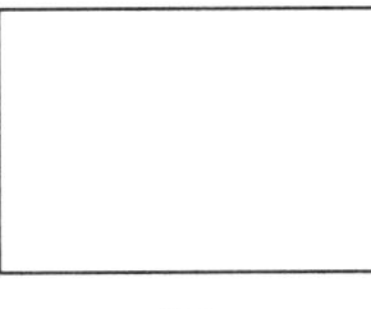

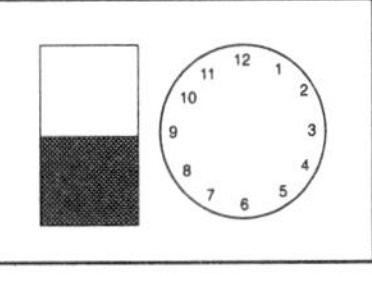

[Y] [Y] [ ] [ ] [Y]

$$\frac{\text{Matches: } 5}{\text{Characteristis listed: } 10} = .50 \times 100 = 50\%$$ Percentage of characteristics matches

Tasks I like

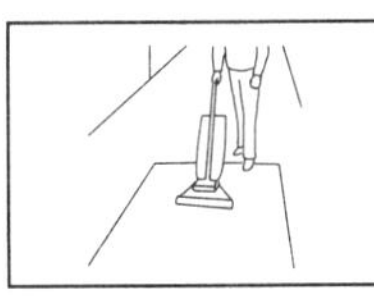

[Y]  [ ] [ ] [Y]

$$\frac{\text{Matches: } 3}{\text{Tasks listed: } 5} = .60 \times 100 = 60\%$$ Percentage of tasks matches

Jobs I like

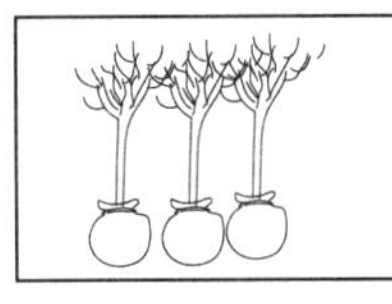

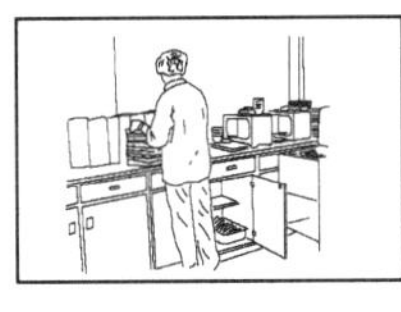

[ ] [ ] [Y] [Y] [Y]

$$\frac{\text{Matches: } 3}{\text{Jobs listed: } 5} = .60 \times 100 = 60\%$$ Percentage of job matches

My Employment Plan: Form B (page 2)

Skills I need to improve: Write a Y in the box for each skill you can improve.

Y

Y

Y

Y

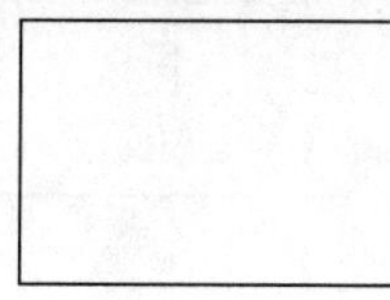

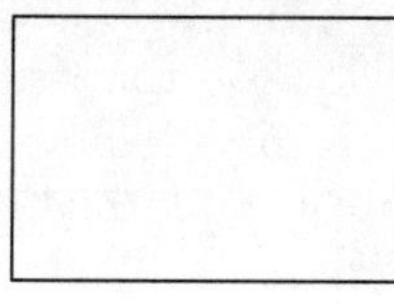

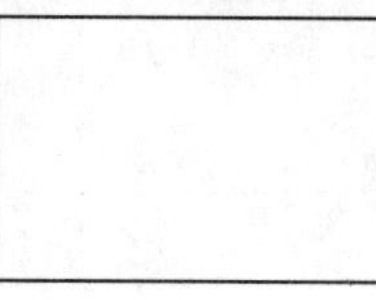

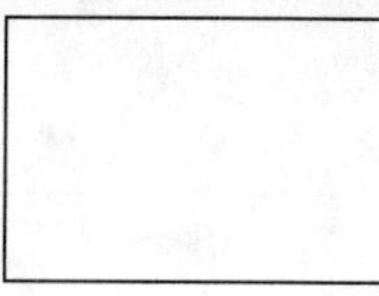

$$\frac{\text{Y's: } 4}{\text{Skills } 5} = .80 \times 100 = 80\%$$ Percentage of skills matches

My job choice

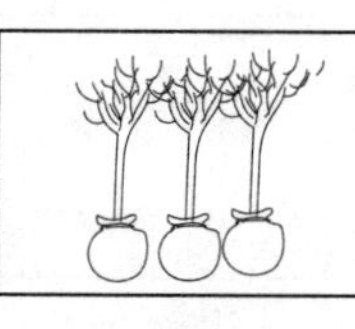

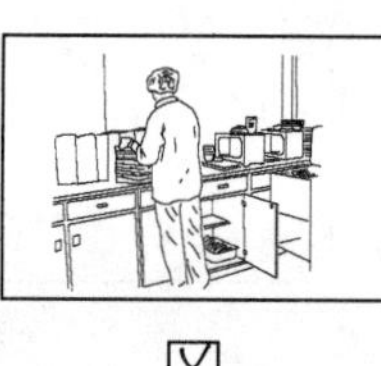

Y

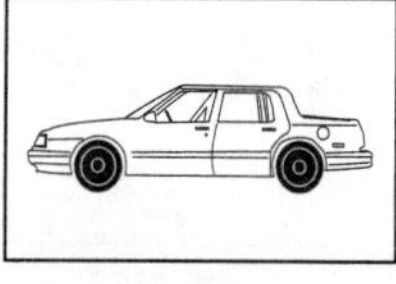

$$\frac{\text{Sum of matches: } 250}{4} = 63\%$$ Average percentage of matches

Signature: Pat Sample Date: June 25, 2002

2. If the individual is not employed, ask him or her to check the box next to each characteristic that he or she would want on a job.

3. Count the number of matches (the number of check-marks), and divide by the number of characteristics listed. Multiply the answer by 100. This yields the "Percentage of job matches."

E. With the individual, determine the work, social, and personal problems that exist on the job, and write or place pictures of these in the "Skills I need to improve" section. It may be helpful to review specific Can I Do This Job? Forms along with the Can I Do This Job? Summary completed in Objective 19. Also the Supervisor Evaluation Cards: Forms A or B along with the Monitor Supervisor Feedback Graph will provide valuable information.

1. Ask the individual whether he or she thinks he or she can improve the listed problems. Write "Y" in the box next to the skill that the individual thinks he or she can improve.

2. Count the number of "Y"s and divide by the number of skills listed. Multiply the answer by 100 to get the "Percentage of skills matches."

F. Perform the calculations in the box to determine the average percentage of matches.

1. Add the "Percentage of characteristics matches," the "Percentage of tasks matches," the "Percentage of job matches," and the "Percentage of skills matches." Divide this sum by 4. This yields the "Average percentage of matches."

G. Ask the person to indicate his or her three top-ranked job choices in the "My job choice" section. Instruct the individual to circle his or her most preferred job choice. If the individual is employed, instruct him or her to circle the job he or she currently has, and then check the box next to the top-ranked job choice. If the individual is not employed, ask him or her to circle only the job he or she wants.

H. Instruct the individual to sign and date My Employment Plan if it represents his or her plans for employment. Individuals are making a contract with themselves, not with the employment specialist.

Monitor and assist with new plan

A. After the original presentation of My Employment Plan, follow up at least once per week with a new one. Explore each response with the individual in detail. Check for consistent responses in each section over time. After each plan is completed, ask yourself:

1. Does the individual know the areas that need improvement?

2. Does the individual know his or her job choice?

3. Does the individual want to change his or her job?

Determine the next step if the job ends

Materials Needed
Job Termination Follow-Up Report

A. If the job does not work out, then arrange a meeting with the individual within 2 weeks. Revise this form or use pictures, if appropriate (see p. 358). An example of the Job Termination Follow-Up Report is shown on pages 197–198. It is important that individuals know that the employment specialist is not going to immediately go out and find them another job. Employment specialists should not reinforce "job hopping" behavior.

1. In the "Why did I lose my job?" and the "Tasks I didn't do" sections, offer a menu of applicable choices that are consistent with the reason behind the actual job loss. When listing the reasons for job loss, be sure to offer additional responses that are not related to the job loss but may match the individual's beliefs.

2. Instruct individuals to check one or more reasons for the job loss. Discuss each choice with the individual. Discuss other items on the menu that were not chosen. If the individual's choices are not accurate, do not try to persuade the individual to make a different choice at this time.

3. Find out if the individual still wants a job in the community. Perhaps a change of mind has taken place as a result of the termination experience. Find out what the person is thinking.

4. Find out if the individual still wants to participate in supported employment. Perhaps there is a personality conflict and the individual does not want to work with a particular employment specialist. If this is a possibility, arrange for a different staff member to support him or her at the next job.

5. Instruct the individual to check an area of work that is preferred in the "Kinds of jobs I would like to have" questions. Revise the job choices as needed to fit your community. Is it the same or different from the last job? Discuss the job choice.

B. Continue to present the first page of the Job Termination Report on a frequent basis until consistent choices are made over time. Based on the responses, some individuals may need to complete this procedure weekly while others may benefit from completing it once every other week.

C. After the individual has given honest answers and has made consistent choices over time, introduce the second page. The

II:E:20:3

Job Termination Follow-up Report (page 1)

Finding a Job

Name: Pat Sample Date: May 5, 2002

Why did I lose my job?

_____ Job was too hard
_____ Not the job area for me
_____ Bored
_____ I couldn't do the tasks
__X__ I didn't do the tasks
__X__ Boss was unfair
_____ Did not like co-workers
_____ Supervisor expected too much
__X__ I was disrespectful
_____ I only did what I wanted

Tasks I didn't do

__X__ I avoided price checks
__X__ I didn't keep carts filled
__X__ I avoided clean-up
__X__ I avoided take-backs

Important questions

Do I want a job in the community? (Yes) No

Do I want to participate in supported employment? (Yes) No

Kinds of jobs I would like to have:

__X__ Store _____ Food service _____ Janitorial _____ Other:

_____ Laundry _____ Factory _____ Maid service

Work issues I need to address in order to maintain a job in the community

Problem: I avoid the tasks I do not like to do.

Solution: Do all the tasks I was hired to do.

Problem: I blame the boss when I get caught

Solution: Take responsibility for my actions by admitting my mistakes.

II:E:20:3

Job Termination Follow-up Report (page 2)

Finding a Job

Name: Pat Sample Date: May 5, 2002

Social issues I need to address in order to maintain a job in the community

Problem: I need to do what is expected of me and not blame others when I don't do the task

Solution: Make a list of all the things I need to do, then do them daily.

Problem: ______

Solution: ______

Personal issues I need to address in order to maintain a job in the community

Problem: ______

Solution: ______

Problem: ______

Solution: ______

Personal contract

I will work hard to do all I can to maintain my next job opportunity in the community. (Yes) No

Signature: Pat Sample Date: 6/19/02

second page addresses work, social and personal problems that need to be addressed to maintain a job in the community. Discuss actual problems and solutions for each problem identified in the work, social, or personal areas. If there are no issues in any of these areas, disregard them. Often, concerns surface that should be resolved before attempting the next job (e.g. medical issues, family dynamics, abuse of alcohol or other drugs). Assist the individual to

1. Identify all concerns or problems
2. Discuss possible solutions
3. Develop an action plan with a time line
4. Take action to resolve concerns
5. Review success and make adjustments, if needed
6. Find and start the new job only after the concerns are resolved

D. Ask the individual to sign the contract at the bottom of the page. The contract is with the individual him- or herself to work hard to maintain the next job. A "No" response is also available. Encourage the individual to be honest in responding. If the individual chooses to stop the supported employment program, call the team together to decide what next steps should be taken.

II:E:20

Objective 20: What If?

What if the individual completes the Job Termination Follow-Up Report but never admits to what actually happened that cost him or her the job?	*Review the events that led up to the termination and the reasons given by the supervisor for the termination. Some individuals may need more internship experiences to enhance their problem-solving skills. Others may not want to work at this time.*
What if the individual completes the Job Termination Follow-Up Report honestly and accurately but keeps losing jobs?	*Try a different format for the report, or discuss events and reasons given in detail, and determine if the individual really wants to work. Consider internships as an appropriate method to try out intervention strategies. You may need to back track and repeat the job match process.*

INTRODUCTION TO SECTION II.

Goal F: Solving On-The-Job Problems

The Self-Directed Employment (SDE) approach supports the idea that teaching self-management and problem-solving empowers the individual and is a cost-effective and efficient method for enhancing long-term employment success. Most individuals with severe disabilities, however, seldom use self-management and problem-solving skills. This chapter describes a straightforward and easy-to-follow approach to teach on-the-job self-management and problem solving. The individual with a severe disability needs assistance, support, time, and practice to learn these skills.

MATCH CONTRACT

Self-evaluation, the ability to record or report one's performance and compare it with a standard, is the first self-management skill introduced. It is the foundational concept for the on-the-job problem-solving system. Workers who need to improve their self-evaluation skills use a Match Contract. Various Match Contract formats are provided to meet the unique learning needs of different workers. All Match Contract formats provide a simple method for the individual to:

1. Self-evaluate work, social, and personal performance
2. Obtain daily performance standard feedback from the supervisor
3. Match his or her self-evaluations to the supervisor's evaluation
4. Plan adjustments for the next day's performance based on today's self-evaluation and feedback

IMPROVEMENT CONTRACT

Individuals who can accurately self-evaluate use Improvement Contracts to learn on-the-job problem-solving skills. Like the Match Contract, several different Improvement Contract formats are available. Choose a format that matches the individual. All formats provide a simple method for the individual to:

1. Solicit supervisor feedback
2. Identify problems
3. Identify solutions
4. Replace a work problem with a work solution
5. Replace a social problem with a social solution
6. Replace a personal problem with a personal solution
7. Follow through on adjustments

MY CHANGE PLAN

My Change Plan is a strategy to enhance long-term employment and career advancement. My Change Plan offers a systematic procedure for individuals to periodically evaluate themselves and their vocational environment. With this information they can set goals, make plans, act on their plans, evaluate the results of their actions, and make needed adjustments in order to meet their stated goals. Complete My Change Plan at least every 6 months or when sudden changes in attitude, motivation, performance, or behavior occurs.

ROLE SUMMARY

Using the SDE approach, both the worker with a severe disability and the employment specialist have specific duties and roles. The worker must:

- Become proficient in using an effective problem-solving method
- Continue to seek out honest and timely supervisor feedback
- Learn to make adjustments independently

The employment specialist will need to:

- Establish a long-term visitation schedule with the supervisor
- Keep in close contact with the individual's family or residential staff
- Determine with the individual whether a problem-solving format change is needed
- Help the individual to develop and implement intervention strategies
- Support the individual in monitoring performance and behavior
- Be aware of changes in the employment setting and monitor the need for re-training, advancement, or job change
- Facilitate natural on-the-job supports
- Serve as a technical resource for career planning, transportation concerns, education/ training, and social security and other benefit issues

The following table is a graphic organizational tool that will assist and guide you through the placement and follow-along process found in this chapter and book section. You may also want to refer to the Implementation Reference Guide.

Goal	Gather data	Graph data	Put summary together
F. Solving On-the-Job Problems	Basic Match Contract Match Contract: Alternate 1 Match Contract: Alternate 2 Supervisor Evaluation Card: Form A or B Objective 21	Match Data Summary Objective 21	Objective 21
	Problems and Solutions List		Objective 22
	Basic Improvement Contract Improvement Contract: Alternate 1 Improvement Contract: Alternate 2 Improvement Contract: Alternate 3 Improvement Contract: Alternate 4 Objective 22	Improvement Contract Data Summary Quarterly Placement Summary Objective 23	Objective 23
	My Change Plan: Form A or B Objective 24		Objective 24

Section II. Placement and Follow-Along: Self-Management

Goal F: Solving On-the-Job Problems

Objective 21: Checking Supervisor Match

CONTENTS

Introduction
Determine need
Performance evaluation introduction
Teach Basic Match Contract
Teach Match Contract: Alternate 1
Teach Match Contract: Alternate 2
Monitor progress

MATERIALS NEEDED

Basic Match Contract (II:F:21:1)
Match Contract: Alternate 1 (II:F:21:2) and Alternate 2 (II:F:21:3)
Supervisor Evaluation Card: Form A (II:E:17:1)
Match Data Summary (II:E:21:4)

PURPOSE

To provide a process for individuals to make honest self-evaluations based on timely and accurate supervisor feedback

LOCATION

Office
Employment Site

Introduction

A. Self-evaluation is a powerful, yet simple, self-management strategy that can often improve behavior just by itself. If, however, more specific antecedent or consequent interventions are needed, Objective 21 will show you how to use an effective problem solving system.

Determine need

A. Based on the individual's matching skills evaluated in assessment, determine if there is a need for the person to learn to match his or her self-evaluations with the supervisor's evaluations. To do this, answer the questions:

1. Did the individual realistically evaluate his or her work performance?
2. Did the individual realistically evaluate his or her work, social, and personal behaviors?
3. Did the individual consistently match supervisor evaluations 75% to 80% of the time?

Note: If your answer is yes to *all three questions,* then go to Objective 22. Otherwise, continue to follow the procedures in this objective.

Performance evaluation introduction

A. Explain performance evaluation to the individual and why it is important:

1. Stress that it is important for a person to understand how well he or she is doing on the job.
2. Suggest to individual to check the differences and similarities between his or her evaluation and the supervisor's.
3. The formal paper-and-pencil supervisor evaluation process is used to formalize what is often unspoken co-worker or supervisor judgments.

B. Several different match contracts are provided to teach the individual the performance evaluation process. Choose a format that will best fit the individual. All match contract formats presented provide a simple method for the individual to:

1. Self-evaluate the work day. It teaches the individual to be honest about how he or she feels he or she is doing on-the-job and helps him or her realize the importance of self-evaluation.
2. Seek daily feedback from the supervisor. It teaches the individual to secure feedback often.
3. Match his or her self-evaluations to the supervisor's evaluations. Matching teaches the individual how to discover supervisor expectations.
4. Demonstrate realistic on-the-job self-evaluations.
5. Make the adjustments needed for the next day's performance.

Teach Basic Match Contract

Materials Needed
Basic Match Contract

A. The Basic Match Contract is designed for individuals who need a method to match their performance evaluations with their supervisor's (see p. 360). You can also insert illustrations for individuals who have been using the Form B format throughout this process. Prepare the form to meet the skills of the individual. An example of a completed form is on page 206.

B. Before beginning the day's work, sit down with the individual, and explain the purpose of the form.

1. Have the supervisor present it the first day, if possible. If not, the employment specialist may need to fill in temporarily as the supervisor.

II:F:21:1

Basic Match Contract

Solving On-the-Job Problems

Name: Kelly Sample

Date: September 7, 2002

Goal	My evaluation	Supervisor's evaluation	Match	Comment	Next goal
Work: Empty all trash cans. Don't miss any.	(Yes) No	Yes (No)	Yes (No)	Missed trash cans in rooms 102 and 105	Empty all trash cans. Don't miss any.
Social: Keep hands to self.	(Yes) No	(Yes) No	(Yes) No	Great!	
Personal: Take shower before work.	(Yes) No	Yes (No)	Yes (No)	Body odor: Needs to take a shower before work, wash uniform, and use deodorant	Good hygiene

2. Specific concerns of the job will need to be addressed in the work, social, or personal areas. Discuss them with the individual. Decide with the individual if there are any concerns that need immediate attention. These concerns can be pictured or written in the boxes labeled under the "Goal" column.

3. Each goal box is labeled with an area: work, social, or personal. Explain to the individual that he or she will be evaluated in all areas, regardless of the goal.

C. For each work day, instruct the individual to choose the goal he or she would like to work on by checking the box located to the right of each goal. The individual can choose more than one. Model the process for the individual and the supervisor, if necessary.

D. The individual should evaluate his or her performance at the end of the shift in the work, social, and personal areas, even if there is no goal checked. The individual should consider how he or she performed overall for each goal listed. Does the individual think that the requirements of the job were met? Instruct the individual to circle the appropriate answer in the section labeled "My evaluation."

E. After performing the self-evaluation, instruct the individual to ask the supervisor to evaluate his or her performance. As the supervisor completes each "Supervisor's evaluation" box, make sure an explanation is given for each response in the "Comment" column. It is very important for the individual to understand why a supervisor's "Yes" or "No" is circled.

F. Sit down in a quiet place with the individual to discuss the match between the individual's self-evaluation, and the supervisor evaluation. Assist the individual with the match process. Ask the individual to explain the reasoning for his or her self-evaluation, the supervisor's evaluation, and the match (or mismatch). Assist the individual, if appropriate, to circle "Yes" or "No" in the "Match" column.

G. If the individual receives a negative evaluation, ask the individual what he or she would like to work on the next day. Suggest to the individual that it may be a good idea to work on goals that have been negatively evaluated again. If so, have him or her check the box on the right side of the "Next goal" column. If individual met the requirement of the job in the work, social or personal areas, he or she may choose the same goal or opt to work on another goal. The individual may opt *not* to choose a goal at all. That's okay! The person will be evaluated in all the goal areas for that day.

H. The individual needs to attain, independently, a match on at least 75% of all sections of the contract over a 10-day period. This will be summarized in the Match Data Summary form discussed in the next part of this objective.

I. The next time the individual is scheduled to work, for the first few days or until the process is learned, refer to the "Next goal" section from the prior day's work. Show the individual the items he or she set as a next goal. Instruct the individual to check the same items in the "Goal" section of their new contract. If needed, review the prior day's contract.

J. If necessary, simplify the form so that the individual is able to learn and perform this process with little or no help. The idea is to get the individual to be able to operationalize the match contract independently. If not, you may need to look at some of the alternate match contracts and determine which one might work better.

Teach Match Contract: Alternate 1

Materials Needed
Match Contract: Alternate 1

A. The Match Contract: Alternate 1 is designed for individuals whose reading skills are limited or nonexistent and who need a simple method to match their evaluations with their supervisors' evaluations (see p. 361).

B. Before beginning the day's work, sit down with the individual and explain the purpose and how this form works.

   1. Have the supervisor present if possible on the first day. If not, the job coach will need to fill in temporarily as the supervisor.

   2. If specific items of concern need to be addressed in the work, social, or personal areas, these items can be pictured or written into the corresponding box. You can download pictures from www.brookespublishing.com/picturebank.

   3. The Match Contract: Alternate 1 can also be adapted to list specific work tasks or a schedule that the individual must perform daily.

C. The individual should evaluate him- or herself at the end of the shift in the work, social, and personal areas. The person should consider daily how he or she performed across each area. Does the person think he or she met the requirements of the job? Have the person circle "Yes" or "No" in the "My evaluation" column.

D. After performing the self-evaluation, the individual should take the contract to his or her supervisor. As the supervisor completes each section, make sure an explanation is given to the worker. It is very important for the individual to understand why a "Yes" or a "No" is being given.

E. Sit down in a quiet place with the individual to discuss the results.

1. Discuss the match between the individual's self-evaluation and the supervisor's evaluation. Assist the individual with the match process. Ask the individual to explain the reasoning for his or her self-evaluation, the supervisor's evaluation, and the match. Instruct the worker to circle the corresponding "Yes" or "No" in the "Match" section.
2. Based on the day's performance, determine the work, social, or personal performance categories the individual needs to work on the next day. Check the corresponding "Next goal" section.

F. Model the process for the individual and supervisor, if appropriate.

G. The individual should attain, independently, a match on at least 75% of all sections of the contract over a 10-day period. If not, continue the process. You may need to reevaluate the effectiveness of this form. Are there some revisions that would help? Is there another format that might work better?

Teach Match Contract: Alternate 2

Materials Needed
- Match Contract: Alternate 2
- Supervisor Evaluation Card: Form A

A. The Match Contract: Alternate 2 should only be used with individuals who

1. Are comfortable using their reading and writing skills
2. Have the skill to develop their own daily goals without a checklist
3. Need to learn to match their self-evaluations with the supervisor's evaluations and need the opportunity to begin simple problem solving

B. The Supervisor Evaluation Card: Form A should be used along with the Match Contract: Alternate 2 (see pp. 343 and 362).

C. The individual should decide which performance areas he or she needs to improve: work, social, or personal. Individuals can choose to work in one, two, or all of these areas. Prior to starting work, ask the worker to write what he or she would like to improve in the work, social, and personal blanks. Also, make sure the individual has provided the supervisor with a Supervisor Evaluation Card: Form A.

D. After work,

1. The individual needs to self-evaluate his or her own performance. Teach the person to circle "Yes" or "No" to answer the question "Did I meet the requirements of the job?"
2. Instruct the individual how to collect the Supervisor Evaluation Cards. Emphasize courtesy when picking up the card.

3. The individual should decide if his or her evaluation matches the supervisor's evaluation and answer the question "Does this match the supervisor's evaluations?" by circling "Yes" or "No." The supervisor should have given *all* "Yes"s on the Supervisor Evaluation Card in order for the individual to meet the requirements of the job.

E. If the individual's evaluation did not match the supervisor's evaluation, instruct him or her to write the concern in the "Next time I need to improve" section. Eventually, this process should be performed independently. If individual met the requirements of the job, he or she may choose to improve in the same areas or choose new ones.

F. The individuals needs to attain, independently, at least 80% of all sections of the contract over a 10-day period.

Monitor progress

Materials Needed
Match Data Summary

Completed:
Basic Match Contract
or Match Contract: Alternates 1 or 2

A. To monitor individual match contracts, use the Match Data Summary. For each contract, transfer the information from the Match Contract to the Match Data Summary (see p. 363).

1. *Set Goal:* Does the individual set his or her goal based on the previous day's supervisor evaluation and "Next goal"? Enter 1 for "Yes" and 0 for "No."

2. *Solicited supervisor feedback:* Does the individual give the supervisor his or her form or evaluation card independently? Enter 1 for "Yes" and 0 for "No."

3. *Self-evaluated:* Does the individual independently complete his or her self-evaluation? Enter 1 for "Yes" and 0 for "No."

4. *Evaluated matches:* Does the individual's evaluation match the supervisor's evaluation? Enter 1 for "Yes" and 0 for "No."

5. *Followed through on adjustment:* Look at the day's supervisor evaluation. Does the individual's "Next goal" match the supervisor's evaluation? Enter 1 for "Yes" and 0 for "No."

B. After 2 weeks or 10 consecutive days of work, add the scores for each section of the Match Data Summary. Divide by the total number of possible entries in that section to obtain a percentage score for that section.

1. Review each section's percentage score with the individual. Scores can be used for Individual Program Plan development.

2. If the individual is maintaining an 80% match, introduce the Improvement Contract (see Objective 22).

C. If the individual's evaluations are not matching with his or her supervisor's evaluations and he or she is not able to reach the 80% criterion on the Match Contract, consider the following:

1. If the individual seems to understand the format used, perhaps he or she just needs more time working at the job and using the Match Contract.

2. The individual is not drawing honest or realistic conclusions about his or her skills and performance. Perhaps the format is not working or being understood by the individual. Explain the format to the individual again using more modeling or physical prompting. Extend the period of instruction until the resulting match takes place. Use another format or create an individualized one. For example, an audiotape cassette can be very effective with some individuals.

3. The supervisor may not be giving honest or fair feedback in his or her evaluations. The individual, with the employment specialist's assistance, needs to decide if he or she wants to discuss any concerns with the supervisor or think about moving on to a new job.

Objective 21: What If?

What if, after an extended period of time, the individual's evaluations are still not consistently matching the supervisor's because the individual is constantly giving him- or herself negative self-evaluations?

More time needs to be spent going over the reasons for the supervisor's positive evaluations. A structured reinforcement program might assist the individual to build confidence and self-esteem. Use a concrete approach when having the individual self-evaluate. Say, for example, "Did you come to work on time today? Did you do what you were told quickly? Did you put your supplies away before you punched out?" Using an Improvement Contract may empower the individual to build confidence because he or she can see his or her plans working (see Objective 22).

What if, after an extended period of time, the individual's evaluations are still not consistently matching the supervisor's evaluations? The individual gives him- or herself positive evaluations despite the negative evaluations of the supervisor.

Self-evaluation by itself is not a powerful enough strategy to change his or her behavior. Implement the Improvement Contract described in Objective 22.

Section II. Placement and Follow-Along: Self-Management

Goal F: Solving On-The-Job Problems

Objective 22: Teaching a Problem-Solving System

CONTENTS

Advance to a system of structured problem solving
Introduce Basic Improvement Contract
Develop a written format
Develop a picture format
Develop Improvement Contract: Alternates 1, 2, 3, and 4

MATERIALS NEEDED

Problems and Solutions List (II:F:22:1)
Basic Improvement Contract (II:F:22:2)
Improvement Contract: Alternates 1 (II:F:22:3), 2 (II:F:22:4), 3 (II:F:22:5), and 4 (II:F:22:6)
Completed:
Supervisor Feedback Card: Forms A (II:E:17:1)
Can I Do This Job? Forms A (II:E:19:1) or Form B (II:E:19:2)
Basic Match Contract (II:F:21:1)

PURPOSE

To provide a process for the individual to problem solve and make adjustments at work by using supervisor feedback and self-determined strategies

LOCATION

Office
Employment Site

Advance to a system of structured problem solving

Materials Needed
Problems and Solutions List

Completed:
Can I Do this Job? Form
Supervisor Feedback Cards
Match Contracts

A. There are two ways to arrive at this objective:

1. Objective 17: Establishing Supervisor Feedback and Support referred you here because the individual is receiving consistent negative supervisor evaluations in the work, social, or personal areas.
2. The individual completed Objective 21: Teaching Supervisor Match and needs to move to the next step of problem solving. If problems occur later, you should refer again to this objective and implement an improvement contract.

Note: If an individual consistently receives positive supervisor evaluations, continue to collect Supervisor Feedback Cards on a weekly basis. There is no need to use an improvement contract at this time. The improvement contract is driven by negative evaluations. It is useful only if a structured problem-solving system is needed to change negative evaluations into positive ones.

B. Individuals who demonstrate poor problem-solving skills and have reading skills that are limited or nonexistent will benefit from forms that have pictures or illustrations. The individual must have picture discrimination skills. Add word descriptions under each picture.

C. Develop with the individual one to three goals or problems that he or she would like to improve. Discuss any problems he or she is experiencing in the work, social, and personal areas. If needed, review the behaviors associated with the work, social, and personal skill areas.

D. If the individual does not set improvement goals or struggles identifying problems, develop a Problems and Solutions List (see p. 364).

1. Review completed Can I Do This Job? forms, Supervisor Feedback Cards, and Match Contracts, if applicable. Are there any behaviors listed that could be improved?
2. Identify reoccurring on-the-job problems. Assist to find three possible solutions to each problem.
3. Meet with the supervisor to identify and discuss strengths and weaknesses.
4. Using the Problems and Solutions List as a guide, prompt the individual to choose several problems and the solution to each that would work the best. Allow the individual to choose his or her own solutions. Review possible consequences for each solution. Allow the individual to make the final choices. Illustrate problems and solutions using pictures downloaded from www.brookespublishing.com/picturebank. You may also add your own photographs or drawings.

Introduce Basic Improvement Contract

A. The Improvement Contract provides a flexible instructional tool to learn and practice problem solving (see pp. 365–369). Explain that problem solving provides a method to achieve job success. It allows individuals to set goals and make plans to achieve their chosen goals. Several different improvement contracts are provided to teach the individual a problem-solving system. Choose a format that will best fit the individual. Present one of the following formats that the individual can use independently.

Develop a written format

Materials Needed
- Improvement Contract
- Problems and Solutions List

Completed:
- Can I Do This Job? Forms
- Supervisor Evaluation Cards
- Match Contracts

A. Individuals who demonstrate good reading and writing skills may want to design their Improvement Contract using an open-ended methodology. An open-ended contract allows individuals to develop and change their plans and solutions to address their own concerns or the concerns of the supervisor on a daily basis.

B. The column labeled "Goal" is the problem statement section of the contract. Develop with the goals or problems that the individual would like to improve. Discuss any problems that the individual might be experiencing in the work, social, and personal areas of the job. If necessary, review the behaviors associated with the work, social, and personal areas. Instruct the individual to decide on one or more goals, problems, or concerns that he or she would like to work on. Instruct the individual to define each item as a work, social, or personal goal. Write the item in the corresponding goal box.

C. If the individual does not set goals or struggles identifying problems, develop a Problems and Solutions List.

1. Review the completed Can I Do This Job? forms, Supervisor Evaluation Cards, and Match Contracts, if applicable. Are there any behaviors listed that could be improved?

2. Identify reoccurring on-the-job problems. Assist to find three possible solutions to each problem. Allow the individual to choose his or her own solutions. Review possible consequences for each solution. Allow the individual to make the final choices.

3. Meet with the supervisor to identify and discuss worker strength and weaknesses.

4. Using the Problems and Solutions List as a guide, prompt the individual to write in the problems discussed. If specific solutions were suggested by the supervisor, write them in the "Solutions" section.

D. Discuss with the employee one to three actions that, when demonstrated, could solve the problem. Use the Problems and Solutions List that was just developed, if necessary. Discuss what action the individual plans to demonstrate in order to accomplish the daily goal. In the "Plan" section, the individual should write in how he or she is going to work on each stated goal.

F. After completing the "Goal" and "Plan" sections of the Improvement Contract, the individual should begin his or her shift and concentrate on achieving the stated goals. At the end of the work shift, follow these steps:

1. For each goal, instruct the individual to evaluate him- or herself and determine if the goal was accomplished. Instruct the individual to indicate whether the goal was accomplished in the "My evaluation" column.

2. Instruct the individual to give the Improvement Contract to the supervisor for an evaluation of the day's performance. The supervisor should respond by indicating whether he or she thinks the goal was met in the "Supervisor's eval-

uation" column. Have the supervisor explain each evaluation in the column labeled "Comments" Discuss the completed evaluation with the supervisor.

3. Instruct the individual to determine if the answers in the "Supervisor's evaluation" matches those in "My evaluation," and circle the corresponding response in the "Match" column.

G. Adjustments to evaluations can be made by writing them into the corresponding boxes in the column labeled "Next goal."

Note: Individuals may discover from supervisor feedback that the goals they are setting are appropriate but find that the solutions proposed to meet the goals are not working. If so, you may need to refer back to the Problems and Solutions List to look at new solutions to the goals. The individual should determine what solution will lead to a positive evaluation and use it on the next day's Improvement Contract.

H. Encourage the individual to think about how long to keep the same goal and when to move on to a new goal. The individual also needs to determine whether his or her solutions are working. Encourage the individual to give solutions enough time to work.

I. For the next day, instruct the individual to refer to the "Next goal" section from the previous day's Improvement Contract to set his or her goals for the new working day in the section labeled "Goal."

J. The individual should attain independent matches for at least 80% for all components of the Improvement Contract over the 10-day period. It is important that Improvement Contracts are updated periodically with the individual. Problem solving is an ongoing process that addresses current job demands. Do not allow the process to stagnate. As the individual becomes successful, assure new goals are set for job improvement at least every 2 weeks.

Develop a picture format

Materials Needed
Basic Improvement Contract

Completed:
Problems and Solutions List

A. For individuals needing an illustrated Improvement Contract, attach pictures that best illustrate the individual's job improvement needs in the column labeled "Goals." Place improvement needs in the appropriate work, social or personal goal boxes. A completed example of an illustrated Basic Improvement Contract is on page 217.

B. With the employee, develop one to three actions that if demonstrated could solve the identified problem in the "Goal" boxes. Use the Problems and Solutions List, if necessary. Place the chosen solutions in the column labeled "Plan."

II:F:22:2

Basic Improvement Contract

Solving On-the-Job Problems

Name: Pat Sample

Date: July 21, 2003

Goal	Plan	My evaluation	Supervisor's evaluation	Match	Comments	Next goal
✓ Clean restrooms	Mop well	(Yes) No	(Yes) No	(Yes) No	(Floor was dry mopped) Floor was too wet	✓ Clean restrooms
✓ Follow directions	Check to see if I'm being stubborn	(Yes) No	Yes (No)	Yes (No)	Asked boss Checked list (Refused directions)	✓ Follow directions
☐		Yes No	Yes No	Yes No		☐

C. For positive supervisor evaluations, copy and place the pictures from the "Plan" column into the "Comments" column. Add one or two new pictures that the individual could chose from that illustrate possible negative outcomes.

D. Copy and place the picture from the "Goals" column into the "Next goal" column. Develop these with the individual, and add one or two new pictures from which the individual can choose.

E. Explain and model the procedures of the Improvement Contract.

1. Choose goals to work on for the day by circling the corresponding pictures in the boxes of the "Goals" column. Write in keywords that best describe the problem under the picture.

2. Circle the picture that best illustrates how the chosen goal will be accomplished in the shaded column labeled "Plan." Write in keywords that best describe the pictured item.

3. After work, the individual should evaluate his or her performance for each goal by circling "Yes" or "No" in the corresponding box in the column labeled "My evaluation."

4. Instruct the employee to give the contract to the supervisor. Ask the supervisor to circle "Yes" or "No" in the "Supervisor's evaluation" column. Ask the supervisor to explain the positive or negative evaluation for each goal circled in the "Goal" column. Write the information in the "Comments" column. Convert to illustrations.

5. For each goal circled, compare the "My evaluation" section to the "Supervisor's evaluation" section. Evaluate if they are the same or different and circle "Yes" or "No" response in the "Comments" column.

6. Determine why the evaluation matched or did not match by circling the picture in the "Comments" column that best describes the reasoning.

F. If the individual received a "No" from the supervisor, instruct him or her to repeat the goal by checking the box in the section labeled "Next goal" in the corresponding work, social, or personal area of the contract. If the individual met the requirements of the job and received a "Yes," he or she may choose the same next goal or opt for a new one.

G. Assist the individual through the process as much as needed or until the individual can perform the process independently.

H. Determine whether the individual understands the format and can productively use it. Individuals must independently meet the 80% problem-solving criterion over a 10-day period.

I. It is important that the Improvement Contract be updated periodically with the individual. This should be an ongoing working process for the individual that addresses current job demands. Do not allow the process to stagnate.

J. The employment specialist should encourage the individual to become as independent as possible, assisting only when needed.

Develop Improvement Contract: Alternates 1, 2, 3, and 4

Materials Needed
Improvement Contract: Alternates 1, 2, 3, and 4

Completed:
Supervisor Evaluation Card: Form A.

A. Samples of some alternative improvement contracts are included that can be used to individualize the decision-making and problem-solving processes (see pp. 366–369). These are only a few of the many adaptations that can be made. A few individuals may choose to use an audiotape recorder or some other media instead of a pictorial or written format. No matter what form or method is used, be sure to include the choose, manage, evaluate, and adjust model. Remember some individuals may need to develop a Problems and Solutions List.

B. Improvement Contract: Alternates 1 and 2 are very similar in design. Start by developing the problems and solutions. Pictures can be used to illustrate the "Goal" (i.e., the problem) and "Plan" (i.e., the solution) sections, or they can be written in. The individual checks the box that identifies the problem and the solution he or she chooses to work on. One or more can be chosen daily.

1. Improvement Contract: Alternate 1 allows for only one problem that can be chosen in the work, social, and personal areas. Improvement Contract: Alternate 2 allows for two problems for each work, social, and personal area.

2. Improvement Contract: Alternates 1 and 2 request the supervisor to write in any concerns that may be developing. Concerns typically are not about requirements of the job but about things that may be bothering the supervisor that may, if not corrected, affect the individual's job.

3. Ask the employee to choose the goal and plan for the day by checking the specified work, social, and personal box. Picture or written formats can be used. The "Next time" adjustment section requires individuals to make a plan for the next day based on the supervisor's feedback for the day and to check the box indicating his or her choice.

C. Improvement Contract: Alternate 3 is a written form that should be used *with* the Supervisor Evaluation Card: Form A. This contract does not have the self-evaluation component.

1. The contract should be shared with the supervisor so that he or she knows specifically what the employee is working toward.

2. Once the Supervisor Evaluation Card: Form A is returned to the employee, he or she needs to determine if he or she met the goals and what goals will be needed for the next day's work.

3. Individuals who become good problem solvers may learn to use this contract on a weekly basis.

D. Improvement Contract: Alternate 4 is designed for use with individuals who find that their emotions may get in the way of their employment success. The contact relates performance to positive and negative feelings the person is experiencing. This is an open-ended format for individuals who also demonstrate good writing skills.

  1. Each time you use this contract, assist the individual through the process as much as needed or until the individual can perform the process independently.

  2. To determine if the individual understands and can productively use this format, he or she must meet the 80% problem-solving criterion over a 10-day period. If the criterion is not met, change the format or use another form.

E. It is important that improvement contracts be updated periodically with the individual. This should be an ongoing process for the individual that addresses current needs.

F. Do not allow the process to stagnate. As the individual becomes successful, make sure that new goals are set for job improvement at least every 2 weeks.

Objective 22: What If?

What if the individual is using an illustrated improvement contract and is unable to meet the criterion of 80% matches?

The individual may not understand the process or may need additional modeling or more time to practice using the contract or a new format. If the individual's evaluation consistently fails to match his or her supervisor's evaluation, the individual may need to return to the match contract. If the individual is having difficulty with checking appropriate goals, then reduce the number of items from five to three or from three to two. Consider other possible formats other than paper and pencil. Perhaps an audiotape or verbal methodology would work better.

What if the individual is having difficulty with developing problems and solutions for his or her improvement contract?

Use the Problems and Solutions List. This form offers a method to develop a general list of problems and solutions for the individual to refer to at any time. Each form has space for one problem and several positive and negative solutions. Allow the individual to determine his or her own problems and solutions to choose from. If the employment specialist finds some solution inappropriate, do not intervene. Let the individual learn from his or her own mistakes. Update the list on a regular basis.

What if the individual keeps choosing the same problems and solutions?

As long as the supervisor's evaluations continue to be positive, that's okay. Some individuals may need to choose these goals time and again. You can challenge the individual to try something new that might help him or her advance. Work on developing a new Problems and Solutions List. Be careful not to disrupt the individual's system if it seems to be working.

What if new problems have surfaced from the supervisor's evaluations, but the individual keeps choosing the same problems and solutions?

Review the supervisor's evaluations with the individual. Develop a new Problems and Solutions List. If needed, complete some new Can I Do This Job? forms.

What if the individual is having difficulty with developing problems and solutions for his or her improvement contract?

Use the Problems and Solutions List. This form offers a method to develop a general list of problems and solutions for the individual to refer to at any time. Each form has space for one problem and several positive and negative solutions. Allow the individual to determine his or her own problems and solutions to choose from. If the employment specialist finds some solution inappropriate, do not intervene. Let the individual learn from his or her own mistakes. Update the list on a regular basis.

Section II. Placement and Follow-Along: Self-Management

Goal F: Solve On-the-Job Problems

Objective 23: Teaching Ongoing Adjustments

CONTENTS

Monitor progress
Facilitate adjustments
Modify specific problems and solutions

MATERIALS NEEDED

Improvement Contract Data Summary (II:F:23:1)
Quarterly Placement Summary (II:F:23:2)
Completed:
Problems and Solutions List (II:F:22:1)
Improvement Contracts (II:F:22:2–6)

PURPOSE

To provide a method for individuals to monitor their progress overtime on a periodic basis

LOCATION

Office
Employment Site

Monitor progress

Materials Needed
Improvement Contract Data Summary

A. To monitor individual's Improvement Contracts use the Improvement Contract Data Summary. Gather the Improvement Contracts used by the individual for the week. For each contract date, transfer the information to the Improvement Contract Data Summary (see p. 370).

1. *Solicited supervisor feedback.* Does the individual get the evaluation section or card filled out by the supervisor? Enter 1 for "Yes" and 0 for "No."

2. *Identified problems.* Is there a goal or problem listed in this section? If the supervisor gave a "No" on the last evaluation, there needs to be a goal or problem listed. If the supervisor gave a "Yes," the individual may list a goal or problem of his or her own, but it is not required. The individual receives feedback in three areas: work, social, and personal. Give partial credit (.33, .50, or 1, depending on how many goals were set to be worked on) in each area for listing a needed goal or problem or if the individual received a "Yes" in that area in the previous evaluation. Concerns listed by the supervisor should be treated as a "No."

3. *Identified solutions.* Is there a plan or solution listed? If the supervisor gave a "No" on the last evaluation or if a goal or problem is listed, there should be a plan or solution listed. Give partial credit (.33, .50, or 1) depending on how many goals were set to be worked on) for each section.

4. *Replaced work problems with work solutions.* Does the individual get or maintain an improved "Yes" evaluation in the work section? Score 1 for "Yes" and 0 for "No." Concerns listed by the supervisor should be treated as a "No."

5. *Replaced social problems with social solutions.* Does the individual get or maintain an improved "Yes" evaluation in the social section? Score 1 for "Yes" and 0 for "No." Concerns listed by the supervisor should be treated as a "No."

6. *Replaced personal problems with personal solutions.* Does the individual get or maintain an improved "Yes" evaluation in the personal section? Score 1 for "Yes" and 0 for "No." Concerns listed by the supervisor should be treated as a "No."

7. *Followed through on adjustment.* Does the individual have a "Next time" goal in the work, social, or personal area where he or she received a "No" or a "Concern" for that day? Give partial credit (.33, .50, or 1, depending on how many goals were set to be worked on) for each work, social and personal section. Give partial credit (.33, .50, or 1, depending on how many goals were set to be worked on) in each area for listing a needed goal or problem or if the individual received a "Yes" in that area in the previous evaluation.

B. Data entry on a weekly basis is preferable. Monitor progress toward meeting the criterion of 80% matches for all components of the contract that were used. Identify any problems.

C. If the individual is only receiving Supervisor Feedback Cards, record the data for columns 3, 4, and 5 only.

D. Every 2 weeks, add the entries for each section of the Improvement Contract Data Summary. Divide by the total number of entries to obtain a percentage score for that section.

E. Gather all the Improvement Contract Data Summary Forms, and summarize weekly progress on the Quarterly Placement Summary. Calculate the total averages for the quarter. Review the Quarterly Placement Summary with the individual. Progress information can be used for planning and development of an annual Individual Program Plan or Individual Written Rehabilitation Plan. An example of a completed Quarterly Placement Summary is shown on page 225.

II:F:23:2

Quarterly Placement Summary

Solving On-the-Job Problems

Name: Pat Sample Jobsite: Do Drop Inn Start date: 3/15/2003

Week	Date	Percentage of days per week feed-back was required	Percentage of days per week feed-back was provided	Minimum feedback provided	Percentage of days per week the goal matched the supervisor's previous evaluation	Percentage of days per week individual's next day's plan matched the next day's goal	Followed through on adjustment
1	4/8	100%	100%	(Yes) No	100%	100%	0%
2	4/13	100%	100%	(Yes) No	100%	95%	60%
3	4/20	100%	100%	(Yes) No	100%	90%	60%
4	4/27	100%	100%	(Yes) No	100%	90%	60%
5	5/3	100%	100%	(Yes) No	100%	90%	60%
6	5/10	100%	100%	(Yes) No	100%	90%	65%
7	5/17	100%	100%	(Yes) No	100%	85%	65%
8	5/24	100%	100%	(Yes) No	100%	85%	65%
9	6/1	80%	80%	(Yes) No	100%	75%	65%
10	6/8	80%	80%	(Yes) No	100%	75%	70%
11	6/15	80%	80%	(Yes) No	100%	85%	70%
12	6/22	80%	80%	(Yes) No	100%	85%	70%
13	6/29	80%	80%	(Yes) No	100%	85%	70%
Total averages		92%	92%	100%	100%	87%	60%

Facilitate adjustments

A. Emphasize on a regular basis that the individual has a way of controlling his or her daily performance by using a problem-solving system. It is up to him or her to get control of his or her job and follow through.

1. Individualize the Improvement Contract so that the individual can use it as independently as possible. He or she needs to be able to stay in control and advance later in the job.
2. When the individual is not following his or her plan, discuss the "Plan" section of the Improvement Contract until he or she realizes this fact.
3. If the individual is getting "No"s and continues to choose the same problems and solutions, begin every day with a review. Have the individual come up with new possible problems and solutions. Have the individual review his or her current Problems and Solutions List.

B. During the beginning or early stages of problem solving, work with the individual to write down problems and solutions he or she is struggling with on the Problems and Solutions List. The individual needs to build up a list of consistent and appropriate problems and solutions.

Modify specific problems and solutions

A. Monitor Improvement Contracts and the Improvement Contract Data Summary on a regular basis.

B. If the individual is getting "No" responses or items of concern written by the supervisor for 3 or more days, or if the individual lists the same goals and plans on a regular basis that are no longer concerns or does not list goals at all, here are some solutions:

1. Develop a new Problems and Solutions List with the individual by using Improvement Contracts that have been completed in the past. Identify strengths and needs.
2. Identify recurring on-the-job problems with the individual and assist him or her in finding three possible solutions to each problem identified.
3. Meet with the supervisor to identify and discuss strong areas and areas that need improvement.
4. Problems and Solution Lists can be illustrated using pictures, if appropriate.

C. If the individual is successful with the Improvement Contract but seems to be getting bored with the format he or she is using, develop new formats for the individual to demonstrate his or her problem-solving skill.

1. Set up an audiotape recorder for the individual so that he or she can state his or her goals, plans, evaluation, and adjustment.
2. Set up a journal format for the individual.
3. DayTimers or weekly planners can be useful to the individual to track his or her daily progress and determine his or her needs and plans.

Objective 23: What If?

What if the individual did not have an opportunity to complete one part of the contract?

When recording data, write "N/A" (i.e., not applicable) in the blank section of the Improvement Contract Data Summary.

SECTION II. PLACEMENT AND FOLLOW-ALONG: SELF-MANAGEMENT

GOAL F: SOLVING ON-THE-JOB PROBLEMS

Objective 24: Monitoring Changes and Adjustments

CONTENTS

On-going support procedures
Introduce My Change Plan
Determine time lines and supports
Implement plan
Outcomes and adjustments

MATERIALS NEEDED

My Change Plan: Form A (II:F:24:1) and Form B (II:F:24:2)
Completed:
Improvement Contracts (II:F: 22:2–6)
Improvement Contract Data Summary (II:F: 23:1)
Quarterly Placement Summary (II:F:23:2)

PURPOSE

To provide a method for individuals to use their own continuous choices, develop their own methods of self-evaluation and problem solving, and implement their own interventions

LOCATION

Employment Site
Office
Community

On-going support procedures

Materials Needed

Completed:
Improvement Contracts
Improvement Contract Data Summary
Quarterly Placement Summary

A. As individuals successfully maintain their employment status they must:
    1. Become proficient in using an effective problem-solving method
    2. Schedule supervisor evaluation feedback on a daily, weekly, or bimonthly basis
    3. Make needed adjustments independently

B. The employment specialist must establish a long-term visitation schedule with the supervisor.
    1. Monitor individual-directed procedures for problem solving.
    2. Serve as a liaison for the supervisor, coworkers, and individual.
    3. Serve as a liaison for home or residential staff.
    4. Establish and maintain a system of natural supports.

C. The employment specialist must periodically determine if a change in Improvement Contracts is appropriate. Work with the individual to develop simple procedures for adapting his or her own method of problem solving and on-the-job evaluations.

D. The employment specialist must, when necessary, implement an intervention strategies package and assist the individual to develop his or her own interventions.

E. The employment specialist must continue to maintain a database through the use of the Improvement Contract Data Summary form and the Quarterly Placement Summary.

F. The employment specialist must look at changes in the business setting and monitor the need for retraining, advancement, or growth.

G. The employment specialist must 1) teach the business to respect the new employee's input and respect him or her as much as other employees, 2) teach co-workers any necessary intervention procedures, and 2) teach the employee to the point of independence and then fade and support the employer.

1. Structure the sacred principals of problem solving (i.e., self-set goals, self-developed plans, supervisor feedback, self-evaluation, self-directed adjustment) to fit the needs of the employer.

2. Be an on-call resource for the individual and the business. Teach the supervisor and co-workers to distinguish problems and concerns. Teach the supervisor and the individual to use the list of concerns by plugging concerns into the Improvement Contract.

3. Work with new supervisors to establish rapport, and educate them about problem solving. Teach them the flexibility and simplicity of the model.

4. Establish natural supports when necessary so that support is provided by co-workers and not always by the job coach.

5. Serve as a technical resource for the individual (e.g., transportation, schooling, Social Security).

6. Continue to work with the individual on career planning and possible future career moves.

H. When meeting with the individual, be productive.

1. Set up a comfortable atmosphere. Meet for lunch, ice cream, or some other relaxed occasion. Routine meetings at the jobsite may not be the best place nor the most natural environment for someone to talk about him- or herself openly.

2. Share something that has happened in your life since the last time you met. Inquire how things are going for the individual.

3. Discuss how things are going at work, such as any changes that have taken place and how are these changes affecting him or her.

4. Reinforce positive statements and discuss concerns.

5. Complete or go over the Improvement Contracts. Discuss goals as they relate to career or life advancement. Discuss plans as they relate to the goals. Listen to evaluations, and use many positive comments. Note, without reprimand, any concerns that are discussed. Acknowledge any necessary adjustment statements. Reinforce the recognition of the supervisor's concerns and the individual's efforts to correct or work on them.

6. Be aware and look for signs of boredom regarding the completion of the Improvement Contract. Discuss the format and timeline, and find out if new goals are needed.

7. Periodically check the hours worked and money earned. Note any sudden change in hours worked and how it is affecting the individual.

Introduce the My Change Plan

Materials Needed
My Change Plan: Form A or B

A. As the individual becomes proficient in his or her problem-solving skills, My Change Plan should be introduced as a long-term strategy for successful employment maintenance and as a vehicle for career advancement (see pp. 372–373).

B. My Change Plan offers a systematic procedure for the individual to periodically evaluate him- or herself and the environment in which he or she works. It affords the individual a further opportunity to evaluate his or her current needs, set goals, make plans, act on plans, evaluate the results of his or her actions, and make needed adjustments in order to meet stated goals. My Change Plan should be completed at least every 6 months or when sudden changes in attitude, motivation, performance, or behavior are noticed.

C. Form A is open ended. Individuals who choose to use this form should have some writing skills. Pictures should be used to illustrate individual preferences and outcomes when using Form B (see www.brookespublishing.com/picturebank). An example of a completed My Change Plan: Form A is shown on page 232.

D. Discuss each work, social, personal, schedule, wages, and education category in depth. Find out which existing demand areas are okay or any factors the individual may want to change. If the individual wants to make a goal change, help him or her to record the new goals in the section labeled "Goal." If the individual feels that there are no changes, then suggest they write "Okay." Accept the individual's response.

II:F:24:1

My Change Plan: Form A

Solving On-the-Job Problems

Name: Kelly Sample Date: September 15, 2003

	Work	Social	Personal	Schedule	Wages	Education
Goal	Work in an office	okay	okay	okay	okay	Improve my reading
Plan	Ask my boss					Ask Mom for help
By what month?	November					January
My results	My boss said I have to improve my reading					Mom helps me two times per week
Month	November					January
Next goal	I still want to work in an office.					I still want to work in an office.

E. If a goal is chosen, help the individual to develop several possible actions that may lead to realizing the new goal. The individual should choose one solution or plan. Place the phrase or picture representing the phrase in the section labeled "Plan."

Determine time lines and supports

A. For each "Goal" section in which a change is identified, assist the individual to determine realistic timelines that will be needed for successful change. Discuss support needs or resources the individual may use to help accomplish the written plan in the "Plan" section. Write the month the goal will be accomplished in the "By what month?" section.

Implement the plan

A. Individuals should implement the plan stating the supports needed to accomplish the goal by the date written in the row labeled "Month." The employment specialist should periodically monitor how the individual is progressing. If barriers are identified, assistance may be needed so the individual can remove them if possible.

1. Provide a copy of My Change Plan for the individual to refer to during the implementation period.
2. Initiate frequent contact and take an interest in the progress of each goal.

Outcomes and adjustments

A. Assist the individual to record the outcomes of his or her actions in the "My results" section of the plan. When using Form A, indicate the month that the action took place. When using Form B, circle the appropriate picture. When talking about the progress, the individual should determine if there is a match to the month chosen in the "My results" section. No notation of the match should be made on the form.

B. Based on the outcomes stated in the "My results" section, explore all possible adjustments that could be made to meet the goal set by the individual in the "My goals" section. Assist the individual to record his or her adjustment statement (use pictures when using Form B) in the section labeled "Next goal." Use the adjustment statements to develop a new My Change Plan, and repeat the process for the next 6 months with a new My Change Plan.

Objective 24: What If?

What if, after several opportunities to complete My Change Plan, the individual continues to state that everything is fine and no changes are needed?

Don't push too hard. The individual may be very happy, satisfied, and successful. However, make sure the individual understands that change is possible. You might want to develop a list of possible changes for each section of the plan for him or her to think about. Make sure you develop a plan list to support the items on the proposed change list. Some individuals may feel they do not have the control or ability to make the suggested changes. Assure them that they do.

10 STORIES

This chapter tells some the life stories of the more than 750 participants in the Self-Directed Employment (SDE) Program at the University of Colorado at Colorado Springs. These stories, collected during the program's 11 years of operation, represent a small part of the human drama that occurs daily in transition and supported employment programs. Unique to these stories are the methods that the individuals used as they discovered their interests, tested jobsites, and worked in the community. These individuals learned to use a system of methods and supports to achieve their own vocational goals. Although the self-directed employment methods usually worked, sometimes the approaches and procedures needed adjustment. As you read and enjoy these stories, pay particular attention to the methods. Hopefully, you will find these stories useful as you implement the Self-Directed Employment procedures.

The 20 stories in this chapter include both non–data-based narratives and case studies. To protect identities, the character names and circumstances have been changed, and many stories are composite accounts of several individuals. The first part of the chapter includes narrative stories, and the second describes data-based case studies. Stories begin during the assessment process and follow the person through their on-the-job experiences.

NARRATIVE STORIES

Mariah: My Story

In preparation for a presentation given at a national Association of People in Supported Employment (APSE) conference in Denver, Mariah wrote the following story about her job search. It is here as she wrote it, with only identifying names and places removed. A more poignant message, typical in the lives of those involved in supported employment, comes through just below the story line—the liberating effect of choosing her own goal. Here's Mariah's story in her own words, with only punctuation edited in order to keep Mariah's voice.

When I was a senior at my high school in my staffing, I was told about the various programs available after graduation. I decided I wanted to attend the self-determination project at UCCS [University of Colorado at Colorado Springs]. I met with a counselor at vocational rehabilitation. She thought it was a good idea. She told me vocational rehabilitation would pay for this program for me.

I have been in the self-determination program since August. I had my evaluation with Eva. Then I went on six job shadowing. I went to a day care center, hotel laundry, store, restaurant, a small family grocery store, and worked in the Special Education Office at UCCS. After all those tryouts, I still felt that I wanted to do store work. All during this time, I attended the Thursday job skills classes.

I worked with a job coach. She helped me learn how to fill out job applications. She took me to fill out applications to many places. I put in over 20 applications. At first, it was really hard for me to ask for an application because I was shy. But she told me I needed to go out of my comfort zone to ask for an application. She told me to just go into a store and have a smile on my face and say, "May I have an application, please?" She was a big help to me when I got discouraged. She told me that you don't always get the first job that you put in an application for. Don't worry, she would say. That just wasn't the job for you. It will come. I know the perfect job is still out there waiting for you. Just be patient. It is better to wait for the right one than take one that you won't like and be unhappy. She told me to keep trying, Mariah. I know that job is out there, Mariah. We just haven't found it yet.

She also told me about what questions they would ask me. My job coach pretended that she was the employer and asked me some interview questions. This practice really helped me gain confidence and courage. It helped me to be calm in the interview.

On December the 4th, I was hired at Wal-Mart. I had to get a drug test, and fill out an employee attitude survey. I wanted part time instead of full time. I work Monday, Tuesday, Thursday, and Friday 9:15–3:15. I had a 90-day training period. I have just finished with that and had an evaluation with my supervisor. I got a raise. I now make $6.25 per hour. I am called an associate because I am a part-time worker. I work 20 hours a week. I get paid every 2 weeks, I have an employee card. I get 10% off of everything in the store, even at the snack bar.

I work in soft lines. That is in the women's, men and children's departments. Twice a week, I water the plants. My uniform is a Wal-Mart vest and dark pants. Sometimes I can wear dresses and my vest. I ride the city bus to work. I went to ARC [Association for Retarded Citizens] and got a handicapped card so I can buy the pass for $.35 a ride.

I want to thank everyone for helping me get a job. I like my job, and it is in the area I was interested in. I am glad I waited and kept trying. I just want to say hang in there and be successful in life. It will happen if you stick to your goal.

Lesson from Mariah's Story This is the story of a shy young woman who stayed the course. It describes her excitement about learning to go out of her comfort zone to ask for applications. She explains that she had to learn how to fill out an application and then complete 20 applications in her effort to find employment and become a self-sufficient, productive person. Her joy is evident as she describes her schedule, department, title, uniform, and the other particulars of her job. Through the self-discovery process during the SDE program, Mariah was able to gain employment at a job she wanted. In so doing, she learned about planning, setting goals, expanding her comfort zone, being persistent, and developing patience in pursuit of her life goals.

Joe: Now Owns a Business

Joe acquired a brain injury from a drug overdose and as a result can only use one side of his body. During our first meeting, he mentioned what he does around the house, and said that he liked to mow his lawn. He described a technique of putting a crescent wrench onto the handle of the lawn mower, which enables him to control the mower with one hand.

On his initial Jobs I Want to Do form, Joe chose, in order of importance, outdoor maintenance, animal care, janitorial work, office work, and store work. His Characteristics I Like form reflected his job choices, too. He wanted part-time work in the daytime that was outside and allowed him to have some physical activity. He designated these as his four most important characteristics. When we discussed the tasks involved and the availability of office work, Joe decided that he could not compete in this job area. This left three job areas to explore and test.

Joe went directly to the Testing Choices phase and completed a series of internships that matched his preferred job choices and characteristics. Joe tried store work first, and his overall characteristics match from the Characteristics I Like versus What Is Here form was in the 80% range. He liked putting stock back on shelves and organizing the merchandise. Joe did the tasks accurately but slowly. Next, Joe went to a dog kennel to see if he liked this job as much as he thought he would. The job consisted of spraying the runways and kennels with disinfectant, scrubbing the walls and floors of the runs, and feeding and watering the dogs. Speed was once again a concern. His Work, Social, Personal, and Task Improvement forms showed a 100% self-evaluation skills match, and his performance was rated as "Great" in nearly all categories but speed. The Characteristics I Like versus What Is Here form showed only a 75% match, which was not quite as high as it was for store work.

After 1 day at the kennel, Joe wanted to try outdoor maintenance. Joe arrived at the outdoor maintenance site equipped with a lawnmower, rake, shovels, push broom, pen, and paper! The Characteristics I Like versus What Is Here form indicated a 95% match. The four most important characteristics ranged from 75% to 100%. The one characteristic that did not match was Joe's preference for a part-time job. Unfortunately, the available outdoor maintenance jobs were full-time work, and Joe only wanted part-time. His evaluations at this jobsite were uniformly positive.

His specific evaluations reflected his very good work skills, with the exception of speed. His decision-making skills from the Adaptability Graph, including self-evaluation and goal-setting skills, were above 90%. Joe said several times how good it was to be working again. He expressed a preference for outdoor maintenance. He said, at one point, "This is for me—getting dirty!" With support from staff and the local rehabilitation services office, he started his own outdoor maintenance business. He got $100 worth of business the first day and has been going strong ever since.

Lesson from Joe's Story Joe's understanding of job characteristics drove his final placement decision. He knew what he wanted but needed support to get it. Placement staff and his counselor from the Colorado Division of Vocational Rehabilitation worked together to help Joe start his own lawn care business. Being his own boss, his only job limitation (i.e., working slowly) was not a problem.

Richard: Learned to Do What He Liked

Richard enrolled in the supported employment program immediately after graduating from high school. School staff reported that he had limited academic and vocational skills and did not express himself easily or fully. Reports indicated that he could read functional words and that he had very basic math addition skills. One of his individualized education program (IEP) goals was to learn to count up to eight items.

On his initial Jobs I Want to Do form, Richard's job choices included store work, food service, child care, and maid service. Richard verbally stated that he did not want to do janitorial work. He had done janitorial work as part of his school transition program. He preferred food service and told the assessment staff that he wanted a food preparation job.

In the Exploring Choices phase, Richard shadowed store work at a drug store and food preparation in a Mexican restaurant. Although Richard stated that he liked this the drug store and could do everything there, his supervisor evaluations told a different story. The supervisor said he required constant encouragement to stay on task, and he received many prompts to complete the tasks successfully.

Next, Richard tried food preparation at a Mexican restaurant. He had a difficult time applying pressure with knives to cut vegetables, did not like working with kitchen equipment, and was frightened by the noisy equipment. His Work, Personal, and Task Improvement forms noted the need for improvement in personal and work skills. He neglected his personal hygiene, had trouble stacking dishes, and tended to leave too much food on the dirty plates. But he still wanted to do this type of work. He said, "It's for me!"

The staff arranged an extended internship at a cafeteria where they thought he had a good chance of getting hired if he demonstrated that he could do the job. While at the cafeteria, the staff carved tasks for him to do. At the end of each workday, he reviewed the areas that needed improvement and developed strategies to improve his performance. The assessment staff used many of the procedures identified in Chapters 7, 8, and 9. The daily performance feedback, strategy identification, and assistance in implementing his change strategies enabled Richard to dramatically improve his performance. After about a month, he worked accurately and independently, came to work on time, and improved his personal hygiene. Before leaving the site each day, Richard thanked the manager of the cafeteria for letting him learn how to work in the cafeteria, and shook his hand before leaving.

Richard liked this jobsite very much; the overall Characteristics I Like versus What Is Here forms showed matches ranging from 80% to 90%. His four most important characteristics matched the jobsite's characteristics 100%. On the last day of the internship session, the assessment staff noticed a "Help Wanted" sign hanging in the window, picked up an application, and helped Richard fill it out. The manager of the cafeteria called Richard a few days later and asked him when he could start. Richard loves working at the cafeteria. His job performance now matches that of his fellow employees.

Lesson from Richard's Story After the Exploring Choices phase, Richard's most preferred choice remained food service work. From the internship at the Mexican restaurant, staff learned that general food preparation work was not a good job match. The staff then carved internship tasks within a food service setting that matched both his skills and preferences. As a result of the internship experience and job carving, he obtained and maintained a cafeteria job. Assessment sites often provide opportunities to develop placements, especially those where job carving identifies unique employer needs that match a worker's skills and interests.

Nina: Listen and Do

Nina was a young woman with mental retardation who had exceptionally well-developed social skills. She liked to dress in western clothes and loved country-western line dancing. At the beginning of assessment, we wanted to know how she learned new line dances, as these are complex and the speed often changes. She said that she watches the dance performed, tries it, then sits down and watches once again to get the details. However, a year-old knee injury affected her hobby and job. After the knee injury, she needed to give up her cleaning job because of the physical endurance needed. She now wanted a job that combined sitting and standing to lessen the strain on her knee.

Her initial job choices included kennel work, office work, maid service work, and warehouse work. The characteristics she chose as the most important described work that was full time, enabled her to sit down, and offered a different job every day. She also expressed a preference for working with lots of people around, at an easy job, inside, and in the mornings. The appearance of a jobsite did not matter to her, but she wanted work that involved thinking and attention to detail, that happened in the daytime, and that was in a large business. Because Nina was an experienced worker, she went directly to the Testing Choices phase, bypassing the Exploring Choices phase.

Nina agreed that maid service exceeded her physical limitations, but she wanted to try out the others. She completed internships at two different store jobs, one that involved shelving merchandise and one where she placed new compact discs in security trays and priced them. She did not particularly like store work, even though she was good at both jobs. She tried kennel work next. She liked this job and did well, but physical demands and holiday work kept her from pursuing employment. Next, she completed an internship in an office. She needed constant supervision and lacked basic computer keyboarding skills. While at the office, she verbally expressed interest in factory work. She interned at a bicycle-helmet manufacturing facility assembling straps and buckles. She learned this complex assembly task quickly.

Of all the places where she interned, she obtained the best Social and Personal Improvement forms skill evaluations at the bike factory, but the job didn't match her task or job preferences. For instance, on the Task Improvement form, she liked only two of the four assigned duties. Also, she received low evaluations on the Work Improvement form for not maintaining a good pace for the job, not working accurately, not coming to work on time (she was extremely late on one occasion), and not working independently. She replaced most of her negative evaluations with positive ones, and for the most part, her evaluations matched those of her job coach. She had trouble in two areas of decision making: choosing the areas for the next day's goals and setting goals based on the previous day's evaluations. Nina did not admit to making errors, a trait consistent with her reluctance to set goals.

During this internship, an individual with visual impairments began his internship at the same site. Nina taught the new worker the assembly tasks within five trials. As a result of sharing her skills, Nina became more enthusiastic, pleasant, helpful, patient, and proud of her ability to help. Nina decided then that she wanted to pursue human service work, and soon afterwards she did.

Lesson from Nina's Story This is a good example of how informed choice is obtained. Nina simply did not know what she wanted to do. Because of her physical work limitations, she needed to find an alternate available community job matching her skills and preferences. The self-directed assessment approach provided the staff with an active listening method to help Nina determine alternate choices.

Several internships are often needed to help individuals identify job preferences. Learning what someone does not want is often as important as finding out what someone does want. As individuals observe and interact in a varied setting, the opportunity to make choices expands when new options occur. In Nina's case, her opportunity to teach someone else a task revealed a potentially satisfying career. Although this particular situation was not planned, the different internships provided her with the experience of new options to choose from. Plus, the employment specialist's observations at the jobsite made other opportunities possible.

Renee: The Match Minimized Behavior Problems

Renee, a recent high school graduate, entered our program shortly after losing her job as a child care worker at a children's entertainment center, which she got while in high school. School staff warned us that her extremely inappropriate questions, aggressiveness, and other inappropriate behaviors would cause problems at assessment and placement sites. We decided to give her the opportunity to try out various jobs. Often, a job match is determined when typical behavior problems do not arise at a particular site. Despite her recent firing, Renee decided that she wanted to continue to pursue child care. She also chose animal care, store work, and office work.

When shadowing store work, Renee paid little attention to the tasks and required many prompts to focus on watching the workers. At the office internship site, Renee's poor task and social skills caused problems. She obtained a 50% match on the Characteristics I Like versus What Is Here forms. Renee did not like office work; she found it too challenging, and it did not provide enough social interaction.

Renee next completed a shadowing and internship experience at a child care center. Renee constantly obstructed others' work, and she asked many irrelevant questions. She presented the teachers with more problems than the children did. Even though she obtained a 75% match on the Characteristics I Like versus What Is Here forms, she could not do the tasks, and the supervisor reported that she would not hire a person with Renee's skill level and inappropriate social skills.

Renee needed a jobsite that kept her very busy so that she would not have time for distractions. She found such a jobsite at a busy skating rink running the snack bar, taking money, and serving people. The snack bar presented tasks similar to those found in store work, one of Renee's job choices. The skating rink charged for everything in multiples of 25 cents; as a result, Renee counted change quickly and accurately.

She liked the skating rink job better than any other jobsite she experienced. Her Characteristics I Like versus What Is Here forms showed matches that ranged from 68% to 93%. Her four most important characteristics matched 100%. Because the skating rink was so busy, Renee had no time to ask questions or make statements that might be perceived as inappropriate or rude by her coworkers, supervisors, or customers.

Renee's performance improved over time. Initially she received poor work, social, personal, and task improvement evaluations, much like those from the office and child care center. After receiving task instruction, having time to practice, and getting feedback, her performance improved dramatically. Renee did a very good job adjusting day to day. She set the next day's goals to improve negative performance evaluations. She was soon hired to assist the operation of the concession stand. Renee found permanent employment at the skating rink.

Lesson from Renee's Story Renee came to the program with a prediction for failure. Finding a characteristic, task, and job environment match minimized the likelihood of inappropriate behaviors occurring. For Renee, a creative internship placement led to a successful job.

Inappropriate behavior at jobsites occur for numerous reasons. When a person enters the job match process with a history of behavior problems, at least one of two options exists. First, as in Renee's case, a location must be identified that matches the person's skills and interests. A good match will often reduce the problem behaviors. Second, a jobsite must be developed where the person's behavior matches co-workers' and supervisors' expectations.

To further illustrate, John, another participant in the supported employment program, had been fired from numerous jobs for inappropriate social behavior before he came into our program. Rather than attempting to change his behavior in the few weeks that we had to work with him, we focused on finding a job that he liked in which his social skills matched the setting. After a detailed job match assessment process, he went to work at a recycling plant where his behavior matched that of his colleagues. He stayed at this job for almost 2 years—the most successful job he had ever had.

Martha: The Job Match Made Success Happen

Martha, a 44-year-old homemaker with paranoid schizophrenia and severe learning disabilities, came into our program with *no* past paid work experience. Martha had lived in abusive situations throughout her childhood and teenage years and recently attempted suicide when her boyfriend broke off their relationship.

Martha completed our assessment process with preferences for store and warehouse work but wanted any kind of job *immediately.* Martha and the job developer believed that assembly work in a large factory closely resembled warehouse work. This related match, plus Martha's desire for an immediate job, prompted her to accept a job assembling bicycle helmets. After 2 weeks of satisfactory performance, her production rate fell far below standards, and she lost this job. A second assembly job lasted a couple of weeks longer, but she eventually lost this one, too.

Martha realized that not only was the job important, but her preferences, skills, limits, and support needs had to match the job environment. Martha needed a business that would provide support and give her time to learn how to do the job without a lot of pressure. We found such a place at a nonprofit consignment store sorting, tagging, and pricing clothing in the backroom warehouse environment.

Martha thrived in this environment. The Supervisor Evaluation Cards, Characteristics I Like versus What Is Here, Jobs I Want forms verified the job match. Martha experienced few problems on the job but missed work for a week or more several times due to disability-related episodic issues. The business understood and kept the job open for her, one of their most productive workers.

Lesson from Martha's Story Martha initially didn't care what she did—she just wanted a job quickly. So she got a job and then another; neither of which worked out. After two failures, Martha agreed to look at her preferences and characteristic matches to guide a job match. Until she experienced failure, she did not want to consider preferences and support factors. If we had mandated a job match assessment process prior to placement, Martha would have most likely left the program. The failures counted against the overall success of the program but ended up producing success for Martha.

Steve: Part-Time Jobs Led to Full-Time Employment

Steve was a 33-year-old man who had mental health problems and Usher's syndrome (resulting in a significant hearing impairment and a gradual loss of sight) when he entered the supported employment program. He had not been employed for 4 years. Based on his own skill assessment, Steve wanted a job at a local school for students with hearing and vision impairments.

Steve started our assessment program knowing exactly what he wanted to do. The Initial Job and Task Preferences Graphs confirmed Steve's wishes. We bypassed the remainder of the assessment process and proceeded to the placement phase. After a few months of persistent job development, he secured a part-time interpreter's position, working 10 hours per week at $7.00 per hour with a promise for increased hours. In the first month of Steve's employment, he also obtained a private contract to teach sign language, increasing his workweek to 13 hours. A year later, Steve's record and references were sufficient to seek permanent employment as a teacher's aide or interpreter. Steve established monthly goals and plans to make this happen. At the beginning of the school year, a local school district employed Steve full-time to work as a one-on-one interpreter at $12.53 per hour. He finally had his dream job.

Lessons from Steve's Story One supported employment belief is that every placement should be at a job working at least 20 hours per week from the first day of employment. Steve illustrates the myth behind this belief—especially for people with unique job interests. Steve got his dream job, but it took a series of part-time jobs, each building on the other, in order to make the connections, establish a work record, and build references to move into his dream position.

Larry: Won the Worker of the Month Award

Larry, a 20-year-old high school graduate with mental retardation, came into the supported employment program directly out of high school. After he finished the assessment phase, library and store work emerged as his two top-ranked job choices. Larry secured a courtesy clerk job at a grocery earning above minimum wage and working 20 hours per week.

We began collecting daily, then weekly Supervisor Evaluation Cards, which the supervisors used to describe his excellent performance. Because of a lack of any problems, we did not implement an improvement contract. After 2 weeks, Larry completed the Characteristics I Like versus What Is Here form, the Job and Tasks I Like forms, and the Can I Do This Job? form, which verified an excellent preference match to his current job. In the beginning, we met with Larry twice per week. As Larry maintained his excellent performance, we gradually decreased our on-site visits from once per week to once per month. During these follow-up visits, we completed follow-along procedures and discussed career advancement.

After about a year on the job, Larry received the grocery store's Worker of the Month Award. Excellent work performance brought increased work hours. His next step up would be a promotion to a customer service position. He is very involved socially at work, and he is finishing up driving lessons in hopes of getting his driver's license.

Lesson from Larry's Story More often than not, the supported employment process works well. Larry represents just one of many individuals who learned what he wanted to do, did it, and became successful. Because of a lack of openings in the city's libraries, Larry first job choice was not an option. He happily entered his second choice. This is why the self-directed assessment approach identifies at least two top-ranked job choices.

Pam: My Change Plan Identified a Switch in Preferences

Pam's initial assessment indicated that she was a 23-year-old woman with mental retardation and low adaptive behavior scores who moved slowly and initiated few conversations. During assessment, her job choices were somewhat scattered, but she appeared to prefer food service or store work. After entering the job development phase of our program, she completed two internships to check out her inconsistent job choices. One was completed at a store and the other at a fast-food restaurant.

While participating in these internships, Pam completed the Characteristics I Like versus What Is Here form and the Job and Tasks I Like form daily. We set up a match contract for her to use daily to monitor her performance. We wanted to see how realistic she would be in evaluating her own performance. During these internships, Pam smiled a lot but spoke very little. The internships resulted in a strong preference for food service. She also performed her best work at this location.

Pam became employed for the same food service chain where she completed an internship but at a different site. Pam worked as a bun warmer for about 20 hours per week at minimum wage. This was the same job she had trained for during her internship. We set up an improvement contract for Pam to complete daily. After 1 week of employment in the new restaurant, she completed the Characteristics I Like versus What Is Here form and the Job and Tasks I Like form. The preference and skills forms indicated that Pam truly did prefer and could do this job.

Pam happily maintained her job. The problem-solving system, in which she used the improvement contracts, became a part of her routine and helped her maintain satisfactory work performance and social behavior. Over the years, Pam has had a few problems along the way, but these do not get in the way of her success. She usually corrects any concerns the supervisor has the next day. About every 6 months, Pam completes a change plan to determine if she is still happy with this job or would want to move onto another. On her last change plan, she asked if she could wrap potatoes and stack the french fry rack. She developed a plan to facilitate this change and presented her request to the supervisor. She soon began doing this new job.

Lesson from Pam's Story Pam's story demonstrates a key to long-term job success. Often, jobs are inadvertently sabotaged because workers' preferences change, and they do not communicate their desire for change in a proactive manner. These individuals often do not show up for work or they come in late or decrease their productivity level until they are terminated. To decrease the likelihood of this happening, Pam completed the proactive My Change Plan form twice a year. The change plan provides a window to observe a preference switch. As her preferences shifted, Pam created a plan to make these changes. If this would involve leaving the present job for a different job, this change could happen in an orderly and respectful manner. This planned departure helps to preserve the placement for a future worker, and provides a reference for the new job.

Judy: Cooperation with Families Leads to Multiple Jobs

When Judy began the supported employment program, she was almost 21 years old and completing her last year of high school transition programming. Her parents were very knowledgeable and influential in their child's life and in the lives of many other individuals with developmental disabilities and their families. The family's goal was for Judy to secure a permanent job after high school.

The parents first secured Judy a public school–funded work-study job in the dining room of a large business. She was paid sub-minimum wages from the public school transition program to work 20 hours per week as a kitchen helper. The parents asked us to work with the school's transition team to facilitate a smooth transition from her public school–subsidized job to one where the school paid her at least minimum wage.

Judy eventually obtained three part-time jobs. Judy started her day by working at the dining hall as a lounge attendant for 10 hours per week. Next, she walked to a near-by restaurant, where she worked as a custodian for 4 hours per week. After finishing lunch, she walked back to the library, where she worked as a library assistant for an hour per day. Judy's parents developed the dining hall job and also secured the job at the library. We developed the custodian position at a nearby restaurant. Together, these jobs provided her sufficient hours.

Lesson from Judy's Story Judy wanted to work as many hours a week as possible. Unfortunately, she could not work any more hours at the dining hall or library. Working collaboratively with Judy and her parents, we developed a third placement. Together, these three jobs provided her varied tasks and sufficient work hours. At times, uniquely developed jobs do not provide sufficient hours. As in Judy's case, she worked at three sites to gain sufficient hours.

Alan: The Road Often Has Detours

Alan, a 29-year-old man with Down syndrome, a history of heart and knee surgeries, and speech impediments, was one of the first participants in the supported employment program. Alan had spent the previous 8 years in a local sheltered workshop, and as he said, "It was time for change." He was adamant about getting a community job. Alan's dream was to get a job in an office. To reach this goal, we used extended internships to carve jobs and build coworker support. The road ahead would be a rocky one, but it would eventually lead to "an outside job." Alan began his job development internship at a local sports training center, doing collating and filing. Because of the numerous social and job concerns, we implemented improvement contracts to change his grooming skills, argumentative on-the-job interactions, inappropriate social skills, and poor work productivity. This internship site did not turn into a placement.

In the next few months, Alan completed two more office internships. During these internships, similar behaviors surfaced, but with each internship and continued use of his improvement contracts, Alan's work and social skills improved. However, one thing became very apparent. The likelihood of employment in the clerical field for Alan was very slim. As a result of completing a series of preference and skill assessments, food service became an alternative job choice.

We procured a job for Alan at a quaint sandwich shop as a dishwasher working 9 hours per week at minimum wage. The owner and staff were great with Alan and had high expectations for the quality of his work. Alan thrived in this setting. By this time, Alan was using, understanding, enjoying, and benefiting from the feedback provided by the Improvement Contract. He willingly completed the forms every work day. Unfortunately, the business closed. Although he had a good experience in food service, he wanted to try office work again.

Next, Alan went to work in an office as a minister's assistant. Alan enjoyed this experience, but the part-time job ended because of a lack of work available for Alan to do. Next, we found a placement for Alan at a local restaurant as a host and busser, working 15 hours per week at minimum wage. Alan did very well at this job. He continued to complete daily improvement contracts, even though we suggested that he could do them once per week. One year later, new owners made drastic changes. Duties were changed, shifts were changed, hours were reduced, and several employees were laid off. Alan was kept on, but his hours were reduced steadily until he was only working 2 hours per week. He was also taken off lounge duties and told that this was the responsibility of the manager. He was instead assigned to do work he considered demeaning—picking up cigarette butts in the parking lot.

A new placement was developed at another local restaurant. Alan was hired as a bun warmer, working 16 hours per week at minimum wage. The restaurant was close to his apartment, and the hours were perfect. Alan has difficulty with endurance, so the short shifts he worked and the location made this an ideal job. Today, Alan continues to work at the restaurant.

Lesson from Alan's Story Like people without disabilities, beginning workers with disabilities often shift jobs during their first several years of working. The profile of individuals with disabilities who enter the workplace for the first time is often like Alan's. He knew what he wanted but needed to modify his initial dream because of a lack of availability. He chose another job and then had to move several times until he found a stable position. Alan was able to persevere in his job search, which led to his success.

Bob: He Kept On Trying

Bob started doing manual labor jobs when he was 9 years old. In school, he participated in football and wrestling. In his teens and early adulthood, he was a boxer, a bicycle racer, a body builder, and a professional rodeo cowboy. When he was 24 years old, Bob was working three jobs. One evening while delivering horses to a nearby ranch, he fell asleep at the wheel and had a major accident in which he was thrown through the windshield. The doctors believed Bob survived his accident because of his excellent physical condition, the result of many years of manual labor and bodybuilding. Bob was in a coma for 6 months and remained in a rehabilitation hospital for another 6 months.

Bob came to our program 2 years after his traffic accident. He had sustained a traumatic brain injury and had many physical limitations:

- He was in a wheelchair.
- He was only able to lift 10–25 pounds.
- He had poor but improving standing balance.
- His reflexes on the left side were slow.
- His visual/perceptual speed was impaired.
- His fine motor skills were impaired.
- His ability to work at a fast pace was limited but improving.
- His mental endurance was poor.
- He was not realistic about his capabilities.

Bob wanted his old lifestyle back. He had little patience for our procedures, our assistance, or our suggestions. His assessment took a long time and was not very successful as a result of his frequent absences. One internship began the chain of events that changed Bob's life. Bob agreed to do an internship at a local movie theater, where he would work in the box office. The first day went fine. On the second day, Bob called and said he would have to cancel due to a headache. Later, he called and said that he decided that he no longer wanted to continue the internship at the theater. He also stated that he was not sure if he was ready for a job.

We knew that if we continued with our standard procedures we would lose him, so we went in a different direction. We contacted a new horseback riding therapy program. Because they only had volunteers, Bob would not be able to get a paid job, but it still seemed like a great low-pressure setting for him to volunteer. Bob reluctantly agreed to try helping at the stables, but he did not think he could do much. Eventually, he found many tasks that he could complete. He started feeling good about himself again. He was back in the outdoors on a ranch with animals he loved. Bob thrived in this setting, and he was able to do more and more as time went by. Eventually, he was able to ride again—an impossible feat according to the information in his records.

Three months after riding, Bob said he was ready to go to work. He was soon hired as an arcade attendant. He excelled at this job and made many friends. The location of the arcade was ideal. It was close enough for Bob to get to work on his own. Also during this period, Bob started using crutches more and more. Bob worked at the arcade for about a year until it closed. We returned to the movie theater where he first started. Bob interviewed with a new manager, who was very impressed. Bob was hired on the spot to work in the box office. Bob quickly learned this job and established an immediate and very close friendship with his boss. The manager was new to the area, and he and Bob were about the same age. Bob began showing him the town, and they frequently watched videos together at Bob's house. Bob learned all he could, as quick as he could about the movie business. He ended up on the management track at the movie theater and started talking about opening his own gym.

Lesson from Bob's Story Read again the first paragraphs of Bob's story, and you will see just how far Bob has come. Before Bob would think about working, he needed a successful experience. Volunteering at the horse therapy program provided him with an excellent opportunity to regain his self-confidence. If we had tried to use only the procedures described in Chapters 3–9, he would have left the program. It is definitely an asset to be able to adapt and adjust the program to meet each individual's needs.

Sam: Satisfaction Remained Elusive

Sam came to our program with these diagnoses: dysthymia (i.e., low-level depression), posttraumatic stress disorder, avoidant personality disorder, very low self-esteem, and lumbar strain with a lifting restriction. At one of the initial meetings with the vocational rehabilitation office, Sam said he

- Felt hopeless
- Had lost his direction in life
- Was in school and had an assignment hanging over his head all semester, afraid to get started
- Had decided not to apply for Social Security because his family considers it a form of welfare
- Had a real fear of going to work but wanted to do so

The rehabilitation counselor, in consultation with Sam, decided that he should wait before seeking employment.

About 9 months later, Sam entered our program. He had completed his bachelor's degree in psychology and was ready to start a human services career. Sam said that he would be interested in working with the people who had mental health issues or developmental disabilities. He preferred an entry-level counseling job but was willing to start in any entry-level human service position. We skipped assessment and went directly to placement.

During the first month, Sam seemed to be dragging his feet whenever we would give him job leads that matched his expressed preferences. In the second month, Sam followed up on a job lead to work as an enclave site supervisor, where he would be working with individuals with severe developmental disabilities. Sam was interviewed and hired. He worked about 15 hours per week at slightly above minimum wage.

Conditions were so strenuous at this site that the lead supervisor quit just 3 days after Sam started. Sam accepted the position of lead supervisor, working a few more hours per week at about $2 per hour more. Sam never received training for this position, the contract he supervised was under bid, and the staff he was given could not do the job. Sam found himself doing the majority of the work and working into all hours of the night. His hours were now up to about 32 hours per week. At this point Sam told me that he wanted to quit but not until he had another job. So, he kept working until another job became available.

During the next few months, Sam did not follow up on several job leads, and many very good opportunities passed by. Finally, Sam got a job as a full-time case manager with a local supported employment agency. Sam accepted the position. By the end of the first week, he quit, stating that it was just too much to learn, too many people in close surroundings, and too much responsibility. He was not ready for this. He said that his old job at the enclave was becoming more appealing. He went back to the original agency and was given a job coach position. Within a few weeks, Sam become bored with this job and wanted more of a challenge. He got a job as a full-time workshop supervisor position, and he has maintained that position.

Lesson from Sam's Story He is working in the field of his choice, and he has maintained employment. Sam often was dissatisfied with any job he had, and he changed jobs to experience what he thought might be a better situation. He went through several jobs until he found one that fit him. His job match process went beyond initial assessment and into placement. His initial match got him into the field he wanted to work, but he needed to explore that field in order to determine what he really wanted. His job switching shows up in the cumulative data presented in Chapter 12. On one hand, job switching like Sam's could be viewed as a negative; on the other hand, his exploration resulted in a permanent job that he liked and was successful at.

Amy Sue: The New Supervisor Syndrome

Amy Sue was one of the first four participants in the Colorado Springs Self-Directed Employment Program. Records indicated that Amy Sue had moderate to severe mental retardation, epilepsy, an eating disorder, poor balance and coordination, and very poor communication skills. The records also said that Amy Sue was very shy and spent most of her time twirling her lower lip. The information in her old records did not state any positive features or strengths. We immediately questioned this report after meeting Amy Sue. We saw that she was happy, smiled a lot, made friends quickly, and knew what she wanted to do. After completing the assessment process Amy Sue expressed consistent interest in office or store work.

We began job development by having Amy Sue complete an extended internship at a major insurance company's office. For over a month while she worked at different tasks, we noticed who did what and what did not get finished. After completing the internship, we sat down with Amy Sue's supervisor and discussed the possibility of a job for Amy Sue. At first, the supervisor said that the company did not have any jobs available. We then explained what we learned during a month of observations. Upper-level employees were completing many simple tasks (e.g., opening mail, stuffing envelopes, stamping envelopes, filing) when they had time, and often these tasks went undone. The employees also hated doing these tasks, as it kept them from more important work. The tasks were very crucial to the business, but they were not completed in a timely fashion. We also talked about costs. Did the company really want upper-level employees completing entry-level tasks at upper-level salaries? These points were very convincing.

Amy Sue was hired as an office assistant working 20 hours per week at above minimum wage. Amy Sue worked at this site for more than 5 years. Amy Sue needed a lot of training before she could accomplish the many tasks involved. Picture-cued improvement contracts, task schedules, behavior programs, Characteristics I Like versus What Is Here forms, Job and Tasks I Like forms, and Can I Do This Job? forms were used throughout the process. Amy Sue's supervisors and coworkers were friendly, appreciated Amy Sue, and took her with them to many office social functions.

Unfortunately, after several years, the company acquired automated mailing machines, and Amy Sue was unable to operate these complex computer-based machines. She was assigned to other duties. Then, three mergers and corporate takeovers changed the office. Amy Sue's job responsibilities changed, then increased. The new supervisors finally decided that Amy Sue could not meet these new demands, and she was fired. She lost her health benefits, a good job, and association with her work friends.

After months of renewed job development, we found a job for Amy Sue at a local discount store. Her tasks were to straighten shelves and take care of defective items. Her job went from daytime to night, which resulted in transportation problems. The city buses did not run late enough, and the residential staff would not transport Amy Sue at these late hours. Our staff took Amy Sue to and from the jobsite for several weeks as we tried to come up with alternatives, but we could not find any. Amy Sue had to quit the job.

Amy Sue's next job was at a clothing store near her home. She placed clothes on hangers and then placed them in the rack for 18 hours per week at minimum wage. After several weeks on the job, where she received positive supervisor evaluations, a new boss changed her quota to 10 racks of clothes every day, and Amy Sue was completing about four racks. The new supervisor gave Amy Sue 30 days to get her production up to seven racks per day, then up to 10 racks per day in 2 months. The outcome is easy to guess.

Lesson from Amy Sue's Story Amy Sue lost two successful jobs because her supervisors changed. Despite two corporate mergers and automation she maintained her first job for several years. However, the third corporate change put new supervisors in Amy Sue's office. When Amy Sue got laid off, the new supervisors told her that they needed employees who could complete multiple tasks and could take over duties of another worker if that person is out of the office. This happened again a few months later at a different jobsite.

We saw this pattern repeat itself, so we often started calling it the "new supervisor syndrome." The syndrome became a problem usually when the person with a disability worked at tasks carved from other positions. Time after time, we saw successful workers who had received repeated positive evaluations terminated by new supervisors. Shortly after new supervisors started, the person with disabilities would be laid off. The supervisor would cite productivity problems, inability to complete a variety of tasks, decreased business, and similar concerns. Follow-up staff were not at a jobsite with enough frequency to always learn about the supervisory change and so could not advocate for continued employment. Co-workers were often at a disadvantage because they also had to adjust to a new supervisor and thus could not successfully advocate for the person's continued employment.

John: Success over Time

John was 26 years old and had a long record of starting and stopping various jobs. He would get a job, and within a few months, he would either quit or get fired. He had been expelled from all the other employment programs in the city, and we were his last chance. John had a dual diagnosis of mental retardation and mental illness.

The assessment process indicated John wanted factory or store work. Because of his poor work history, we thought that completing a successful factory internship at a site that was hiring would be the best method to find a placement. John did well during the internship and was hired for a 6-week position, with the promise that this may lead to a permanent job. During the first week, John called in sick twice. The next week, his supervisor listed several concerns: he poked others, called others names, came in late from breaks and lunches, and needed to increase production. In the third week, John kept falling asleep on the job. After checking, the residential staff said that he was staying up most of the night. The next week John's stepfather died, so he took off 3 days for the funeral, and then he took some time off to drive his wife on different errands. At the end of the sixth week, John decided to ask about a permanent job. His supervisor told him that the company was not hiring, so John quit on the spot, saying, "You can't fire me. I quit."

Over the next 6 years, John had found and then lost more than 20 different jobs. His success in these jobs could be measured by his degree of involvement in our program and whether he was completing his improvement contracts. When John was active and meeting with us, he would generally do well. The times that he met with us coincided with his more lengthy job experiences. But as soon as he would drop out of sight or not complete contracts, he would usually get fired or quit his job. The same concerns followed him from job to job: impulsivity, poor attendance, tardiness, poor temper, and frequent illness or injury. He would take off work to see doctors or to take his wife to the doctor, as she was also often sick. When supervisors would talk with him about improvements he needed to make, he would quit. We measured success by the increasing length of time he stayed with a job. The last job he had with our program lasted almost 22 months, the longest he had ever kept the same job.

Lesson from John's Story During the time we knew John, we supported him at four jobs. In addition, he had 16 other jobs that we knew about. When he interacted with our program, he saw increasingly longer periods of success. John, like many individuals in our program, found success when he used the improvement contracts to solicit feedback and then make changes in his on-the-job performance. Once he quit using the improvement contracts, he lost his jobs. We would always welcome John back into our program because with each try he worked a longer and longer stretch. For John, getting the job was easy and as John learned more about what he wanted and used his improvement forms, the jobs lasted longer. His last job lasted almost 2 years—a major success!

Paula: When Do You Quit?

Paula was 21 years old when she came to our program with her records indicating that she had a learning disability, cerebral palsy, a dependent personality disorder with avoidant traits, attention deficit disorder, and hemiparesis (i.e., slight paralysis affecting one side of the body). Like so many others, her records indicated no strengths. As always, we ignored these negative records and started asking her what she wanted. Paula's finished assessment stated that her top-ranked job choices were working at a car wash and doing car detailing.

We started job development by securing an internship for Paula at a neighborhood car wash. Her biggest problem during the first 2 weeks was not listening to or following her supervisor's requests. For example, Paula was asked to concentrate on vacuuming instead of pulling the cars forward. She needed to be reminded of this several times. She used Improvement Contracts to change these behaviors. A few weeks later, she was hired, but speed became an issue on busy days when her erratic pace often held up the assembly line. After being constantly urged to work faster, she decided to quit the car wash and look for a different job.

Paula was then hired to be an on-call employee at a store that sold music and books. This store would only hire from their pool of on-call employees. Paula began the job stocking shelves, but her speed was a concern. The business said they would like Paula to try maintenance tasks. Paula was doing satisfactory work, and she was being called in to work on a regular basis. Then, Paula approached one of her supervisors with very explicit sexual suggestions. She was told not to return to work.

Following this situation, we re-evaluated Paula's job choices with her. She stated that she was interested in store or food service. We were able to find a job for Paula at a fast-food restaurant at an Army base doing food preparation. She started out working about 8 hours per week at minimum wage with the option to add more hours after gaining experience and showing satisfactory performance. Immediately, Paula had difficulties, and she was impatient with her coworkers. We initiated an adapted improvement contract to meet the needs of her jobsite and the Characteristics I Like versus What Is Here form, the Job and Tasks I Like form, and the Can I Do This Job? form. Paula was confronted three times during the month regarding her inappropriate language. Her personal appearance was an additional concern. Although Paula's behavior improved during the next few months, other concerns began to surface: working too slowly, not completing work before leaving for the day, calling the restaurant at peak hours, and talking too much on the job. Speed continued to be the major issue, so her supervisor asked if she would like to learn how to work in the lounge. Eventually, social interaction issues with customers emerged that led to her immediate termination. Paula's supervisor said that she was terminated for the following reasons:

- Swearing
- Working too slowly. The supervisor said that he could tolerate this in isolation; however, he could not tolerate it in combination with

Paula disappearing from the workstation or taking the long way around in getting back to her workstation
- Showing little respect for co-workers and customers

We spoke often about all of these issues, and Paula had goals and made plans to address these behaviors in a Job Termination and Follow Up form, but she had limited success.

We were able to find another job for Paula at a grocery store as a courtesy clerk. Paula had immediate problems and again was uncooperative at work and with program staff. She would not listen to anyone. Her third day review included the following problems:

- Packing bags too heavy
- Being unfriendly with customers
- Needing to be more productive bagging
- Needing to work on controlling her anger

When a job coach or peer trainer tried to make suggestions to Paula, she asked them to leave. As the month wore on, more concerns surfaced:

- She continued to show a disinterest in working.
- When the manager tried to help, she would walk away or become very argumentative.
- As she became more comfortable with her environment, her productivity decreased.
- Paula was deliberately doing the opposite of what she was asked to do.

Paula was terminated before the end of the month. We met with Paula, her mother, and her rehabilitation counselor. We all decided it was time to close her case.

Lesson from Paula's Story We worked with more than 700 individuals in the supported employment program. Paula is a notable example of the individual who did not maintain employment. In spite of our best attempts, Paula represents a case in which the self-directed employment approach did not achieve its goal of successful continued employment. Supported employment programs funded through vocational rehabilitation offices offer, by definition, short-term intervention. Some situations require more intensive intervention, and some individuals have characteristics that make continued employment very difficult. The Self-Directed Employment procedures did not achieve positive long-term results for Paula.

DATA-BASED CASE STUDIES

This section shows the method used to achieve success by four participants in the Self-Directed Employment program in a more quantitative way. We used single-subject AB (baseline, then intervention) designs to show behavior change. In each case, we used the procedures discussed in the previous chapters and supplemented them with various self-management strategies.

The first case study presents Jane, who, at age 32, had a partially debilitating heart attack that led to brain injury. Jane learned a four-step self-instruction method to improve and maintain an acceptable level of production and record keeping. The second case study describes Tate, a 21-year-old man with Down syndrome. Tate used a self-monitoring package supplemented with color-coded Supervisor Evaluation Cards to improve his work production. The third case study presents the story of Freddy, a 35-year-old woman who had a brain injury caused by an automobile accident. Freddy used a social improvement contract to stop inappropriately touching male co-workers. Ty, des cribed in the fourth case study, was a 28-year-old man with traumatic brain injury. Five years after his severe motorcycle accident, he wanted to get a job. Ty used a self-monitoring package plus Supervisor Evaluation Cards to help him set his own goal, measure his own success, and make adjustments to achieve on-the-job success.

Case Study 1: Jane

Method Jane, a 32-year-old woman, had brain injury as the result of a heart attack and subsequent lack of oxygen to the brain. Jane was highly motivated, friendly, and interacted well with almost everyone. She had been working for about a month and had received training from her co-workers, when Jane's supervisor requested additional support. Jane at first didn't want job coaches on site but agreed when her supervisor explained that the typical training program did not work for her, and she needed additional training from her job coach to keep her job.

Setting Jane entered the SDE program and completed the job match assessment process. Jane chose factory and janitorial jobs as her first and second choices. She initially had a janitorial position but left for a factory job that paid more. She took a new job at a plastic molding factory where she worked on the operations floor. Jane had to stack the output of two plastic presses uniformly on a rack. As she took a large piece from the press, Jane turned the piece several times trying to find the correct fit. As a result, she fell behind, and the assembly line waited for her. Jane found it difficult to distinguish subtle differences in the various pieces that came out of the press. She felt that she could do the job, but it would take time and intense concentration for her to learn how to stack the pieces quickly. To save the expense of additional training, the supervisor moved Jane to the plastic bagging area, which was cooler, less noisy, and less stressful.

Dependent Measures Jane's job in the bagging area consisted of filling a 15 cubic foot bag with plastic filling, securing the bag at the top, counting and marking it on the inventory sheet, weighing every tenth bag, and stacking the bags in the appropriate area. The percentage of correct bags was chosen as the dependent measure. Tying was evaluated per unit. The job coach inspected each bag for holes or gaps at the top of the bag. The counting and marking step was vitally important because the supervisor used the sheet for inventory. Because Jane was required to weigh every tenth bag, it was decided that her accuracy should be measured in counting blocks of 10. If she missed one of 10, she missed the whole block. Multiple errors within blocks were noted but did not figure in her overall score. The supervisor indicated that the average worker performed the task at 98% accuracy, so this became the criterion. An ABA design across tasks was used to assess the effectiveness of the intervention.

Baseline and Intervention During baseline, Jane received praise, error feedback, and limited error correction. We collected baseline measures three times (3 hours a day for 3 consecutive days). During posttreatment, Jane received the same praise, error feedback, and limited error correction. Posttreatment measures were collected four times.

Procedure First, Jane received explicit feedback on her baseline performance. Jane's biggest problem was the counting/marking step. She would consistently mark the wrong column or forget to mark the sheet. She helped devise a new inventory sheet that included clear column borders and color-coded columns. Next, she received detailed training in the use of self-instruction procedures that would be used to support her efforts to get to the desired level of performance.

The self-instructional package contained four steps that were repeated for seven consecutive workdays. Jane's self-instructional chant was, "Mark in yellow, weigh in blue." For the first 10 bags of the session, Jane would fill, tie, and stack as usual, but the job coach said the phrase aloud and marked the inventory sheet. For the next 10, Jane would say the phrase aloud while marking the appropriate column, with the job coach whispering next to her. The next time, Jane would whisper while marking, with the job coach mouthing the words and prompting if necessary. Finally, Jane would mouth the words while marking, while the job coach observed. After the session, data were collected across all tasks.

Interobserver Agreement Interobserver agreement was measured by the total number of checks in agreement divided by the total number of inspections, multiplied by 100. Bags received a plus or a minus after inspection. A second job coach independently inspected the bag, graded accordingly, and independently recorded her evaluations. Agreement measures were 98% and were obtained on approximately 25% of the observations.

Results Figure 10.1 shows data from 13 probes over a 2-month period. Her supervisor indicated that the counting and marking portion of the work was most critical. The baseline reflects an average score of 20%, which is well below the 98% criterion. On the first probe after introducing the four-step self-instruction model, efficiency increased to 70%. Continual increases were recorded during the month of intervention; the final three probes scored 100% accuracy. Maintenance scores of 80%, 100%, and 90% were all much better than baseline. Jane's tying ability was a few percentage points below criterion at baseline. Her scores continued below criterion during intervention and increased to slightly above the criterion of 98%. Improvement continued during maintenance, progressing from criterion of 98% to 100%. Jane's stacking ability received baseline scores below tying and above counting and marking on inventory sheet. The stacking data increased slightly from baseline and stayed at this level.

Discussion The results of this study indicated that a brief self-instructional intervention in conjunction with a color-cue for completing the inventory significantly increased Jane's work performance. About 2 weeks after the intervention ended, Jane's supervisor reported that Jane had made a column-related counting error. When asked about this, Jane said that she had run out of the color-coded inventory sheets and had to keep a tally on one of the regular sheets. Jane said that the ones with the grid and the color-coding were much easier to see and she could remember which column to mark in ("mark in yellow, weigh in blue"). Jane's supervisor was impressed with the increases that the data had indicated and was pleased that the job coaches faded out of the picture.

Case Study 2: Tate

Method Tate, a young man with moderate mental retardation, began the supported employment program when he was almost 21 years old and was completing his last year of high school transition programming. We worked with the school transition team to facilitate a smooth transition from a public school–subsidized job to one in which he got paid at least minimum wage. Before he left his school program, Tate was hired as a dishwasher at a site where he completed a school sponsored internship.

Setting Tate's job was as a dishroom attendant for a cafeteria. His duties consisted of loading and unloading a high-output dishwasher, sorting silverware, and wiping down tables in the cafeteria. Tate could perform his basic duties but was extremely distractible and had a tendency to wander off. These behaviors resulted in negative evaluations from his coworkers, and his supervisor warned about possible termination. Tate's duties were reduced to loading only, as the supervisor felt this might reduce his wandering.

Dependent Measures We implemented a modified version of the supervisor evaluation card. Tate was evaluated with a green index card if he had a "great" day (i.e., less than three prompts to stay on task or reprimands for wandering), a yellow index card if he had an "okay" day (i.e., three to six prompts or reprimands), or a blue card if he had a "bad" day (more than six prompts or reprimands). The percentage of "okay" or "great" days was the dependent mea-

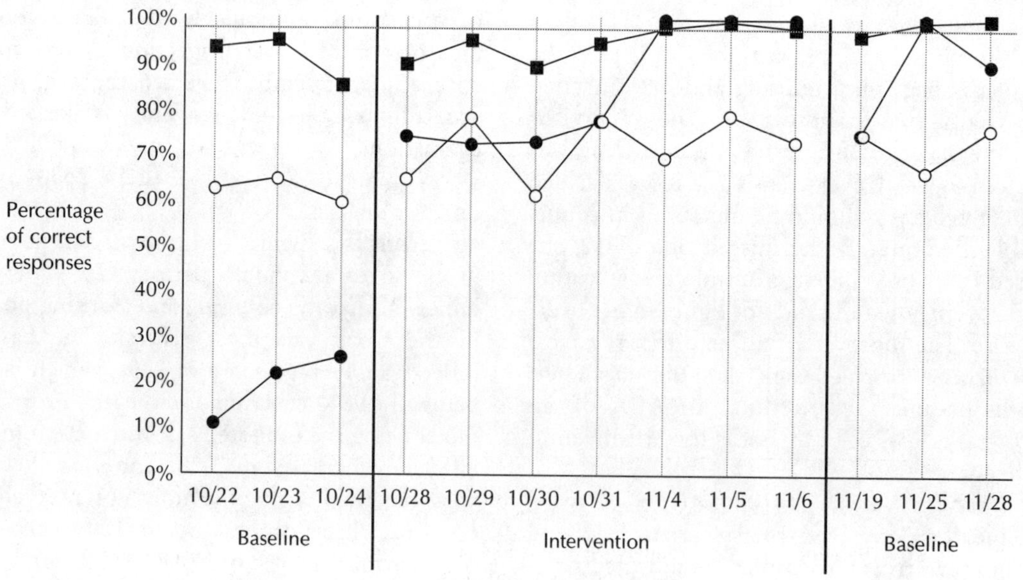

Figure 10.1. Jane's responses over a 1-month period. (*Key:* ● Counting and marking on the inventory sheet; ■ Tying bags; O Stacking)

sure. The supervisor wanted Tommy to have 80% of his work days evaluated as "okay" or "great." An ABA design was used to determine the overall effectiveness of a self-monitoring package paired with feedback from the modified supervisor evaluation card.

Baseline and Intervention During baseline assessment, Tate received praise and error feedback. Pretreatment measures were collected once per day for 3 days. During posttreatment, Tate received praise and error feedback. Posttreatment measures were collected every 10 days.

Procedure Prior to intervention, the supervisor reviewed Tate's performance, and he told Tate that improvement was needed for him to remain employed. Tate was given a month to improve his performance. The procedure to be used was discussed, and the desired levels of performance were set. Tate began his shift by verbally setting a goal (e.g., "blue card today"). His co-workers evaluated his performance with the color-coded cards. Tate acknowledged his evaluation and set a goal for the next day.

Results During the 3 days of baseline, Tate's performance was deemed unacceptable by his co-workers. As depicted in the graph in Figure 10.2, after introduction of the card system, Tate received "okay" or "great" evaluations on 91% of his probationary work days. After removal of the instructional components, Tate received "okay" or "great" evaluations on nine of 10 additional work days. His supervisor was so impressed with the performance improvement that Tate not only kept his job but also received a raise after another 30 days.

Discussion We modified the supervisor feedback form into a format understandable to Tate. The combination of goal setting, getting a supervisor feedback card with specific feedback as to what to change, and being praised for successfully accomplished steps improved Tate's performance. The supported employment staff tried not to become involved in task training issues, leaving this up to the employer and the typical process. When a person received a warning, supported employment staff would intervene to attempt to improve performance. If the person knew how to do the task, a goal setting feedback loop was established as the first method to change performance. This approach often worked, as it did with Tate.

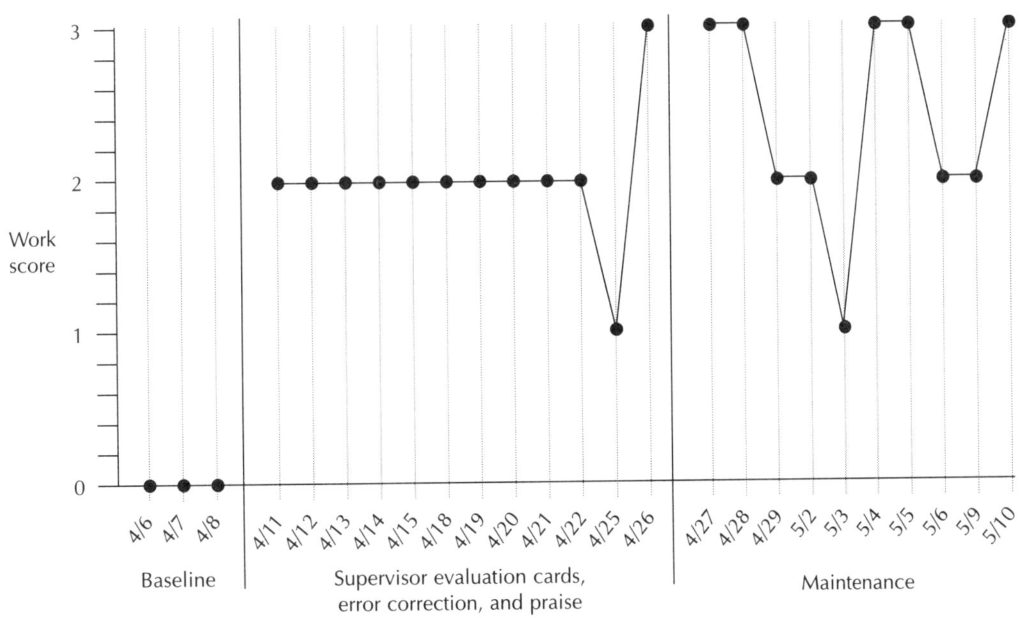

Figure 10.2. Tate's responses over a 1-month period.

Case Study 3: Freddy

Method Freddy was a 35-year-old woman when she entered the supported employment program. A few years earlier, she acquired a severe traumatic brain injury when she was thrown from a truck during an accident.

Setting Prior to her accident, Freddy worked as a janitor, and she expressed a desire to return to that line of work. Freddy was placed in a janitorial position at a local business. Her duties included sweeping, mopping, emptying trash, and cleaning bathrooms. She had been working for 2 months when her supervisor requested additional support.

Dependent Measures Freddy's work performance was consistently adequate, and she often received praise for a job well done. But as she became more acquainted with the staff, Freddy began initiating physical contact with the male co-workers. As the complaints increased, Freddy was given a warning to stop or she would lose her job. The percentage of positive social evaluations became the dependent measure. The supervisor set 100% positive evaluation as the criterion. An AB teaching design was used across evaluation domains to assess the effectiveness of the intervention.

Baseline and Intervention During baseline assessment, Freddy received daily supervisor evaluation cards and verbal warnings for problem behavior. The supervisor evaluated Freddy's work, social, and personal behavior by checking "Yes" for acceptable behaviors and "No" for unwanted work, social and personal behaviors. A percentage was also included in her daily evaluations for tasks done correctly.

Intervention A daily social improvement contract was added to the daily feedback card routine. Using the improvement contract, Freddy set a daily social goal before starting work and described what she would do to attain her goal. She would write down both her goal and how she would accomplish it after reviewing the goal and strategy with a job coach or a co-worker. At the end of the day, she received her supervisor evaluation card and made adjustments for the next day's goal. At the start of each day, she received instruction to set her social goal based on the previous day's feedback.

Results Figures 10.3 and 10.4 indicate the results. Baseline assessment consisted of 43 days of work, social, and personal evaluations in addition to assessment of the percentage of tasks done correctly. The "No" scores on the social graph depict the days when she received negative supervisor feedback for inappropriately touching male co-workers. During baseline, Freddy received a "Yes" on 79% of the days and "No" on 21%.

Following the introduction of the improvement contract, Freddy received a "Yes" on all 23 days that she received supervisor feedback over a 3-month period. Her work and personal graph also showed 100% for both baseline and intervention on all but one of the 66 total probes. The only "No" in the work and personal behavior coincided with a "No" on social behavior, and a 52% drop in task quality.

The task quality data fluctuated but stayed within the range of what was acceptable to her supervisor. During baseline assessment, her percentage of tasks done well was 100% on 76% of the days over the 2½-month period. During the 3-month improvement contract period, Freddy improved from 76% to 82% of the 23 probes measured.

Discussion Freddy's case shows the advantage of collecting daily supervisor evaluation cards during the first few weeks that a person begins working. As her negative social evaluations began to accumulate, Freddy and her job coach used the data to show her positive performance in other work areas. This positive data more than likely kept her employed long enough to change her social behavior.

For many people, getting daily supervisor feedback improves behavior. In Freddy's case, simple feedback was insufficient. The data showed that Freddy worked several days at a time with correct social behavior, so she knew what to do. We implemented a simple improvement contract to motivate her positive behavior. Each day, she set a social goal based in part on feedback from the previous day. She wrote down the goal on her improvement contract and identified what she would do to attain the goal. At the end of the day, she would get feedback and make an adjustment statement by writing what she would do differently, if anything, the next day. Supervisor feedback and warnings did not change the behavior, but following the introduction of the improvement contract, her social behavior improved.

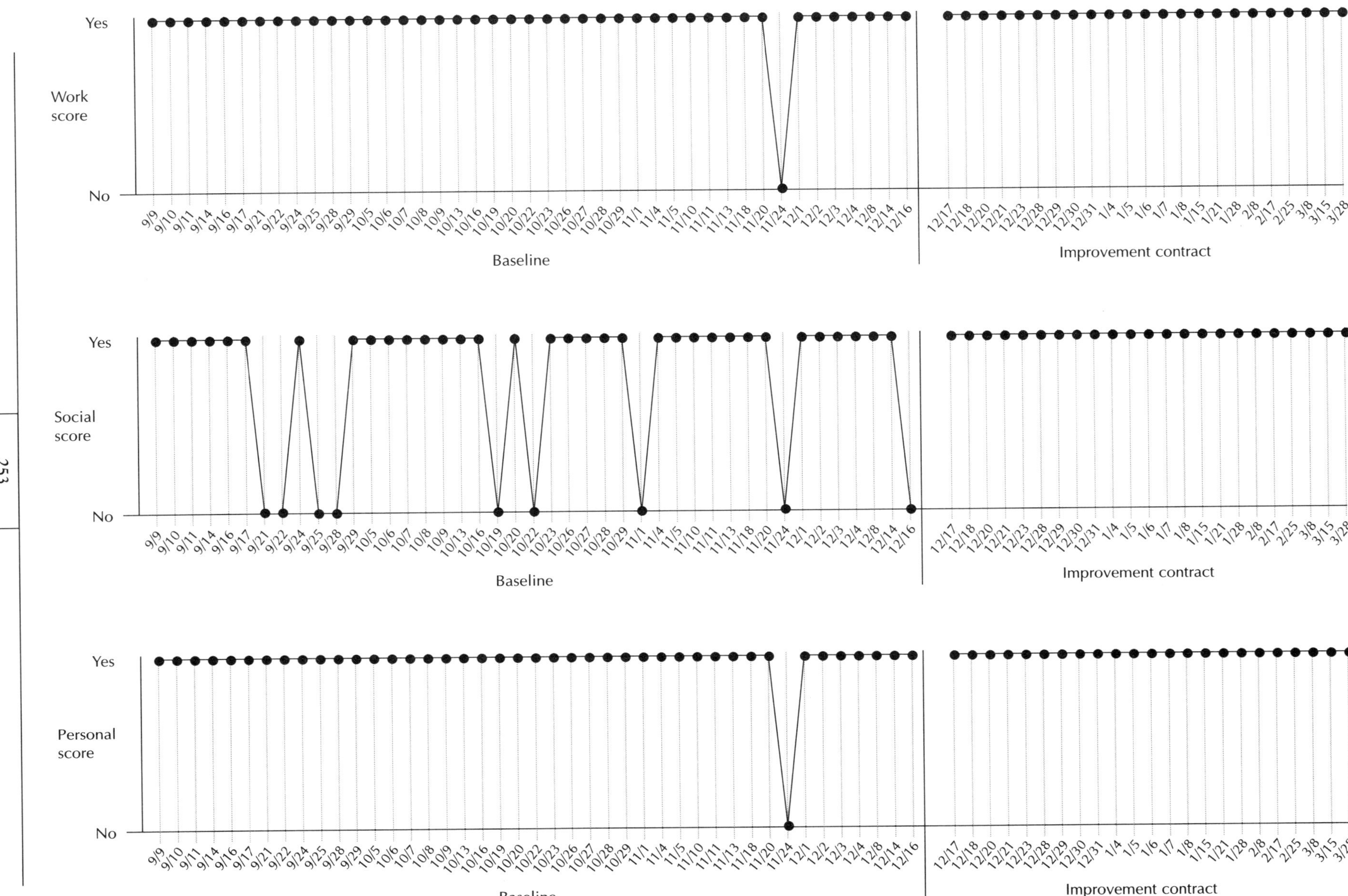

Figure 10.3. Freddy's responses to improvement contracts for work, social, and personal issues.

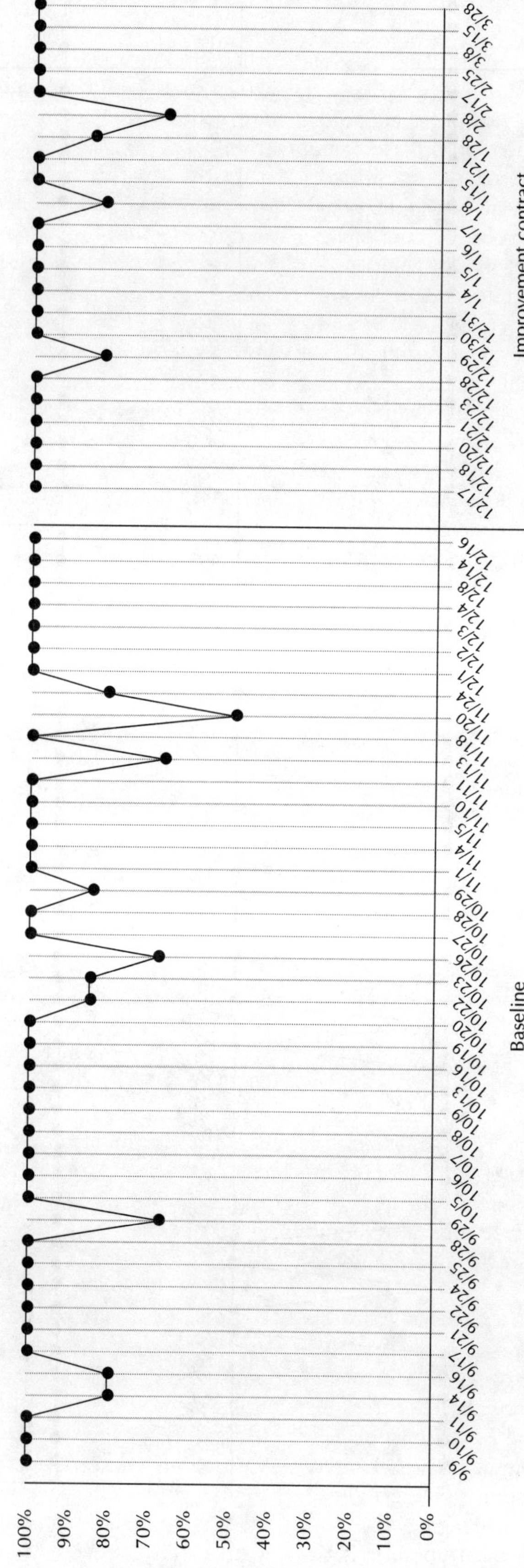

Figure 10.4. Freddy's responses to improvement contracts for task issues.

Case Study 4: Ty

Method Ty was a 28-year-old male who had acquired a brain injury in a motorcycle accident 5 years before he entered the supported employment program. When he began the program, he also continued to receive counseling from the hospital regarding his mood swings, significant anger outbursts, independent living options, and money management skills. Ty's records indicated that he had difficulty with attention to detail, visual perceptual function, speed of response, endurance, distractibility, work and social judgment, and problem solving. The reports also noted that Ty required a job with repetitive tasks that had little variation in routine, and that he needed to work in an environment that did not distract him from his primary tasks. As a result of his injury, he had expressive language dysfunction; could not read more than a single paragraph at a time; and had poor attention, concentration, rate of response, and short-term memory. An evaluation indicated that assembly-line tasks were not recommended. The report suggested that, with proper supervision and instruction, Ty could be allowed to try light machining, construction, and drilling activities where he could self-pace with minimal distractions and interruptions.

Finally, the reports emphasized that Ty had difficulty with recognizing his deficits and that his long-range vocational and educational goals were not appropriate given his cognitive status. When he entered our program, he expressed a strong desire to go back to college and become an engineer after saving money from working at the job we would help him get.

Prior to his brain injury, Ty worked as a machinist while he was going to college, and he wanted to return to this type of work more than any other. Three years following his injury, he worked at several food service jobs. He found these jobs himself but did not stay at any job for very long.

Setting After exposure to many types of jobs during the assessment process, his first and second job choices were to work at a machine shop or a factory. Ty quickly secured a part-time job at a local machine shop as a machinist helper. His tasks included unloading deliveries of stock material, measuring and cutting stock, grinding, de-burring, counting and packaging finished products for shipment, daily clean-up duties, and other duties assigned by the owner. The owner agreed to assess Ty's machining skills after a 90-day probationary period. Ty was expected to achieve a performance and productivity rating of at least 80% of the shop standard. Ty had been working for 2 weeks when the owner became concerned about his productivity levels. His co-workers gave him additional support, and the owner restated the expectations. They all liked Ty and wanted him to succeed, but he had to do his own work. Ty also received negative evaluations on his daily supervisor evaluation cards. His performance did not improve.

Dependent Measures Ty struggled the most with de-burring, counting, and packing a variety of finished machined items into boxes for shipping. The number produced per hour for each part was set as the dependent measure. An AB design was used to assess the effectiveness of a self-monitoring package, paired with feedback from the daily supervisor evaluation card.

Baseline and Intervention Ty received daily supervisor feedback forms at the end of his shift, and unplanned suggestions and prompts from co-workers while he was on the job. Ty also received praise, specific error feedback, and owner prompting and correction. The owner once again reviewed Ty's performance and indicated what areas needed to be improved in order for him to remain employed. The intervention procedure was then described to Ty.

Ty was given a package of modified production sheets that he would complete daily. He was to tell his supervisor the name of the part that he would be working on for each hour, get the shop standard from his supervisor, set his own goal for how many pieces he would produce each hour, count the number he actually produced at the end of the hour, determine if he met his goal for each hour, and discuss the results with the supervisor while getting instructions on what part to do next. He repeated this procedure for each new batch. At the end of the day, Ty verbally summarized to his supervisor whether he met his goals and then stated what he would do the next day to improve his performance, if any improvement was needed. Ty self-monitored his own progress using the production sheet. The owner randomly verified his count. When Ty met the shop production rate for the parts he produced, the supervisor would mark the supervisor evaluation card with a "Yes;" if not, a "No" was circled.

Results During baseline assessment, Ty received five "No" evaluations, which prompted a change in strategy. The addition of praise, specific error feedback, and peer instruction improved the situation, but his performance was still not at an acceptable level. During this intervention, he earned six positive evaluations and seven negative supervisor evaluations. Next, Ty began using the social improvement contract, which used goal setting, self-monitoring, self-strategy production, plus the previous intervention components. For the next 3 days, Ty tried unsuccessfully to increase his production level. On the fourth day, he succeeded with a production level that met the shop production level, which earned him a "Yes" evaluation. He continued to receive a "Yes" on the supervisor's evaluation card for the remaining 18 days. After this, he continued to use the modified inventory form, the improvement contract was discontinued, and his production rate remained satisfactory (see Figure 10.5).

Discussion The results indicated that the goal attainment improvement contract Ty used significantly increased his performance. The improvement contract combined several self-management strategies into one package to help facilitate behavior change. Ty also worked in a very supportive environment, and this environment must have increased Ty's willingness to continue trying. The owner of the shop, his supervisor, and co-workers all wanted him to succeed. However, the typical training and support methods the shop crew used to support and train Ty didn't work. The crew and Ty were ready for a different approach.

SUMMARY

Every person associated with transition and supported employment programs can tell stories about their experience. We included this chapter for two reasons. First, it allowed us to share a few of the ups and downs of the individuals who participated in the Self-Directed Employment Program at the University of Colorado at Colorado Springs. Second, it provided a means of showing how the procedures presented in Chapters 4–9 actually work. Sometimes the methods did not work by themselves, and we had to implement other strategies to achieve success. One story tells of abandoning the self-directed methods while the person spent time at a stable. Another describes using self-instructions to teach someone to learn a task. Detailing all these additional strategies goes beyond the purpose of this book, and other materials are readily available. At times, you may need to supplement the methods discussed in this book, but for many other people, these methods worked well. The next chapter covers the summary statistics of how the program functioned at different points in time. As you read Chapter 11, remember the people in Chapter 10—their lives are included in the data summaries.

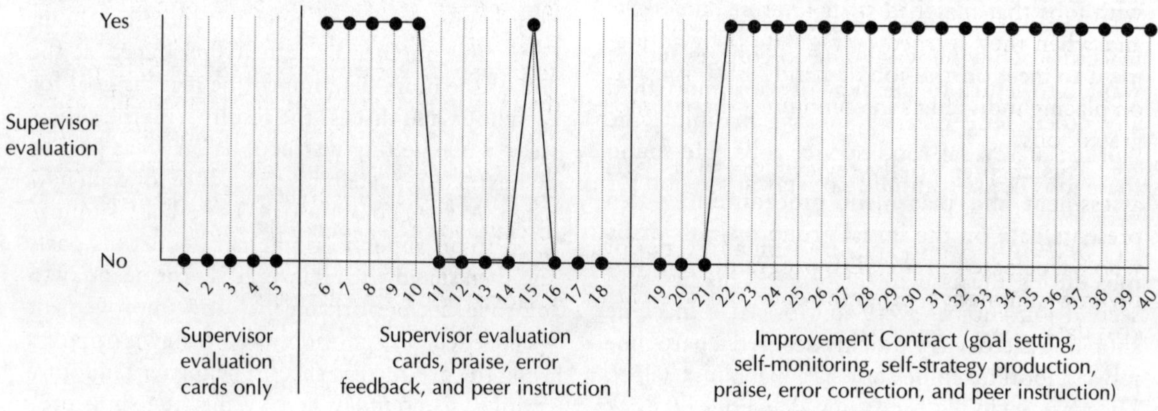

Figure 10.5. Ty's responses to strategies for improving his supervisor's evaluation scores.

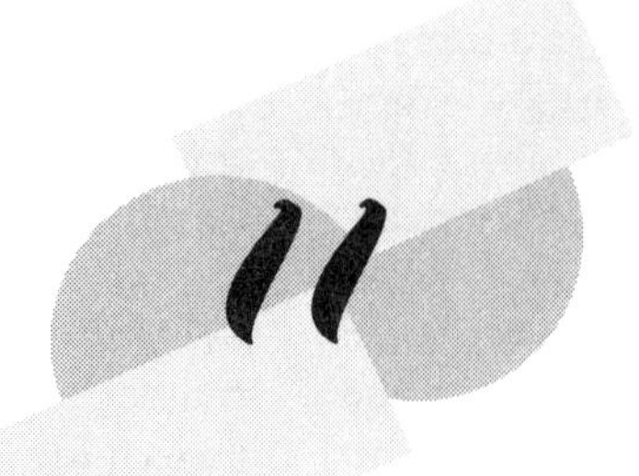

THE NUMBERS

We developed the Self-Directed Employment (SDE) Program to demonstrate that workers with disabilities, who have the right to control their own job choices, would benefit from a program that empowered that right. SDE demonstrated that workers with disabilities would be more likely to achieve success when provided with jobs that matched their interests and skills and when they learned to regulate their adjustment to meet on-the-job demands. SDE focused on placing individuals in community-based integrated jobs.

This chapter briefly reviews the basic SDE assessment and placement procedures. It also presents data on the initial group of individuals who participated in the SDE program. Finally, it reviews summative program data and presents cost data.

PROCEDURAL OVERVIEW

SDE consisted of three consecutive phases: assessment, placement, and follow-along. First, over a 6 to 12 week period, SDE provided individuals with the opportunity to complete a repeated-measures, community-based, situational assessment. Second, SDE worked with individuals to secure a job that matched their interests, skills, and limits, and provided opportunities for workers to learn on-the-job problem-solving skills. Third, SDE provided long-term follow-up services, which focused on job adjustment and career advancement. SDE procedures enabled individuals to systematically think about and then answer critical questions. Central to this decision-making process were repeated community-based assessments that presented discrepancy problems to the individual.

Discrepancy Problems

SDE choice and work adjustment situations created discrepancy problems that workers had to solve. In assessment, these problems arose when chosen job, task, and characteristic interests did not match specific jobs. In placement, the discrepancy occurred when workers' self-evaluation of their performance did not match the supervisors' written evaluations. Discrepancies diminished when the person worked at a jobsite that matched expressed interests or when self-evaluations of performance matched the supervisor's evaluations. Logical choice making happened when chosen preferences matched the task and characteristics at available jobs. Likewise, systematic feedback, the reactive effect of self-monitoring, or the use of other problem-solving strategies produced workers' self-evaluations that matched those from the supervisor.

Assessment: Choice Management

SDE's structure enabled the individuals to answer specific questions across four curriculum goals: 1) making choices, 2) exploring choices, 3) testing choices, and 4) final choices. The assessment procedures identified the workers' strengths, skills, and preferences and depicted how these matched available jobs. Through a series of community-based experiences, each person narrowed his or her choices to two available jobs that matched stated preferences.

Through this process, individuals with disabilities thought about and made their own decisions by using a series of written or illustrated forms. For instance, prior to visiting a community jobsite, a person would identify preferred job characteristics by circling words or illustrations describing the characteristics. After visiting the jobsite, each person would compare the characteristics from the site to previously expressed interests. If the stated preferences existed at the site, a match existed; if not, the discrepancy indicated the lack of a logical match. This process was repeated across numerous sites until at least two consistent matches were obtained.

Placement and Follow-Along: Self-Management

SDE provided support and opportunities for individuals with disabilities to find a job that would match skills and preferences and to solve on-the-job problems. Using assessment information, SDE staff and the individual jointly developed jobs.

Job Match Once a person began a job, the position was not considered a match until many of the assessment procedures again determined across time that this specific position still matched the person's interests, skills, and limits. We repeated the assessment process at placement sites because many environmental differences exist from one jobsite to another, which helped to ensure a positive match.

Job Training At many sites, co-workers provided job training. In difficult situations, employment specialists or peer job coaches would at times enter the sites to facilitate skill development. Across all situations, and often completed off-site, employment specialists would teach the workers self-management strategies, such as self-instructions, to use with typical self-evaluation feedback methods. SDE employment specialists did not perform the work for the individual because each person needed to assume the responsibilities associated with each position.

Solving On-the-Job Problems Once a worker learned what to do at a jobsite, the next step focused on fluency, maintenance of learned skills, and adjustment to changing job demands. As the worker approached mastery of the required job duties, this phase of the SDE procedures began. Based on supervisor feedback from the previous day, the worker established a short-term plan to solve identified problems, and then he or she implemented the plan, evaluated progress, compared self-evaluations to the supervisor's evaluations, stated any needed adjustments, and repeated the entire process the next day. Workers used various improvement contracts and strategies to facilitate this problem-solving process.

Follow-Along Once a worker's case was closed by the Colorado Division of Vocational Rehabilitation, SDE supplied on-going follow-up support. Unfortunately, some of the individuals did not have a source of long-term funding because they were on waiting lists or lacked long-term funding for their particular disabilities. For these workers without long-term financial support, SDE provided subsidized private-pay follow-along services, which the workers paid out of earnings directly to the SDE program.

Those involved in follow-along often continued to use their improvement contracts, although less frequently than before. Twice per year, workers used a change plan to compare what they wanted at a jobsite to their current situation. If discrepancies existed, the person developed and implemented a plan to remove the discrepancies. This plan targeted, for instance, getting a different job, securing a promotion, or asking for a pay increase.

PROGRAM ACCOMPLISHMENTS

Eleven years of accumulated information strongly suggest that long-term success was not related to disability categories but rather to factors such as a successful job match or a worker's commitment to regularly use his or her acquired on-the-job problem-solving skills. The data indicate that the percentage of workers who became successfully employed was significantly greater when they completed the SDE assessment process. More than 93% of the placements matched a person's first or second job choices. In a few cases, other factors, such as guardian opposition to a particular job or travel concerns, forced the person to take a job outside of his or her chosen line of work. According to data provided us by Colorado Rehabilitation officials, most Colorado programs typically averaged a 60%–65% successful supported employment closure rate. In contrast, the Colorado Springs Rehabilitation Office successfully closed 60%–73% of its referrals to the SDE program. Given these numbers, the self-directed methodology used by SDE was at least as effective and often more so than the staff-directed approach practiced by most Colorado programs.

JUMP START: THE BEGINNING

Prior to 1988, Colorado Springs did not have a supported employment program, and many employment providers questioned the viability of community-based employment options. A partnership between the Colorado Springs's Office of the Colorado Division of Rehabilitation, the local developmental disabilities funding board, and the Special Education Program at the University of Colorado at Colorado Springs (UCCS) was formed to jump start the city-wide development and use of supported employment methodologies. Together, we created a state-approved employment agency at UCCS, and individuals with mental retardation from three sheltered workshops had the opportunity to participate in this new program.

Fifty-eight names were chosen using a randomly selected, stratified design, in which the level of mental retardation served as the defining variable. The list of participants and their levels of mental retardation matched the proportion of the levels of mental retardation served by each workshop. If a person declined to participate, someone else was selected from the pool whose level of mental retardation closely matched the person he or she was replacing. The end result was a group of individuals who wanted a community job and whose level of mental retardation closely matched the profile of who was served by the sheltered workshops.

Results

From October 1988 to April 1990, 61% of the initial Jump Start workers became employed at a community job and 19% were involved in job development activities (most looking for second or third jobs). The remainder left Jump Start for a variety of reasons:

- Some families did not want their adult sons or daughters working outside of a sheltered workshop.
- Some individuals had poor attendance or on-the-job behavior problems and were fired.
- Some individuals wanted to return to sheltered workshops.
- A few individuals moved to other cities.
- Illness caused removal of some from the program.

We interviewed those still working and asked them, "What has changed in your life as a result of your job?" We were able to group many of their responses into categories, but a few responses were unique and stood alone. Listed in decreasing frequency, individuals said they:

- Were not bored at work anymore
- Could get out into the community
- Had more friends
- Had more money
- Felt more like human beings
- Could buy things for themselves
- Had money now to go on trips, buy new clothes, visit relatives, and so forth

Parents were asked, "What has changed in your child's life as a result of the job?" Most parents had many positive comments to make, which also clustered around similar themes. Listed by decreasing frequency, parents said that their adult son or daughter:

- Learned responsibility, punctuality, and diligence
- Learned to interact with a variety of people
- Was being seen now as normal and more ordinary rather than disabled
- Made a positive move in leaving sheltered workshop
- Became more outgoing and confident
- Was not lonely anymore
- Handled more responsibility
- Became more aware of others in his or her surroundings

SUMMATIVE DATA

When the Jump Start group started returning to their original program for long-term follow-up, SDE began serving individuals with severe vocational disabilities on a direct referral basis from the Colorado Division of Vocational Rehabilitation. As these individuals became successful workers, SDE started providing long-term follow-along services. Periodically during the next 9 years, we evaluated SDE's results. This section presents the results of these analyses—snapshots of the program at different points in time.

PROFILE OF THOSE SERVED

SDE provided self-determined oriented services for 751 individuals with disabilities between October 1988 and November 1999. During these 11 years, the program strove to demonstrate the viability of self-determination practices across a range of individual needs and across different disability categories[1]. We accomplished this outcome with the same funding that the Colorado Division of Vocational Rehabilitation, Colorado Division of Developmental Disabilities, and other funding sources paid similar Colorado community metro-area agencies. We closed SDE 11 years after it began due to funding cuts caused in part by statewide tax limitation constraints.

The chart in Figure 11.1 shows, by percentage of the total number, the distribution across different disability labels. The numbers show that among program participants

- 234 people had mental retardation
- 145 people had chronic mental illness
- 113 people had a severe learning disability
- 102 people had physical disabilities
- 96 people had other types of primary disabilities, including autism,
- 61 people had traumatic brain injury

Often individuals who entered the program had different diagnoses at different times in their lives, or they had multiple diagnoses, such as mental retardation and mental illness, when they began the program. We tracked the disability classification in their files at the time they started SDE. Altogether, approximately 53% of the individuals had one diagnosis, 44% had two, and the remainder had three or more diagnoses.

We wanted to demonstrate the utility of the SDE procedures across a wide range of disabilities and make supported employment opportunities available to more people. In comparison to national data, SDE provided services to a broader group of individuals than typically served in supported employment programs (Kregel & Wehman, 1997). Most national programs provided supported employment services primarily to individuals with mental retardation (70% compared with SDE's 32%). SDE made community employment opportunities available to those with physical disabilities, traumatic brain injuries, and severe learning disabilities to a much greater percentage than other programs across the country (Table 11.1).

[1]A grant from the National Institute on Disability and Rehabilitation Research enabled us to initially develop many of the procedures that we then refined during the next several years.

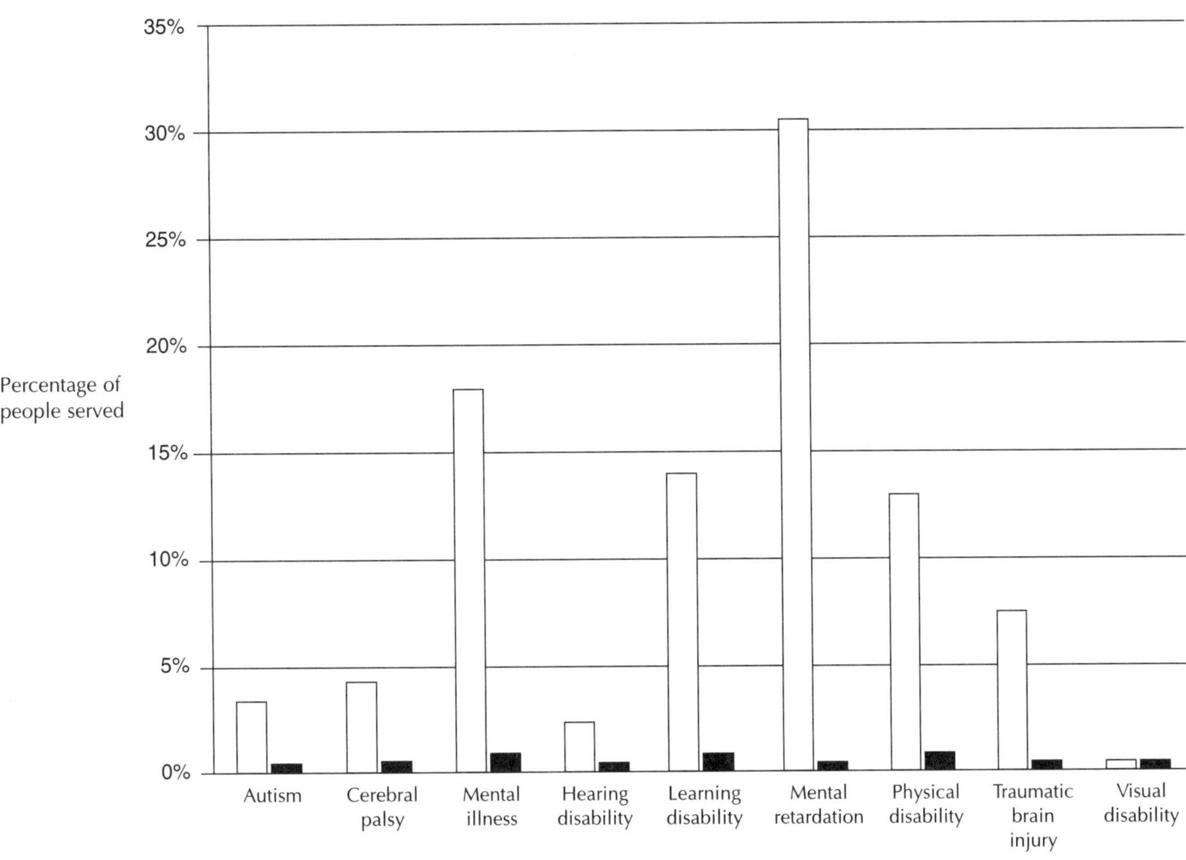

Figure 11.1. Primary and secondary diagnoses of participants in the Self-Directed Employment Program (N = 751). (*Key:* □ Primary diagnosis; ■ Secondary diagnosis)

Age When Started SDE

Individuals came into SDE primarily through referrals from the Colorado Division of Vocational Rehabilitation at two different life stages (see Figure 11.2). About 23% of the individuals entered SDE while involved in their high school transition program. Most (73%) of the individuals came into SDE in early or middle adulthood. Only about 4% entered after age 50. Within the age range of 22–35, more males than females entered SDE. This profile was reversed in the next age group; more females than males began the program between the ages of 36 and 50.

Completing Assessment and Successful Closures

About 70% of individuals who entered SDE completed the assessment process; the other 30%

Table 11.1. Diagnoses of participants in the Self-Directed Employment Program, compared with diagnoses of participants in other programs

Diagnosis	Percentages of SDE participants	National average percentages of participants in other programs (Kregel & Wehman, 1997)
Mental retardation	32	70
Mental illness	20	19
Physical disability	15	2
Traumatic brain injury	9	2
Severe learning disabilities	15	0
Other or undisclosed	3	7

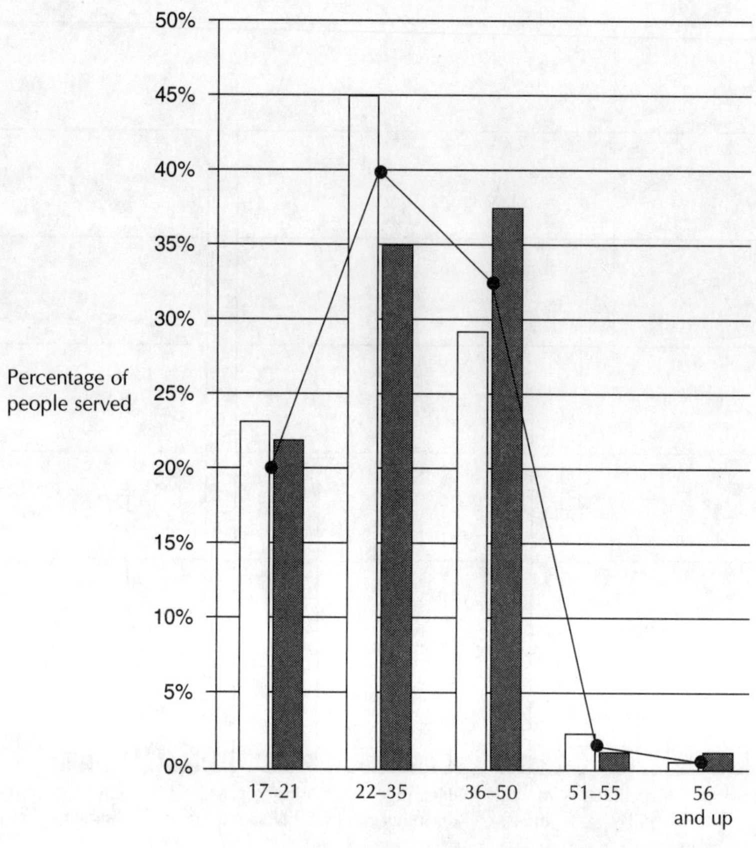

Figure 11.2. Age groups of people referred to the Self-Directed Employment Program by the Colorado Division of Vocational Rehabilitation (*N* = 652). (*Key:* □ Percentage of men; ■ Percentage of women; —●— Percentage of total)

did not begin or finish the assessment process. Those who completed assessment had a significantly greater chance (Chi square $p < .05$) of successfully closing their case with the Colorado Division of Rehabilitation than those who did not finish or begin the assessment process (Martin, Mithaug, Husch, Frazier, & Huber Marshall, 2002). About 69% of participants who finished assessment were successful, compared with 31% of participants who did not finish assessment and were successful.

Number of Jobs Before Closure

Of those successful, about 92% of the individuals closed their case with the Colorado Division of Vocational Rehabilitation within two job placements. Most (about 75%) reached this success benchmark after only one placement. Another 20% of cases were successfully closed after the second job. The remaining obtained a successful closure after three, four, or five placements (see Figure 11.3). Males and females experienced similar success rates. The number of jobs before closure varied somewhat by disability category.

Number of Jobs Before Closure by Disability Across disability categories, most of the closures came with the first job placement. This varied from 58% of workers with traumatic brain injury to 79% of workers with chronic mental illness (see Figure 11.4). A significant difference existed between the percentage of closures that came with the first job compared to the second (Chi square $p < .01$), indicating that many more closures were obtained with the first job than with the second.

When Closures Occurred

The Colorado Division of Vocational Rehabilitation closed unsuccessful cases during both

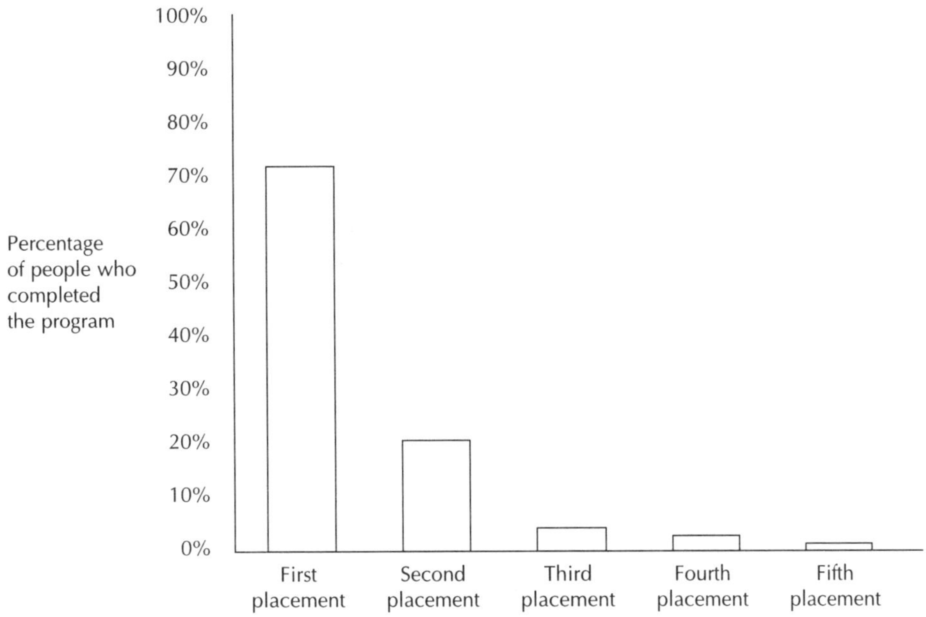

Figure 11.3. Number of placements required before successful closure for participants in the Self-Directed Employment Program.

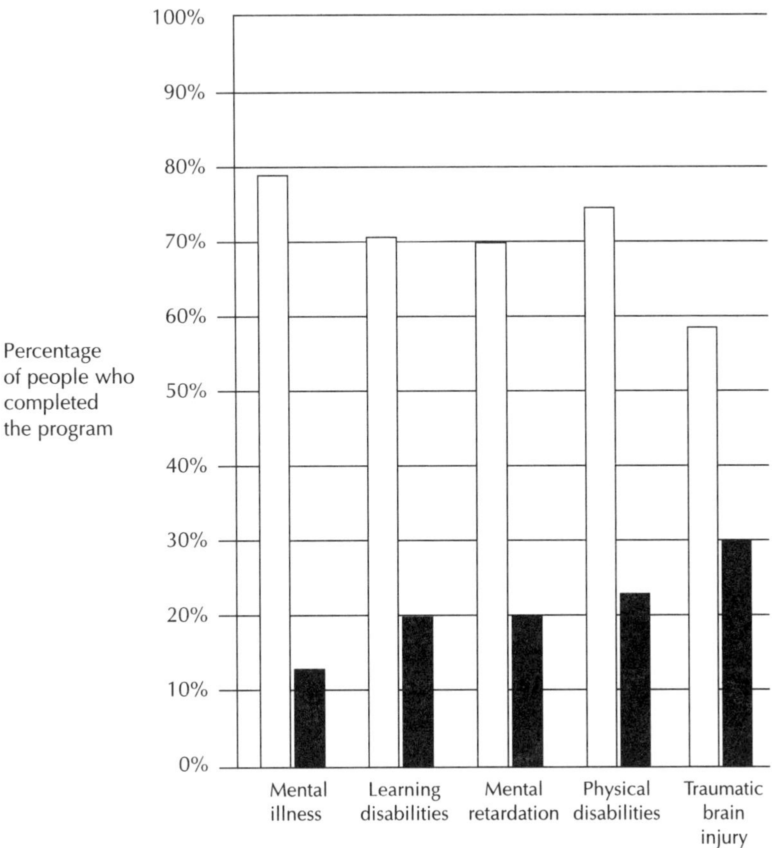

Figure 11.4. Percentages of closures across disabilities. (*Key:* □ First job; ■ Second job)

assessment and placement phases. Data from the first 9 of the 11 years SDE operated indicated that almost 20% of the closures happened during assessment. Of these, 13% of the closures during assessment were successful, and 87% were unsuccessful. The majority of those in the unsuccessful group simply stopped coming to the assessment program or meeting with their vocational rehabilitation counselors. Almost all the workers who successfully closed during assessment obtained a job at one of their assessment sites.

Time Employed at the Job

A 5-year cumulative SDE analysis showed that 3 months after placement, 88% of the individuals were still working, 55% were at the same job, 33% were at a different job, and 12% were no longer employed. Two years after placement, 12% of the individuals still worked at their first job, 39% worked at subsequent jobs, and the remainder were no longer employed. Kregel and colleagues (1990), in their analysis of supported employment data in Virginia, indicated similar percentages 3 and 24 months after placement (see Figure 11.5). In Virginia, however, more workers stayed at their first job and fewer worked at subsequent jobs.

Number of Work and Support Hours

Seven and a half years of data indicate that after 2 months on-the-job, workers clocked between 90 and 105 hours per month, with an average schedule of 95 hours per month. The number of SDE staff support hours averaged 32 hours the first month, 21 the second, 16 the third, and decreased to 13 by the fifth month. During months 6 through 18, staff typically provided about 7 hours of support. This level remained fairly stable until about the sixth year, when the number of work hours increased and the service hours doubled. When work hours decreased, the service hours returned to their previous levels.

Support Ratio Kregel and colleagues (1990) indicated in a study of a large group of workers with mental retardation that for the first 12 months of employment, an average of 175 support hours were provided for each worker with mental retardation. Figures 11.6 and 11.7 depict an extension of this analysis for another 6 years. The

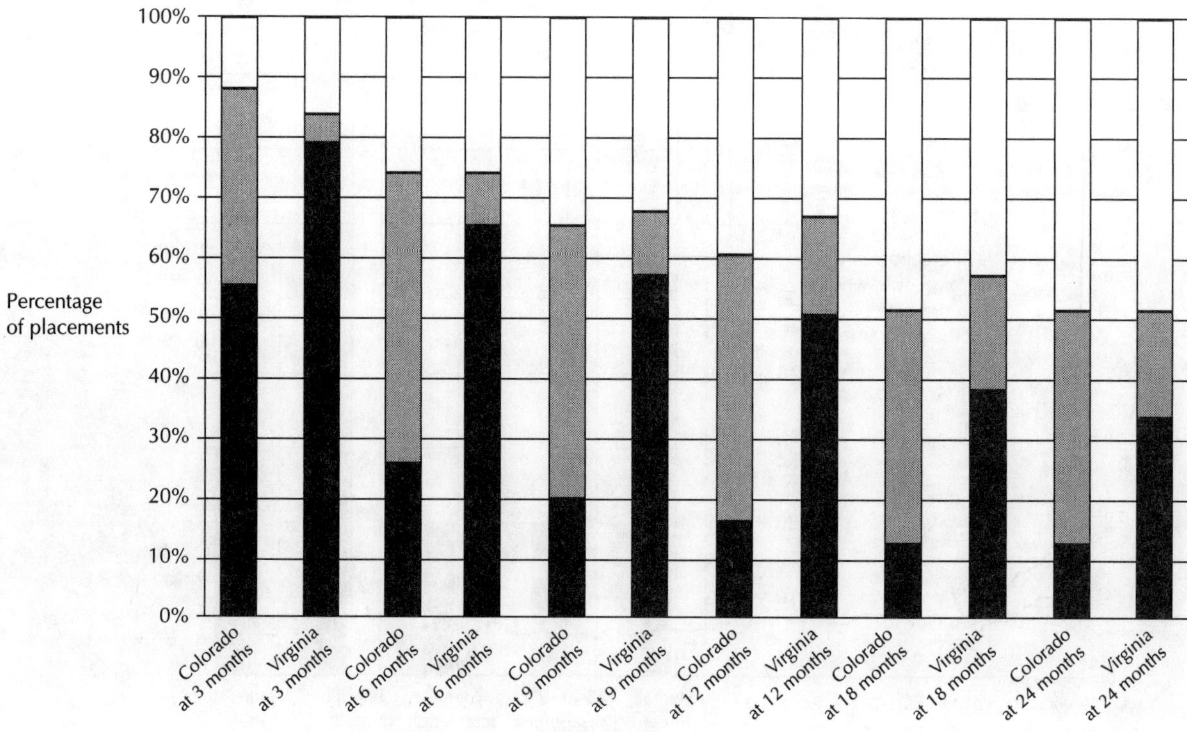

Figure 11.5. Job status of participants in the Self-Directed Employment Program in Colorado and Virginia over a period of 2 years. (*Key:* ■ Still at first job; ▒ Employed at a subsequent job; □ No longer employed)

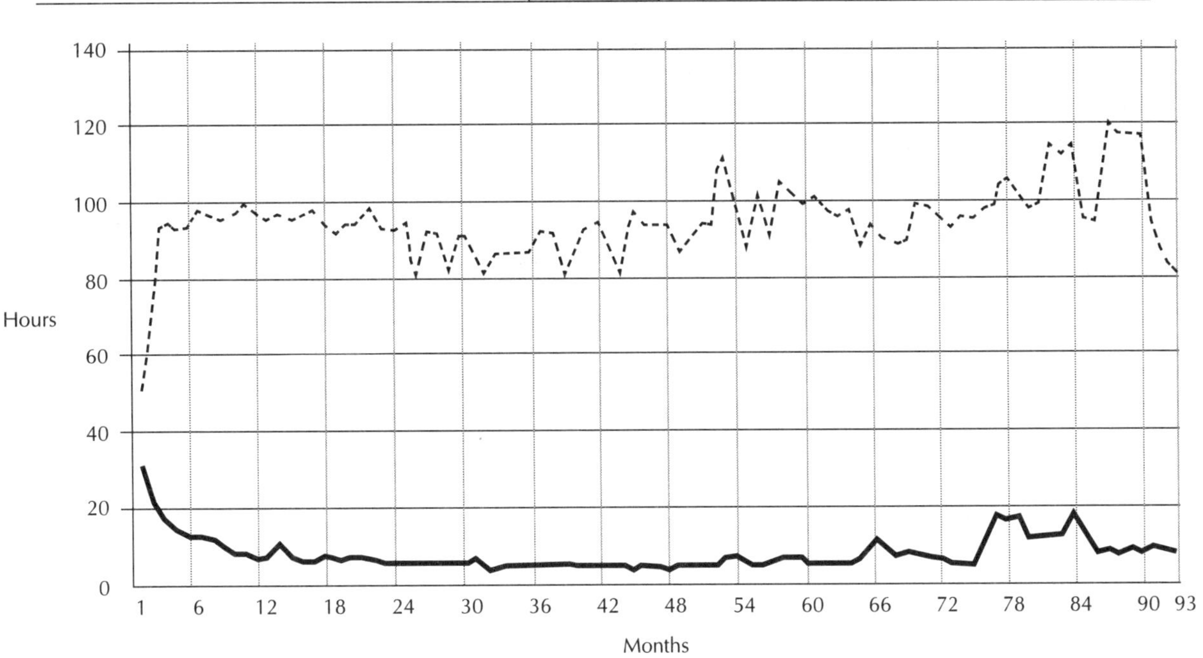

Figure 11.6. Average number of work hours compared with average number of support hours for workers with mental retardation over a period of 93 months. (*Key:* -------- Work hours; ▬▬▬ Support hours)

support ratio is calculated by dividing the number of support hours by the number of hours worked. The service ratio stabilized for a period of 5 years after the initial 12 months. Although the average number of service hours increased in year 7, the average number of work hours also increased.

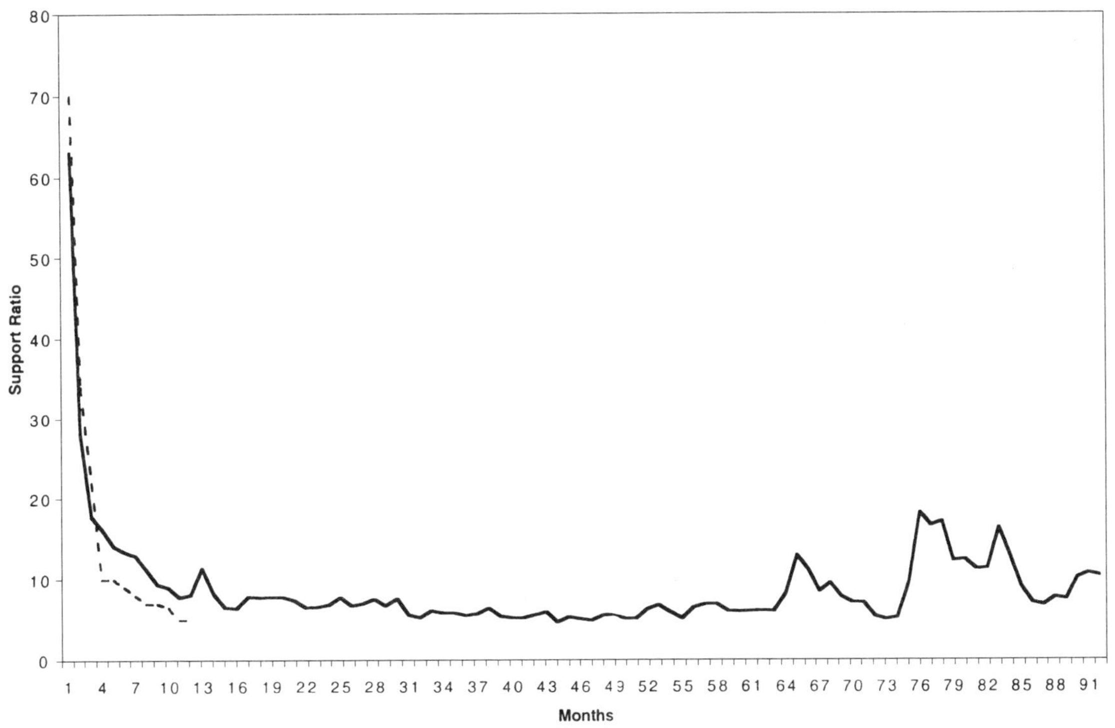

Figure 11.7. Support ratios across 91 months in Colorado and 12 months in Virginia. (*Key:* -------- Virginia; ▬▬▬ Colorado)

Wehman and colleagues (1988) indicated that an average of 266 hours of support time was needed for a group of individuals with traumatic brain injuries. In contrast, SDE provided an average of 168 hours of support the first year for individuals across disability labels. The average number of hours of support decreased and then increased over the years:

- 87 hours in year 2
- 68 hours in year 3
- 59 hours in year 4
- 89 hours in year 5
- 153 hours in year 6

During the last 8 months of the final year, this decreased to 70 hours or 105 hours prorated across 12 months.

Levels of Integration

Besides earning a wage, workplace integration is one of the primary reasons behind the development of supported employment programs (Wehman & Moon, 1986). In support of this philosophical notion, Kregel and colleagues (1990) presented data depicting the level of integration experienced by workers in their model supported employment program in Virginia. About 40% of their workers experienced frequent work-related interactions with individuals without disabilities. Another 40% had moderate levels of work-related interactions. Ten percent of the Virginia workers had no work-related interactions with individuals without disabilities. A 5-year comparison shows that 80% of SDSE workers had frequent work-related interactions with individuals without disabilities, and another 19% had moderate levels of interactions. Those who did not have frequent interactions chose jobs that provided the opportunity to work alone, without having to frequently interact with others. The high level of integration directly reflects SDE's individual job placement practices. Figure 11.8 depicts the levels of integration with workers without disabilities in the Colorado program and the Virginia program.

Reasons for Job Separations

In their seminal chapter, Kregel and colleagues (1990) presented a list of reasons why workers in their supported employment program left their jobs. Using SDE's first 5 years of data, we compared SDE separations to the Virginia data (see Figure 11.9). The greatest proportion of SDE workers (15%) left for a better job. Other reasons included, in order of prevalence, economic layoffs, seasonal layoffs, and poor attendance and tardiness. In Virginia, the largest group left their jobs due to economic layoffs. Other reasons included that the individuals did not want to work, wanted a better job, or had a poor work

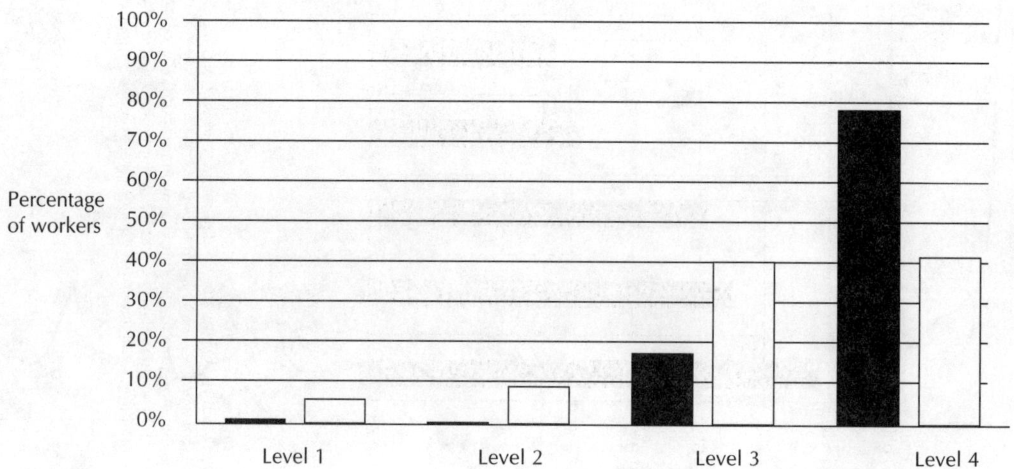

Figure 11.8. Levels of integration between participants in the Self-Directed Employment Program and workers without disabilities in Colorado and Virginia. Level 1 indicates complete segregation or general physical separation. Level 2 indicates no work-related interaction. Level 3 describes a moderate level of work-related interaction. Level 4 indicates frequent work-related interaction. (*Key:* ■ Colorado; □ Virginia)

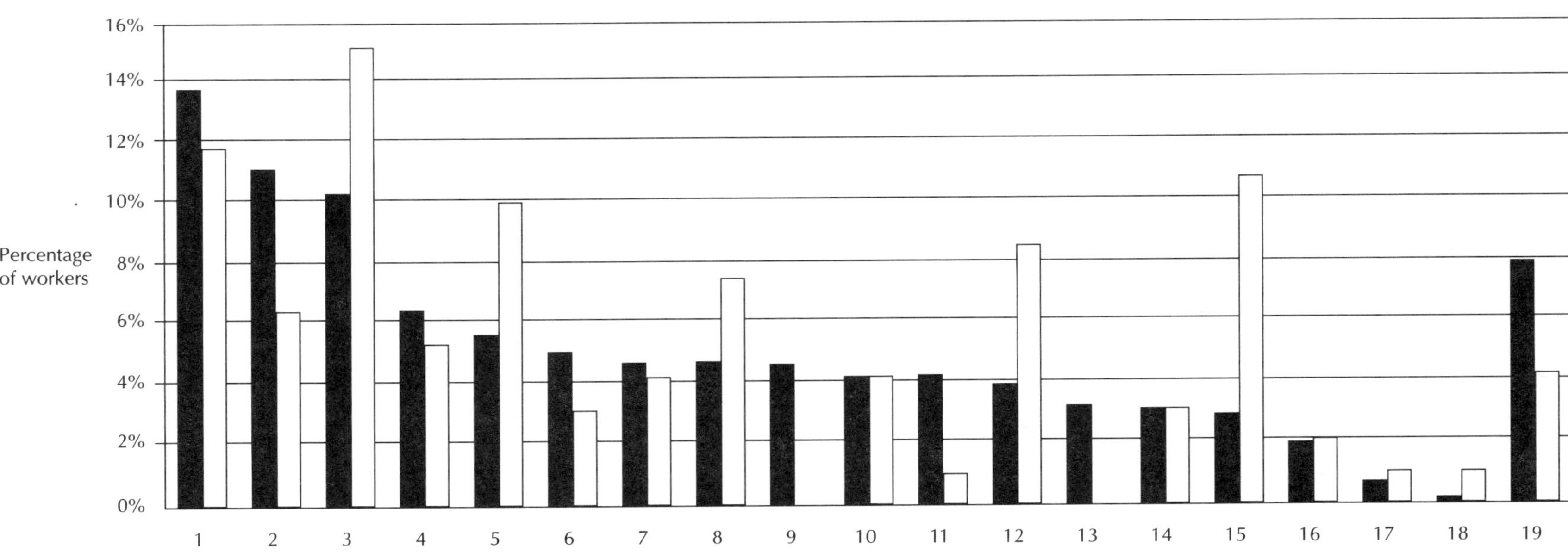

Figure 11.9. Nineteen reasons for workers' separations from jobs. Workers had the following reasons for leaving or being fired from jobs (each reason corresponds with numbered columns in the graph): 1) an economic layoff occurred; 2) the person did not want to work; 3) the person resigned to take a better job; 4) the person had a poor work attitude; 5) the person had a history of poor attendance at the job or tardiness; 6) the employer was uncomfortable with the arrangements; 7) the person worked too slowly; 8) it was a poor job match; 9) the person's parent or guardian initiated the person's resignation; 10) the person did low-quality work; 11) the person displayed insubordinate behavior; 12) the person experienced a medical or health problem; 13) the person displayed aberrant behavior; 14) the person required continual prompting; 15) a seasonal layoff occurred; 16) a transportation problem arose; 17) there was parental interference; 18) the person experienced a conflict with Supplemental Security Income (SSI) or Social Security Disability Insurance (SSDI); 19) the person had other or undisclosed reasons. (*Key:* ■ Virginia; □ Colorado)

attitude. Maybe SDE's emphasis on self-directed practices caused the search for a job that better matched workers' interests.

Types of Jobs

In 1995, 7 years into the program, 37% of the individuals had obtained service jobs, 28% had clerical and sales jobs, and 16% had professional, technical, and managerial jobs (see Figure 11.10). These percentages reflected the Colorado Springs entry-level job market. During the last 4 years SDE operated, the percentages remained near these levels.

To examine the service jobs closer, we broke down this category into its occupational divisions (see Figure 11.11). Of the 35% of all the workers involved in service work, almost half of those workers (45%) choose food and beverage preparation jobs, 16% chose building maintenance and related services, and about 13% chose service jobs in the lodging industry.

COSTS

Supported employment costs reflect local expenses and reimbursement rates. Costs differ among rural and urban locations and across the country. SDE maintained open books, and we shared our costs with the Colorado Springs Office of the Colorado Division of Vocational Rehabilitation for many years to determine a fair reimbursement rate. We used Hill's (1988) per hour cost formula to determine SDE per hour costs. This section details the steps to Hill's formula and uses 1999 SDE costs to describe how to determine per hour costs. Colorado Association for Persons in Supported Employment (APSE) undertook a statewide cost study in response to a change from

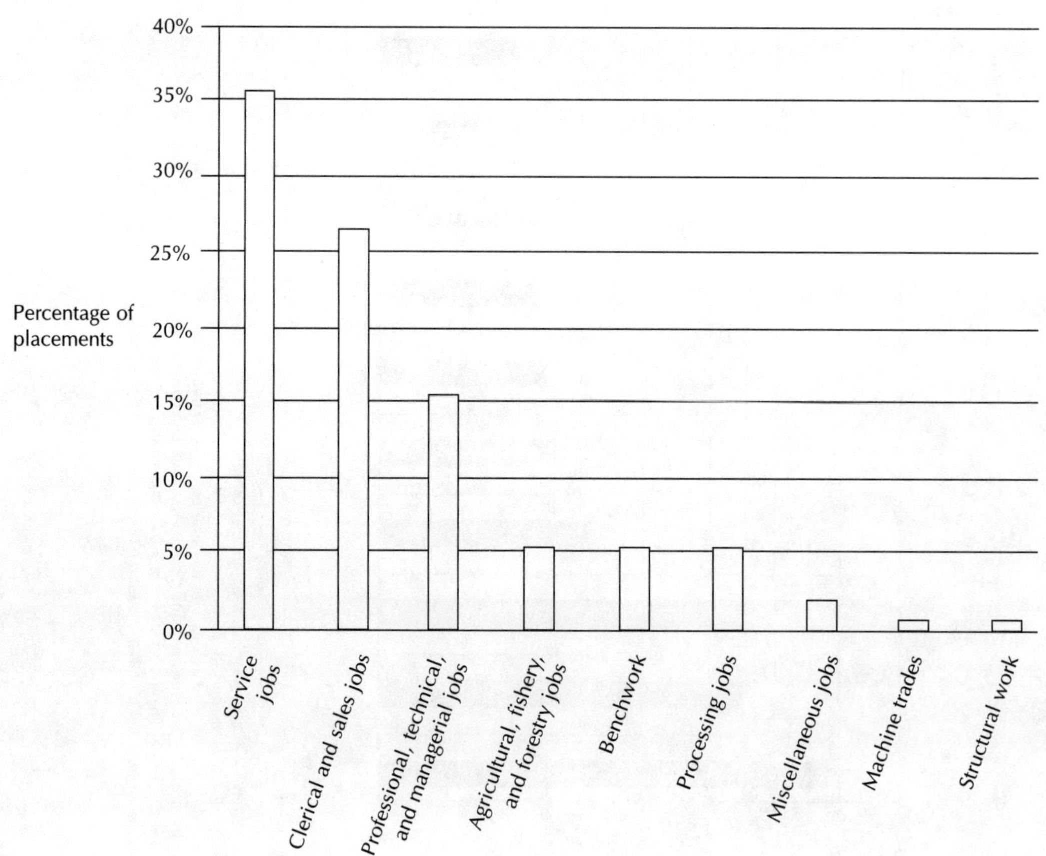

Figure 11.10. Types of jobs that participants in the Self-Directed Employment Program obtained.

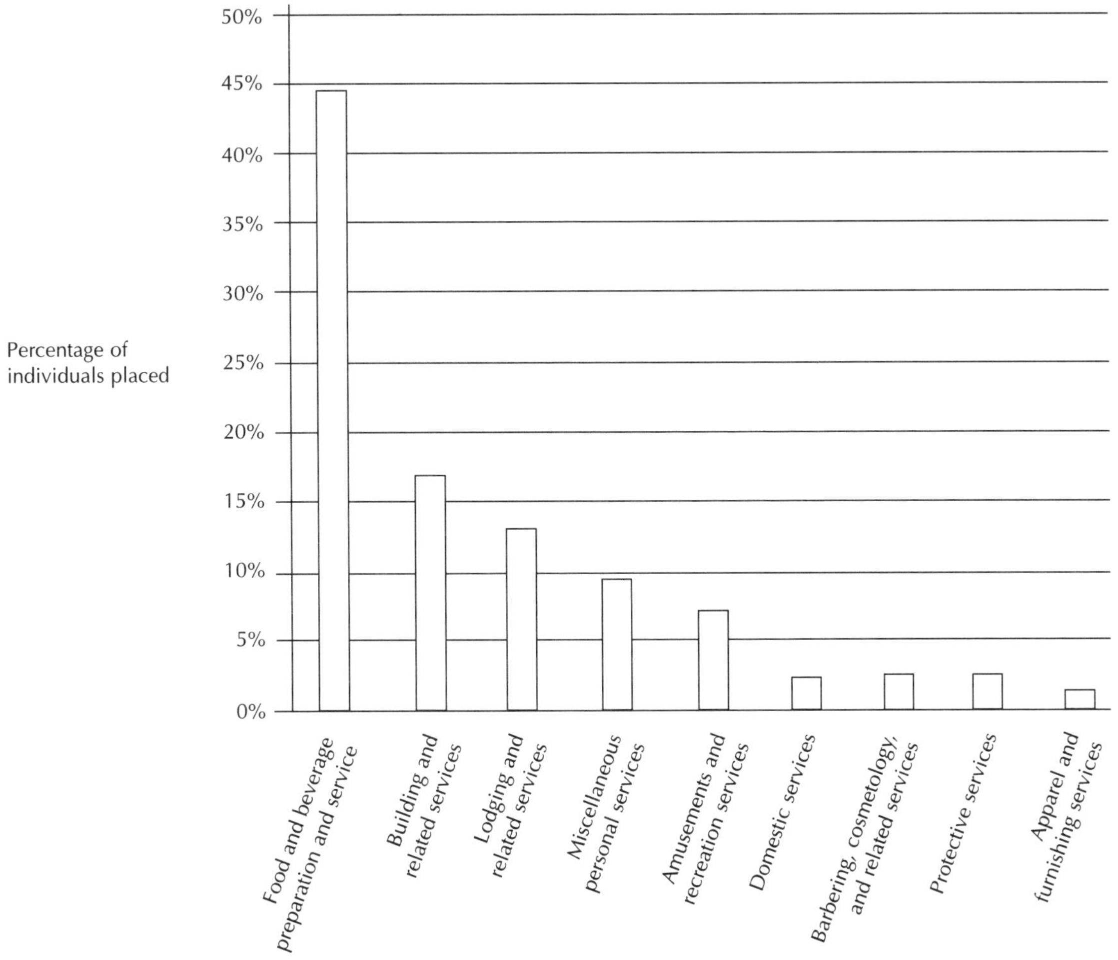

Figure 11.11. Types of service jobs that participants in the Self-Directed Employment Program obtained.

locally negotiated vocational rehabilitation rates to a lower state established level (Martin & Lawhead, 1999). These data show how Hill's formula worked across a variety of supported employment programs.

Hourly Cost Formula

The sum of three cost factors produces a per hour supported employment cost: 1) direct service staff costs, 2) support staff costs, and 3) support costs. By 1999, SDE had already begun closing down in an attempt to cut costs to stay within new lower statewide mandated reimbursement rates. In 1995, SDE employed more than 15 direct service full-time employees (FTEs), which decreased to 4.3 by 1999. Table 11.2 shows the steps to determine costs. Table 11.3 presents SDE's costs for 1999. As SDE decreased staff during 1997 to 1999, the total budget decreased, but the cost per hour increased as the program lost economy of scale.

Colorado 1999 Cost Study

Colorado APSE trained supported employment agencies across Colorado to use Hill's (1988) per hour cost formula (Martin & Lawhead, 1999). Colorado APSE requested that these agencies submit their per hour costs. Several agencies reported that they could not get specific support staff and support cost figures from their agency because of the way their program kept nonprogram-specific financial records. A total of eight agencies submitted their costs. Two of these agencies served rural areas, and the other six served urban regions. The programs served between 10 and 50 individuals per year funded

Table 11.2. Steps used to determine the total hourly cost of the Self-Directed Employment program

Cost factor	Step	Formula	Example
Direct service hourly costs	1	Divide the total amount of the direct service cost (i.e., salaries and benefits) by the number of direct service full-time employees (FTEs). This yields the average yearly direct service FTE costs.	($89,413 + $16, 310) ÷ 4.3 = $24,587
	2	Subtract the total amount of time off (i.e., vacation, sick, and holiday leave) from 52 weeks. This yields the total number of work weeks	52 weeks − 10 weeks = 42 work weeks
	3	Multiply the number of work weeks by 40 hours. Multiply the answer by the direct service time factor.[a] This yields the available yearly FTE staff intervention hours.	(42 × 40) × .65 = 1,092
	4	Divide the average yearly direct FTE costs (from Step 1) by the available yearly direct service FTE service hours (from Step 3). This yields the direct service hourly cost.	$24,587 ÷ 1,092 = $22.52
Support staff hourly costs	5	Determine support staff salary and benefit costs. Support staff includes secretaries, supervisors, and any other administrator or support person who supports the program.	
	6	Divide the nondirect staff support costs (i.e., salaries and benefits) by the direct service FTEs. Divide this answer by the available yearly direct service FTE hours (from Step 3). This yields the nondirect service hourly cost.	($68,467 ÷ 4.3) ÷ 1,092 = $14.58
Support costs	7	Determine the total supports costs, including rent, utility bills, accounting, supplies, travel expenses, training expenses, telephone bills, cost of mail, copier expenses, liability insurance, and so forth.	The Self-Directed Employment (SDE) program's largest support item was travel reimbursement at $12,000. The university donated office space, utilities, insurance, and accounting as a community service.
	8	Divide the total support cost by the number of direct service FTEs. Divide this number by the available yearly direct service FTE hours (from Step 3). This yields the hourly support costs.	($25,600 ÷ 4.3) ÷ 1,092 = $5.45
Total hourly cost	9	Add the direct service hourly cost, the nondirect service hourly cost, and the support hourly cost. This yields the total hourly cost.	$22.52 + $14.58 + $5.45 = $42.55

[a] Hill (1998) recommends a .65 direct services intervention time factor. Our own experience verified this amount, as our staff were rarely able to attain billable hours above this level.

Table 11.3. The 1999 costs for the Self-Determined Employment program

Cost factors	Percentage of total hourly cost	Hourly cost
Direct service staff	53	$22.52
Support staff	34	$14.58
Support costs	13	$ 5.45
Total hourly cost	100	$42.55

by the Colorado Division of Vocational Rehabilitation, and a total of 39 to 150 individuals per year. The two rural programs average per hour cost was $31.76. The six urban programs averaged $39.65 per hour, with a range of $31.55 to $42.65 per hour. SDE per hour costs ended up being high because of the university's generous vacation and sick leave policy. SDE salaries matched the other urban programs.

In 1999, the developmental disability system reimbursed between $25 and $35 per hour for job coaching. Vocational rehabilitation would reimburse between $15 to $20 per hour for situational assessment, between $400 and $600 for job development, and between $10 to $30 per hour for job coaching (up to $900 per month). The amount that vocational rehabilitation reimbursed also decreased if the person was not successful. Simply put, no urban program received reimbursement that covered their costs.

Colorado APSE used these costs figures to argue for a fair reimbursement rate from the Colorado Division of Vocational Rehabilitation and Division of Developmental Disabilities. Both the Colorado Division of Vocational Rehabilitation and the Division of Developmental Disabilities did not increase their 1999 reimbursement rates but did promise that they would continue to examine the issue. Faced with a situation where the reimbursement rates were lower than the cost of operation, SDE closed its doors.

12

CONCLUSION

Today more and more educators and supported employment providers are beginning to believe that people with disabilities should be provided with the same right to self-determination routinely afforded to people without disabilities. There is less awareness, however, of how to implement that right in a functional and realistic way. Should providers offer individuals with disabilities as many choices as possible and then see what happens? Should providers help individuals with disabilities make a connection between choice and experience so that there is a sense of self-determination in meeting important goals in their lives?

In this book, we have argued for the latter. When individuals with disabilities have opportunities to learn to choose and then to experience the consequences of their choice, they discover for themselves what they like, what they can do, and what works best for them. They learn to be self-determined. The purpose of this book is to show how connections between choice and experience can lead to finding a job, the most difficult challenge facing any adult entering the workforce. When faced with this challenge, people with disabilities respond much like any person with limited experience. They make choices based on unrealistic expectations, inaccurate information about different jobs, and limited knowledge of what is available. However, when they get the information they need about themselves, about different work conditions, and about jobs that are available, they choose as rationally as any other self-determined job seeker. This outcome was only possible, however, when we used procedures and user-friendly formats that allowed choices and experiences to match during an adjustment process that led to a self-determined job and successful on-the-job problem solving.

SELF-DETERMINATION

The concept of self-determination inspires and revolutionizes those who understand its meaning. Historically, John Locke's discussion of self-determination inspired early American colonists and helped them to justify seeking independence from Britain (Unterberger, 1996). Today, self-determination still inspires revolutionary change by creating opportunities in educational and employment programs for people with disabilities to make their own decisions and to become actively involved in solving their own problems. Although the institutions being targeted for change are different than those affected by the American Revolution, the situation is not. Far too many people with disabilities lack the opportunity to make their own fundamental choices and decisions.

COMMUNITY EMPLOYMENT

The idea that individuals with disabilities could obtain and maintain employment in community jobs changed the type of vocational services available to and the quality of life for people with disabilities. No longer are sheltered workshops the primary employer of youth and adults with disabilities. No longer do people with disabilities need to spend their adulthood working in sheltered jobs earning less than minimum wage. Today, increasing numbers of youth with disabilities obtain competitive community jobs while involved in their high school transition programs. Today, many adult employment programs support individuals with disabilities as they secure and work in community-based competitive jobs.

Community employment led to increased opportunities for individuals with disabilities to determine their own future. At first, however, individuals involved in supported employment programs took any available jobs. As workers with disabilities gained experience and enjoyed the freedom of working outside of sheltered workshops, some began asking for other types of work either directly or through their behavior. The opportunities to support individuals in community settings also affected employment staff involved in direct service and support roles, who began thinking about what types of jobs would best match individual workers. As self-determination practices entered schools and employment programs, more individuals with disabilities began asking for specific jobs. Staff also started thinking about ways they could provide opportunities for individuals to learn for themselves what they want to do. This led to another simple idea: self-directed employment.

SELF-DIRECTED EMPLOYMENT

The right to express preferences and make decisions about employment is fundamental. When workers have job options and a means of regulating their adjustments in order to act on them, the likelihood of vocational success improves (Martin et al., 2002). Self-directed employment applies this concept to long-term and daily job decisions. It attempts to improve "the prospects for self-determined pursuits by building capacity and improving opportunity" (Mithaug, 1996, p. 239).

DISCREPANCY METHODOLOGY

The SDE procedures described in Chapters 3–9 explain the systematic, data-driven, discrepancy approach we developed to provide individuals with severe disabilities the opportunity to learn how to direct their own employment decisions and problem solving. These procedures create two major types of discrepancy problems, which individuals solve each time they make a choice or evaluate a situation (Martin et al., 1990). First, discrepancies occur when an initially preferred task, setting, or job characteristic does not match what is present at a particular jobsite. Second, discrepancy situations also happen when workers' self-evaluations differ from evaluations completed by a supervisor. Preference discrepancies disappear when individuals adjust choices so that initial preference selections match those made after visiting at a site. Evaluation discrepancies disappear when workers adjust their behaviors so that their self-reports match supervisor performance ratings (Martin et al., 2002).

These SDE methods provide the opportunity to build each worker's capacity to engage in opportunities that match their own needs, interests, skills, and desire. The stories in Chapter 10 provide a window into the lives of a few people who became involved with the SDE Program in Colorado. Chapter 11 presents summative data that show that the SDE procedures produced outcomes equal to, and often better, than staff-directed programs.

SELF-MANAGEMENT INFLUENCE

The SDE methods use many powerful self-management strategies, especially self-monitoring, self-evaluation, antecedent cue regulation, and goal setting. Self-management strategies, either alone or in combination, produce generalized behavior change across vocational and other skill areas (Agran & Martin, 1987; Martin, Burger, Elias-Burger, & Mithaug, 1988). Self-management strategies empower self-determined behavior (Wehmeyer et al., 1998).

Implementation

The SDE curriculum, introduced in Chapter 3, contains 6 goals and 24 objectives across two sections (see Table 12.1). The assessment section of the curriculum creates opportunities for each individual to manage his or her own vocational choice making through participation in a systematic, repeated measures, situational assessment. The person first chooses a job, works at that site, and then chooses again. Over time, most individuals develop a consistent pattern of choices after they have learned their likes and dislikes. Accompanying graphic data summaries depict the pattern of choices. The placement and follow-along sections of the curriculum teach on-the-job self-management, by first providing structured support to enable each worker to find a job that matches his or her interests and skills and then by solving on-the-job problems.

Opportunity

Increases in individuals' capacity to act in self-determined ways result from employment programs that emphasize self-determination and implement self-determined procedures. Chapter 3 introduced a Self-Directed Employment Staff Profile, which teachers and employment specialists complete by answering three questions: 1) have I learned this? 2), do I do this? and 3) how important is this to my program? (see pp. 281–284). When all three occur, maximum opportunity exists for individuals involved in employment programs to act in self-determined ways.

Colorado's Example The U.S. Department of Education's Rehabilitation Services Administration awarded the University of Colorado at Colorado Springs a 3-year grant to train rural and urban employment program staff to use the SDE procedures. Supported employment staff from 10 rural and 5 urban areas participated in a year-long training program. All direct-service staff and their administrators from the participating agencies first completed a 1-day training workshop. Next, 71 supported employment specialists attended a 3-day intensive training, which involved seminar participating and completing field internships in the SDE Program. Each program then systematically introduced the SDE curriculum starting with assessment, while receiving technical assistance from SDE staff. After implementing the assessment phase, performance checks found staff implementing an average of 90.8% of the staff profile assessment competencies and 85% of the placement competencies.

Before training began, we did a pretest evaluation on each SDE curriculum objective by presenting the Self-Directed Employment Staff Profile to 94 field personnel involved with the participating employment programs. Those who completed the form included administrative personnel (about 30 people) and employment specialists. Only a few individuals who completed the pre- and posttests forms attended the SDE internships and were involved in the subsequent follow-up technical assistance visits. Using a three-point Likert scale, respondents were asked, "Have I learned this?" "Do I do this?" and "How important is this to my agency?" on each of the 61 items. We summed the responses within the assessment, placement, and follow-along categories.

Only 32 people completed the posttest. This drop off occurred primarily because of job changes and turnover. Still, the generalized effect of intensively training a few employment specialists showed in the data. After training, 30% more staff implemented the assessment procedures, and 27% more implemented the placement methods. Even greater numbers of staff learned how to implement the follow-along methods. Yet, a large discrepancy remained between what was important and what was actually done. After training, the employment programs valued more than 90% of the profile items and implemented 61–71% of the profile items.

Table 12.1. Supported employment curriculum guide

Goals	Objectives				
Section I. Assessment: Choice Management					
A. Making Choices	1. Getting Started	2. Completing the Jobs I Want to Do: Form A or B	3. Completing the Characteristics I Like: Form A or B	4. Summarizing Making Choices	5. Constructing a Résumé
B. Exploring Choices	6. Completing Shadowing Skills and Preference Match	7. Completing the Characteristics I Like versus What Is Here: Form A or B	8. Doing the Situational Interview (optional)	9. Completing the Shadowing Summary	
C. Testing Choices	10. Facilitating Internships	11. Completing the Characteristics I Like versus What Is Here: Form A or B	12. Doing the Improvement Forms	13. Completing the Job Requirements and Accommodations: Form A or B	
D. Final Choices	14. Completing the Job Internship Summary Graphs	15. Facilitating Postassessment Staffing			
Section II. Placement and Follow-Along: Self-Management					
E. Finding a Job Matching Skills and Preferences	16. Individualizing Job Development	17. Collecting and Evaluating Supervisor Feedback	18. Completing the Do I Have the Job I Like? Forms	19. Completing the Can I Do This Job? Forms	20. Completing the My Employment Plan
F. Solving On-the-Job Problems	21. Checking Supervisor Match	22. Teaching a Problem-Solving System	23. Teaching Ongoing Adjustments	24. Monitoring Changes and Adjustments	

THE CHALLENGE LIES IN IMPLEMENTING WHAT IS VALUED

Valuing self-determination is easy. Turning this value into opportunities for individuals with disabilities to develop the capacity to act in self-determined ways requires system change. This requires a commitment on the part of educators, employment specialists, supervisors, administers, parents, and individuals with disabilities to implement and follow through with procedures and structures that produce self-determined outcomes. The challenge truly does lie in implementing what is valued! We hope that the procedures in this book will facilitate this process.

Appendix

Self-Directed Employment Staff Profile (page 1)

First score: ________

Second score: ________

Name: ____________ Title: ____________ Program: ____________ Date: ________

Instructions: Respond to each item by circling a number from 0 to 3 in each of the three answer columns. A rating of 0 indicates "Not at all." A rating of 3 in the first answer column indicates "Very well"; in the second answer column, it indicates "Frequently"; and in the third answer column, it indicates "Very important. "Add the number of points at the end of each section for the "Have I learned this?" "Do I do this?" and "Is this important to my program?" categories. Complete the profile by following the instructions for calculating your score on the last page.

	Section I. Assessment: Choice Management	Have I learned this?	Do I do this?	Is this important to my program?
Making Choices	1. Facilitate job choices	0 1 2 3	0 1 2 3	0 1 2 3
	2. Discuss choices	0 1 2 3	0 1 2 3	0 1 2 3
	3. Teach Characteristics I Like forms	0 1 2 3	0 1 2 3	0 1 2 3
	4. Construct a résumé with an individual	0 1 2 3	0 1 2 3	0 1 2 3
	5. Determine specific jobsites	0 1 2 3	0 1 2 3	0 1 2 3
Exploring Choices	6. Teach shadowing	0 1 2 3	0 1 2 3	0 1 2 3
	7. Teach skills matching	0 1 2 3	0 1 2 3	0 1 2 3
	8. Teach preference matching	0 1 2 3	0 1 2 3	0 1 2 3
	9. Teach jobsite evaluation	0 1 2 3	0 1 2 3	0 1 2 3
	10. Teach job availability	0 1 2 3	0 1 2 3	0 1 2 3
	11. Teaching Shadowing Summary form	0 1 2 3	0 1 2 3	0 1 2 3
	12. Develop internships	0 1 2 3	0 1 2 3	0 1 2 3
Testing Choices	13. Facilitate internships	0 1 2 3	0 1 2 3	0 1 2 3
	14. Teach goal setting and planning on improvement forms	0 1 2 3	0 1 2 3	0 1 2 3
	15. Be an individual's job coach	0 1 2 3	0 1 2 3	0 1 2 3
	16. Teach self-evaluation and matching	0 1 2 3	0 1 2 3	0 1 2 3
	17. Teach adjustment	0 1 2 3	0 1 2 3	0 1 2 3
	18. Teach Job Requirements and Accommodations forms	0 1 2 3	0 1 2 3	0 1 2 3
	19. Teach preference matching	0 1 2 3	0 1 2 3	0 1 2 3

Self-Directed Employment Staff Profile (page 2)

	Section I. Assessment: Choice Management (continued)	Have I learned this?	Do I do this?	Is this important to my program?
Final Choices	20. Teach the Job Preferences Summary form	0 1 2 3	0 1 2 3	0 1 2 3
	21. Teach the improvement summaries	0 1 2 3	0 1 2 3	0 1 2 3
	22. List natural and other supports	0 1 2 3	0 1 2 3	0 1 2 3
	23. Facilitate postassessment staffing	0 1 2 3	0 1 2 3	0 1 2 3
Section I. Assessment: Choice Management scores				
Section II. Placement: Self-Management				
Finding a Job	24. Review and discuss assessment results	0 1 2 3	0 1 2 3	0 1 2 3
	25. Identify jobs	0 1 2 3	0 1 2 3	0 1 2 3
	26. Individualize job development	0 1 2 3	0 1 2 3	0 1 2 3
	27. Complete the placement process	0 1 2 3	0 1 2 3	0 1 2 3
Matching Job to Choices	28. Teach Characteristics I Like versus What Is Here forms	0 1 2 3	0 1 2 3	0 1 2 3
	29. Teach Tasks I Like forms	0 1 2 3	0 1 2 3	0 1 2 3
	30. Teach Jobs I Like forms	0 1 2 3	0 1 2 3	0 1 2 3
	31. Record and analyze data	0 1 2 3	0 1 2 3	0 1 2 3
	32. Monitor and assist with the plan	0 1 2 3	0 1 2 3	0 1 2 3
Matching Job to Skills	33. Collect supervisor feedback	0 1 2 3	0 1 2 3	0 1 2 3
	34. Teach Can I Do the Job? forms	0 1 2 3	0 1 2 3	0 1 2 3
	35. Monitor and assist with adjustments	0 1 2 3	0 1 2 3	0 1 2 3

Self-Directed Employment Staff Profile (page 3)

	Section II. Placement: Self-Management (continued)	Have I learned this?	Do I do this?	Is this important to my program?
Identify and Use Supports	36. Teach the Initial Support Ratio Graph	0 1 2 3	0 1 2 3	0 1 2 3
	37. Facilitate on-the-job supports	0 1 2 3	0 1 2 3	0 1 2 3
	38. Facilitate personal supports	0 1 2 3	0 1 2 3	0 1 2 3
	39. Facilitate community supports	0 1 2 3	0 1 2 3	0 1 2 3
	40. Facilitate financial supports	0 1 2 3	0 1 2 3	0 1 2 3
Use Learning Strategies	41. Identify and develop learning strategies	0 1 2 3	0 1 2 3	0 1 2 3
	42. Teach learning strategies	0 1 2 3	0 1 2 3	0 1 2 3
	43. Teach learning strategy evaluation	0 1 2 3	0 1 2 3	0 1 2 3
	44. Teach learning strategy adjustments	0 1 2 3	0 1 2 3	0 1 2 3
Problem Solve	45. Teach performance evaluation	0 1 2 3	0 1 2 3	0 1 2 3
	46. Teach a problem-solving system	0 1 2 3	0 1 2 3	0 1 2 3
	47. Facilitate use of the problem-solving system	0 1 2 3	0 1 2 3	0 1 2 3
	48. Monitor the problem-solving system	0 1 2 3	0 1 2 3	0 1 2 3
	49. Facilitate modifications and adjustments	0 1 2 3	0 1 2 3	0 1 2 3
When a Job Ends	50. Teach the Job Termination Follow-Up Report form	0 1 2 3	0 1 2 3	0 1 2 3
	51. Assist with planning the next step	0 1 2 3	0 1 2 3	0 1 2 3
	52. Facilitate implementation of the plan for the next step	0 1 2 3	0 1 2 3	0 1 2 3
	53. Monitor the plan for the next step	0 1 2 3	0 1 2 3	0 1 2 3
	54. Facilitate modifications	0 1 2 3	0 1 2 3	0 1 2 3
Section II. Placement: Self-Management scores				

Self-Directed Employment Staff Profile (page 4)

	Follow Along: Change Management	Have I learned this?	Do I do this?	Is this important to my program?
Review Problem Solving	55. Teach evaluation of problem-solving strategies	0 1 2 3	0 1 2 3	0 1 2 3
	56. Teach a new problem-solving system	0 1 2 3	0 1 2 3	0 1 2 3
Review the vocational plan	57. Teach needs, goals, and plans sections in change plans	0 1 2 3	0 1 2 3	0 1 2 3
	58. Assist with time lines	0 1 2 3	0 1 2 3	0 1 2 3
	59. Facilitate support analysis	0 1 2 3	0 1 2 3	0 1 2 3
	60. Monitor the vocational plan	0 1 2 3	0 1 2 3	0 1 2 3
	61. Teach results and adjustment sections in change plans	0 1 2 3	0 1 2 3	0 1 2 3
	Follow Along: Change Management scores			

Fill in the chart for each section's score. Visually compare each score to the percentage arrow at the bottom of the chart.

Assessment: Choice Management	0	6	13	20	27	34	41	48	55	62	69
Placement: Self-Management	0	9	18	27	37	46	55	65	74	83	93
Follow-Along: Change Management	0	2	4	6	8	10	12	14	16	18	21
Percentages	0	10	20	30	40	50	60	70	80	90	100

I:A:1:1	**Self-Directed Employment Orientation Matrix**	Making Choices

Phases	Purpose	Schedule	What happens
Assessment: Choice management	Find a job you like, that you can do, and that is available	1–4 times per week for about 1–3 months	*Making Choices:* Choose jobs you want to explore *Exploring Choices:* Learn more about job choices *Testing Choices:* Try out job choices until you find a good match *Final Choices:* Prepare an assessment summary and present this at a postassessment staff meeting
Placement: Self-management	Get a job and learn it Get help and support on the job Learn to self-manage work in order to keep the job Become as independent as possible through self-management	About 2–3 months after starting your job	*Finding a Job Matching Skills and Preferences:* Start a job, with support from a job coach *Solving On-the-Job Problems:* Master work demands through learning self-management techniques
Follow-along: Self-management	Receive ongoing support Receive support with job changes Receive support with career	About once per week, for as long as you need or want support	*Solving On-the-Job Problems:* Work with your job coach, case manager, or another person who provides support occasionally (about once per week). Continue doing your job using self-management procedures. Determine any new changes and begin long-term career planning.

Notes or drawings

1:A:2:1

Jobs I Want to Do: Form A

Making Choices

Name: ______________________ Date: ______________________

For the first and last columns, rank the jobs 1–4, with 4 indicating the job or task you like most.

Rank each job	Job type	Job title	Have I done this job?	Did I like this job?	Job tasks (list four)	Rank best tasks
			Yes No	Yes No	______ ______ ______ ______	______ ______ ______ ______
			Yes No	Yes No	______ ______ ______ ______	______ ______ ______ ______
			Yes No	Yes No	______ ______ ______ ______	______ ______ ______ ______
			Yes No	Yes No	______ ______ ______ ______	______ ______ ______ ______

Can't think of choices? Here are some examples:

Some job types	Some job tasks		
Store work Laundry work Food service (restaurant) work Maid service work Janitorial work Factory work Office work Child care work Animal care work	Stocking and pricing items Bringing carts inside Running a cash register Folding laundry Pressing laundry Wiping tables Serving food Washing dishes Cleaning a kitchen	Working on an assembly line Bussing tables Cooking or baking Cleaning bathrooms Vacuuming Making beds Dusting Washing windows Mopping floors	Emptying trash Typing Mailing Filing Answering phones Playing with children Talking with children Disciplining children Watching children Cleaning animal cages

I:A:2:2	**Jobs I Have Done**	Making Choices

Name: ____________________ Date: ____________________

Circle jobs you have done.

Store work	Laundry	Food service	Maid service	Child care	Janitorial work
Animal care	Outdoor maintenance	Warehouse work	Office work	Factory work	Other

Circle tasks you have done.

$ .39 Pricing	Folding	Ironing	Wiping tables	Serving food	Vacuuming
Cooking/baking	Washing dishes	Washing cars	Making beds	Dusting	Mowing lawns
Sanding	Taking out trash	Dusting videos	Carrying boxes	Weedeating	Gathering carts
Mailing	Working with machines	Washing windows	Watching children	Mopping/ sweeping	Cleaning bathrooms
Disciplining children	Bagging groceries	Filling condiments	Straightening books	Playing with children	Stocking
Other	Other	Other	Other	Other	Other

I:A:2:3

Jobs I Want to Do: Form B

Making Choices

Name: ______________________ Date: ______________________

Circle at least four jobs you like. Rate them 1–4. A rank of 4 shows the job you like best.

Store work	Laundry	Food service	Maid service	Child care	Janitorial work
Animal care	Outdoor maintenance	Warehouse work	Office work	Factory work	Other

Circle tasks you like. Rate them 1–4. A rank of 4 shows the task you like best.

$ .39 Pricing	Folding	Ironing	Wiping tables	Serving food	Vacuuming
Cooking/baking	Washing dishes	Washing cars	Making beds	Dusting	Mowing lawns
Sanding	Taking out trash	Dusting videos	Carrying boxes	Weedeating	Gathering carts
Mailing	Working with machines	Washing windows	Watching children	Mopping/ sweeping	Cleaning bathrooms
Disciplining children	Bagging groceries	Filling condiments	Straightening books	Playing with children	Stocking
Other	Other	Other	Other	Other	Other

I:A:3:1

Characteristics I Like: Form A

Making Choices

Name: ____________________ Date: ____________________

First, circle the preferred item in each pair. Second, draw a star in the ★ column for the 10 characteristics that are most important to you. Third, check your four most preferred characteristics in the "Top Four" column.

Characteristics		★	Top four
Work alone	Work with others		
Work in a quiet workplace	Work in a noisy workplace		
Work part-time	Work full-time		
Work weekdays only	Works weekends, too		
Work at a hard job	Work at an easy job		
Work inside	Work outside		
Have few rules	Have well-defined rules		
Work standing up	Work sitting down		
Work mornings	Work evenings		
Work in an attractive place	Looks of place do not matter		
Dress up for work	Do not dress up		
Do physical work	Do thinking work		
Detail is important	Detail is not important		
Do the same tasks every day	Do different tasks every day		
Work with people	Work with things		
Working fast is important	Speed does not matter		
Work with little supervision	Work with a lot of supervision		
Work in the daytime	Work at night		
Work in a small business	Work in a large business		
Other:			
Other:			
Other:			
Other:			

I:A:3:2

Characteristics I Like: Form B

Making Choices

Name: ______________________ Date: ______________________

For each pair, circle the one you like best.		★	Top 4	For each pair, circle the one you like best.		★	Top 4
Work alone	Work with others			Dress up for work	Do not dress up		
Work in a quiet place	Work in a loud place			Physical work	Thinking work		
Work part-time	Work full-time			Important to work fast	Speed is not important		
S M Tu W Th F S / X ✓ ✓ ✓ ✓ ✓ X Work weekdays only	S M Tu W Th F S / ✓ ✓ ✓ ✓ ✓ ✓ ✓ Work weekends, too			Same job every day	Different job every day		
Work a hard job	Work an easy job			Work with people	Work with things		
Work inside	Work outside			A little supervision	A lot of supervision		
Have few rules	Have lots of rules			Daytime work	Nighttime work		
Work standing up	Work sitting down			Small business	Large business		
Work mornings	Work afternoons			Other	Other		
Attractive place	Looks of place do not matter			Other	Other		
Detail important	Detail not important			Other	Other		

I:A:4:1

Initial Job Preferences Graph

Making Choices
Final Choices

Name: ______________________ Date: ______________________

Job	Rank Day 1	Rank Day 2	Rank Day 3	Check if done	Job preference graph
					1 2 3 4 5 6 7 8 9 10 11 12
					1 2 3 4 5 6 7 8 9 10 11 12
					1 2 3 4 5 6 7 8 9 10 11 12
					1 2 3 4 5 6 7 8 9 10 11 12
					1 2 3 4 5 6 7 8 9 10 11 12
					1 2 3 4 5 6 7 8 9 10 11 12
					1 2 3 4 5 6 7 8 9 10 11 12
					1 2 3 4 5 6 7 8 9 10 11 12
					1 2 3 4 5 6 7 8 9 10 11 12
					1 2 3 4 5 6 7 8 9 10 11 12
					1 2 3 4 5 6 7 8 9 10 11 12
					1 2 3 4 5 6 7 8 9 10 11 12

Four top-ranked jobs	Have I done this job?	Do I need to shadow this job?
______________________	Yes No	Yes No
______________________	Yes No	Yes No
______________________	Yes No	Yes No
______________________	Yes No	Yes No

I:A:4:2

Initial Task Preferences Graph

Making Choices
Final Choices

Name: ______________________ Date: ______________________

Task	Rank Day 1	Day 2	Day 3	Check if done	Task preference graph
					1 2 3 4 5 6 7 8 9 10 11 12
					1 2 3 4 5 6 7 8 9 10 11 12
					1 2 3 4 5 6 7 8 9 10 11 12
					1 2 3 4 5 6 7 8 9 10 11 12
					1 2 3 4 5 6 7 8 9 10 11 12
					1 2 3 4 5 6 7 8 9 10 11 12
					1 2 3 4 5 6 7 8 9 10 11 12
					1 2 3 4 5 6 7 8 9 10 11 12
					1 2 3 4 5 6 7 8 9 10 11 12
					1 2 3 4 5 6 7 8 9 10 11 12
					1 2 3 4 5 6 7 8 9 10 11 12
					1 2 3 4 5 6 7 8 9 10 11 12

Four top-ranked tasks	Have I done this task?		Do I need to shadow this task?	
______________________	Yes	No	Yes	No
______________________	Yes	No	Yes	No
______________________	Yes	No	Yes	No
______________________	Yes	No	Yes	No

1:A:4:3

Characteristics Summary Graph

Making Choices
Exploring Choices
Testing Choices
Final Choices

Name: ______________________ Date: ______________

Work alone	1	2	3	4	5	6	7	8	9	10	11	12	13	14	15	16	17	18
Work with others	1	2	3	4	5	6	7	8	9	10	11	12	13	14	15	16	17	18
Work in a quiet workplace	1	2	3	4	5	6	7	8	9	10	11	12	13	14	15	16	17	18
Work in a noisy workplace	1	2	3	4	5	6	7	8	9	10	11	12	13	14	15	16	17	18
Work part-time	1	2	3	4	5	6	7	8	9	10	11	12	13	14	15	16	17	18
Work full-time	1	2	3	4	5	6	7	8	9	10	11	12	13	14	15	16	17	18
Work weekdays only	1	2	3	4	5	6	7	8	9	10	11	12	13	14	15	16	17	18
Works weekends, too	1	2	3	4	5	6	7	8	9	10	11	12	13	14	15	16	17	18
Work at a hard job	1	2	3	4	5	6	7	8	9	10	11	12	13	14	15	16	17	18
Work at an easy job	1	2	3	4	5	6	7	8	9	10	11	12	13	14	15	16	17	18
Work inside	1	2	3	4	5	6	7	8	9	10	11	12	13	14	15	16	17	18
Work outside	1	2	3	4	5	6	7	8	9	10	11	12	13	14	15	16	17	18
Have few rules	1	2	3	4	5	6	7	8	9	10	11	12	13	14	15	16	17	18
Have well-defined rules	1	2	3	4	5	6	7	8	9	10	11	12	13	14	15	16	17	18
Work standing up	1	2	3	4	5	6	7	8	9	10	11	12	13	14	15	16	17	18
Work sitting down	1	2	3	4	5	6	7	8	9	10	11	12	13	14	15	16	17	18
Work mornings	1	2	3	4	5	6	7	8	9	10	11	12	13	14	15	16	17	18
Work evenings	1	2	3	4	5	6	7	8	9	10	11	12	13	14	15	16	17	18
Work in an attractive place	1	2	3	4	5	6	7	8	9	10	11	12	13	14	15	16	17	18
Looks of place do not matter	1	2	3	4	5	6	7	8	9	10	11	12	13	14	15	16	17	18
Dress up for work	1	2	3	4	5	6	7	8	9	10	11	12	13	14	15	16	17	18
Do not dress up	1	2	3	4	5	6	7	8	9	10	11	12	13	14	15	16	17	18
Do physical work	1	2	3	4	5	6	7	8	9	10	11	12	13	14	15	16	17	18
Do thinking work	1	2	3	4	5	6	7	8	9	10	11	12	13	14	15	16	17	18
Detail is important	1	2	3	4	5	6	7	8	9	10	11	12	13	14	15	16	17	18
Detail is not important	1	2	3	4	5	6	7	8	9	10	11	12	13	14	15	16	17	18
Do the same tasks every day	1	2	3	4	5	6	7	8	9	10	11	12	13	14	15	16	17	18
Do different tasks every day	1	2	3	4	5	6	7	8	9	10	11	12	13	14	15	16	17	18
Work with people	1	2	3	4	5	6	7	8	9	10	11	12	13	14	15	16	17	18
Work with things	1	2	3	4	5	6	7	8	9	10	11	12	13	14	15	16	17	18
Working fast is important	1	2	3	4	5	6	7	8	9	10	11	12	13	14	15	16	17	18
Speed does not matter	1	2	3	4	5	6	7	8	9	10	11	12	13	14	15	16	17	18
Work with little supervision	1	2	3	4	5	6	7	8	9	10	11	12	13	14	15	16	17	18
Work with a lot of supervision	1	2	3	4	5	6	7	8	9	10	11	12	13	14	15	16	17	18
Work in the daytime	1	2	3	4	5	6	7	8	9	10	11	12	13	14	15	16	17	18
Work at night	1	2	3	4	5	6	7	8	9	10	11	12	13	14	15	16	17	18
Work in a small business	1	2	3	4	5	6	7	8	9	10	11	12	13	14	15	16	17	18
Work in a large business	1	2	3	4	5	6	7	8	9	10	11	12	13	14	15	16	17	18
Other:	1	2	3	4	5	6	7	8	9	10	11	12	13	14	15	16	17	18
Other:	1	2	3	4	5	6	7	8	9	10	11	12	13	14	15	16	17	18
Other:	1	2	3	4	5	6	7	8	9	10	11	12	13	14	15	16	17	18
Other:	1	2	3	4	5	6	7	8	9	10	11	12	13	14	15	16	17	18

I:A:4:4

Four Most Important Characteristics Graph

Making Choices
Exploring Choices
Testing Choices
Final Choices

Name: ______________________________ Date: ____________________

Work alone	1	2	3	4	5	6	7	8	9	10	11	12	13	14	15	16	17	18
Work with others	1	2	3	4	5	6	7	8	9	10	11	12	13	14	15	16	17	18
Work in a quiet workplace	1	2	3	4	5	6	7	8	9	10	11	12	13	14	15	16	17	18
Work in a noisy workplace	1	2	3	4	5	6	7	8	9	10	11	12	13	14	15	16	17	18
Work part-time	1	2	3	4	5	6	7	8	9	10	11	12	13	14	15	16	17	18
Work full-time	1	2	3	4	5	6	7	8	9	10	11	12	13	14	15	16	17	18
Work weekdays only	1	2	3	4	5	6	7	8	9	10	11	12	13	14	15	16	17	18
Works weekends, too	1	2	3	4	5	6	7	8	9	10	11	12	13	14	15	16	17	18
Work at a hard job	1	2	3	4	5	6	7	8	9	10	11	12	13	14	15	16	17	18
Work at an easy job	1	2	3	4	5	6	7	8	9	10	11	12	13	14	15	16	17	18
Work inside	1	2	3	4	5	6	7	8	9	10	11	12	13	14	15	16	17	18
Work outside	1	2	3	4	5	6	7	8	9	10	11	12	13	14	15	16	17	18
Have few rules	1	2	3	4	5	6	7	8	9	10	11	12	13	14	15	16	17	18
Have well-defined rules	1	2	3	4	5	6	7	8	9	10	11	12	13	14	15	16	17	18
Work standing up	1	2	3	4	5	6	7	8	9	10	11	12	13	14	15	16	17	18
Work sitting down	1	2	3	4	5	6	7	8	9	10	11	12	13	14	15	16	17	18
Work mornings	1	2	3	4	5	6	7	8	9	10	11	12	13	14	15	16	17	18
Work evenings	1	2	3	4	5	6	7	8	9	10	11	12	13	14	15	16	17	18
Work in an attractive place	1	2	3	4	5	6	7	8	9	10	11	12	13	14	15	16	17	18
Looks of place do not matter	1	2	3	4	5	6	7	8	9	10	11	12	13	14	15	16	17	18
Dress up for work	1	2	3	4	5	6	7	8	9	10	11	12	13	14	15	16	17	18
Do not dress up	1	2	3	4	5	6	7	8	9	10	11	12	13	14	15	16	17	18
Do physical work	1	2	3	4	5	6	7	8	9	10	11	12	13	14	15	16	17	18
Do thinking work	1	2	3	4	5	6	7	8	9	10	11	12	13	14	15	16	17	18
Detail is important	1	2	3	4	5	6	7	8	9	10	11	12	13	14	15	16	17	18
Detail is not important	1	2	3	4	5	6	7	8	9	10	11	12	13	14	15	16	17	18
Do the same tasks every day	1	2	3	4	5	6	7	8	9	10	11	12	13	14	15	16	17	18
Do different tasks every day	1	2	3	4	5	6	7	8	9	10	11	12	13	14	15	16	17	18
Work with people	1	2	3	4	5	6	7	8	9	10	11	12	13	14	15	16	17	18
Work with things	1	2	3	4	5	6	7	8	9	10	11	12	13	14	15	16	17	18
Working fast is important	1	2	3	4	5	6	7	8	9	10	11	12	13	14	15	16	17	18
Speed does not matter	1	2	3	4	5	6	7	8	9	10	11	12	13	14	15	16	17	18
Work with little supervision	1	2	3	4	5	6	7	8	9	10	11	12	13	14	15	16	17	18
Work with a lot of supervision	1	2	3	4	5	6	7	8	9	10	11	12	13	14	15	16	17	18
Work in the daytime	1	2	3	4	5	6	7	8	9	10	11	12	13	14	15	16	17	18
Work at night	1	2	3	4	5	6	7	8	9	10	11	12	13	14	15	16	17	18
Work in a small business	1	2	3	4	5	6	7	8	9	10	11	12	13	14	15	16	17	18
Work in a large business	1	2	3	4	5	6	7	8	9	10	11	12	13	14	15	16	17	18
Other:	1	2	3	4	5	6	7	8	9	10	11	12	13	14	15	16	17	18
Other:	1	2	3	4	5	6	7	8	9	10	11	12	13	14	15	16	17	18

Four most
important characteristics ________________ ________________ ________________ ________________

I:A:5:1

Application for Employment (page 1)

Making Choices

Personal information

Name: ______________________________ Phone number: ____________
Last First Middle

Current address: ______________________________
Street City State Zip code

Permanent address: ______________________________
Street City State Zip code

Social security number: ______________ Are you 18 or older? Yes No

Are you a U.S. citizen? Yes No If not, are you authorized to work in the U.S.? Yes No

Employment goals

Position: ______________ Date you can start: ________ Requested salary: ________

Are you employed now? Yes No May we contact your present employer? Yes No

Have you applied to this company before? Yes No When? ______________

Who referred you to this company? ______________________________

Education

Level of education	Name and location of school	Years	Did you graduate?	Subjects studied
Grammar school				
High school				
College				
Trade, business, or correspondence school				

General information

Subjects of special study or research work: ______________________________

____

Special skills: ______________________________

____

Activities (e.g., volunteer work, sports): ______________________________

U.S. military service: ____________ Rank: ________ National Guard or Reserves: ________

I:A:5:1 — Making Choices

Application for Employment (page 2)

Former employers List at least three employers, starting with the most recent one.

Dates of employment	Name and address of employer	Salary	Position	Reason for leaving

References Give the names of three people who are not related to you who you have known for at least a year.

Name	Address and phone number	Relationship	Number of years

In case of emergency, call: ______________________________

Name — Address — Phone number

I certify the facts contained in this application are true and complete to the best of my knowledge and understand that, if employed, falsified statements on this application shall be grounds for dismissal.

I authorize investigation of all statements in the application, including the references listed, to obtain any information concerning my previous employment and any other pertinent information.

Signature: ______________________________ Date: ____________

Do not write in the shaded box below.

Interviewed by: ______________________________ Date: ____________

Remarks: ______________________________

____

____

____

____

Hired? Yes No Date: ____________ Position: ______________ Salary: ____________

Kelly Sample

29 Red Horse Road
Fountain, Colorado 80917
(719) 555–9987

Career Objective

An entry-level position in an office, copy store, or mail room, which takes advantage of my attention to detail and good organizational skills.

Education

1990	Graduated from Fountain-Fort Carson High School
1990–1992	Attended Pikes Peak Community College. Took graphic arts and printing courses.

Work Experience

1987–1990 (Summers)	Camp counselor at Otis Park. Aide at a day camp for children with disabilities. Supervised children on field trips; helped with arts and crafts, physical education, music, and drama activities.

Volunteer Experience

1990	Consumer-directed supported employment. Participated in a program to determine my skills and preferences as a worker.
1989–1990	Teacher's aide at Jefferson Elementary School. Duties included copying instructional materials; filing completed work; and tutoring math, spelling, and reading.
September – November 1989	Mushroom Monday. Washed silk-screens and scrubbers.

References furnished on request.

Pat Sample

1536 Perry Drive ■ Miller's Creek, Mississippi 38655 ■ (601) 555-5548

■ *Career Objective*

To obtain a long-term position that allows me to apply and expand my skills and interests in cooking or working with cars

■ *Education*

1990 Graduated from Harrison High School

1990–1992 Attended Anderson College. Earned a certificate in the Food Service Program.

■ *Work Experience*

Food Service
Peterson Air Force Base, assistant cook and meal preparer
Louie's Pizza, pizza maker and delivery driver
Subway Sandwich Shop, sandwich maker and delivery driver
Little Caesar's Pizza, delivery driver

Mechanical
United States Navy, Gas Turbine Systems Technician, served in the Persian Gulf
Fort Carson, military pool civilian overhaul division, mechanic assistant
Conoco Gas Station, station attendant

References furnished on request.

Aaron Sample

23244 North Albert Street, Apartment 4
Boston, Massachusetts 02114
(617) 555-1212

Career Objective

A position that allows me to use my skills and interest in the areas of maintenance work or fitness

Qualifications

Maintenance

- Welding
- Light plumbing
- Mowing
- Furniture repairs
- Use of power tools
- Sprinkler system repair
- Janitorial duties
- Delivery and warehouse duties
- Painting

Fitness

- Played football
- Ran track
- Wrestled
- Studied physical education on the college level

Education

Widefield High School, High School Diploma
Jones Junior College, Physical Education

Work Experience

TRW—10 years as a maintenance man
Apollo Park Apartments—3 years as a maintenance man
Ingalls Ship Building—4 years as a welder/shipfitter, welder/tacker

References furnished on request.

I:B:6:1	**Assessment Event Organizer**	Exploring Choices

Use this form to keep track of shadowing, internships, summaries, telephone calls, appointments, résumés, staffings, and any other important events.

Week: ________________________________

Individual's name	Assessment events to do	When	Done	Staff responsible

I:B:6:2

Questions for Shadowing

Exploring Choices

Name: ______________________ Date: ______________________

Jobsite: ______________________ Interviewee: ______________________

Main factors describing this job (Required work skills)
Characteristics of a person who is good at this job (Required social and personal skills)
Duties of this job (Required task skills)
Daily routines
Experience, licenses, and education required for this job
How often do you hire for this position? Other positions?
How much does a person doing this job get paid?

Shadowing: Form A

Name: ______________________ Jobsite: ________________ Date: ______________

Part 1: What I can do

Skills I need for this job (Get the answers from the Questions for Shadowing Form)	Skills I have (write the number of each)	Matches
Work skills		/
Social skills		/
Personal skills		/
Task skills		/
Job experiences, licenses, and education		/

$$\frac{\text{Skills I have:}}{\text{Skills I need:}} = \_\_\_ \times 100 = \_\_\_\%$$ Percentage of average skill match

Part 2: What I like

Two jobs I like most	Is this job one of my top choices?	Matches
	Yes No Yes No	/ = Site match

Two tasks I like most	Is this task performed here?	Matches
	Yes No Yes No	/ = Task match

$$\frac{\text{Site match + Task match + Characteristics match*:}}{3} = \_\_\_ \times 100 = \_\_\_\%$$ Percentage of average preference match

**From the Characteristics I Like versus What Is Here Form*

I:B:6:4

Shadowing: Form B

Exploring Choices

Name: ______________________ Jobsite: ______________ Date: ______________

Row	
	Jobs I like (Before): Circle two.
1	
	Tasks I like (Before): Circle two.
2	
	The job here: Circle one.
3	
	Tasks here: Circle all the tasks that are here.
4	
	Tasks here I can do: Circle all the tasks you can do.
5	
	Tasks here I have done: Circle all the tasks you have done.
6	
	Tasks here I like: Circle all the tasks you like.
7	
	Jobs I like (After): Circle two.
8	

1. Matches for Rows 1 and 3 =
2. Matches for Rows 1 and 8 =
3. Items circled in Row 2 divided by total of Row 7 =
4. Characteristics match (from I.B.7.2) =

Sum of 1–4: ______ / 4 = ___.___ x 100 = ______ % Percentage of preference match

5. Items circled in Row 5 divided by total of Row 4 =
6. Items circled in Row 6 divided by total of Row 4 =

Sum of 5 and 6: ______ / 2 = ___.___ x 100 = ______ % Percentage of skill match

I:B:7:1

Characteristics I Like versus What Is Here: Form A

Exploring Choices
Testing Choices

Name: ______________________ Jobsite: ______________ Date: ____________

What I like (Before)		★	✓	What is here (After)		Matches	
Work alone	Work with others			Work alone	Work with others	Yes	No
Quiet workplace	Noisy workplace			Quiet workplace	Noisy workplace	Yes	No
Part-time	Full-time			Part-time	Full-time	Yes	No
Weekdays only	Weekends, too			Weekdays only	Weekends, too	Yes	No
Hard job	Easy job			Hard job	Easy job	Yes	No
Work inside	Work outside			Work inside	Work outside	Yes	No
Few rules	Defined rules			Few rules	Defined rules	Yes	No
Work standing up	Work sitting down			Work standing up	Work sitting down	Yes	No
Mornings	Evenings			Mornings	Evenings	Yes	No
Attractive place	Looks of place do not matter			Attractive place	Looks of place do not matter	Yes	No
Detail is important	Detail is not important			Detail is important	Detail is not important	Yes	No
Dress up for work	Do not dress up			Dress up for work	Do not dress up	Yes	No
Physical work	Thinking work			Physical work	Thinking work	Yes	No
Important to work fast	Speed is unimportant			Important to work fast	Speed is unimportant	Yes	No
Same tasks every day	Different tasks every day			Same tasks every day	Different tasks every day	Yes	No
Work with people	Work with things			Work with people	Work with things	Yes	No
Little supervision	A lot of supervision			Little supervision	A lot of supervision	Yes	No
Daytime work	Nighttime work			Daytime work	Nighttime work	Yes	No
Small business	Large business			Small business	Large business	Yes	No
Other:	Other:			Other:	Other:	Yes	No
Other:	Other:			Other:	Other:	Yes	No

Number of matches: ______
Available matches: ______

= ___.___
Characteristics match
x 100
= ____ %
Percentage of characteristics match

100%
Good match
75%
Okay match
50%
Poor match
25%
Not a match
0%

After determining the four top-ranked characteristics and checking them, write "okay" beside each checked item that matches the characteristic circled in the "What is here" column.

Number of okays: ______
4
x 100 = ____ %
Percentage of most important characteristics match

I:B:7:2

Characteristics I Like versus What Is Here: Form B (page 1)

Exploring Choices
Testing Choices

Name: ______________________ Jobsite: ______________________

What I like (Before)		★	✓	What is here (After)		Matches
Work alone	Work with others			Work alone	Work with others	Yes No
Work in a quiet place	Work in a loud place			Work in a quiet place	Work in a loud place	Yes No
Work part-time	Work full-time			Work part-time	Work full-time	Yes No
S M Tu W Th F S / X ✓ ✓ ✓ ✓ ✓ X Work weekdays only	S M Tu W Th F S / ✓ ✓ ✓ ✓ ✓ ✓ ✓ Work weekends, too			S M Tu W Th F S / X ✓ ✓ ✓ ✓ ✓ X Work weekdays only	S M Tu W Th F S / ✓ ✓ ✓ ✓ ✓ ✓ ✓ Work weekends, too	Yes No
Work a hard job	Work an easy job			Work a hard job	Work an easy job	Yes No
Work inside	Work outside			Work inside	Work outside	Yes No
Have few rules	Have lots of rules			Have few rules	Have lots of rules	Yes No
Work standing up	Work sitting down			Work standing up	Work sitting down	Yes No
Work mornings	Work afternoons			Work mornings	Work afternoons	Yes No
Attractive place	Looks of place do not matter			Attractive place	Looks of place do not matter	Yes No
Detail important	Detail not important			Detail important	Detail not important	Yes No

I.B.7.2

Characteristics I Like versus What Is Here: Form B (page 2)

Exploring Choices
Testing Choices

What I like (Before)		★	✓	What is here (After)		Matches
Dress up for work	Do not dress up			Dress up for work	Do not dress up	Yes No
Physical work	Thinking work			Physical work	Thinking work	Yes No
Important to work fast	Speed is not important			Important to work fast	Speed is not important	Yes No
Same job every day	Different job every day			Same job every day	Different job every day	Yes No
Work with people	Work with things			Work with people	Work with things	Yes No
A little supervision	A lot of supervision			A little supervision	A lot of supervision	Yes No
Daytime work	Nighttime work			Daytime work	Nighttime work	Yes No
Small business	Large business			Small business	Large business	Yes No
Other	Other			Other	Other	Yes No

Number of matches: ______ / Matches available: = .____ x 100 = ____% Percentage of characteristics match

After determining the four top-ranked characteristics and ranking them, write "okay" beside each ranked item that matches the same characteristic circled in the "What is here" column.

Number of okays: ______ / 4 = .____ x 100 = ____% Percentage of most important characteristics match

100%	
Good match	
75%	
Okay match	
50%	
Poor match	
25%	
Not a match	
0%	

I:B:8:1	**Situational Interview (page 1)**	Exploring Choices

Name: ______________________ Jobsite: ______________ Date: ______________

Work characteristics questions

What I like (Before)		Matches	What is here (After)	
Work alone	Work with others	Yes No	Work alone	Work with others
Quiet workplace	Noisy workplace	Yes No	Quiet workplace	Noisy workplace
Part-time	Full-time	Yes No	Part-time	Full-time
Weekdays only	Weekends, too	Yes No	Weekdays only	Weekends, too
Hard job	Easy job	Yes No	Hard job	Easy job
Work inside	Work outside	Yes No	Work inside	Work outside
Few rules	Defined rules	Yes No	Few rules	Defined rules
Work standing up	Work sitting down	Yes No	Work standing up	Work sitting down
Mornings	Evenings	Yes No	Mornings	Evenings
Attractive place	Looks of place do not matter	Yes No	Attractive place	Looks of place do not matter
Dress up for work	Do not dress up	Yes No	Dress up for work	Do not dress up
Physical work	Thinking work	Yes No	Physical work	Thinking work
Detail is important	Detail is not important	Yes No	Detail is important	Detail is not important
Same tasks every day	Different tasks every day	Yes No	Same tasks every day	Different tasks every day
Work with people	Work with things	Yes No	Work with people	Work with things
Important to work fast	Speed is unimportant	Yes No	Important to work fast	Speed is unimportant
Little supervision	A lot of supervision	Yes No	Little supervision	A lot of supervision
Daytime work	Nighttime work	Yes No	Daytime work	Nighttime work
Small business	Large business	Yes No	Small business	Large business

Number of characteristics match: / Number of available matches: = ___.___ x 100 = ____% Percentage of characteristics match

Company culture questions	Is the answer okay?	
1. If you need help, who do you go to?	Okay	Not okay
2. How do you ask for help on this job?	Okay	Not okay
3. How do you make friends on this job?	Okay	Not okay
4. If you had an idea about how to do your job better, who would you go to?	Okay	Not okay
5. What motivates you to work hard?	Okay	Not okay
6. What kind of training do workers receive?	Okay	Not okay
7. How do people get promoted?	Okay	Not okay

Number of culture items okay: / Number of available answers: = ___.___ x 100 = ____% Percentage of culture match

I:B:8:1

Situational Interview (page 2)

Exploring Choices

Work skills questions

1. What are the responsibilities of this job?
2. How fast do people need to work here?
3. How do workers maintain quality on this job?
4. How do workers address safety?
5. What is the typical daily routine of this job?
6. What experience must individuals have to start work here?

Social skills questions

1. What is the best way to interact with co-workers on this job?
2. How do workers make sure that they respond properly to the supervisor's demands and feedback?
3. How should workers treat customers at this job?

Personal skills questions

1. What is the dress code here?
2. What kind of attitude should workers have here?
3. What items must workers bring to work (e.g., uniform, work shoes, lunch)?

Task skills questions

1. What are the tasks that workers must learn and know to do this job?

Requirements questions

1. What are the hours of this job?
2. What are the physical demands here?
3. What kind of machines do workers operate?
4. Do workers need a license or take a special test to do this job?
5. How often do you hire for this job?
6. What is the entry-level wage?
7. What benefits can workers receive here?

I:B:8:2	**Situational Interview Summary**	Exploring Choices

Name: ______________________ Jobsite: ______________ Date: ______________

Part 1: What I can do

Skills I need for this job (Get the answers from the Situational Interview Form)	Skills I have (write the number of each)	Matches
Work skills		/
Social skills		/
Personal skills		/
Task skills		/
Job needs, requirements, and conditions		/

$$\frac{\text{Skills I have:}}{\text{Skills I need:}} = \underline{\ .\ \ \ } \times 100 = \underline{\ \ \ \ \%}$$ Percentage of average skill match

Part 2: What I like

The job I like most	Is this job one of my top choices?	Site match
	Yes No	$\frac{\ }{1}$ =

$$\frac{\text{Site match + Culture match}^{a} + \text{Characteristics match}^{b}\text{:}}{3} = \underline{\ .\ \ \ } \times 100 = \underline{\ \ \ \ \%}$$ Percentage of average preference match

[a] *From the Situational Interview (page 1)*
[b] *From the Characteristics I Like versus What Is Here Form (page 1)*

I:B:9:1

Exploring Choices
Testing Choices

Shadowing Summary Graph

Name: ______________________ Date: ______________________

	Shadowed site 1			Shadowed site 2			Shadowed site 3			Shadowed site 4			Shadowed site 5			Shadowed site 6		
100%																		
Good match																		
80%																		
Okay match																		
60%																		
Poor match																		
20%																		
Not a match																		
Percentage match for category	Skill match	Prefer-ence match	Culture match	Skill match	Prefer-ence match	Culture match	Skill match	Prefer-ence match	Culture match	Skill match	Prefer-ence match	Culture match	Skill match	Prefer-ence match	Culture match	Skill match	Prefer-ence match	Culture match

Three internship sites:

I:C:12:1

Work Improvement: Form A

Testing Choices

Name: ______________ Jobsite: ______________ Date: ______________ Session: ______

Key: Score a "1" for "great!" ".67" for "okay," ".33" for "needs improvement," and "0" for "poor." I and .67 are positive scores. .33 and 0 are negative.

Goal	Plan (How will I do this?)	My evaluation	Job coach evaluation	Comments	Match	Improve next
Follow company rules		1 .67 .33 0	1 .67 .33 0		Yes No	Follow company rules
Come to work		1 .67 .33 0	1 .67 .33 0		Yes No	Come to work
Come to work on time		1 .67 .33 0	1 .67 .33 0		Yes No	Come to work on time
Call if you miss work		1 .67 .33 0	1 .67 .33 0		Yes No	Call if you miss work
Work accurately		1 .67 .33 0	1 .67 .33 0		Yes No	Work accurately
Pay attention to work		1 .67 .33 0	1 .67 .33 0		Yes No	Pay attention to work
Work at the right pace		1 .67 .33 0	1 .67 .33 0		Yes No	Work at the right pace
Work safely		1 .67 .33 0	1 .67 .33 0		Yes No	Work safely
Take specified breaks		1 .67 .33 0	1 .67 .33 0		Yes No	Take specified breaks
Listen and use feedback		1 .67 .33 0	1 .67 .33 0		Yes No	Listen and use feedback

Number of matches with job coach: / Available matches: x 100 =	Number of positive job coach answers: / Available answers: x 100 =
____ % Percentage of work matches	____ % Percentage of positive job coach work answers
Note: Positive scores match as do negative scores.	*Note: Score any evaluation of 1 or .67 as positive.*

I:C:12:2

Social Improvement: Form A

Testing Choices

Name: ____________ Jobsite: ____________ Date: ________ Session: ______

Key: Score a "1" for "great!" ".67" for "okay," ".33" for "needs improvement," and "0" for "poor." I and .67 are positive scores. .33 and 0 are negative.

Goal	Plan (How will I do this?)	My evaluation	Job coach evaluation	Comments	Match	Improve next
Talk the right amount		1 .67 .33 0	1 .67 .33 0		Yes No	Talk the right amount
Behave appropriately		1 .67 .33 0	1 .67 .33 0		Yes No	Behave appropriately
Ask when I need help		1 .67 .33 0	1 .67 .33 0		Yes No	Ask when I need help
Follow directions		1 .67 .33 0	1 .67 .33 0		Yes No	Follow directions
Work independently		1 .67 .33 0	1 .67 .33 0		Yes No	Work independently
Express my needs and feelings		1 .67 .33 0	1 .67 .33 0		Yes No	Express my needs and feelings
Talk about the right things		1 .67 .33 0	1 .67 .33 0		Yes No	Talk about the right things
Feel comfortable talking		1 .67 .33 0	1 .67 .33 0		Yes No	Feel comfortable talking
Other:		1 .67 .33 0	1 .67 .33 0		Yes No	Other:

Number of matches with job coach: ________ x 100 = Available matches: ______ % Percentage of social matches *Note: Positive scores match as do negative scores.*	Number of positive job coach answers: ________ x 100 = Available answers: ______ % Percentage of positive job coach social answers *Note: Score any evaluation of 1 or .67 as positive.*

I:C:12:3	**Personal Improvement: Form A**	Testing Choices

Name: ______________ Jobsite: ______________ Date: __________ Session: ______

Key: Score a "1" for "great!" ".67" for "okay," ".33" for "needs improvement," and "0" for "poor." I and .67 are positive scores. .33 and 0 are negative.

Goal	Plan (How will I do this?)	My evaluation	Job coach evaluation	Comments	Match	Improve next
Use good grooming skills		1 .67 .33 0	1 .67 .33 0		Yes No	Use good grooming skills
Have a positive attitude		1 .67 .33 0	1 .67 .33 0		Yes No	Have a positive attitude
Show good hygiene		1 .67 .33 0	1 .67 .33 0		Yes No	Show good hygiene
Wear clean clothes		1 .67 .33 0	1 .67 .33 0		Yes No	Wear clean clothes
Wear clothes that match		1 .67 .33 0	1 .67 .33 0		Yes No	Wear clothes that match
Have the things I need		1 .67 .33 0	1 .67 .33 0		Yes No	Have the things I need
Other:		1 .67 .33 0	1 .67 .33 0		Yes No	Other:
Other:		1 .67 .33 0	1 .67 .33 0		Yes No	Other:
Other:		1 .67 .33 0	1 .67 .33 0		Yes No	Other:

Number of matches with job coach: / Available matches: x 100 =	Number of positive job coach answers: / Available answers: x 100 =
____% Percentage of personal matches	____% Percentage of positive job coach personal answers
Note: Positive scores match as do negative scores.	*Note: Score any evaluation of 1 or .67 as positive.*

I:C:12:4

Testing Choices

Task Improvement: Form A

Name: ________________ Jobsite: ________________ Date: ________________ Session: ________

Goal	Concern	Plan	Tried to improve	My evaluation	Job coach evaluation	My performance was	Matches	Improve next	Like this task?
Task 1	Independence	by:	Independence	Yes No	Yes No	Great	Yes No	Independence	Yes
	Speed		Speed	Yes No	Yes No	Okay	Yes No	Speed	
	Quality		Quality	Yes No	Yes No	Not good	Yes No	Quality	No
Task 2	Independence	by:	Independence	Yes No	Yes No	Great	Yes No	Independence	Yes
	Speed		Speed	Yes No	Yes No	Okay	Yes No	Speed	
	Quality		Quality	Yes No	Yes No	Not good	Yes No	Quality	No
Task 3	Independence	by:	Independence	Yes No	Yes No	Great	Yes No	Independence	Yes
	Speed		Speed	Yes No	Yes No	Okay	Yes No	Speed	
	Quality		Quality	Yes No	Yes No	Not good	Yes No	Quality	No
Task 4	Independence	by:	Independence	Yes No	Yes No	Great	Yes No	Independence	Yes
	Speed		Speed	Yes No	Yes No	Okay	Yes No	Speed	
	Quality		Quality	Yes No	Yes No	Not good	Yes No	Quality	No

Tasks I like: / Tasks I did: = .___ x 100 = ___% Percentage of task preference matches (TP)

Matches made: / Available matches: = .___ x 100 = ___% Percentage of task matches (TM)

Positive job coach answers: / Tasks I did: = .___ x 100 = ___% Percentage of positive job coach task answers (PA)

100%
Good match
75%
Okay match
50%
Poor match
25%
Not a match
0%

I:C:12:5

Work Improvement: Form B

Testing Choices

Name: ____________________ Jobsite: ________________ Date: __________ Session: ______

Goal	Plan	Evaluation			Great	Match	Next
Follow company rules		I think ☐ Job coach thinks ☐	Follow company rules	Break company rules ☐ ☐		Yes No	
M Tu W Th F ✓ ✓ ✓ ✓ ✓ Come to work		I think ☐ Job coach thinks ☐	M Tu W Th F ✓ ✓ ✓ ✓ ✓ Come to work	M Tu W Th F ✓ X ✓ X X Miss work ☐ ☐		Yes No	
Come to work on time		I think ☐ Job coach thinks ☐	Come to work on time	Come to work late ☐ ☐		Yes No	
Call if you miss work		I think ☐ Job coach thinks ☐	Call if you miss work	Miss work without calling ☐ ☐		Yes No	
Work accurately		I think ☐ Job coach thinks ☐	Work accurately	Make mistakes ☐ ☐		Yes No	
Pay attention to work		I think ☐ Job coach thinks ☐	Pay attention to work	Pay little attention ☐ ☐		Yes No	
Work at the right pace		I think ☐ Job coach thinks ☐	Work at the right pace	Work too fast or too slow ☐ ☐		Yes No	
Work safely		I think ☐ Job coach thinks ☐	Work safely	Work unsafely ☐ ☐		Yes No	
Take specified breaks		I think ☐ Job coach thinks ☐	Take specified breaks	Take too many breaks ☐ ☐		Yes No	
Listen and use feedback		I think ☐ Job coach thinks ☐	Listen and use feedback	Reject feedback ☐ ☐		Yes No	

Number of matches: ____ / Available matches: = ___.___ x 100 = ____% Percentage of work matches

Number of positive job coach answers: ____ / Available answers: = ___.___ x 100 = ____% Percentage of positive job coach work answers

I:C:12:6

Social Improvement: Form B

Testing Choices

Name: ____________ Jobsite: ____________ Date: ____________ Session: ______

Goal	Plan	Evaluation			Great	Match	Next
Talk the right amount		I think ☐ Job coach thinks ☐	Talk the right amount	☐ Talk too much or too little ☐		Yes No	
Behave appropriately		I think ☐ Job coach thinks ☐	Behave appropriately	☐ Behave inappropriately ☐		Yes No	
Ask when I need help		I think ☐ Job coach thinks ☐	Ask when I need help	☐ Not ask for needed help ☐		Yes No	
Follow directions		I think ☐ Job coach thinks ☐	Follow directions	☐ Not follow directions ☐		Yes No	
Work independently		I think ☐ Job coach thinks ☐	Work independently	☐ Need lots of supervision ☐		Yes No	
Express my needs and feelings		I think ☐ Job coach thinks ☐	Express my needs and feelings	☐ Repress my needs and feelings ☐		Yes No	
Talk about the right things		I think ☐ Job coach thinks ☐	Talk about the right things	☐ Talk about the wrong things ☐		Yes No	
Feel comfortable talking		I think ☐ Job coach thinks ☐	Feel comfortable talking	☐ Feel uncomfortable talking ☐		Yes No	

Number of matches: ______ / Available matches: = ______ x 100 = ______ % Percentage of social matches	Number of positive job coach answers: ______ / Available answers: = . ______ x 100 = ______ % Percentage of positive job coach social answers

I:C:12:7	**Personal Improvement: Form B**	Testing Choices

Name: ______________ Jobsite: ______________ Date: __________ Session: ______

Goal	Plan	Evaluation	Great	Match	Next
Use good grooming skills		I think ☐ ☐ Job coach thinks ☐ Use good grooming skills / Use poor grooming skills ☐		Yes No	
Have a positive attitude		I think ☐ ☐ Job coach thinks ☐ Have a positive attitude / Have a bad attitude ☐		Yes No	
Show good hygiene		I think ☐ ☐ Job coach thinks ☐ Show good hygiene / Show poor hygiene ☐		Yes No	
Wear clean clothes		I think ☐ ☐ Job coach thinks ☐ Wear clean clothes / Wear dirty clothes ☐		Yes No	
Wear clothes that match		I think ☐ ☐ Job coach thinks ☐ Wear clothes that match / Wear clothes that clash ☐		Yes No	
Have the things I need		I think ☐ ☐ Job coach thinks ☐ Have the things I need / Need things I don't have ☐		Yes No	

Number of matches: ______ / Available matches: = ___.___ x 100 = ___% Percentage of personal matches

Number of positive job coach answers: ______ / Available answers: = ___.___ x 100 = ___% Percentage of positive job coach personal answers

I:C:12:8

Task Improvement: Form B

Testing Choices

Name: ______ Jobsite: ______ Date: ______ Session: ______

Task	Concern	Plan	Tried to improve	My evaluation	Job coach evaluation	Matches	Improve next	Like this task?
	Speed		Speed	Yes No	Yes No	Yes No	Speed	
	Independence		Independence	Yes No	Yes No	Yes No	Independence	Yes No
	Quality		Quality	Yes No	Yes No	Yes No	Quality	
	Speed		Speed	Yes No	Yes No	Yes No	Speed	
	Independence		Independence	Yes No	Yes No	Yes No	Independence	Yes No
	Quality		Quality	Yes No	Yes No	Yes No	Quality	

Tasks I like: / Tasks I did: = .___ x 100 = ___% Percentage of task preference matches (TP)

Matches made: / Available matches: = .___ x 100 = ___% Percentage of task matches (TM)

Positive job coach answers: / Available answers: = .___ x 100 = ___% Percentage of positive job coach task answers (PA)

100%
Good match
75%
Okay match
50%
Poor match
25%
Not a match
0%

I:C:12:9

Testing Choices

Self-Determined Improvement Form

Name: ____________ Jobsite: ____________ Date: ____________ Session: ______

Goal: List the behaviors you want to improve	Plan	My evaluation	Job coach evaluation	Matches	Improve next
Work behavior		Great 1 Okay .50 Not at all 0	Great 1 Okay .50 Not at all 0	Yes No	
Work behavior		Great 1 Okay .50 Not at all 0	Great 1 Okay .50 Not at all 0	Yes No	
Social behavior		Great 1 Okay .50 Not at all 0	Great 1 Okay .50 Not at all 0	Yes No	
Social behavior		Great 1 Okay .50 Not at all 0	Great 1 Okay .50 Not at all 0	Yes No	
Personal behavior		Great 1 Okay .50 Not at all 0	Great 1 Okay .50 Not at all 0	Yes No	
Personal behavior		Great 1 Okay .50 Not at all 0	Great 1 Okay .50 Not at all 0	Yes No	
Task-related behavior		Great 1 Okay .50 Not at all 0	Great 1 Okay .50 Not at all 0	Yes No	
Task-related behavior		Great 1 Okay .50 Not at all 0	Great 1 Okay .50 Not at all 0	Yes No	

Matches made: / Available matches: = .____ x 100 = ____% Percentage of task matches (TM)

Positive job coach answers: / Available answers: = .____ x 100 = ____% Percentage of positive job coach task answers (PA)

100% Good match 75%	Okay match 50%	Poor match 25%	Not a match 0%

I:C:13:1

Job Requirements and Accommodations: Form A

Testing Choices

Name: ____________ Jobsite: ____________ Date: ____________ Session: ________

Tasks required at this job	Can I do this now?	Job coach evaluation	Matches	I can change	Plan	Who can help?	Can I do this with changes?
Transportation	Yes No	Yes No	Yes No	The task My skills The tools I use			Yes No
Hours	Yes No	Yes No	Yes No	The task My skills The tools I use			Yes No
Walking or climbing?	Yes No	Yes No	Yes No	The task My skills The tools I use			Yes No
Lifting, pushing, or pulling?	Yes No	Yes No	Yes No	The task My skills The tools I use			Yes No
Bending or reaching?	Yes No	Yes No	Yes No	The task My skills The tools I use			Yes No
Standing or sitting?	Yes No	Yes No	Yes No	The task My skills The tools I use			Yes No
Fine motor skills?	Yes No	Yes No	Yes No	The task My skills The tools I use			Yes No
Other?	Yes No	Yes No	Yes No	The task My skills The tools I use			Yes No

______ + ______ = ______

Tasks I can do now + Tasks I can do with accommodations = Tasks I can do

Tasks I can do: ______ / Tasks required at this job: ______ = ___.___ x 100 = ______ % Percentage of job requirements and accommmodations match

I:C:13:2	**Job Requirements and Accommodations: Form B (page 1)**	Testing Choices

Name: ______________________ Jobsite: __________________ Date: __________ Session: _____

Required tasks	Can I do this now?	Job coach evaluation	Match
Walking	Yes No	Yes No	Yes No
Climbing stairs/ladders	Yes No	Yes No	Yes No
Bending/ reaching	Yes No	Yes No	Yes No
Having reliable transportation	Yes No	Yes No	Yes No
Pushing/ pulling	Yes No	Yes No	Yes No
Standing and sitting	Yes No	Yes No	Yes No
Manipulating small objects	Yes No	Yes No	Yes No
Lifting	Yes No	Yes No	Yes No
Working required hours	Yes No	Yes No	Yes No
Driving	Yes No	Yes No	Yes No
Using the phone	Yes No	Yes No	Yes No
Reading (Manual: Read the instructions in this book for the job.)	Yes No	Yes No	Yes No
Writing	Yes No	Yes No	Yes No

Tasks I can do now: ____

Tasks required at this job:

= ___.____

x 100

= ____ %

Percentage of tasks I can do now

100%	
Good match	
75%	
Okay match	
50%	
Poor match	
25%	
Not a match	
0%	

I:C:13:2

Job Requirements and Accommodations: Form B (page 2)

Testing Choices

Name: ____________ Jobsite: ____________ Date: ____________ Session: ______

Tasks I can't do now	Can I do this with changes?	Who can help?
Walking	Yes No	
Climbing stairs/ladders	Yes No	
Bending/ reaching	Yes No	
Having reliable transportation	Yes No	
Pushing/ pulling	Yes No	
Standing and sitting	Yes No	
Manipulating small objects	Yes No	
Lifting	Yes No	
Working required hours	Yes No	
Driving	Yes No	
Using the phone	Yes No	
Reading (Manual: Read the instructions in this book for the job.)	Yes No	
Writing	Yes No	

Tasks I can do with accommodations: ______

+

Tasks I can do now: ______

= ______

Total number of tasks I can do now and with accommodations

Tasks I can do now and with accommodations:
―――――――――――
Tasks required at this job:

= ___.___

x 100

= ______%

Percentage of job requirements and accommodations match

100%

Good match

75%

Okay match

50%

Poor match

25%

Not a match

0%

I:D:14:1

Final Choices

Work Strength Evaluation Graph

Name: ____________________ Date: ____________________

100%										
75%										
50%										
25%										
0%	Follow company rules	Come to work	Come to work on time	If I miss work, call	Work accurately	Pay attention to work	Work at the right pace	Work safely	Take specified breaks	Listen and use feedback
Internship 1	Day 1	Day 1	Day 1	Day 1	Day 1	Day 1	Day 1	Day 1	Day 1	Day 1
	Day 2	Day 2	Day 2	Day 2	Day 2	Day 2	Day 2	Day 2	Day 2	Day 2
	Day 3	Day 3	Day 3	Day 3	Day 3	Day 3	Day 3	Day 3	Day 3	Day 3
Internship 2	Day 1	Day 1	Day 1	Day 1	Day 1	Day 1	Day 1	Day 1	Day 1	Day 1
	Day 2	Day 2	Day 2	Day 2	Day 2	Day 2	Day 2	Day 2	Day 2	Day 2
	Day 3	Day 3	Day 3	Day 3	Day 3	Day 3	Day 3	Day 3	Day 3	Day 3
Internship 3	Day 1	Day 1	Day 1	Day 1	Day 1	Day 1	Day 1	Day 1	Day 1	Day 1
	Day 2	Day 2	Day 2	Day 2	Day 2	Day 2	Day 2	Day 2	Day 2	Day 2
	Day 3	Day 3	Day 3	Day 3	Day 3	Day 3	Day 3	Day 3	Day 3	Day 3
	My score	My score	My score	My score	My score	My score	My score	My score	My score	My score
	Number of scores	Number of scores	Number of scores	Number of scores	Number of scores	Number of scores	Number of scores	Number of scores	Number of scores	Number of scores
	My average score	My average score	My average score	My average score	My average score	My average score	My average score	My average score	My average score	My average score

I:D:14:2

Final Choices

Social Strength Evaluation Graph

Name: ______________________ Date: ______________________

100%								
75%								
50%								
25%								
0%	Talk the right amount	Behave appropriately	Ask for help when I need it	Follow directions	Work independently	Express my needs and feelings	Talk about the right things	Feel comfortable with talking
Internship 1	Day 1	Day 1	Day 1	Day 1	Day 1	Day 1	Day 1	Day 1
	Day 2	Day 2	Day 2	Day 2	Day 2	Day 2	Day 2	Day 2
	Day 3	Day 3	Day 3	Day 3	Day 3	Day 3	Day 3	Day 3
Internship 2	Day 1	Day 1	Day 1	Day 1	Day 1	Day 1	Day 1	Day 1
	Day 2	Day 2	Day 2	Day 2	Day 2	Day 2	Day 2	Day 2
	Day 3	Day 3	Day 3	Day 3	Day 3	Day 3	Day 3	Day 3
Internship 3	Day 1	Day 1	Day 1	Day 1	Day 1	Day 1	Day 1	Day 1
	Day 2	Day 2	Day 2	Day 2	Day 2	Day 2	Day 2	Day 2
	Day 3	Day 3	Day 3	Day 3	Day 3	Day 3	Day 3	Day 3
	My score	My score	My score	My score	My score	My score	My score	My score
	Number of scores	Number of scores	Number of scores	Number of scores	Number of scores	Number of scores	Number of scores	Number of scores
	My average score	My average score	My average score	My average score	My average score	My average score	My average score	My average score

I:D:14:3

Final Choices

Personal Strength Evaluation Graph

Name: ____________________ Date: ____________________

100%						
75%						
50%						
25%						
0%						
	Use good grooming skills	Have a positive attitude	Show good hygiene	Wear clean clothes	Wear clothes that match	Have the things I need
Internship 1	Day 1	Day 1	Day 1	Day 1	Day 1	Day 1
	Day 2	Day 2	Day 2	Day 2	Day 2	Day 2
	Day 3	Day 3	Day 3	Day 3	Day 3	Day 3
Internship 2	Day 1	Day 1	Day 1	Day 1	Day 1	Day 1
	Day 2	Day 2	Day 2	Day 2	Day 2	Day 2
	Day 3	Day 3	Day 3	Day 3	Day 3	Day 3
Internship 3	Day 1	Day 1	Day 1	Day 1	Day 1	Day 1
	Day 2	Day 2	Day 2	Day 2	Day 2	Day 2
	Day 3	Day 3	Day 3	Day 3	Day 3	Day 3
	My score	My score	My score	My score	My score	My score
	Number of scores	Number of scores	Number of scores	Number of scores	Number of scores	Number of scores
	My average score	My average score	My average score	My average score	My average score	My average score

I:D:14:4

Final Choices

Task Strength Evaluation Graph

Name: ____________________ Date: ____________________

For each task, multiply the average score (listed in the last box of each column) by 100 and mark it on this graph.

	100%										
	75%										
	50%										
	25%										
	0%										
Task											
Day 1	Independence										
	Speed										
	Quality										
Day 2	Independence										
	Speed										
	Quality										
Day 3	Independence										
	Speed										
	Quality										
Total: / Days worked x 3:											
My average score											

I:D:14:5

Job Requirements and Accommodations Graph

Final Choices

Name: ____________________ Date: ____________________

Internship 1:	Internship 2:	Internship 3:
Tasks required that I can do: / Number of required tasks: = . ___ x 100 = ___% Percentage of tasks I can do now	Tasks required that I can do: / Number of required tasks: = . ___ x 100 = ___% Percentage of tasks I can do now	Tasks required that I can do: / Number of required tasks: = . ___ x 100 = ___% Percentage of tasks I can do now
Number of tasks I can do now: + Number of tasks I can do with accommodations: / Number of required tasks: = . ___ x 100 = ___% Percentage of tasks I can do with accommodations	Number of tasks I can do now: + Number of tasks I can do with accommodations: / Number of required tasks: = . ___ x 100 = ___% Percentage of tasks I can do with accommodations	Number of tasks I can do now: + Number of tasks I can do with accommodations: / Number of required tasks: = . ___ x 100 = ___% Percentage of tasks I can do with accommodations
Number of matches: / Number of required tasks: = . ___ x 100 = ___% Percentage of task matches	Number of matches: / Number of required tasks: = . ___ x 100 = ___% Percentage of task matches	Number of matches: / Number of required tasks: = . ___ x 100 = ___% Percentage of task matches

	Percentage I can do now	Percentage I can do with accommodations	Percentage of matches	Percentage I can do now	Percentage I can do with accommodations	Percentage of matches	Percentage I can do now	Percentage I can do with accommodations	Percentage of matches
100%									
75%									
50%									
25%									

I:D:15:1

Evaluation Across Internships Graph (page 1)

Final Choices

Name: ______________________ Date: ______________________

To complete page 1, find the percentages of matches and positive answers for each session, find the percentages for each group of improvement forms, add them, and divide by the number of sessions. Record the percentages in the following tables. To find the average percentage of positive answers, add the percentages from the three sessions, and divide by the number of sessions.

Internship 1:	Job type interned:							
	Work issues		Social issues		Personal issues		Task issues	
	Matches	Positive answers	Matches	Positive answers	Matches	Positive answers	Matches	Positive answers
Session 1	%	%	%	%	%	%	%	%
Session 2	%	%	%	%	%	%	%	%
Session 3	%	%	%	%	%	%	%	%
Average percentage of positive answers		%		%		%		%

Internship 2:	Job type interned:							
	Work issues		Social issues		Personal issues		Task issues	
	Matches	Positive answers	Matches	Positive answers	Matches	Positive answers	Matches	Positive answers
Session 1	%	%	%	%	%	%	%	%
Session 2	%	%	%	%	%	%	%	%
Session 3	%	%	%	%	%	%	%	%
Average percentage of positive answers		%		%		%		%

Internship 3:	Job type interned:							
	Work issues		Social issues		Personal issues		Task issues	
	Matches	Positive answers	Matches	Positive answers	Matches	Positive answers	Matches	Positive answers
Session 1	%	%	%	%	%	%	%	%
Session 2	%	%	%	%	%	%	%	%
Session 3	%	%	%	%	%	%	%	%
Average percentage of positive answers		%		%		%		%

Sum of all percentages of positive answers: / Number of percentages of positive answers: = ___% Replace: Overall average percentage of positive answers

Sum of all percentages of matches: / Number of percentages of matches: = ___% Match: Overall average percentage of matches

I:D:15:1

Evaluation Across Internships Graph (page 2)

Final Choices

To complete page 2, graph the "Average percentage of positive answers" for each issue across internships.

100%												
Good match												
80%												
Okay match												
60%												
Poor match												
30%												
Not a match												
	Work	Social	Personal	Task	Work	Social	Personal	Task	Work	Social	Personal	Task
	Internship 1:				Internship 2:				Internship 3:			

I.D.15.2

Final Choices

Adaptability Summary (page 1)

Name: ______________________ Date: ______________________

Category	A. Negative answers last time	B. Goals set for negative answers	C. Choose: B divided by A	D. Goals set	E. Plans made for goals set	F. Manage: E divided by D	G. Negative answers today	H. Improve next for today	I. Adjust: H divided by G
Session 1.1									
Work									
Social									
Personal									
Task									
Session 1.2									
Work									
Social									
Personal									
Task									
Session 1.3									
Work									
Social									
Personal									
Task									
Session 2.1									
Work									
Social									
Personal									
Task									
Session 2.2									
Work									
Social									
Personal									
Task									

I.D.15.2

Adaptability Summary (page 2)

Final Choices

Category	A. Negative answers last time	B. Goals set for negative answers	C. Choose: B divided by A	D. Goals set	E. Plans made for goals set	F. Manage: E divided by D	G. Negative answers today	H. Improve next for today	I. Adjust: H divided by G
Session 2.3									
Work									
Social									
Personal									
Task									
Session 3.1									
Work									
Social									
Personal									
Task									
Session 3.2									
Work									
Social									
Personal									
Task									
Session 3.3									
Work									
Social									
Personal									
Task									

Choose: Add all of the numbers in Column C and divide by the total number of entries: ______

Manage: Add all of the numbers in Column F and divide by the total number of entries: ______

Adjust: Add all of the numbers in Column I and divide by the total number of entries: ______

I:D:15:3

Adaptability Graph

Final Choices

Name: ______________________________ Date: ______________________________

To complete this graph, refer to the bottom of the first page of the Evaluation Across Internship Graph (I:D:15:1). Locate the two shaded boxes labeled "Replace: Overall average percentage of positive answers" and "Match: Overall average percentage of matches." Graph those percentage for Replace and Match in the appropriate columns. Then, find page 2 of the Adaptability Summary (I:D:15:2). Graph the percentages for Choose, Manage, and Adjust in the appropriate columns.

100%					
90%					
80%					
70%					
60%					
50%					
40%					
30%					
20%					
10%					
0%					
	Choose	Manage	Replace	Adjust	Match

I:D:15:4

Internship Preference Graph

Final Choices

Name: ______________________ Date: ______________________

	Internship 1:			Internship 2:			Internship 3:		
100%									
90%									
80%									
70%									
60%									
50%									
40%									
30%									
20%									
10%									
0%	Characteristics match	Four most important characteristics match	Task match	Characteristics match	Four most important characteristics match	Task match	Characteristics match	Four most important characteristics match	Task match

	Percentage of characteristics match	Percentage of four most important characteristics match	Percentage of characteristics match	Percentage of four most important characteristics match	Percentage of characteristics match	Percentage of four most important characteristics match
Session 1						
Session 2						
Session 3						
Average						

Tasks at Internship 1	1	2	3	Tasks at Internship 2	1	2	3	Tasks at Internship 3	1	2	3

Internship 1	Internship 2	Internship 3
Total: / Number of entries: =	Total: / Number of entries: =	Total: / Number of entries: =
.____ x 100 = ____% Percentage of tasks match	.____ x 100 = ____% Percentage of tasks match	.____ x 100 = ____% Percentage of tasks match

I:D:15:5	**Initial Support Ratio Graph**	Final Choices

Initial Support Ratio Calculations Field

1	Use information in the Job Requirements and Accommodations Graph (I:D:14:5). Sum of the percentages of tasks I can do with accommodations: / Number of internships: = ____% Average percentage of tasks I can do Now, use information in the Evaluations Across Internships Graph (I:D:15:1) (Overall average percentage of positive answers + Average percentage of tasks I can do) / 2 = ____% Average percentage of positive skill answers
2	Use information in the Adaptability Graph (I:D:15:3). Choose + Manage + Replace + Adjust + Match: / 5 = ____% Average percentage of independent decision making
3	Use information in the Internship Preference Graph (I:D:15:4). Sum of the percentages of task matchs: / Number of internships: = ____% Average percentage of task performance
4	Use information from the above numbers to find the Initial Support Ratio Sum of first three averages on this page: / 3 = Result: ____% 100% – Result = ____% Initial support ratio

100%				
90%				
80%				
70%				
60%				
50%				
40%				
30%				
20%				
10%				
0%				
	Average percentage of positive skill answers	Average percentage of independent decision making	Average percentage of task performance	Initial support ratio

I:D:15:6

Self-Determined Job Match Summary (page 1)

Final Choices

Job seeker's name: ______________________ Begin date: __________

Name of assessing organization: ______________________ End date: __________

Job preferences

Job of first choice: ______________________ DOT: __________

Job of second choice: ______________________ DOT: __________

Four most important characteristics	Match first job choice?		Match second job choice?		Preferred tasks
________	Yes	No	Yes	No	________
________	Yes	No	Yes	No	________
________	Yes	No	Yes	No	________
________	Yes	No	Yes	No	________

Job evaluation

Job with highest overall skill and requirement evaluations: ______________________

Job with second highest overall skill and requirement evaluations: ______________________

Work, social, personal, and task skills with highest evaluations	Work, social, personal, and task skills with lowest evaluations	Independent decision making skills			
		Choose	Yes	No	____%
		Manage	Yes	No	____%
		Replace negative answers with positive answers	Yes	No	____%
		Adjust	Yes	No	____%
		Self-evaluation	Yes	No	____%
		Able to use forms	Yes	No	____%
					Initial support ratio

Type of form recommended: open-ended written pictorial

I:D:15:6

Self-Determined Job Match Summary (page 2)

Final Choices

Support recommendations and personal notes

What next?

Summary of the assessment process

FOR OFFICE USE ONLY

Summary prepared by: ______________________ Date: ________

Summary approved by: ______________________ Date: ________

Consumer: ______________________ Date: ________

Parent or Guardian (if applicable): ______________________ Date: ________

Vocational Rehabilitation Counselor: ______________________ Date: ________

Other support professional: ______________________ Date: ________

II:E:16:1

Preplacement Information (page 1)

Finding a Job

Name: ______________________ Date of completed assessment: ____________

1. Review the individual's educational history as it relates to his or her top-ranked job choices.

2. Review the individual's vocational history as it relates to his or her top-ranked job choices.

3. What successful experiences did the individual have during internships and on past jobs?

4. What problems did the individual have during internships and on past jobs?

5. Besides program staff, who gives the individual vocational support? How do they do this (e.g., rides, pep talks, modeling, assisting with job seeking)?

6. Determine the individual's degree of motivation to work.

7. Determine the individual's work persistence.

8. Determine the individual's attendance and punctuality history.

9. Determine the approximate amount of time it might take the individual to learn his or her job.

10. Determine the individual's independence level.

11. Determine the individual's work speed.

12. Determine the individual's work quality.

13. Determine the individual's decision-making ability.

14. Determine the individual's problem-solving ability.

15. Determine how the individual learns best.

16. Is the individual taking medication at this time?

17. How does this affect the individual's vocational program?

18. Are there any medical concerns?

19. How does this affect the individual's vocational program?

Preplacement Information (page 3)

20. Are there any limits or restrictions? ______________________________

____

21. What accommodations have been used successfully to overcome them?

____

____

22. Is the individual receiving any Social Security or other benefits? ______________________________

____

____

23. Is the individual receiving assistance from any outside sources?

____

____

____

24. Please list any other important information or comments. ______________________________

____

____

____

____

____

____

____

____

____

____

____

____

____

II:E:16:2

Job Development Information

Finding a Job

Name: ____________________ Date of completed assessment: __________

Address: ____

____________________________ Telephone number: __________

Top-ranked job choices	Top-ranked characteristic preferences
____________________	____________________
____________________	____________________
____________________	____________________

Means of transportation: ________________________________

Prefers to work ☐ Part time ☐ Full time

☐ Days ☐ Nights ☐ Weekends

Education, training, or experience: ________________________

____

____

Needed accommodations, limitations, or restrictions: ______________

____

____

Self-Directed Employment case manager: ____________________

Vocational rehabilitation counselor: ______________________

Other case manager(s): ______________________________

Contact information for a parent or significant other: ____________

____

Parents or residential staff who desire ongoing contact: __________

Job coach support needed or desired? ______________________

Concerns: ____

____

____

II:E:16:3	**Job Development Record (page 1)**	Finding a Job

Name: ______________________ Date: ____________

Program phase: ______________ Billing phase: ______________

Activity	Date	Hours	Initials
Match SDE case manager			
Review file/assessment notes			
Meet with assessment personnel			
Attend postassessment staffing			
Review assessment summary			
Attend initial job development meeting			
Complete Preplacement Information form			
Report job changes to VR office			
Contact businesses for jobs			
Check newspapers			
Do cold calls			
Complete applications/interviews			
Canvas the local area			
Conduct a door-to-door job search			
Set up temporary services			
Contact job lines			
Set up internship			
Send out résumé			
Follow up on leads			
Give job leads to the individual			
Follow up on the individual's results			
Help with skills building			
Check out a job club			
Contact VR			
Contact a parent or significant other			
Miscellaneous:			

II:E:16:3

Job Development Record (page 2)

Finding a Job

Concerns

Outcomes and placement		
Start date: ____________	Placement: ____________	Job title: ____________
End date: ____________	Average hours per week: ________	Number of weeks worked: ________
Wage: ____________	Total wage earned: ____________	Number of internship hours: ________

Other significant events: Enter events, the dates they occurred, and staff initials. Hours should be noted on page 1.

Other staff activities: Enter events, the dates they occurred, and staff initials. Hours should be noted on page 1.

Supervisor Evaluation Cards: Form A

Supervisor's Evaluation

Name: ______________________ Date: ____________

Category	Requirements	Concern
Work	Yes No	
Social	Yes No	
Personal	Yes No	

Supervisor's Evaluation

Name: ______________________ Date: ____________

Category	Requirements	Concern
Work	Yes No	
Social	Yes No	
Personal	Yes No	

Supervisor's Evaluation

Name: ______________________ Date: ____________

Category	Requirements	Concern
Work	Yes No	
Social	Yes No	
Personal	Yes No	

Supervisor's Evaluation

Name: ______________________ Date: ____________

Category	Requirements	Concern
Work	Yes No	
Social	Yes No	
Personal	Yes No	

II:E:17:2

Supervisor Evaluation Cards: Form B

Finding a Job

Supervisor's Evaluation

Name: ____________________ Date: ____________

Category	Requirements	Comment
Work	Yes No	
Social	Yes No	
Personal	Yes No	

Supervisor's Evaluation

Name: ____________________ Date: ____________

Category	Requirements	Comment
Work	Yes No	
Social	Yes No	
Personal	Yes No	

Supervisor's Evaluation

Name: ____________________ Date: ____________

Category	Requirements	Comment
Work	Yes No	
Social	Yes No	
Personal	Yes No	

Supervisor's Evaluation

Name: ____________________ Date: ____________

Category	Requirements	Comment
Work	Yes No	
Social	Yes No	
Personal	Yes No	

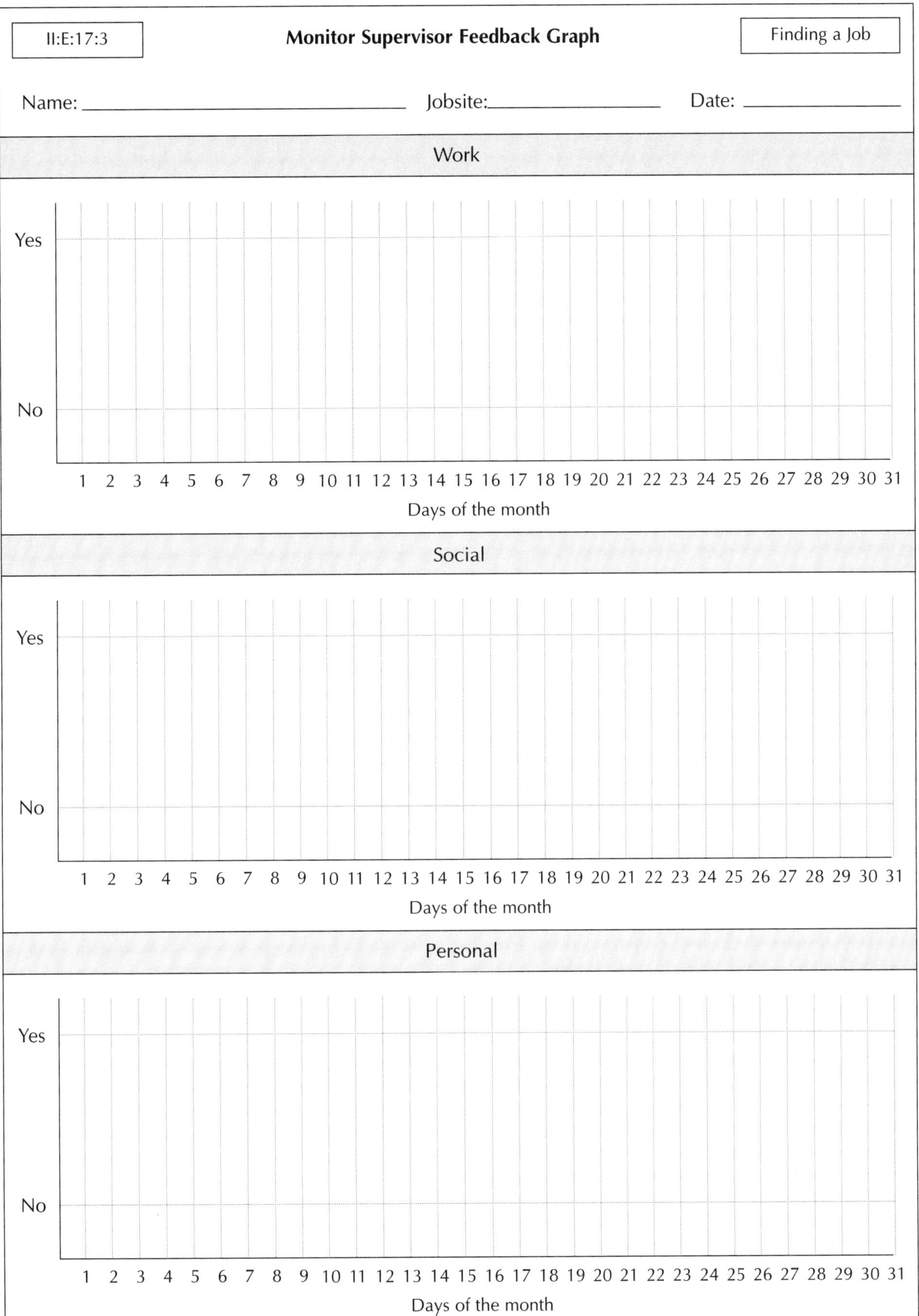

II:E:17:3

Monitor Supervisor Feedback Graph

Finding a Job

Name: ____________________ Jobsite: ____________ Date: ____________

Work

Social

Personal

II:E:18:1

Characteristics I Like versus What Is Here: Form A

Finding a Job

Name: ______________________ Jobsite: ______________ Date: ____________

What I like (Before)		★	✓	What is here (After)		Matches
Work alone	Work with others			Work alone	Work with others	Yes No
Quiet workplace	Noisy workplace			Quiet workplace	Noisy workplace	Yes No
Part-time	Full-time			Part-time	Full-time	Yes No
Weekdays only	Weekends, too			Weekdays only	Weekends, too	Yes No
Hard job	Easy job			Hard job	Easy job	Yes No
Work inside	Work outside			Work inside	Work outside	Yes No
Few rules	Defined rules			Few rules	Defined rules	Yes No
Work standing up	Work sitting down			Work standing up	Work sitting down	Yes No
Mornings	Evenings			Mornings	Evenings	Yes No
Attractive place	Looks of place do not matter			Attractive place	Looks of place do not matter	Yes No
Detail is important	Detail is not important			Detail is important	Detail is not important	Yes No
Dress up for work	Do not dress up			Dress up for work	Do not dress up	Yes No
Physical work	Thinking work			Physical work	Thinking work	Yes No
Important to work fast	Speed is unimportant			Important to work fast	Speed is unimportant	Yes No
Same tasks every day	Different tasks every day			Same tasks every day	Different tasks every day	Yes No
Work with people	Work with things			Work with people	Work with things	Yes No
Little supervision	A lot of supervision			Little supervision	A lot of supervision	Yes No
Daytime work	Nighttime work			Daytime work	Nighttime work	Yes No
Small business	Large business			Small business	Large business	Yes No
Other:	Other:			Other:	Other:	Yes No
Other:	Other:			Other:	Other:	Yes No

Number of matches: ______

Available matches:

= ___.___

Characteristics match

x 100

= ______%

Percentage of characteristics match

100%

Good match

75%

Okay match

50%

Poor match

25%

Not a match

0%

After determining the four top-ranked characteristics and checking them, write "okay" beside each checked item that matches the characteristic circled in the "What is here" column.

Number of okays: ______

4

x 100 = ______%

Percentage of most important characteristics match

II:E:18:2	**Characteristics I Like versus What Is Here: Form B (page 1)**	Finding a Job

Name: ______________________ Jobsite: ______________________

What I like (Before)		★	✓	What is here (After)		Matches	
Work alone	Work with others			Work alone	Work with others	Yes	No
Work in a quiet place	Work in a loud place			Work in a quiet place	Work in a loud place	Yes	No
Work part-time	Work full-time			Work part-time	Work full-time	Yes	No
S M Tu W Th F S X ✓ ✓ ✓ ✓ ✓ X Work weekdays only	S M Tu W Th F S ✓ ✓ ✓ ✓ ✓ ✓ ✓ Work weekends, too			S M Tu W Th F S X ✓ ✓ ✓ ✓ ✓ X Work weekdays only	S M Tu W Th F S ✓ ✓ ✓ ✓ ✓ ✓ ✓ Work weekends, too	Yes	No
Work a hard job	Work an easy job			Work a hard job	Work an easy job	Yes	No
Work inside	Work outside			Work inside	Work outside	Yes	No
Have few rules	Have lots of rules			Have few rules	Have lots of rules	Yes	No
Work standing up	Work sitting down			Work standing up	Work sitting down	Yes	No
Work mornings	Work afternoons			Work mornings	Work afternoons	Yes	No
Attractive place	Looks of place do not matter			Attractive place	Looks of place do not matter	Yes	No
Detail important	Detail not important			Detail important	Detail not important	Yes	No

II:E:18:2	**Characteristics I Like versus What Is Here: Form B (page 2)**	Finding a Job

What I like (Before)		★	✓	What is here (After)		Matches	
Dress up for work	Do not dress up			Dress up for work	Do not dress up	Yes	No
Physical work	Thinking work			Physical work	Thinking work	Yes	No
Important to work fast	Speed is not important			Important to work fast	Speed is not important	Yes	No
Same job every day	Different job every day			Same job every day	Different job every day	Yes	No
Work with people	Work with things			Work with people	Work with things	Yes	No
A little supervision	A lot of supervision			A little supervision	A lot of supervision	Yes	No
Daytime work	Nighttime work			Daytime work	Nighttime work	Yes	No
Small business	Large business			Small business	Large business	Yes	No
Other	Other			Other	Other	Yes	No

Number of matches: / Matches available: = ___.___ x 100 = ___% Percentage of characteristics match

After determining the four top-ranked characteristics and ranking them, write "okay" beside each ranked item that matches the same characteristic circled in the "What is here" column.

Number of okays: / 4 = ___.___ x 100 = ___% Percentage of most important characteristics match

100%	
Good match	
75%	
Okay match	
50%	
Poor match	
25%	
Not a match	
0%	

II:E:18:3

Jobs and Tasks I Like: Form A

Finding a Job

Name: ______________________ Jobsite: ______________ Date: ______________

Jobs

Two top-ranked jobs from assessment: ______________________________

Four jobs I like	This job	Match	
______________			
______________			
______________	______________	Yes	No
______________			

Do I have a job I like? Yes No

Do I have a job I said I wanted in assessment? Yes No

Tasks

Four top-ranked tasks from assessment: ______________________________

Tasks at this job	Do I like this task?	
______________________________	Yes	No
______________________________	Yes	No
______________________________	Yes	No
______________________________	Yes	No
______________________________	Yes	No
______________________________	Yes	No
______________________________	Yes	No
______________________________	Yes	No

Tasks I like: ________ / Tasks at this job: ________ = . ____ x 100 = ____ % Percentage of tasks I like

0%	Not a match	25%	Poor match	50%	Okay match	75%	Good match	100%

Do I like most of the tasks here? Yes No

II:E:18:4

Jobs and Tasks I Like: Form B

Finding a Job

Name: ______________ Jobsite: ______________ Date: ______________

Jobs

Two top-ranked jobs from assessment:

Four jobs I like

This job	Match	
	Yes	No
Do I have a job I like?	Yes	No
Do I have a job I said I wanted in assessment?	Yes	No

Tasks

Four top-ranked tasks from assessment:

Tasks that are here (circle the ones you like):

$$\frac{\text{Tasks I like:}}{\text{Tasks at this job:}} = \underline{\;.\;\;\;} \times 100 = \underline{\;\;\;\;}\%$$ Percentage of tasks I like

0% Not a match 25% Poor match 50% Okay match 75% Good match 100%

Do I like most of the tasks here?

Yes No

II:E:18:5

Do I Have the Job I Like? Summary

Finding a Job

Name: ______________________ Jobsite: ______________ Date: ______________

Characteristics I like versus what is here		Job I like		Tasks I like	
Percentage of characteristics match	Date of match	Percentage of jobs I like (100 or 0)	Date of score	Percentage of tasks I like	Date of match
______	______	______	______	______	______
______	______	______	______	______	______
______	______	______	______	______	______
______	______	______	______	______	______
______	______	______	______	______	______
Total score / Number of days = ___% Average percentage of characteristics match		Total score / Number of days = ___% Average percentage of jobs I like		Total score / Number of days: = ___% Average percentage of tasks I like	

Preference for this job

______ Average percentage of characteristics match + ______ Average percentage of jobs I like + ______ Average percentage of tasks I like = ______ Total average percentage

Total average percentage: / 3 = ___% Average percentage of preference for this job

0% – 25%	25% – 50%	50% – 75%	75% – 100%
Not a match	Poor match	Okay match	Good match

Do I have the job I like? Yes No

(Circle "Yes" for a score of 50% or higher.)

II:E:19:1

Can I Do This Job? Form A

Finding a Job

Name: ____________________ Jobsite: ____________ Date: __________

Job requirements	My evaluation		Supervisor's evaluation		Match	
	Yes	No	Yes	No	Yes	No
	Yes	No	Yes	No	Yes	No
	Yes	No	Yes	No	Yes	No
	Yes	No	Yes	No	Yes	No
	Yes	No	Yes	No	Yes	No
	Yes	No	Yes	No	Yes	No
	Yes	No	Yes	No	Yes	No
	Yes	No	Yes	No	Yes	No
	Yes	No	Yes	No	Yes	No
	Yes	No	Yes	No	Yes	No
	Yes	No	Yes	No	Yes	No
	Yes	No	Yes	No	Yes	No
	Yes	No	Yes	No	Yes	No
	Yes	No	Yes	No	Yes	No
	Yes	No	Yes	No	Yes	No
	Yes	No	Yes	No	Yes	No
	Yes	No	Yes	No	Yes	No
	Yes	No	Yes	No	Yes	No
	Yes	No	Yes	No	Yes	No
	Yes	No	Yes	No	Yes	No

Number of supervisor's yeses: 1 2 3 4 5 6 7 8 9 10 11 12 13 14 15 16 17 18 19 20

Number of matches: 1 2 3 4 5 6 7 8 9 10 11 12 13 14 15 16 17 18 19 20

Can I do this job? Yes No

II:E:19:2

Can I Do This Job? Form B

Finding a Job

Name: ______________________ Jobsite: ______________ Date: ______________

Job requirements	My evaluation		Supervisor's evaluation		Match	
	Yes	No	Yes	No	Yes	No
	Yes	No	Yes	No	Yes	No
	Yes	No	Yes	No	Yes	No
	Yes	No	Yes	No	Yes	No
	Yes	No	Yes	No	Yes	No
	Yes	No	Yes	No	Yes	No
	Yes	No	Yes	No	Yes	No
	Yes	No	Yes	No	Yes	No

Number of supervisor's yeses: 1 2 3 4 5 6 7 8

Number of matches: 1 2 3 4 5 6 7 8

Can I do this job? Yes No

II:E:19:3

Can I Do This Job? Summary

Finding a Job

Name: ______________________ Jobsite: ______________ Start date: __________

Date criterion met: __________ Dates covered in this summary: ______________________

Date	My evaluation yeses	Supervisor's yeses	Available yeses	Matches
Total				

Total matches: / Total yeses available: = ___.___ x 100 = ____% Percentage of matches (M)

Total supervisor's yeses: / Total yeses available: = ___.___ x 100 = ____% Percentage of positive answers (P)

0%	Not a match	25%	Poor match	50%	Okay match	75%	Good match	100%

Can I do this job? Yes No

II:E:20:1

My Employment Plan: Form A

Finding a Job

Name: ______________ Job site: ______________ Date: ______________

If employed, check what's here and determine the match. If unemployed, check the boxes for the items that you want in your next job.

Characteristics I like

______________ ☐ ______________ ☐ ______________ ☐
______________ ☐ ______________ ☐ ______________ ☐
______________ ☐ ______________ ☐ ______________ ☐
______________ ☐

Matches: / Characteristis listed: = .____ x 100 = ____% Percentage of characteristics matches

Tasks I like

______________ ☐ ______________ ☐ ______________ ☐
______________ ☐ ______________ ☐

Matches: / Tasks listed: = .____ x 100 = ____% Percentage of tasks matches

Jobs I like

______________ ☐ ______________ ☐ ______________ ☐
______________ ☐ ______________ ☐

Matches: / Jobs listed: = .____ x 100 = ____% Percentage of job matches

Skills I need to improve: Write a Y in the box for each skill you can improve.

______________ ☐ ______________ ☐ ______________ ☐
______________ ☐ ______________ ☐ ______________ ☐

Y's: / Skills = .____ x 100 = ____% Percentage of skills matches

My job choice

______________ ☐ ______________ ☐ ______________ ☐

Sum of matches: / 4 = .____ x 100 = ____% Average percentage of matches

Signature: ______________ Date: ______________

II:E:20:2

My Employment Plan: Form B (page 1)

Finding a Job

Name: ______________________ Jobsite: ______________ Date: ____________

If employed, check what's here and determine the match. If unemployed, check the boxes for the items that you want in your next job.

Characteristics I like

☐ ☐ ☐ ☐ ☐

☐ ☐ ☐ ☐ ☐

Matches: / Characteristics listed: = . ____ x 100 = ____% Percentage of characteristics matches

Tasks I like

☐ ☐ ☐ ☐ ☐

Matches: / Tasks listed: = . ____ x 100 = ____% Percentage of tasks matches

Jobs I like

☐ ☐ ☐ ☐ ☐

Matches: / Jobs listed: = . ____ x 100 = ____% Percentage of job matches

II:E:20:2

My Employment Plan: Form B (page 2)

Finding a Job

Skills I need to improve: Write a Y in the box for each skill you can improve.

☐ ☐ ☐ ☐ ☐

☐ ☐ ☐ ☐ ☐

Y's: ______ / Skills: = .____ x 100 = ____% Percentage of skills matches

My job choice

☐ ☐ ☐ ☐ ☐

Sum of matches: ______ / 4 = .____ x 100 = ____% Average percentage of matches

Signature: ______________________________ Date: ______________

II:E:20:3

Job Termination Follow-Up Report (page 1)

Finding a Job

Name: ______________________ Date: ______________________

Why did I lose my job?

Tasks I didn't do

Important questions

Do I want a job in the community? Yes No

Do I want to participate in supported employment? Yes No

Kinds of jobs I would like to have:

____ Store ____ Food service ____ Janitorial ____ Other:

____ Laundry ____ Factory ____ Maid service

Work issues I need to address in order to maintain a job in the community

Problem: ______________________

____

Solution: ______________________

____

Problem: ______________________

____

Solution: ______________________

____

II:E:20:3

Job Termination Follow-Up Report (page 2)

Finding a Job

Social issues I need to address in order to maintain a job in the community

Problem: ______________________________

____

Solution: ______________________________

____

Problem: ______________________________

____

Solution: ______________________________

____

Personal issues I need to address in order to maintain a job in the community

Problem: ______________________________

____

Solution: ______________________________

____

Problem: ______________________________

____

Solution: ______________________________

____

Personal contract

I will work hard to do all I can to maintain my next job opportunity in the community. Yes No

Signature: ______________________ Date: __________

II:F:21:1

Basic Match Contract

Solving On-the-Job Problems

Name: ______________________ Date: ______________________

Goal	My evaluation	Supervisor's evaluation	Match	Comment	Next goal
Work	Yes No	Yes No	Yes No		
Social	Yes No	Yes No	Yes No		
Personal	Yes No	Yes No	Yes No		

II:F:21:2

Match Contract: Alternate 1

Solving On-the-Job Problems

Name: ______________________ Date: ______________________

Goal	My evaluation	Supervisor's evaluation	Match	Comment	Next goal
Work	Yes No	Yes No	Yes No		
	Yes No	Yes No	Yes No		
Social	Yes No	Yes No	Yes No		
	Yes No	Yes No	Yes No		
Personal	Yes No	Yes No	Yes No		
	Yes No	Yes No	Yes No		

II:F:21:3

Match Contract: Alternate 2

Solving On-the-Job Problems

Name: ______________________ Date: ______________

Things I need to improve today

Work: ______________________

____

____

Social: ______________________

____

____

Personal: ______________________

____

____

Important questions

Did I meet the requirements of the job? Yes No

Does this match the supervisor's evaluations? Yes No

Next time I need to improve

Work: ______________________

____

____

Social: ______________________

____

____

Personal: ______________________

____

____

II:F:21:4

Match Data Summary

Solving
On-the-Job Problems

Name: ____________ Jobsite: ____________ Start date: ____________

Days of the week	Date	Set goal	Solicited supervisor feedback	Self-evaluated	Evaluated matches	Followed through on adjustment
Week:						
Monday						
Tuesday						
Wednesday						
Thursday						
Friday						
Saturday						
Sunday						
Week:						
Monday						
Tuesday						
Wednesday						
Thursday						
Friday						
Saturday						
Sunday						

II:F:22:1

Problems and Solutions List

Solving On-the-Job Problems

Name: ____________________ Date: ____________

	Problem	Solutions
Work		
Social		
Personal		

II:F:22:2

Basic Improvement Contract

Solving On-the-Job Problems

Name: ____________________ Date: ____________________

Goal	Plan	My evaluation	Supervisor's evaluation	Match	Comments	Next goal
		Yes No	Yes No	Yes No		
		Yes No	Yes No	Yes No		
		Yes No	Yes No	Yes No		

II:F:22:3

Improvement Contract: Alternate 1

Solving On-the-Job Problems

Name: ______________________ Date: ______________

	Work	Social	Personal
Goal			
Plan			
My evaluation	Yes No	Yes No	Yes No
Supervisor evaluation	Yes No	Yes No	Yes No
Match	Yes No	Yes No	Yes No
Comments			
Next goal			

II:F:22:4

Improvement Contract: Alternate 2

Solving On-the-Job Problems

Name: ______________________ Date: ______________

	Work		Social		Personal	
Goal	☐	☐	☐	☐	☐	☐
Plan						
My evaluation	Yes No	Yes No	Yes No	Yes No	Yes No	Yes No
Supervisor evaluation	Yes No	Yes No	Yes No	Yes No	Yes No	Yes No
Match	Yes No	Yes No	Yes No	Yes No	Yes No	Yes No
Comments						
Next goal	☐	☐	☐	☐	☐	☐

II:F:22:5

Solving On-the-Job Problems

Improvement Contract: Alternate 3

Name: ______________________ Date: ______________________

	My goal for today	Plan	Did I meet the goal?	Get supervisor's card	Next goal
Work			Yes No	Yes No	
			Yes No	Yes No	
Social			Yes No	Yes No	
			Yes No	Yes No	
Personal			Yes No	Yes No	
			Yes No	Yes No	

II:F:22.6

Improvement Contract: Alternate 4

Solving On-the-Job Problems

Name: ______________________ Date: ______________

1. How do I feel? ____

____

____

2. How can I use these positive feelings in order to have a good day? ______________

____

____

3. What problems could my negative feelings cause? ______________________

____

____

4. How am I going to deal with these negative feelings or potential problems in order to have a good day? ____

____

____

5. Did I recieve my evaluation from my supervisor? Yes No

6. Did I meet my goals today?

Work	Yes	No
Social	Yes	No
Personal	Yes	No

7. Here are some comments about my performance: ______________________

____

____

8. What am I going to try to do tomorrow to keep or gain positive feelings and cope with negative feelings in order to have good days? ______________________

____

____

____

____

II:F:23:1

Improvement Contract Data Summary

Solving On-the-Job Problems

Name: ____________ Jobsite: ____________ Start date: ____________

Days of the week	Date	Solicited supervisor feedback	Identified problems	Identified solutions	Replaced work problems with work solutions	Replaced social problems with social solutions	Replaced personal problems with personal solutions	Followed through on adjustment
Week:								
Monday								
Tuesday								
Wednesday								
Thursday								
Friday								
Saturday								
Sunday								
Week:								
Monday								
Tuesday								
Wednesday								
Thursday								
Friday								
Saturday								
Sunday								

II:F:23:2

Quarterly Placement Summary

Solving On-the-Job Problems

Name: ______________ Jobsite: ______________ Start date: ______________

Week	Date	Percentage of days per week feed-back was required	Percentage of days per week feed-back was provided	Minimum feedback provided	Percentage of days per week the goal matched the supervisor's previous evaluation	Percentage of days per week individual's next day's plan matched the next day's goal	Followed through on adjustment
1				Yes No			
2				Yes No			
3				Yes No			
4				Yes No			
5				Yes No			
6				Yes No			
7				Yes No			
8				Yes No			
9				Yes No			
10				Yes No			
11				Yes No			
12				Yes No			
13				Yes No			
Total averages							

II:F:24:1

My Change Plan: Form A

Solving On-the-Job Problems

Name: ______________________ Date: ______________

	Work	Social	Personal	Schedule	Wages	Education
Goal						
Plan						
By what month?						
My results						
Month						
Next goal						

II:F:24:2

My Change Plan: Form B

Solving On-the-Job Problems

Name: ______________________ Date: ______________

	Work	Social	Personal	Schedule	Wages	Education
Goal						
Plan						
By what month?						
My results						
Month						
Next goal						

References

Agran, M., & Martin, J.E. (1987). Applying a technology of self-control in community environments for mentally retarded individuals. In M. Hersen, R.M. Eisler, & P.M. Miller (Eds.), *Progress in behavior modification* (Vol. 21, pp. 108–151). Thousand Oaks, CA: Sage Publications.

Agran, M., & Morgan, R.L. (1991a). Current transition assessment practices. *Research in Developmental Disabilities, 12,* 113–126.

Agran, M., Test, D., & Martin, J.E. (1994). Employment preparation of students with severe disabilities. In E. Cipani & F. Spooner (Eds.), *Curricular and instructional approaches for persons with severe disabilities* (pp. 184–212). Needham, MA: Allyn & Bacon.

Anderson, P., & Wisener, K. (1996). *Open employment services for people with disabilities 1995: The first year of National Information Management System (NIMS) data.* Canberra: Australian Institute of Health and Welfare.

Anthony, W.A., & Blanch, A. (1987). Supported employment for persons who are psychiatrically disabled: A historical and conceptual perspective. *Psychosocial Rehabilitation Journal Special Issue: Supported employment for persons with severe mental illness, 11*(2), 5–23.

Association of Persons in Supported Employment (APSE). (2001). *APSE supported employment quality indicators.* Richmond, VA: Author. (Available: http://www.apse.org/products.html)

Bambara, L.M., & Koger, F. (1995). *Innovations: Opportunity for daily choice making.* Washington, DC: American Association on Mental Retardation (AAMR).

Bambara, L.M., Koger, F., Katzer, T., & Davenport, T.A. (1995). Embedding choice in the context of daily routines: An experimental case study. *The Journal of The Association for Persons with Severe Handicaps, 20*(3), 185–195.

Barlsen, J., & Bungart, J. (1997, March). *Supported employment in Germany.* Paper presented at the Third Conference of the European Union of Supported Employment, Oslo, Norway.

Bellamy, G.T., Horner, R.H., & Inman, D.P. (1979). *Vocational habilitation of severely retarded adults: A direct service technology.* Baltimore: University Park Press.

Bellamy, G.T., Rhodes, L.E., Mank, D.M., & Albin, J.M. (1988). *Supported employment: A community implementation guide.* Baltimore: Paul H. Brookes Publishing Co.

Bent, E. (1997, March). *Why supported employment?* Paper presented at the Third Conference of the European Union of Supported Employment, Oslo, Norway.

Berkell, D.E. (1987). Vocational assessment of students with severe handicaps: A review of the literature. *Career Development of Exceptional Individuals, 10*(2), 61–75.

Beyer, S., & Kilsby, M. (1997). Supported employment in Britain. *Tizard Learning Disability Review, 2,* 6–14.

Beyer, S., Kilsby, M., & Willson, C. (1995). Interaction and engagement of workers in supported employment: A British comparison between workers with and without learning disabilities. *Mental Handicap Research, 8*(3), 137–155.

Blystad, R., & Spjelkavik, O. (1997). *A Norwegian approach to supported employment.* Oslo, Norway: Work Research Institute.

Bodgan, A. (1996). Customer driven approach to organizational change. *Journal of Vocational Rehabilitation, 6,* 63–68.

Brigham, T.A. (1979). Some effects of choice on academic performance. In L.D. Perlmuter & R.A. Monte (Eds.), *Choice and perceived control* (pp. 131–142). Mahwah, NJ: Lawrence Erlbaum Associates.

Brooke, V., Wehman, P., Inge, K., & Parent, W. (1995). Toward a customer-driven approach. *Education and Training in Mental Retardation and Developmental Disabilities, 30*(4), 308–320.

Brown, F., Belz, P., Corsi, L., & Wenig, B. (1993). Choice diversity for people with severe disabilities. *Education and Training in Mental Retardation, 28*(4), 318–326.

Browning, P.L. (1997). *Transition in action.* Auburn, AL: Rehab and Special Education, Auburn University.

Buschner, P.C., Watts, M.B., Siders, J.A., & Leonard, R.L. (1989). Career interest inventories: A need for analysis. *Career Development for Exceptional Individuals, 12*(2), 129–137.

Callahan, M.J., & Garner, J.B. (1997). *Keys to the workplace: Skills and supports for people with dis-*

abilities. Baltimore: Paul H. Brookes Publishing Co.

Caught in the act. (2001, May). *Mouth Magazine,* p. 4.

Chadsey-Rusch, J., & Rusch, F.R. (1988). Ecology of the workplace. In R. Gaylord-Ross (Ed.), *Vocational education for persons with handicaps* (pp. 234–256). Mountain View, CA: Mayfield.

Cross, T., Cooke, N.L., Wood, W.M., & Test, D.W. (1999). Comparison of the effects of MAPS and ChoiceMaker on student self-determination skills. *Education and Training in Mental Retardation and Developmental Disabilities, 34*(4), 499–510.

Culver, J.B., Spencer, K.C., & Gliner, J.A. (1990). Prediction of supported employment placements by job developers. *Education and Training in Mental Retardation, 25*(3), 237–242.

Dattilo, J., & Rusch, F.R. (1985). Effects of choice on leisure participation for persons with severe handicaps. *Journal of The Association for Persons with Severe Handicaps, 10*(4), 194–199.

Deci, E.L., & Ryan, R.M. (1985). *Intrinsic motivation and self-determination in human behavior.* Plenum, NY: Klumer Academic/Plenum Publishers.

Deci, E.L., Vallerand, R.J., Pelletier, L.G., & Ryan, R.M. (1991). Motivation and education: The self-determination perspective. *Educational Psychologist, 26*(3/4), 325–346.

Developmental Disabilities Act of 1984, PL 98-527, 42 U.S.C. §§ 6000 *et seq.*

DiLeo, D., McDonald, R., & Killam, S. (1996). *Ethical guidelines for professionals in supported employment.* Richmond, VA: Association for Persons in Supported Employment (APSE).

Dudley, J.R. (1997). *Confronting the stigma in their lives.* Springfield, IL: Charles C. Thomas.

Edgerton, D. (1990). Quality of life from a longitudinal research perspective. In R. Schalock (Ed.), *Quality of life: Perspectives and issues* (pp. 149–160). Washington, DC: American Association of Mental Retardation (AAMR).

Eisenman, L.T. (2001). Conceptualizing the contribution of career-oriented schooling to self-determination. *Career Development for Exceptional Individuals 24,* 3–17.

Ellis, W.K., Rusch, F.R., Tu, J.J., & McCaughrin, W. (1990). Supported employment in Illinois. In F.R. Rusch (Ed.), *Supported employment: Models, methods, and issues* (pp. 31–44). Sycamore, IL: Sycamore.

Elrod, G.F., Sorgenfrei, T.B., & Gibson, A.P. (1989). Agreement between the expressed and scales-determined career interests of adolescents with mild handicaps. *Career Development for Exceptional Individuals, 12*(2), 107–116.

European Centre for the Development of Vocational Training. (1986). *Training, employment, and integration of disabled persons.* Luxemburg: Office for the Official Publication of the European Communities.

Everson, J.M. (1996). Using person-centered planning concepts to enhance school-to-adult transition planning. *Journal of Vocational Rehabilitation, 6,* 7–13.

Everson, J.M., & Reid, D.H. (1997). Using person-centered planning to determine employment preferences among people with the most severe developmental disabilities. *Journal of Vocational Rehabilitation, 9*(2), 99–108.

Fabian, E.S., Luecking, R.G., & Tilson, G.P., Jr. (1994). *A working relationship: The job development specialist's guide to successful partnerships with business.* Baltimore: Paul H. Brookes Publishing Co.

Felce, D. (1997). Defining and applying the concept of quality of life. *Journal of Intellectual Disability Research, 41*(2), 126–135.

Ficker-Terrill, C., & Rowitz, L. (1991). Choices. *Mental Retardation, 29*(2), 63–64.

Field, S., & Hoffman, A. (1994). Development of a model for self-determination. *Career Development for Exceptional Individuals, 17*(2), 159–169.

Field, S., & Hoffman, A. (1995). *Steps to self-determination.* Austin, TX: PRO-ED.

Field, S., Martin, J.E, Miller, R., Ward, M., & Wehmeyer, M. (1998a). *A practical guide for teaching self-determination.* Reston, VA: Council for Exceptional Children.

Field, S., Martin, J.E., Miller, R., Ward, M., & Wehmeyer, M. (1998b). Self-determination for persons with disabilities: A position statement of the Division on Career Development and Transition. *Career Development for Exceptional Individuals, 21*(2), 113–128.

Gallup, G., & Gallup, A.M. (1986). *The great American success story: Factors that affect achievement.* Homewood, Illinois: Dow Jones-Irwin.

Garfield, G. (1986). *Peak performers: The new heroes of American business.* New York: Avon.

Gaylord-Ross, R. (1986). The role of assessment in transitional, supported employment. *Career Development for Exceptional Individuals, 9*(2), 129–134.

Gerber, P.J., Ginsberg, R., & Reiff, H.B. (1992). Identifying alterable patterns in employment success for highly successful adults with learning disabilities. *Journal of Learning Disabilities, 25*(8), 475–487.

Gifford, J.L., Rusch, F.R., Martin, J.E., & White, D.M. (1984). Autonomy and adaptability in work behavior of retarded clients. In N.R. Ellis & N.W. Bray (Eds.), *International Review of Research in Mental Retardation.* San Diego: Academic Press.

Gilmore, D.S., Schuster, J.L., Timmons, J.C., & Butterworth, J. (Fall, 2000). An analysis of trends for people with MR, cerebral palsy, and epilepsy receiving services from state vocational rehabilitation agencies. *Rehabilitation Counseling Bulletin, 44*(1), 30–38.

Gilson, S.F., & Tusler, A. (1997). Introduction to special issue on disability empowerment. *Journal of Vocational Rehabilitation, 9,* 3–5.

Gold, M. (1972). Stimulus factors in skill training of the retarded on a complex assembly task: Acquisition, transfer, and retention. *American Journal of Mental Deficiency, 76*(5), 517–526.

Guess, D., Benson, H.A., & Siegal-Causey, E. (1985). Concepts and issues related to choice-making and autonomy among persons with severe disabilities. *The Journal of The Association for Persons with Severe Handicaps, 10*(2), 79–86.

Hagner, D., & DiLeo, D. (1993). *Working together: workplace culture, supported employment, and persons with disabilities.* Cambridge, MA: Brookline Books.

Hagner, D., Helm, D.T., & Butterworth, J. (1996). "This is your meeting": A qualitative study of person-centered planning. *Mental Retardation, 34*(3) 159–171.

Halloran, W.D. (1993). Transition services requirement: Issues, implications, challenge. In R.C. Eaves & P.J. McLaughlin (Eds.), *Recent advances in special education and rehabilitation* (pp. 210–224). Boston: Andover Medical Publishers.

Halpern, A.S. (1994). The transition of youth with disabilities to adult life: A position statement of the Division on Career Development and Transition. *Career Development for Exceptional Individuals, 17*(2), 115–124.

Harchik, A.E., Sherman, J.A., Sheldon, J.B., & Bannerman, D.J. (1993). Choice and control: New opportunities for people with developmental disabilities. *Annals of Clinical Psychiatry, 5,* 151–161.

Harkapaa, K., Jarvikoski, A., Mannila, S., Haapasalo, Valkama, M., Kinnunen, J., & Sintonen, H. (1997, March). *Evaluation and follow-up of two Finnish programs.* Paper presented at the Third Conference of the European Union of Supported Employment, Oslo, Norway.

Hill, M. (1988). *Interagency vendorization: Expanding supported employment services.* Richmond, VA: Rehabilitation Research and Training Center, Virginia Commonwealth University.

Hill, M., & Wehman, P. (1983). Cost benefit analysis of placing moderately and severely handicapped individuals into competitive employment. *Journal of the Association for the Severely Handicapped, 8*(1), 30–38.

Horner, R.H. (1990). Introduction to supported employment methods. In F.R. Rusch (Ed.), *Supported employment: Models, methods, and issues* (pp. 83–86). Sycamore, IL: Sycamore.

Houghton, J., Bronicki, G.J., & Guess, D. (1987). Opportunities to express preferences and make choices among students with severe disabilities in classroom settings. *The Journal of The Association for Persons with Severe Handicaps, 12*(1), 18–27.

Hughes, C., Pitkin, S.E., & Lorden, S.W. (1998). Assessing preferences and choices of persons with severe and profound mental retardation. *Education and Training in Mental Retardation and Developmental Disabilities, 33*(4), 299–316.

Individuals with Disabilities Education Act (IDEA) Amendments of 1991, PL 102-119, 20 U.S.C. §§ 1400 *et seq.*

Individuals with Disabilities Education Act (IDEA) Amendments of 1997, PL 105-17, 20 U.S.C. §§ 1400 *et seq.*

Inge, K.J., & Tilson, G.P. (1997). Ensuring support systems that work: Getting beyond the natural supports versus job coach controversy. *Journal of Vocational Rehabilitation, 9*(2), 133–142.

Johnson, D.R., McGrew, K.S., Bloomberg, L., Bruininks, R.H., & Lin, H.C. (1997). Results of a national follow-up study of young adults with severe disabilities. *Journal of Vocational Rehabilitation, 8,* 119–133.

Kishi, G., Teelucksingh, B., Zollers, N., Park-Lee, S., & Meyer, L. (1988). Daily decision-making in community residences: A social comparison of adults with and without mental retardation. *American Journal of Mental Retardation, 92*(5), 430–435.

Kregel, J., & Wehman, P. (1997). Supported employment: A decade of employment outcomes for individuals with significant disabilities. In W.E. Kiernan & R.L. Schalock (Eds.) *Integrated employment: Current status and future directions* (pp. 31–48). Washington, DC: American Association on Mental Retardation (AAMR).

Kregel, J., Wehman, P., Revell, W.G., & Hill, M. (1990). Supported employment in Virginia. In F.R. Rusch (Ed.) *Supported employment: Models, methods, and issues* (pp. 15–44). Sycamore, IL: Sycamore.

Lancioni, G.E., O'Reilly, M.F., & Emerson, E. (1996). A review of choice research with people with severe and profound developmental disabilities. *Research in Developmental Disabilities, 17*(5), 391–411.

Locke, J. (1715). *An essay concerning human understanding.* London: Black Swan.

Lohrmann-O'Rourke, S., & Browder, D.M. (1998). Empirically based methods to assess the preferences of individuals with severe disabilities. *American Journal on Mental Retardation, 103*(2), 146–161.

Mank, D. (2000, November). *Natural supports research project.* Paper presented at the Employment Conference 2000, South Portland, Maine.

Mank, D., Cioffii, A., & Yovanoff, P. (1997). Patterns of support for employees with severe disabilities. *Mental Retardation, 35*(6), 433–447.

Martin, J.E., Burger, D.L., Elias-Burger, S., & Mithaug, D.E. (1988). Practical application of self-control strategies with individuals who are mentally retarded. In N. Bray (Ed.), *International review of research in mental retardation* (pp. 155–193). San Diego: Academic Press.

Martin, J.E., & Huber Marshall, L. (1995). ChoiceMaker: A comprehensive self-determination transition program. *Intervention In School and Clinic, 30*(3), 147–156.

Martin, J.E., Huber Marshall, L., & Maxson, L. (1993). Transition policy: Infusing student self-determination and self-advocacy into transition programs. *Career Development for Exceptional Individuals, 16*(1), 53–61.

Martin, J.E., & Husch, J.U. (1987). School-based vocational programs and labor laws. *The Journal of The Association for Persons with Severe Handicaps, 12*(2), 140–144.

Martin, J.E., & Lawhead, R. (1999). *Determining per hour supported employment costs.* Colorado Association for Person in Supported Employment (COAPSE) Professional Seminar, Denver and Colorado Springs.

Martin, J.E., & Mithaug, D.E. (1990). Consumer-directed placement. In F.R. Rusch (Ed.), *Supported employment methods, models, and issues* (pp. 87–110). Sycamore, IL: Sycamore.

Martin, J.E., Mithaug, D.E., Agran, M., & Husch, J.V. (1990). Consumer-centered transition and supported employment. In J.L. Matson (Ed.), *Handbook of behavior modification* (2nd ed., pp. 357–389). Plenum, NY: Kluwer Academic/Plenum Publishers.

Martin, J.E., Mithaug, D.E., Husch, J.V., Frazier, E.S., & Huber Marshall, L. (2002). Optimal opportunities and adjustments during job searches by adults with severe disabilities. In D.E. Mithaug, D.K. Mithaug, M. Agran, J.E. Martin, & M. Wehmeyer (Eds.), *Self-determined learning theory: Predictions, prescriptions, and practice.* Mahwah, NJ: Laurence Erlbaum Associates.

Martin, J.E., Oliphint, J., & Weisenstein, G.R. (1994). ChoiceMaker: Transitioning self-determined youth. *Rural Special Education Quarterly, 13*(1), 16–23.

McDonnell, J., Nofs, D., Hardman, M., & Chambless, C. (1989). An analysis of the procedural components of supported employment programs associated with employment outcomes. *Journal of Applied Behavior Analysis, 22*(4), 417–428.

McLoughlin, C.S., Garner, J.B., & Callahan, M.J. (1987). *Getting employed, staying employed: Job development and training for persons with severe handicaps.* Baltimore: Paul H. Brookes Publishing Co.

Menchetti, B.M., & Flynn, C.C. (1990). Vocational evaluation. In F.R. Rusch (Ed.), *Supported employment: Models, methods, and issues* (pp. 111–130). Sycamore, IL: Sycamore.

Miller, A.B., & Keys, C.B. (1996). Awareness, action, and collaboration: How the self-advocacy movement is empowering for persons with developmental disabilities. *Mental Retardation, 34*(5), 312–319.

Mithaug, D.E. (1979). The relation between programmed instruction and task analysis in the prevocational training of severely and profoundly handicapped persons. *AAESPH Review, 4,* 162–178.

Mithaug, D.E. (1991). *Self-determined kids: Raising satisfied and successful children.* Lexington, MA: D.C. Heath.

Mithaug, D.E. (1996). *Equal opportunity theory.* Thousand Oaks, CA: Sage Publications.

Mithaug, D.E., & Hanawalt, D.A. (1978). The validation of procedures to assess prevocational task preferences in retarded adults. *Journal of Applied Behavior Analysis, 11*(1), 153–162.

Mithaug, D.E., & Mar, D.K. (1980). The relation between choosing and working prevocational tasks in two severely retarded young adults. *Journal of Applied Behavior Analysis, 13*(1), 177–182.

Mithaug, D.E., Martin, J.E., & Agran, M. (1987). Adaptability instruction: The goal of transitional programming. *Exceptional Children, 53*(6), 500–505.

Mithaug, D.E, Wehmeyer, M.L., Agran, M., Martin, J.E., & Palmer, S. (1998). The self-determined learning model of instruction: engaging students to solve their learning problems. In M.L. Wehmeyer & D.J. Sands (Eds.), *Making it happen: Student involvement in educational planning, decision-making, and instruction* (pp. 299–328). Baltimore: Paul H. Brookes Publishing Co.

Mithaug, D.E., Wolman, J., & Campeau, P. (1992). *Research in self-determination individuals with disabilities.* Palo Alto, CA: American Institutes for Research.

Mittler, P. (1995). Special needs education: An international perspective. *British Journal of Special Education, 22*(3), 105–108.

Moon, M.S., Goodall, P., Barcus, M., & Brooke, V. (1986). *The supported work model of competitive employment for citizens with severe handicaps: A guide for job trainers.* Richmond: Virginia Commonwealth University, Rehabilitation Research and Training Center on Supported Employment.

Moon, M.S., Inge, K.J., Wehman, P., Brooke, V., & Barcus, J.M. (1990). *Helping persons with severe mental retardation get and keep employment.* Baltimore: Paul H. Brookes Publishing Co.

Moseley, C. (1999). *Making self-determination work.* Durham: University of New Hampshire, National Program Office on Self-Determination. (Available: http://www.self-determination.org/publications1251/publications_show.htm-doc_id=18644.htm)

Murphy, S.T., & Rogan, P.M. (1994). *Developing natural supports in the workplace: A practitioner's guide.* Saint Augustine, FL: Training Resource Network.

Neumayer, R., & Bleasdale, M. (1996). Personal lifestyle preferences of people with an intellectual disability. *Journal of Intellectual and Developmental Disability, 21,* 91–114.

Nirje, B. (1972). The right to self-determination. In W. Wolfensberger (Ed.), *The principal of normalization in human services.* Toronto: National Institute on Mental Retardation.

Nisbet, J. (1992). *Natural supports in school, at work, and in the community for people with disabilities.* Baltimore: Paul H. Brookes Publishing Co.

Nowak, R., Laitinen, R.E., Stowitschek, J.J., & Affleck, J.Q. (1995). Advocates and adults with developmental disabilities: Shared and unshared perceptions of self-determination opportunity and impact. *Journal of Vocational Rehabilitation, 5*(4), 307–317.

O'Brien, C.L., O'Brien, J., & Mount, B. (1997). Person-centered planning has arrived . . . or has it? *Mental Retardation, 35*(6), 480–484.

O'Brien, J. (1987). A guide to life-style planning: Using the activity catalog to integrate services and natural support systems. In B. Wilcox & G.T. Bellamy (Eds.), *A comprehensive guide to the Activities Catalog: An alternative curriculum for youth and adults with severe disabilities* (pp. 175–189). Baltimore: Paul H. Brookes Publishing Co.

Pancsofar, E.L., & Steere, D.E. (1997). The c.a.p.a.b.l.e. process: Critical dimensions of community-based assessment. *Journal of Vocational Rehabilitation, 8*(1), 99–108.

Parent, W. (1996). Consumer choice and satisfaction in supported employment. *Journal of Vocational Rehabilitation, 6,* 23–30.

Parent, W., Unger, D., Gibson, K., & Clements, C. (1994). The role of job coach: Orchestrating community and workplace supports. *American Rehabilitation, 20*(3), 2–11.

Parent, W., Unger, D., & Inge, K. (1997). Customer profile. In V. Brooke, K.J. Inge, A.J. Armstrong, & P. Wehman (Eds.), *Supported employment handbook: A customer-driven approach for persons with significant disabilities.* Richmond: Virginia Commonwealth University, Rehabilitation Research and Training Center on Supported Employment.

Parker, R.M., Szymanski, E.M., & Hanley-Maxwell, C. (1989). Ecological assessment in supported employment. *Journal of Applied Rehabilitation Counseling, 20*(3), 26–33.

Parsons, M.B., & Reid, D.H. (1990). Assessing food preferences among persons with profound mental retardation: Providing opportunities to make choices. *Journal of Applied Behavior Analysis, 23*(2), 183–195.

Pennell, R.L. (2001). Self-determination and self-advocacy: Shifting the power. *Journal of Disability Policy Studies, 11*(4), 223–227.

Phelps, L.A., & Hanley-Maxwell, C. (1997). School-to-work transitions for youth with disabilities: A review of outcome and practices. *Review of Educational Research, 67*(2), 197–226.

Powell, T.H., Pancsofar, E.L., Steere, D.E., Butterworth, J., Itzkowitz, J.S., & Rainforth, B. (1991). *Supported employment: Providing integrated employment opportunities for persons with disabilities.* White Plains, NY: Longman.

President's Committee on Employment of People with Disabilities (1998). Supported employment. Washington, DC: Author. (Available: http://www.pcepd.gov/pubs/fact/supportd.htm#top)

Pumpian, I., Fisher, D., Certo, N.J., & Smalley, K.A. (1997). Changing jobs: An essential part of career development. *Mental Retardation, 35*(1), 39–48.

Rawlings, M., Dowse, L., & Shaddock, A. (1995). Increasing the involvement of people with an intellectual disability in choice-making situations: A practical approach. *International Journal of Disability, Development, and Education, 42*(2), 137–153.

Rehab Brief. (1992). *New directions in supported employment: Bringing research into effective focus, 14*(3).Washington, DC: National Institute on Disability and Rehabilitation Research.

Rehabilitation Act Amendments of 1992, PL 102-569, 29 U.S.C. §§ 701 *et seq.*

Reid, D.H., Parsons, M.B., & Green, C.W. (1998). Identifying work preferences among individuals with severe multiple disabilities prior to beginning supported work. *Journal of Applied Behavior Analysis, 31*(2), 281–285.

Robbins, A. (1997). *Unlimited power.* New York: Fireside.

Rogers-Warren, A., & Warren, S.F. (1977). The developing ecoehavioral psychology. In A. Rogers-Warren & S.F. Warren (Eds.), *Ecological perspectives in behavior analysis* (pp. 3–8). Baltimore: University Park Press.

Rogovsky, E. (1997). A partial history of self-determination and the politics in the disabled community. *Journal of Vocational Rehabilitation, 9*(1), 19–30.

Rusch, F.R. (1986). *Competitive employment issues and strategies.* Baltimore: Paul H. Brookes Publishing Co.

Rusch, F.R. (1990). *Supported employment: Models, methods, and issues.* Sycamore, IL: Sycamore.

Rusch, F.R., Connis, R.T., & Sowers, J. (1978). The modification and maintenance of time spent attending to task using social reinforcement, token reinforcement and response cost in an applied restaurant setting. *Journal of Special Education Technology, 2,* 18–26.

Rusch, F.R., & Hughes, C. (1989). Overview of supported employment. *Journal of Applied Behavior Analysis, 22*(4), 351–363.

Rusch, F.R., & Hughes, C. (1990). Historical overview of supported employment. In F.R. Rusch (Ed.), *Supported employment: Models, methods, and issues* (pp. 5–14). Sycamore, IL: Sycamore.

Rusch, F.R., & Mithaug, D.E. (1980). *Vocational training for mentally retarded adults.* Champaign, IL: Research Press.

Rusch, F.R., & Schutz, R.P. (1979). Nonsheltered employment of the mentally retarded adult: Research to reality? *Journal of Contemporary Business, 8,* 85–98.

Sands, D.J., & Kozleski, E.B. (1994). Quality of life differences between adults with and without disabilities. *Education and Training in Mental Retardation and Developmental Disabilities, 29*(2), 90–101.

Schaller, J.L., & Szmanski, E.M. (1992). Supported employment, consumer choice, and independence. *Journal of Vocational Rehabilitation, 2*(4), 45–50.

Schalock, R.L., & Jensen, C.M. (1986). Assessing the goodness-of-fit between persons and their environments. *The Journal of The Association for Persons with Severe Handicaps, 11*(2), 103–109.

Schloss, P.J., Alper, S., & Jayne, D. (1994). Self-determination for persons with disabilities: Choice, risk, and dignity. *Exceptional Children 60*(3), 215–225.

Serna, L.A., & Lau-Smith, J. (1995). Learning with purpose: Self-determination skills for students who are at risk for school and community failure. *Intervention in School and Clinic, 30*(3), 142–146.

Shevin, M., & Klein, N. (1984). The importance of choice-making skills for students with severe disabilities. *The Journal of The Association for Persons with Severe Handicaps, 9*(3), 159–166.

Simon, M., & Halloran, W. (1994). Community-based vocational education: Guidelines for complying with the Fair Labor Standards Act. *The Journal of The Association for Persons with Severe Handicaps, 19*(1), 52–60.

Smith, D.M. (1992). The dynamics of Dene struggle for self-determination. *Anthropologica, 34,* 21–49.

Snyder-Joy, Z.K. (1992). *American Indian education in the Southwest: Issues of self-determination and local control.* Unpublished doctoral dissertation, Arizona State University, Tempe.

Sowers, J.A., & Powers, L. (1991). *Vocational preparation and employment of students with physical and multiple disabilities.* Baltimore: Paul H. Brookes Publishing Co.

Special education needs: Code of practice. (1997). Cardiff, Wales, United Kingdom: Welsh Office, Department for Education.

Stalker, K., & Harris, P. (1998). The exercise of choice by adults with intellectual disabilities: A literature review. *Journal of Applied Research in Intellectual Disabilities, 11*(1), 60–76.

Targett, P.S., Ferguson, S.S., & McLaughlin, J. (1998). Consumer involvement in vocational evaluation. In P. Wehman & J. Kregel (Eds.), *More than a job: Securing satisfying careers for people with disabilities* (pp. 95–117). Baltimore: Paul H. Brookes Publishing Co.

Test, D.W., & Wood, W.M. (1995). It almost does take a rocket scientist to be an employment specialist. *Journal of Vocational Rehabilitation, 5*(3), 257–259.

Thurman, S.K. (1977). Congruence of behavioral ecologies: A model for special education programming. *Journal of Special Education, 11*(3), 329–333.

United Nations. (1997). *General Assembly resolution 52/113, 12 December, 1997.* New York: Author.

Unterberger, B.M. (1996). The United States and national self-determination: A Wilsonian perspective. *Presidential Studies Quarterly, 26*(4), 926–941.

Verdugo, M.A., Borja, F., Urries, J., Bellver, F, & Martinez, S. (1998). Supported employment in Spain. *Journal of Vocational Rehabilitation, 11*(3), 223–232.

Wagner, B.R. (2000, January/February). Visions for the new millennium: Empowered effective self-advocates. *AAMR's News & Notes, 3,* 13.

Ward, M.J. (1988). The many facets of self-determination. *National Information Center for Children and Youth with Handicaps: Transition Summary 5*(2), 2–3.

Ward, M.J., & Kohler, P.D. (1996). Teaching self-determination: Content and process. In L.E. Powers, G.H.S. Singer, & J.A. Sowers (Eds.), *On the road to autonomy* (pp. 275–290). Baltimore: Paul H. Brookes Publishing Co.

Ward, N. (1996). Supporting self-advocacy in national organizations: Our role and yours. *Mental Retardation, 34,* 121–122.

Wehman, P. (1981). *Competitive employment: New horizons for severely disabled individuals.* Baltimore: Paul H. Brookes Publishing Co.

Wehman, P. (1997). [Editorial for special issue about disability empowerment.] *Journal of Vocational Rehabilitation, 9,* 1.

Wehman, P. (2001). *Life beyond the classroom: Transition strategies for young people with disabilities* (3rd ed.). Baltimore: Paul H. Brookes Publishing Co.

Wehman, P., Hill, J.W., & Koehler, F. (1979). Placement of developmentally disabled individuals into competitive employment: Three case studies. *Education and Training of the Mentally Retarded, 14*(4), 269–276.

Wehman, P., & Kregel, J. (1989). *Supported employment for persons with disabilities: Focus on excellence.* New York: Human Sciences Press.

Wehman, P., & Kregel, J. (Eds.). (1998). *More than a job: Securing satisfying careers for people with disabilities.* Baltimore: Paul H. Brookes Publishing Co.

Wehman, P., Kreutzer, J.S., Stonnington, H.H., & Wood, W. (1988). Supported employment for persons with traumatic brain injury: A preliminary report. *Journal of Head Trauma Rehabilitation, 3*(4), 82–93.

Wehman, P., & Moon, S. (1986). Critical values in employment programs for persons with developmental disabilities: A position paper. *Journal of Applied Rehabilitation Counseling, 18,* 12–16.

Wehman, P., & Revell, W.G. (1997). Transition into supported employment for young adults with severe disabilities: Current practices and future directions. *Journal of Vocational Rehabilitation, 8*(1), 65–74.

Wehmeyer, M.L. (1992). Self-determination and the education of students with mental retardation. *Education and Training in Mental Retardation, 27,* 302–314.

Wehmeyer, M.L. (1996). Self-determination as an educational outcome: Why is it important to children, youth and adults with disabilities? In D.J. Sands & M.L. Wehmeyer (Eds.), *Self-determination across the life span: Independence and choice for people with disabilities* (pp. 15–34). Baltimore: Paul H. Brookes Publishing Co.

Wehmeyer, M.L. (1999). A functional model of self-determination: Describing development and implementing instruction. *Focus on Autism and Other Developmental Disabilities, 14*(1), 53–61.

Wehmeyer, M.L., Agran, M., & Hughes, C. (1998). *Teaching self-determination to students with disabilities.* Baltimore: Paul H. Brookes Publishing Co.

Wehmeyer, M.L., Kelchner, K., & Richards, S. (1995). Individual and environmental factors related to the self-determination of adults with mental retardation. *Journal of Vocational Rehabilitation, 5*(4), 291–305.

Wehmeyer, M.L., Kelchner, K., & Richards, S. (1996). Essential characteristics of self-determined behavior of individuals with mental retardation. *American Journal of Mental Retardation, 100*(6), 632–642.

Wehmeyer, M.L., Palmer, S.P., Agran, M., Mithaug, D.E., & Martin, J.E. (2000). Promoting causal agency: The self-determined learning model of instruction. *Exceptional Children, 66*(4), 439–453.

Wehmeyer, M.L., & Schwartz, M. (1997). Self-determination and positive adult outcomes: A follow-up of youth with mental retardation or learning disabilities. *Exceptional Children, 63*(2), 245–255.

Wehmeyer, M.L., & West, M.D. (1995). Introduction to the special issue on self-determination. *Journal of Vocational Rehabilitation, 5,* 277–279.

West, M. (1995). Choice, self-determination and VR services: systemic barriers for consumers with severe disabilities. *Journal of Vocational Rehabilitation, 5*(4), 281–290.

West, M., & Parent, W. (1992). Consumer choice and empowerment in supported employment: Issues and strategies. In P. Wehman, P. Sale, & W. Parent

(Eds.), *Supported employment: From research to practice* (pp. 47–52). Boston: Andover Medical Publishers.

Whitehead, C.W. (1979). Sheltered workshops in the decade ahead: Work and wages, or welfare. In G.T. Bellamy, G. O'Connor, & O.C. Karan (Eds.), *Vocational rehabilitation of severely handicapped persons* (pp. 71–84). Baltimore: University Park Press.

Wilcox, B., McDonnell, J.J., Bellamy, G.T., & Rose, H. (1988). Preparing for supported employment: The role of secondary special education. In G.T. Bellamy, D.M. Mank, & J.M. Albin (Eds.), *Supported employment: A community implementation guide* (pp. 183–208). Baltimore: Paul H. Brookes Publishing Co.

Williams, R.R. (1990). Creating a new world of opportunity: Expanding choice and self-determination in lives of Americans with severe disability by 1992 and beyond. In R. Perske (Ed.), *Proceedings from the National Conference on Self-Determination* (pp. 16–17). Minneapolis, MN: Institute on Community Integration.

Wilson, M.W. (1997). Self-determination, empowerment and community: A perspective from Ireland. *Journal of Vocational Rehabilitation, 9,* 47–56.

Wilson's Address to Congress. (1918, Feb. 12). *The New York Times,* 1.

Windsor, J., O'Reilly, B., & Moon, M.S. (1993). Preference: The missing link in the job match process for individuals without functional communication skills. *Journal of Vocational Rehabilitation, 3,* 27–42.

Wolman, M., Campeau, P.L., DuBois, P.A., Mithaug, D.E., & Stolarski, V.S. (1994). *AIR self-determination scale and user guide.* Palo Alto, CA: American Institutes for Research.

Wood, D., & Trickey, S. (1996). Transition planning: Process or procedure? *British Journal of Special Education, 23*(3), 120–125.

Index

Page numbers followed by "f" indicate figures; those followed by "t" indicate tables.